tasteofhome
cookies

taste of home cookies

A Taste of Home/Reader's Digest Book

Editor in Chief	Catherine Cassidy
Vice President, Executive Editor/Books	Heidi Reuter Lloyd
Creative Director	Ardyth Cope
Food Director	Diane Werner RD
Senior Editor/Books	Mark Hagen
Editor	Janet Briggs
Art Director	Rudy Krochalk
Content Production Supervisor	Julie Wagner
Design Layout Artists	Emma Acevedo, Catherine Fletcher
Proofreaders	Linne Bruskewitz, Amy Glander
Recipe Asset System	Coleen Martin, Sue A. Jurack
Premedia Supervisor	Scott Berger
Recipe Testing & Editing	Taste of Home Test Kitchen
Food Photography	Taste of Home Photo Studio
Editorial Assistant	Barb Czysz

Chief Marketing Officer	Lisa Karpinski
Vice President/Book Marketing	Dan Fink

The Reader's Digest Association, Inc.

President and Chief Executive Officer	Mary G. Berner
President, RDA Food & Entertaining	Suzanne M. Grimes
President, Consumer Marketing	Dawn Zier

"Timeless Recipes from Trusted Home Cooks"
is a registered trademark of Reiman Media Group, Inc.

For other Taste of Home books and products, visit: ShopTasteofHome.com

For more Reader's Digest products and information, visit rd.com (in the United States)
or see rd.ca (Canada).

International Standard Book Number (10): 0-89821-727-X
International Standard Book Number (13): 978-0-89821-727-8
Library of Congress Control Number: 2008943191

Cover Photography
Photographer	Dan Roberts
Food Stylist	Jennifer Janz
Set Stylist	Stephanie Marchese

Pictured on the front cover
On top from left to right: Fudge-Filled Sandies (p. 143), Raspberry Nut Pinwheels (p. 117), Christmas Sandwich Cookies (p. 309),
Cream Cheese Cutouts (p. 183) and Marble Brownies (p. 217). On bottom: Chocolate Caramel Wafers (p. 283), Five-Chip Cookies (p. 51),
Cream Cheese-Filled Cookies (p. 101), Chocolate Chip Cookie Pizza (p. 282), Linzer Cookies (p. 190) and White Chocolate Macaroons (p. 70).

Pictured on the back cover
Clockwise from top: Dipped Spice Cookies (p. 141), Cranberry Swirl Biscotti (p. 312) and Walnut Oat Brownies (p. 229).

Pictured on the Table of Contents page
From left to right: Versatile Slice 'n' Bake Cookies (p. 100), Raspberry Truffle Brownies (p. 214) and Stawberry Sandwich Cookies (p. 194).

Printed in U.S.A.
3 5 7 9 10 8 6 4

table of contents

cookies 101

before you begin

Read the entire recipe before you begin, and check to see that you have all the ingredients called for. Also make sure you understand the cooking techniques.

Preheat the oven for 10 to 15 minutes before baking. Use an oven thermometer to verify the accuracy of your oven. If the set oven temperature and the oven thermometer do not agree, adjust the oven temperature accordingly.

mixing it up

Always prepare the ingredients before you start mixing. Let the butter soften, toast the coconut, chop the nuts, etc. Measure the ingredients correctly, using the proper technique and the correct measuring utensils. Prepare the recipe according to directions.

Avoid overmixing the cookie dough. If it's handled too much, the cookies will be tough. For even baking, always make cookies the same size and thickness.

Use heavy-gauge, dull aluminum baking sheets with one or two short sides for cookies. For brownies and bars, use dull aluminum baking pans or glass. It's best to use the size of pan called for in the recipe.

When a recipe calls for greased baking sheets or pans, grease them with shortening or cooking spray. For easy removal, line the bottom of the pan with parchment paper and grease the paper.

Unless the recipe states otherwise, place cookie dough 2 to 3 in. apart on a cool baking sheet. For brownies and bars, spread the batter evenly in the pan, otherwise the treats may bake unevenly.

while baking

Leave at least 2 in. around the baking sheet or pan and the oven walls for good heat circulation. For best results, bake only one sheet of cookies at a time. If you need to bake two sheets at once, switch the position of the baking sheets halfway through the baking time.

Use a kitchen timer to accurately time the recipe. Unless otherwise directed, let cookies cool for 1 minute on the baking sheet before removing to a wire rack. Cooling baked goods on a wire rack allows air to circulate around the food and cool completely before storing.

Let baking sheets cool before placing the next batch of cookie dough on it. Otherwise, the heat from the baking sheet will soften the dough and cause it to spread.

---

storing cookies & bars

Cookies tend to switch texture upon storing—soft cookies get hard and crisp cookies get soft. Here are some tips to keep these morsels at peak freshness.

* Allow cookies and bars to cool completely before storing. Cut crisp bar cookies while slightly warm. Allow icing on cookies to completely dry before storing.

* Store soft and crisp cookies in separate airtight containers. If stored together, the moisture from the soft cookies will soften the crisp cookies and they will lose their crunchy texture.

* Flavors can also blend during storage, so don't store strong-flavored cookies with delicate-flavored cookies.

* Arrange cookies in a container with waxed paper between each layer.

* Store cookies in a cool, dry place. Cookies, frosted with a cream cheese frosting, should be covered and stored in the refrigerator.

* If your crisp cookies became soft during storage, crisp them up by heating in a 300° oven for 5 minutes.

* Cover a pan of uncut brownies and bars with foil—or put the pan in a large resealable plastic bag. If the bars are made with perishable ingredients, such as cream cheese, store covered in the refrigerator. Once the bars are cut, store them in an airtight container in the refrigerator.

* For longer storage, place in freezer bags, and freeze for up to 3 months.

* Wrap unfrosted cookies in plastic wrap, stack in an airtight container, seal and freeze.

* Freeze a pan of uncut bars in an airtight container or resealable plastic bag. Or, wrap individual bars in plastic wrap and stack in an airtight container.

* Thaw wrapped cookies and bars at room temperature before frosting and serving.

shipping cookies

Here are some pointers to ensure that cookies arrive at their destination as delicious and attractive as the day you baked them.

First, select cookies that are sturdy and will travel well such as drop, slice and bake and sandwich cookies as well as bars and brownies. Cutouts and other thin cookies might break or crumble during shipping. Cookies requiring refrigeration are a poor choice for shipping because they'll spoil.

Bake and completely cool cookies just before packing and shipping. This way they arrive as fresh as possible.

To help the cookies stay fresh and intact, wrap them in bundles of two (for drop cookies, place

their bottoms together) with plastic wrap (photo 1). Wrap bars individually. Pack crisp cookies, soft cookies and strong-flavored cookies, such as gingersnaps, in separate tins.

Line a tin or box with crumbled waxed paper to cushion the cookies. Snugly pack the cookies to within 1 in. of the top. Use crumpled waxed

paper or bubbly wrap to fill in any gaps between cookies and side of container and to cover the tops of the cookies (photo 2). Close the box or tin.

Wrap cookie container in a cardboard box that is slightly larger and cushion with bubble wrap, crumpled paper or shipping peanuts. Seal box and label "Fragile and Perishable."

problem-solving pointers for cookies & bars

cookies spread too much

* Place cookies on a cool baking sheet.
* Replace part of the butter in the recipe with shortening.
* If using margarine, check label and make sure it contains 80% vegetable oil.

cookies don't spread enough

* Use all butter instead of shortening or margarine.
* Add 1 to 2 tablespoons of liquid such as milk or water.
* Let dough stand at room temperature before baking.

cookies are tough

* The dough was overhandled or overmixed; use a light touch when mixing.
* Too much flour was worked into the dough.

* Add 1 or 2 tablespoons more of shortening or butter or sugar.

cookies are too brown

* Check the oven temperature with an oven thermometer.
* Use heavy-gauged, dull aluminum baking sheets. Dark baking sheets will cause the cookies to become overly brown.

cookies are too pale

* Check the oven temperature with an oven thermometer.
* Use heavy-gauged, dull aluminum baking sheets. Insulated baking sheets cause cookies to be pale in color.
* Use butter, not shortening or margarine.
* Substitute 1 to 2 tablespoons corn syrup for the sugar.

bars bake unevenly

* Spread batter evenly in pan.
* Check to make sure oven rack is level.

bars are overbaked

* Use pan size called for in recipe, too large a pan will cause batter to be thin and dry.
* Check the oven temperature with an oven thermometer.
* Check for doneness 5 minutes sooner than the recommended baking time.

bars are gummy

* Use pan size called for in recipe, too small a pan will cause batter to be thick and may be gummy or cake-like.

food equivalents

item	equivalent
Butter *or* Margarine	1 pound = 2 cups; 4 sticks 1 stick = 8 tablespoons
Chocolate Chips	6 ounces = 1 cup
Cocoa, baking	1 pound = 4 cups
Coconut, flaked	14 ounces = 5-1/2 cups
Cream Cheese	8 ounces = 16 tablespoons
Flour: all-purpose cake whole wheat	 1 pound = about 3-1/2 cups 1 pound = about 4-1/2 cups 1 pound = about 3-3/4 cups
Frozen Whipped Topping	8 ounces = 3-1/2 cups
Graham Crackers	16 crackers = 1 cup crumbs
Honey	1 pound = 1-1/3 cups
Lemons	1 medium = 3 tablespoons juice; 2 teaspoons grated peel
Limes	1 medium = 2 tablespoons juice; 1-1/2 teaspoons grated peel
Marshmallows: large miniature	 1 cup = 7 to 9 marshmallows 1 cup = about 100 marshmallows
Nuts: almonds ground hazelnuts pecans walnuts	 1 pound = 3 cups whole, 4 cups slivered 3-3/4 ounces = 1 cup 1 pound = 3-1/2 cups whole 1 pound = 4-1/2 cups chopped 1 pound = 3-3/4 cups chopped
Oats: old-fashioned quick-cooking	 1 pound = 5 cups 1 pound = 5-1/2 cups
Oranges	1 medium = 1/3 to 1/2 cup juice; 4 teaspoons grated peel
Raisins	15 ounces = 2-1/2 cups
Shortening	1 pound = 2 cups
Sugar: brown sugar confectioners' sugar granulated	 1 pound = 2-1/4 cups 1 pound = 4 cups 1 pound = 2-1/4 to 2-1/2 cups

ingredient substitutions

ingredient	amount	substitution
Apple Pie Spice	1 teaspoon	1/2 teaspoon ground cinnamon + 1/4 teaspoon ground nutmeg, 1/8 teaspoon ground allspice and dash ground cloves or cardamom
Baking Powder	1 teaspoon	1/2 teaspoon cream of tartar + 1/4 teaspoon baking soda
Buttermilk	1 cup	1 tablespoon lemon juice or white vinegar + enough milk to measure 1 cup. Stir and let stand for 5 minutes before using. Or 1 cup plain yogurt
Chocolate, semisweet	1 square (1 ounce)	3 tablespoons semisweet chocolate chips or 1 square (1 ounce) unsweetened chocolate + 1 tablespoon sugar
Chocolate, unsweetened	1 square (1 ounce)	3 tablespoons baking cocoa + 1 tablespoon shortening or canola oil
Corn Syrup, dark	1 cup	3/4 cup light corn syrup + 1/4 cup molasses
Corn Syrup, light	1 cup	1 cup sugar + 1/4 cup water
Cream, half-and-half	1 cup	1 tablespoon melted butter + enough whole mike to measure 1 cup
Egg	1 whole	2 egg whites or 2 egg yolks or 1/4 cup egg substitute
Flour, cake	1 cup	1 cup minus 2 tablespoons (7/8 cup) all-purpose flour
Flour, self-rising	1 cup	Place 1-1/2 teaspoons baking powder and 1/2 teaspoon salt in a measuring cup. Add all-purpose flour to measure 1 cup.
Honey	1 cup	1-1/4 cups sugar + 1/4 cup water
Lemon Juice	1 teaspoon	1 teaspoon cider vinegar
Lemon Peel	1 teaspoon	1/2 teaspoon lemon extract
Milk, whole	1 cup	1/2 cup evaporated milk + 1/2 cup water. Or 1 cup water + 1/3 cup nonfat dry milk powder
Molasses	1 cup	1 cup honey
Pumpkin Pie Spice	1 teaspoon	1/2 teaspoon ground cinnamon + 1/4 teaspoon ground ginger, 1/4 teaspoon ground allspice and 1/8 teaspoon ground nutmeg or cloves
Sour Cream	1 cup	1 cup plain yogurt
Sugar	1 cup	1 cup packed brown sugar or 2 cups sifted confectioners' sugar

cookie jar favorites

chocolate-topped surprise cookies, p. 17

Keep the cookie jar filled

with plenty of family-pleasing treats. These cookies are big on flavor and will appeal to kids of all ages...and are easy to bake! Choose from melt-in-your-mouth sugar cookies, old-time oatmeal cookies, spicy molasses chews and more.

pecan meltaways, p. 16

crisp lemon sugar cookies, p. 19

※ Edith Pluhar, Cohagen, Montana

My sons and grandsons manage our ranch, and they always seem to have one hand in the cookie jar; especially when I bake these crunchy morsels!

white chocolate oatmeal cookies

yield about 5 dozen

1	**cup butter, softened**
1/2	**cup sugar**
1/2	**cup packed brown sugar**
1	**egg**
3	**teaspoons vanilla extract**
1	**teaspoon coconut extract**
6	**squares (1 ounce *each*) white baking chocolate, melted**
1-1/4	**cups all-purpose flour**
1	**teaspoon salt**
1	**teaspoon baking soda**
1-1/2	**cups quick-cooking oats**
1	**cup flaked coconut, toasted**

Additional sugar

In a large bowl, cream the butter and sugars until light and fluffy. Add the egg and extracts; mix well. Stir in the melted chocolate. Combine the flour, salt and baking soda; gradually add to creamed mixture. Stir in the oats and the coconut.

Drop by tablespoonfuls 3 in. apart onto ungreased baking sheets. Flatten with a glass dipped in sugar. Bake at 350° for 9-11 minutes or until golden brown. Cool for 1 minute before removing to wire racks to cool completely.

Carolyn Horne, Tigard, Oregon

Folks can't get enough of these giant cookies. Topped with leftover peanut brittle bits, they take star billing on holiday cookie trays—anytime I serve the tasty treats.

giant peanut brittle cookies
yield 1-1/2 dozen

1/3	cup butter-flavored shortening
1/3	cup creamy peanut butter
1/3	cup sugar
1/3	cup packed brown sugar
2	teaspoons 2% milk
1	egg
1	cup all-purpose flour
1/2	teaspoon baking soda
1/4	teaspoon baking powder
1/8	teaspoon salt
3/4	cup peanut butter chips
2/3	cup crushed peanut brittle

In a small bowl, cream the shortening, peanut butter and sugars until light and fluffy. Beat in milk and egg. Combine the flour, baking soda, baking powder and salt; gradually add to creamed mixture and mix well.

Shape dough into 1-1/2-in. balls. Place 3-1/2 in. apart on ungreased baking sheets. Flatten into 3-in. circles with a glass dipped in sugar.

Bake at 375° for 6-8 minutes or until golden brown. Cool for 2 minutes before removing to wire racks.

In a microwave, melt peanut butter chips; stir until smooth. Spread over half of each cookie; sprinkle with peanut brittle.

editor's note: Reduced-fat or generic brands of peanut butter are not recommended for this recipe.

low-fat oatmeal raisin cookies
yield 44 cookies

1	cup raisins
1/4	cup water
3	egg whites
1	tablespoon molasses
1	cup sugar
1	cup packed brown sugar
1-1/2	teaspoons vanilla extract
1	cup all-purpose flour
1/2	cup nonfat dry milk powder
1-1/2	teaspoons baking powder
1-1/2	teaspoons ground cinnamon
2-1/2	cups quick-cooking oats

In a food processor, combine the raisins, water, egg whites and molasses. Cover and process for 10-15 seconds or until the raisins are finely chopped.

Transfer to a large bowl. Beat in sugars and vanilla. Combine the flour, milk powder, baking powder and cinnamon; gradually add to raisin mixture and mix well. Stir in oats.

Drop by tablespoonfuls 2 in. apart onto baking sheets coated with cooking spray.

Bake at 350° for 8-10 minutes or until edges are golden brown. Remove to wire racks to cool completely.

Julie Hauser
Sheridan, California
The first time I made these sweet chewy cookies, I didn't tell my family they were low in fat. Their reaction when they found out? "No way!"

✳ Rose Mabee, Selkirk, Manitoba
My mother, who is of Scottish heritage, passed this recipe, as with most of my favorite recipes, on to me. When I entered Scottish Shortbread at our local fair, it won a ribbon.

scottish shortbread

yield about 4 dozen

1	**pound butter, softened**
1	**cup packed brown sugar**
4	**to 4-1/2 cups all-purpose flour**

In a large bowl, cream the butter and brown sugar. Add 3-3/4 cups flour; mix well until light and fluffy.

Sprinkle a board with some of the remaining flour. Knead for 5 minutes, adding enough remaining flour to make a soft, nonsticky dough. Roll to 1/2-in. thickness. Cut into 3-in. x 1-in. strips.

Place 1 in. apart on ungreased baking sheets. Prick with fork. Bake at 325° for 20-25 minutes or until cookies are lightly browned. Remove to wire racks to cool.

✳ Pearl Cochenour
Williamsport, Ohio
With four sons in service during World War II, my mother sent these favorite cookies as a taste from home to "her boys" in different parts of the world.

mom's soft raisin cookies

yield 6 dozen

2	**cups raisins**
1	**cup water**
1	**cup shortening**
1-3/4	**cups sugar**
2	**eggs, lightly beaten**
1	**teaspoon vanilla extract**
3-1/2	**cups all-purpose flour**
1	**teaspoon baking powder**
1	**teaspoon baking soda**
1	**teaspoon salt**
1/2	**teaspoon ground cinnamon**
1/2	**teaspoon ground nutmeg**
1/2	**cup chopped walnuts**

Combine raisins and water in a small saucepan; bring to a boil. Cook for 3 minutes; remove from the heat and let cool (do not drain).

In a large bowl, cream shortening until light and fluffy. Gradually add sugar. Add eggs and vanilla. Combine dry ingredients; gradually add to creamed mixture and blend thoroughly. Stir in nuts and raisins.

Drop by teaspoonfuls 2 in. apart on greased baking sheets. Bake at 350° for 12-14 minutes or until set. Remove to wire racks to cool.

Chris Paulsen, Glendale, Arizona ✳

This recipe from my grandmother was my grandfather's favorite. I keep the dough in the freezer because I love to make a fresh batch when company drops in for a visit.

icebox cookies

yield about 7 dozen

1/2	cup butter, softened
1	cup packed brown sugar
1	egg, beaten
1/2	teaspoon vanilla extract
2	cups all-purpose flour
1/2	teaspoon baking soda
1/2	teaspoon cream of tartar
1/2	teaspoon salt
1	cup chopped walnuts, optional

In a large bowl, cream the butter and brown sugar. Add egg and vanilla; beat well. Combine dry ingredients; add to creamed mixture. Stir in nuts if desired.

On a lightly floured surface, shape dough into two 10-in. rolls; wrap each in plastic wrap. Freeze for at least 12 hours.

Unwrap and cut into 3/8-in. slices. Place 2 in. apart on greased baking sheets. Bake at 350° for 6-8 minutes. Remove to wire racks to cool.

Audrey Metzger, Larchwood, Iowa ✳

My daughter substituted crushed malted milk balls in our favorite chocolate chip cookie recipe to create these crisp treats. They're so yummy, especially fresh from the oven.

malted milk cookies

yield about 3 dozen

1	cup butter, softened
3/4	cup packed brown sugar
1/3	cup sugar
1	egg
2	teaspoons vanilla extract
2-1/4	cups all-purpose flour
2	tablespoons instant chocolate drink mix
1	teaspoon baking soda
1/2	teaspoon salt
2	cups malted milk balls, crushed

In a large bowl, cream the butter and sugars until light and fluffy. Beat in egg and vanilla. Combine the flour, drink mix, baking soda and salt; gradually add to creamed mixture. Stir in malted milk balls.

Roll into 1-1/2-in. balls. Place 2 in. apart on greased baking sheets. Bake at 375° for 10-12 minutes or until set. Cool for 1 minute before removing from pans to wire racks.

✳ Virginia Bodner, Sandusky, Ohio
My mother got this recipe in about 1910 when she was a housekeeper and cook for the local physician. The doctor's wife was an excellent cook and taught my mother of lot of her cooking techniques. The cookies are a favorite in our home.

family–favorite oatmeal cookies

yield about 5 dozen

2	cups packed brown sugar
1	cup shortening
3	eggs
3	cups all-purpose flour
1	teaspoon salt
1	teaspoon baking powder
1	teaspoon baking soda
1	teaspoon ground cinnamon
1	cup buttermilk
2	cups rolled oats
1	cup raisins
1	cup chopped walnuts

In a large bowl, cream sugar and shortening until light and fluffy. Add eggs, one at a time, beating well after each addition. Combine flour, salt, baking powder, baking soda and cinnamon; add alternately with buttermilk to the creamed mixture. Stir in the oats, raisins and nuts.

Drop dough by heaping tablespoonfuls onto greased baking sheets. Bake at 350° for about 12 minutes or until lightly browned. Remove to wire racks to cool.

✳ Nancy Tafoya, Ft. Collins, Colorado
I keep the ingredients for these easy-to-make cookies in my pantry. That way I can make a fresh batch in just minutes.

coconut macaroons

yield 1-1/2 dozen

2-1/2	cups flaked coconut
1/3	cup all-purpose flour
1/8	teaspoon salt
2/3	cup sweetened condensed milk
1	teaspoon vanilla extract
9	red *or* green candied cherries, halved, optional

In a bowl, combine coconut, flour and salt. Add milk and vanilla; mix well (batter will be stiff).

Drop by tablespoonfuls 1 in. apart onto a greased baking sheet. Top each with a candied cherry half if desired. Bake at 350° for 15-20 minutes or until golden brown. Remove to wire racks to cool completely.

championship cookies

yield about 5 dozen

2/3	cup shortening
1-1/4	cups packed brown sugar
1	egg
1	teaspoon vanilla extract
1-1/2	cups all-purpose flour
1	teaspoon baking powder
1	teaspoon baking soda
1/2	teaspoon ground cinnamon
1/4	teaspoon salt
2	Snickers candy bars (2.07 ounces *each*), chopped
1/2	cup quick-cooking oats

In a large bowl, cream shortening and brown sugar until light and fluffy. Beat in egg and vanilla. Combine the flour, baking powder, baking soda, cinnamon and salt; gradually add to creamed mixture. Stir in chopped candy bars and oats.

Drop dough by round tablespoonfuls 2 in. apart onto greased or parchment-lined baking sheets. Bake at 350° for 10-12 minutes or until lightly browned. Remove to wire racks to cool.

toffee almond sandies

yield 9 dozen

1	cup butter, softened
1	cup canola oil
1	cup sugar
1	cup confectioners' sugar
2	eggs
1	teaspoon almond extract
4-1/2	cups all-purpose flour
1	teaspoon baking soda
1	teaspoon cream of tartar
1	teaspoon salt
2	cups sliced almonds
1	package English toffee bits (10 ounces) *or* almond brickle chips (7-1/2 ounces)

In a large bowl, cream butter, oil and sugars. Add eggs, one at a time, beating well after each addition. Beat in extract. Combine flour, baking soda, cream of tartar and salt; gradually add to the creamed mixture. Stir in almonds and toffee bits.

Drop by teaspoonfuls 2 in. apart onto ungreased baking sheets. Bake at 350° for 10-12 minutes or until golden brown. Remove to wire racks to cool completely.

✳ Alberta McKay, Bartlesville, Oklahoma
These sugared nut-filled balls are a tradition of ours at Christmastime, but the melt-in-your-mouth treats are great anytime of the year.

pecan meltaways

yield about 4 dozen

1	cup butter, softened
1/2	cup confectioners' sugar
1	teaspoon vanilla extract
2-1/4	cups all-purpose flour
1/4	teaspoon salt
3/4	cup chopped pecans

Additional confectioners' sugar

In a large bowl, cream the butter, sugar and vanilla. Combine the flour and salt; add to creamed mixture. Stir in pecans. Cover and chill until easy to handle.

Roll into 1-in. balls and place 1 in. apart on ungreased baking sheets. Bake at 350° for 10-12 minutes. Roll in confectioners' sugar while still warm. Cool; roll in sugar again.

peanut butter candy cookies

yield 4 dozen

✳ Carol Kitchens
Ridgeland, Mississippi
I prefer chunky peanut butter in this cookie. The candy bars add a touch of chocolate and a sweet crunch. These great cookies don't last long—make a double batch!

1/2	cup butter, softened
3/4	cup sugar
2/3	cup packed brown sugar
2	egg whites
1-1/4	cups chunky peanut butter
1-1/2	teaspoons vanilla extract
1	cup all-purpose flour
1/2	teaspoon baking soda
1/4	teaspoon salt
5	Butterfinger candy bars (2.1 ounces *each*), chopped

In a large bowl, cream butter and sugars. Add egg whites; beat well. Blend in peanut butter and vanilla. Combine flour, baking soda and salt; add to creamed mixture and mix well. Stir in candy bars.

Roll into 1-1/2-in. balls and place on greased baking sheets. Bake at 350° for 10-12 minutes or until golden brown. Remove to wire racks to cool completely.

editor's note: Reduced-fat or generic brands of peanut butter are not recommended for this recipe.

BAKING

making shaped cookies of the same size — Cookies bake more evenly if all the cookies on the baking sheet are the same size. To make the 1-1/2-inch ball of dough called for in the peanut butter candy cookies above, use about 1 tablespoon of dough per cookie.

Veronica Strange, Glocester, Rhode Island ✳

I first tasted these cookies during a cookie swap at work a few years ago. Now I make them every Christmas for our family get-together. People who haven't had them are always delighted by the "hidden treasure" inside.

chocolate-topped surprise cookies

yield 2 dozen

24	maraschino cherries
1/2	cup butter, softened
3/4	cup packed brown sugar
1	tablespoon maraschino cherry juice
1	teaspoon vanilla extract
1-1/2	cups all-purpose flour
1/8	teaspoon salt
1	cup milk chocolate chips, *divided*
1/2	teaspoon shortening

Pat cherries with paper towels to remove excess moisture; set aside. In a large bowl, cream butter and brown sugar until light and fluffy. Beat in cherry juice and vanilla. Combine flour and salt; gradually add to creamed mixture and mix well. Cover and refrigerate for 1 hour or until dough is easy to handle.

Insert a chocolate chip into each maraschino cherry. Wrap a tablespoon of dough around each cherry. Place 1 in. apart on ungreased baking sheets.

Bake at 350° for 15-17 minutes or until set and edges are lightly browned. Remove to wire racks to cool.

In a microwave, melt remaining chips and shortening; stir until smooth. Dip tops of cookies in melted chocolate; allow excess to drip off. Place on wax paper; let stand until set. Store in an airtight container.

Bob Dittmar, Trout Run, Pennsylvania ✳

When I was a child, we kids helped Mom cut these crispy crackers into all sorts of shapes. They're not too sweet, but they are sweet enough that we always wanted a few more.

oatmeal animal crackers

yield about 4 dozen

2	cups sugar
2	cups old-fashioned oats
1	teaspoon baking soda
1/4	teaspoon salt
1/2	cup shortening
1/2	cup hot water
1	tablespoon vanilla extract
2	to 2-1/2 cups all-purpose flour

In a large bowl, combine the sugar, oats, baking soda and salt. Cut in the shortening until crumbly. Add water and vanilla; stir until blended. Add enough flour to form a stiff dough.

On a lightly floured surface, roll dough to 1/8-in. thickness. Cut into rectangles or use floured cookie cutters. Using a floured spatula, transfer to greased baking sheets, placing 2 in. apart. Bake at 350° for 8-10 minutes or until lightly browned. Remove to wire racks to cool.

✳ Lori Daniels, Beverly, West Virginia
I was delighted to find the recipe for these fun cookies. The peanut butter makes them extra-special.

crisp graham cookies

yield 7 dozen

1/2	cup butter-flavored shortening
1/2	cup packed brown sugar
1	egg
1-1/2	teaspoons vanilla extract
1	can (14 ounces) sweetened condensed milk
3	tablespoons creamy peanut butter
1-1/2	cups all-purpose flour
1	cup graham cracker crumbs
1	teaspoon baking soda
1	teaspoon salt
2	cups (1 pound) plain M&M's
1/2	cup chopped pecans

In a large bowl, cream shortening and brown sugar until light and fluffy. Beat in egg. Add vanilla and milk. Blend in peanut butter. Combine dry ingredients; add to the creamed mixture. Stir in the M&M's and nuts.

Drop by teaspoonfuls 1 in. apart on ungreased baking sheets. Bake at 350° for 10-12 minutes or until golden brown. Remove to wire racks to cool completely.

editor's note: Reduced-fat or generic brands of peanut butter are not recommended for this recipe.

✳ Edith MacBeath, Gaines, Pennsylvania
Vanilla Wafer Cookies are chewy and irresistible, and they're a wonderful way to round out a meal when you're on a budget.

vanilla wafer cookies

yield about 3-1/2 dozen

1/2	cup butter, softened
1	cup sugar
1	egg
1	tablespoon vanilla extract
1-1/3	cups all-purpose flour
3/4	teaspoon baking powder
1/4	teaspoon salt

In a large bowl, cream butter and sugar until light and fluffy. Beat in egg and vanilla. Combine dry ingredients; add to creamed mixture and mix well.

Drop by teaspoonfuls 2 in. apart onto ungreased baking sheets. Bake at 350° for 12-15 minutes or until edges are golden brown. Remove to a wire rack to cool.

Dollie Ainley, Doniphan, Missouri

I've had this recipe for 40 years. These cookies are my husband's favorite, so I bake them almost every week. One of my daughter's friends still remembers having my special treats when she stopped in on her way home from school.

crisp lemon sugar cookies

yield 6-1/2 dozen

1/2	cup butter, softened
1/2	cup butter-flavored shortening
1	cup sugar
1	egg
1	tablespoon milk
2	teaspoons lemon extract
1	teaspoon vanilla extract
2-1/2	cups all-purpose flour
3/4	teaspoon salt
1/2	teaspoon baking soda

Additional sugar

In a large bowl, cream butter, shortening and sugar until light and fluffy. Beat in egg, milk and extracts. Combine the flour, salt and baking soda; gradually add to creamed mixture.

Roll into 1-in. balls or drop by rounded teaspoonfuls 2 in. apart onto ungreased baking sheets. Flatten with a glass dipped in sugar. Bake at 400° for 9-11 minutes or until edges are lightly browned. Immediately remove to wire racks to cool.

Isabel Podeszwa, Lakewood, New Jersey

Since my children are grown, I make these light butter cookies for the neighborhood kids.

golden raisin cookies

yield about 6 dozen

1	cup butter, softened
1-1/2	cups sugar
1	tablespoon lemon juice
2	eggs
3-1/2	cups all-purpose flour
1-1/2	teaspoons cream of tartar
1-1/2	teaspoons baking soda
1	package (15 ounces) golden raisins (2-1/2 cups)

In a large bowl, cream butter and sugar until light and fluffy. Add lemon juice and eggs. Combine dry ingredients; gradually add to creamed mixture. Stir in raisins.

Roll into 1-in. balls. Place on greased baking sheets; flatten with a floured fork. Bake at 400° for 8-10 minutes or until lightly browned.

BAKING tip

storing cookies — Cookies should always be completely cooled, and icings should be completely dry before storing. Store crisp cookies separately from soft cookies, and strong-flavored cookies separately from delicate-flavored ones. If you like, place a sheet of waxed paper between each layer of cookies.

✳ Debbie Carlson, San Diego, California
Whenever Mother made these cookies, there never seemed to be enough! Even now when I make them, they disappear quickly. The buttery treats are great with a cold glass of milk or a steaming mug of hot chocolate.

pecan sandies cookies

yield about 5 dozen

2	**cups butter, softened**
1	**cup confectioners' sugar**
2	**tablespoons water**
4	**teaspoons vanilla extract**
4	**cups all-purpose flour**
2	**cups chopped pecans**

Additional confectioners' sugar

In a large bowl, cream butter and sugar until light and fluffy. Add water and vanilla; mix well. Gradually add flour; fold in pecans.

Roll dough into 1-in. balls. Place on ungreased baking sheets and flatten with fingers. Bake at 300° for 20-25 minutes. Remove to wire racks to cool. When cool, dust with additional confectioners' sugar.

tried 'n' true peanut butter cookies

yield about 8 dozen

✳ Emma Lee Granger
La Pine, Oregon
When I want to offer friends and family a tried-and-true cookie, this is the recipe I turn to. Use either creamy or crunchy peanut butter with delicious results.

4	**cups butter-flavored shortening**
4	**cups peanut butter**
3	**cups sugar**
3	**cups packed brown sugar**
8	**eggs**
4	**teaspoons vanilla extract**
2	**teaspoons water**
9	**cups all-purpose flour**
4	**teaspoons baking soda**
4	**teaspoons salt**

In a large bowl, cream shortening, peanut butter and sugars until light and fluffy. Add eggs, one at a time, beating well after each addition. Beat in vanilla and water. Combine flour, baking soda and salt; gradually add to the creamed mixture.

Drop by heaping tablespoons 2 in. apart onto ungreased baking sheets. Flatten with a fork. Bake at 350° for 12-15 minutes or until golden brown. Remove to wire racks to cool.

editor's note: Reduced-fat or generic brands of peanut butter are not recommended for this recipe.

mocha crackle cookies

yield about 5 dozen

- 1/2 **cup butter**
- 5 **squares (1 ounce** *each***) unsweetened chocolate**
- 1 **tablespoon instant coffee granules**
- 4 **eggs**
- 1/8 **teaspoon salt**
- 1 **cup sugar**
- 1 **cup packed brown sugar**
- 2 **cups plus 3 tablespoons all-purpose flour**
- 2 **teaspoons baking powder**
- 1/3 **cup confectioners' sugar**

In a microwave or saucepan, heat butter, chocolate and coffee until chocolate is melted; cool slightly. In a large bowl, combine eggs and salt. Add sugar and brown sugar. Stir in chocolate mixture; mix well. Combine flour and baking powder; gradually add to egg mixture to form a soft dough. Cover and refrigerate for 2 hours or until easy to handle.

Roll dough into 3/4-in. balls. Roll in confectioners' sugar; place 2 in. apart on greased baking sheets. Bake at 350° for 12 minutes or until set. Remove to wire racks to cool.

cookie jar nut cookies

yield 9 dozen

- 1 **cup butter, softened**
- 2 **cups packed brown sugar**
- 2 **eggs**
- 1/4 **cup milk**
- 1 **teaspoon vanilla extract**
- 3 **cups all-purpose flour**
- 1 **teaspoon baking soda**
- 1 **teaspoon salt**
- 1 **teaspoon ground nutmeg**
- 1 **cup chopped walnuts**

In a large bowl, cream butter and brown sugar until light and fluffy. Add eggs, one at a time, beating well after each addition. Beat in milk and vanilla. Combine flour, baking soda, salt and nutmeg; gradually add to the creamed mixture. Stir in the walnuts.

Drop by rounded teaspoonfuls 2 in. apart onto ungreased baking sheets. Flatten with a glass dipped in sugar. Bake at 350° for 10-12 minutes or until lightly browned. Remove to wire racks to cool.

I started collecting cookie recipes when I was a teenager. These chewy spice cookies were some of the first I ever made, and they're still a favorite today. They can be found in my cookie jar whenever someone stops by.

✻ Kelly Ward-Hartman, Cape Coral, Florida
The night before I make these sweet and salty treats, I measure out the pretzels, peanuts, raisins and chocolate. (I've even used a leftover hollow Easter bunny!) Assembly goes quickly the next day.

chunky drop cookies

yield about 6-1/2 dozen

1	cup butter, softened
1	cup packed brown sugar
1/2	cup sugar
2	eggs
3	teaspoons vanilla extract
2-1/2	cups all-purpose flour
3/4	teaspoon baking powder
2	cups halved pretzel sticks
1	cup coarsely chopped dry roasted peanuts
1	cup semisweet chocolate chunks
1	cup raisins

In a large bowl, cream butter and sugars until light and fluffy. Add eggs, one at a time, beating well after each addition. Beat in vanilla. Combine the flour and baking powder; gradually add to the creamed mixture and mix well. Stir in the pretzels, peanuts, chocolate chunks and raisins.

Drop by heaping tablespoonfuls 2 in. apart onto ungreased baking sheets. Bake at 350° for 10-14 minutes or until edges are golden brown. Cool for 2 minutes before removing to wire racks.

✻ Marion Lowery
Medford, Oregon
These spice cookies loaded with raisins and walnuts really do appeal to all generations —I found the recipe in a 1901 South Dakota cookbook! Sour cream adds a wonderful, unique flair.

soft ginger puffs

yield 8 dozen

1/2	cup butter, softened
3/4	cup sugar
3	eggs
1	cup molasses
1	cup (8 ounces) sour cream
3-1/2	cups all-purpose flour
2	teaspoons ground ginger
1	teaspoon baking soda
1/2	teaspoon *each* ground allspice, cinnamon and nutmeg
1-1/2	cups raisins
1-1/2	cups chopped walnuts

In a large bowl, cream the butter and sugar until light and fluffy. Add eggs, one at a time, beating well after each addition. Beat in the molasses and sour cream. Combine the flour, ginger, baking soda, allspice, cinnamon and nutmeg; gradually add to the creamed mixture. Stir in the raisins and walnuts.

Drop by tablespoonfuls 1 in. apart onto greased baking sheets. Bake at 375° for 10-12 minutes or until the edges begin to brown. Remove to wire racks to cool.

Jo Ann Blomquest, Freeport, Illinois ✳
Cookies that melt in your mouth and are practically fat-free...is it any wonder that these meringue morsels
disappear as fast as I can whip them up? Friends and family love them.

cherry kisses

yield 6 dozen

4	**egg whites**
1-1/4	**cups sugar**
1/3	**cup chopped walnuts**
1/3	**cup chopped pitted dates**
1/3	**cup chopped candied cherries**

Place egg whites in a large bowl; let stand at room temperature for 30 minutes. Beat on medium speed until soft peaks form. Gradually beat in sugar, 1 tablespoon at a time, on high until stiff glossy peaks form and the sugar is dissolved. Fold in the walnuts, dates and cherries.

Drop by teaspoonfuls 2 in. apart onto lightly greased baking sheets. Bake at 300° for 20-30 minutes or until lightly browned and firm to the touch. Remove to wire racks to cool. Store in an airtight container.

Jean Dandrea, Burkesville, Kentucky ✳
A friend shared this delicious recipe with me. The chewy cookies are bound to satisfy big and little kids alike. They're truly
a hit wherever I take them.

toffee oat cookies

yield about 4 dozen

3/4	**cup butter, softened**
1	**cup packed brown sugar**
3/4	**cup sugar**
2	**eggs**
3	**teaspoons vanilla extract**
2-1/4	**cups all-purpose flour**
2-1/4	**cups old-fashioned oats**
1	**teaspoon baking soda**
1	**teaspoon baking powder**
1/2	**teaspoon salt**
1	**package English toffee bits 10 ounces) *or* almond brickle chips (7-1/2 ounces)**

In a large bowl, cream butter and sugars until light and fluffy. Add eggs, one at a time, beating well after each addition. Beat in vanilla. Combine the flour, oats, baking soda, baking powder and salt; gradually add to creamed mixture and mix well. Stir in toffee bits.

Drop by rounded tablespoonfuls 2 in. apart onto ungreased baking sheets. Bake at 375° for 10-12 minutes or until golden brown. Cool for 1 minute before removing from pans to wire racks to cool completely.

※ Sarah Miller, Wauconda, Washington

I get lots of compliments on these crunchy cookies. They're always part of my Christmas cookie platter.

cinnamon-sugar crackle cookies

yield 4 dozen

1	cup shortening
1-3/4	cups sugar, *divided*
2	eggs
2-3/4	cups all-purpose flour
2	teaspoons cream of tartar
1	teaspoon baking soda
1/2	teaspoon salt
4	teaspoons ground cinnamon

In a large bowl, cream shortening and 1-1/2 cups sugar until light and fluffy. Add eggs, one at a time, beating well after each addition. Combine the flour, cream of tartar, baking soda and salt; gradually add to creamed mixture and mix well. Cover and chill for 30 minutes or until easy to handle.

In a small bowl, combine cinnamon and remaining sugar; set aside. Shape dough into 1-in. balls; roll in cinnamon-sugar. Place 2 in. apart on ungreased baking sheets.

Bake at 400° for 8-10 minutes or until lightly browned. Cool for 2 minutes before removing to wire racks.

※ Brenda Beachy, Belvidere, Tennessee

The kitchen smells so good when Mom bakes these yummy cookies, which we like to make with sorghum syrup instead of molasses. They're chewy and tender, with a sugary coating. It's hard to eat just one!

mom's molasses cookies

yield 5 dozen

3/4	cup shortening
1-1/4	cups sugar, *divided*
1	egg
1/4	cup molasses
2	tablespoons milk
1	teaspoon vanilla extract
2-1/2	cups all-purpose flour
1-1/2	teaspoons baking soda
1	teaspoon ground cinnamon
3/4	teaspoon salt
3/4	teaspoon ground nutmeg

In a large bowl, cream shortening and 1 cup sugar until light and fluffy. Beat in the egg, molasses, milk and vanilla. Combine the flour, baking soda, cinnamon, salt and nutmeg; gradually add to creamed mixture and mix well. Cover and refrigerate for 1 hour.

Roll into 1-1/4-in. balls; roll in remaining sugar. Place 2 in. apart on greased baking sheets.

Bake at 350° for 10-14 minutes or until tops crack and edges are slightly firm. Remove to wire racks to cool.

Sharon Bretz, Havre de Grace, Maryland ✳
These treats have a delicate lemon and ginger flavor that's ideal with a hot cup of tea in the afternoon.

soft lemon-ginger cookies

yield 2 dozen

- 1/2 **cup butter, softened**
- 1 **cup packed brown sugar**
- 1 **egg**
- 3 **tablespoons sour cream**
- 1/2 **teaspoon lemon extract**
- 1/2 **teaspoon vanilla extract**
- 1-3/4 **cups all-purpose flour**
- 1 **teaspoon baking soda**
- 1 **teaspoon cream of tartar**
- 1 **teaspoon ground ginger**
- 1/4 **teaspoon salt**

In a large bowl, cream butter and brown sugar until light and fluffy. Beat in the egg, sour cream and extracts. Combine the flour, baking soda, cream of tartar, ginger and salt; gradually add to creamed mixture and mix well.

Drop by rounded teaspoonfuls 2 in. apart onto ungreased baking sheets. Bake at 350° for 10-12 minutes or until lightly browned. Immediately remove from pans to wire racks.

pudding sugar cookies

yield 7 dozen

- 1 **cup butter, softened**
- 1 **cup canola oil**
- 1 **cup sugar**
- 1 **cup confectioners' sugar**
- 2 **eggs**
- 1 **teaspoon vanilla extract**
- 1 **package (3.4 ounces) instant lemon pudding mix *or* instant pudding mix of your choice**
- 4 **cups all-purpose flour**
- 1 **teaspoon cream of tartar**
- 1 **teaspoon baking soda**

In a large bowl, cream the butter, oil and sugars until light and fluffy. Beat in eggs, vanilla and dry pudding mix. Combine the flour, cream of tartar and baking soda; gradually add to creamed mixture and mix well.

Drop by tablespoonfuls 2 in. apart onto ungreased baking sheets. Flatten with a glass dipped in sugar.

Bake at 350° for 12-15 minutes or until lightly browned. Remove to wire racks.

Sharon Reed ✳
Catlin, Illinois
This recipe, which was passed on by a friend, has become a year-round favorite at our house. For fun, substitute other flavors of pudding mix.

✳ Cathy Wilson, Midvale, Utah

My mom added nutritional ingredients to recipes whenever she could. Chock-full of nuts and oats, these crispy-chewy cookies are the perfect example.

coconut drop cookies

yield 5-1/2 dozen

1	cup shortening
1	cup sugar
1	cup packed brown sugar
2	eggs
1	teaspoon vanilla extract
2	cups all-purpose flour
2	cups old-fashioned oats
1	teaspoon baking powder
1	teaspoon baking soda
1/2	teaspoon salt
2	cups flaked coconut
1	cup chopped walnuts

In a large bowl, cream shortening and sugars until light and fluffy. Add eggs, one at a time, beating well after each addition. Beat in vanilla. Combine the flour, oats, baking powder, baking soda and salt; gradually add to creamed mixture and mix well. Stir in coconut and walnuts.

Drop by rounded tablespoonfuls 3 in. apart onto greased baking sheets. Flatten slightly.

Bake at 350° for 11-14 minutes or until golden brown. Cool for 2 minutes before removing to wire racks. Store in an airtight container.

✳ Taste of Home Test Kitchen

A delicious "dunker," this biscotti is chock-full of dried cherries and chocolate chips. Wrapped in colored cellophane and curly ribbons, it makes a lovely homemade holiday or hostess gift.

cherry-chocolate chip biscotti

yield 2-1/2 dozen

3/4	cup sugar
1	tablespoon canola oil
2	eggs
2	egg whites
2	teaspoons vanilla extract
1/4	teaspoon almond extract
2-3/4	cups all-purpose flour
1	teaspoon baking powder
1/4	teaspoon baking soda
1/4	teaspoon salt
2/3	cup dried cherries, chopped
1/2	cup miniature semisweet chocolate chips

In a large bowl, beat sugar and oil until blended. Beat in the eggs, egg whites and extracts. Combine the flour, baking powder, baking soda and salt; gradually add to egg mixture and mix well. Stir in cherries and chocolate chips.

Divide dough in half. With lightly floured hands, shape each portion into a 12-in. x 3-in. rectangle; place each on a baking sheet coated with cooking spray.

Bake at 350° for 15-20 minutes or until lightly browned. Carefully remove to wire racks; cool for 5 minutes.

Transfer to a cutting board; cut with a serrated knife into 3/4-in. slices. Place cut side down on ungreased baking sheets. Bake for 5 minutes. Turn and bake 5-7 minutes longer or until firm. Remove to wire racks to cool. Store in an airtight container.

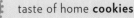

Mary Wilhelm, Sparta, Wisconsin ✳
I have baked these delicious glazed cookies for the Cranberry Festival Cooking Contest in nearby Warrens, where cranberry is "king." They're a favorite of mine.

cranberry cashew jumbles

yield 5 dozen

1/2	cup butter, softened
1	cup packed brown sugar
1/2	cup sour cream
1	egg
1	teaspoon vanilla extract
2	cups all-purpose flour
3/4	teaspoon baking powder
1/4	teaspoon baking soda
1/4	teaspoon salt
1	package (6 ounces) dried cranberries
1	cup chopped cashews

GLAZE:

1	cup confectioners' sugar
2	tablespoons orange juice

In a large bowl, cream butter and brown sugar until light and fluffy. Beat in the sour cream, egg and vanilla. Combine the flour, baking powder, baking soda and salt; gradually add to creamed mixture and mix well. Stir in cranberries and cashews.

Drop by tablespoonfuls 2 in. apart onto ungreased baking sheets. Bake 375° for 10-12 minutes or until lightly browned. Remove to wire racks to cool. Combine glaze ingredients; drizzle over cookies.

Pat Doerflinger, Centerview, Missouri ✳
The smell of peanut butter and chocolate always brings my cookie-hungry family to the kitchen. This recipe is so quick and easy, I often stir up a batch while making dinner.

peanut butter chippers

yield 3-1/2 dozen

6	tablespoons butter, softened
1/4	cup peanut butter
1/2	cup sugar
1/2	cup packed brown sugar
1	egg
1	teaspoon vanilla extract
1-1/4	cups all-purpose flour
1/2	teaspoon baking soda
1/4	teaspoon salt
1	cup milk chocolate chips

In a small bowl, cream the butter, peanut butter and sugars until light and fluffy. Beat in egg and vanilla. Combine the flour, baking soda and salt; gradually add to creamed mixture and mix well. Stir in chocolate chips.

Drop by tablespoonfuls 2 in. apart onto ungreased baking sheets. Bake at 350° for 11-14 minutes or until golden brown. Remove to wire racks.

editor's note: Reduced-fat or generic brands of peanut butter are not recommended for this recipe.

chock-full of chips

banana chocolate chip cookies, p. 32

If you're crazy about chips,

here's a collection of delicious recipes showcasing

semisweet, milk, peanut butter, butterscotch and

vanilla chips. You'll discover new variations on classic

chocolate chip cookies, as well as chips in delicate

meringue cookies and even hearty biscotti.

honey maple cookies, p. 33

pistachio thumbprints, p. 49

❋ Katie Jean Boyd, Roachdale, Indiana

I take these cookies to family gatherings and socials and give them as gifts to friends. The cinnamon flavor and soft frosting make them special.

iced cinnamon chip cookies

yield about 3-1/2 dozen

1	cup butter, softened
3/4	cup sugar
3/4	cup packed brown sugar
2	eggs
1	teaspoon vanilla extract
3	cups all-purpose flour
1	teaspoon baking soda
1	teaspoon salt
1	package (10 ounces) cinnamon baking chips

ICING:

1/4	cup butter, melted
1/4	cup shortening
1-1/4	cups confectioners' sugar
1	tablespoon milk
3/4	teaspoon vanilla extract

In a large bowl, cream the butter and sugars until light and fluffy. Beat in the eggs and vanilla. Combine the flour, baking soda and salt; gradually add to the creamed mixture and mix well. Fold in cinnamon chips.

Drop by rounded tablespoonfuls 2 in. apart onto ungreased baking sheets. Bake at 350° for 10-12 minutes or until golden brown. Remove to wire racks to cool.

In a small bowl, combine icing ingredients; beat on high speed for 1-2 minutes or until fluffy. Spread over cooled cookies.

Dee Derezinski, Waukesha, Wisconsin ✳

This is my favorite Christmas cookie recipe. The cookies remind me of the snowballs I'd packed as a child during the snowy winters here in southeastern Wisconsin.

chocolate snowballs

yield about 4 dozen

3/4	cup butter, softened
1/2	cup sugar
1	egg
2	teaspoons vanilla extract
2	cups all-purpose flour
1/2	teaspoon salt
1	cup chopped nuts
1	cup (6 ounces) chocolate chips

Confectioners' sugar

In a large bowl, cream butter and sugar. Add egg and vanilla; mix well. Combine the flour and salt; stir into creamed mixture. Fold in the nuts and chips.

Roll into 1-in. balls. Place 1 in. apart on ungreased baking sheets. Bake at 350° for 15-20 minutes. Remove to wire racks. Cool cookies slightly before rolling in confectioners' sugar.

raspberry meringues

yield 7-1/2 dozen

3	egg whites
3	tablespoons plus 1 teaspoon raspberry gelatin powder
3/4	cup sugar
1	teaspoon white vinegar
1/8	teaspoon salt
2	cups (12 ounces) semisweet chocolate chips
1/2	cup finely chopped pecans

TOPPING:

1/4	cup semisweet chocolate chips
1	teaspoon shortening

Place egg whites in a small bowl; let stand at room temperature for 30 minutes. Beat the egg whites until soft peaks form. Gradually add gelatin, beating until combined. Gradually add sugar, 1 tablespoon at a time, beating until stiff peaks form. Beat in vinegar and salt. Fold in chocolate chips and nuts.

Drop by rounded teaspoonfuls onto parchment-lined baking sheets. Bake at 250° for 20-25 minutes or until firm to the touch. Turn oven off; leave the cookies in the oven with door ajar for about 1-1/2 hours or until cool. In a microwave or heavy saucepan, melt the chocolate chips and shortening; stir until smooth. Drizzle over cookies.

Iola Egle ✳
McCook, Nebraska
As rosy pink as Santa's cheeks, these merry meringue cookies are drizzled with dark chocolate and are almost too pretty to eat. Pecans add a nice crunch to these chewy treats.

※ Vicki Raatz, Waterloo, Wisconsin
These soft cookies have a cake-like texture and lots of banana flavor that folks love.

banana chocolate chip cookies

yield 3 dozen

1/3	cup butter, softened
1/2	cup sugar
1	egg
1/2	cup mashed ripe banana
1/2	teaspoon vanilla extract
1	cup all-purpose flour
1	teaspoon baking powder
1/4	teaspoon salt
1/8	teaspoon baking soda
1	cup (6 ounces) semisweet chocolate chips

In a small bowl, cream butter and sugar until light and fluffy. Beat in the egg, banana and vanilla. Combine the flour, baking powder, salt and baking soda; gradually add to creamed mixture and mix well. Stir in chocolate chips.

Drop by tablespoonfuls 2 in. apart onto baking sheets coated with cooking spray. Bake at 350° for 9-11 minutes or until edges are lightly browned. Remove to wire racks to cool.

※ Linda Wheeler Sparks
Severna Park, Maryland
With oats, two kinds of chips and a strawberry drizzle on top, each bite of this cookie is packed with fabulous flavor!

special chocolate chip cookies

yield about 4-1/2 dozen

1/2	cup quick-cooking oats
1	Nestle Crunch candy bar (1.4 ounces), broken into pieces
1/4	cup chopped pecans
1	cup butter, softened
3/4	cup packed brown sugar
1/2	cup sugar
2	eggs
3	teaspoons vanilla extract
2	cups all-purpose flour
1	teaspoon baking soda
1/2	teaspoon salt
1	cup semisweet chocolate chips
1	cup vanilla *or* white chips

ICING:

2	cups confectioners' sugar
2	tablespoons milk
2	teaspoons strawberry *or* raspberry extract
1	to 2 drops red food coloring, optional

In a food processor, combine the oats, candy bar and pecans. Cover and process until finely chopped; set aside.

In a large bowl, cream butter and sugars until light and fluffy. Add eggs, one at a time, beating well after each addition. Beat in vanilla. Combine the flour, baking soda, salt and reserved oat mixture; gradually add to creamed mixture and mix well. Stir in chips.

Drop by tablespoonfuls 2 in. apart onto ungreased baking sheets. Bake at 350° for 11-13 minutes or until lightly browned. Cool for 2 minutes before removing to wire racks to cool completely.

Combine the icing ingredients until smooth; drizzle over cookies. Let stand until set. Store in an airtight container.

Bernice Morris, Marshfield, Missouri ✳
These light, crispy cookies are packed with fun ingredients perfect for Halloween.

goblin chewies

yield about 6 dozen

1	cup shortening
1	cup packed brown sugar
1	cup sugar
2	eggs
1	teaspoon vanilla extract
2	cups all-purpose flour
1	teaspoon baking soda
1/2	teaspoon baking powder
1/2	teaspoon salt
1-1/2	cups old-fashioned oats
1	cup crisp rice cereal
1	cup diced candy orange slices
1	cup (6 ounces) semisweet chocolate chips *or* raisins

Additional raisins *or* chocolate chips and candy orange slices

In a mixing bowl, cream shortening and sugars. Add eggs and vanilla; mix well. Combine the flour, baking soda, baking powder and salt; add to creamed mixture. Stir in oats, cereal, orange slices and chips or raisins.

Drop dough by tablespoonfuls 2 in. apart onto greased baking sheets. Flatten slightly with a fork. Decorate with raisin or chocolate chip eyes and orange slice mouths. Bake at 350° for 10-14 minutes. Remove to wire racks to cool.

editor's note: Orange slices cut easier if microwaved for 5 seconds on high and cut with a sharp knife or kitchen scissors.

Barbara Kuder, Tribune, Kansas ✳
Honey and maple syrup make these chocolate chip cookies a little different. The maple flavor is pleasant and subtle.

honey maple cookies

yield 5 dozen

1	cup shortening
3/4	cup honey
3/4	cup maple syrup
2	eggs
1	teaspoon vanilla extract
2-1/2	cups all-purpose flour
1	teaspoon baking soda
1	teaspoon salt
2	cups (12 ounces) semisweet chocolate chips
1	cup chopped pecans

In a large bowl, beat shortening until light and fluffy. Add honey and syrup, a little at a time, beating well after each addition. Add eggs, one at a time, beating well after each addition (mixture will appear curdled). Beat in vanilla. Combine the flour, baking soda and salt. Gradually add to honey mixture and mix until moistened. Stir in chocolate chips and pecans.

Drop by rounded tablespoonfuls onto greased baking sheets. Bake at 350° for 8-10 minutes or until golden brown. Remove to wire racks.

* Dorothy Kollmeyer, Dupo, Illinois
If you like cookies with crunch, you'll love these golden treats. Crushed peanut brittle adds an unexpected kick to the vanilla chips and brown sugar that flavor the dough. It's hard to believe something this simple to make tastes so terrific.

macadamia chip cookies

yield 5-1/2 dozen

1	cup butter, softened
3/4	cup packed brown sugar
1/4	cup sugar
2	eggs
1	teaspoon vanilla extract
2-1/4	cups all-purpose flour
1	package (3.4 ounces) instant vanilla pudding mix
1	teaspoon baking soda
1/4	teaspoon salt
1	package (10 to 12 ounces) vanilla *or* white chips
2	jars (3-1/4 ounces *each*) macadamia nuts, chopped
1/2	cup finely crushed peanut brittle

In a large bowl, cream butter and sugars until light and fluffy. Add eggs, one at a time, beating well after each addition. Beat in vanilla. Combine the flour, dry pudding mix, baking soda and salt; gradually add to creamed mixture and mix well. Stir in the chips, nuts and peanut brittle.

Drop by rounded tablespoonfuls 2 in. apart onto greased baking sheets. Bake at 375° for 10-12 minutes or until golden brown. Remove to wire racks to cool.

* Maria Groff, Ephrata, Pennsylvania
When I baked these moist, fudgy cookies for the first time, my three children loved them! But I like them because they're lower in fat and easy to mix and bake.

crinkle-top chocolate cookies

yield 3-1/2 dozen

2	cups (12 ounces) semisweet chocolate chips, *divided*
2	tablespoons butter, softened
1	cup sugar
2	egg whites
1-1/2	teaspoons vanilla extract
1-1/2	cups all-purpose flour
1-1/2	teaspoons baking powder
1/4	teaspoon salt
1/4	cup water
1/2	cup confectioners' sugar

In a microwave, melt 1 cup chocolate chips. Stir until smooth; set aside. In a small bowl, beat butter and sugar until crumbly, about 2 minutes. Add egg whites and vanilla; beat well. Stir in melted chocolate. Combine the flour, baking powder and salt; gradually add to butter mixture alternately with water. Stir in remaining chocolate chips. Cover and refrigerate for 2 hours or until easy to handle.

Shape dough into 1-in. balls. Roll in the confectioners' sugar. Place 2 in. apart on baking sheets coated with cooking spray. Bake at 350° for 10-12 minutes or until set. Remove to wire racks to cool.

Shauna Stephens, San Diego, California ✳
This recipe will make a cookie-lover's dream come true! Chock-full of pecans, walnuts and three types of chips—semisweet, milk and vanilla—these crisp treats will be a hit with your family.

chips galore cookies

yield 9 dozen

1	cup butter, softened
3/4	cup sugar
3/4	cup packed brown sugar
2	eggs
1	tablespoon almond extract
2-1/4	cups all-purpose flour
1	teaspoon baking soda
1/2	teaspoon salt
1-1/2	cups *each* semisweet chocolate chips, milk chocolate chips and vanilla *or* white chips
1-1/2	cups chopped pecans
1-1/2	cups chopped walnuts

In a large bowl, cream butter and sugars. Add eggs, one at a time, beating well after each addition. Beat in almond extract. Combine the flour, baking soda and salt; gradually add to creamed mixture. Combine chips and nuts; stir into dough. Cover and refrigerate for 1 hour or until easy to handle.

Drop by tablespoonfuls 2 in. apart onto greased baking sheets. Bake at 325° for 18-20 minutes or until golden brown. Remove to wire racks to cool completely.

big chocolate cookies

yield 1 dozen

6	tablespoons butter
6	squares (1 ounce *each*) semisweet chocolate
2	squares (1 ounce *each*) unsweetened chocolate
2	eggs
3/4	cup sugar
2	teaspoons instant coffee granules
1	tablespoon boiling water
2	teaspoons vanilla extract
1/4	cup all-purpose flour
1/2	teaspoon salt
1/4	teaspoon baking powder
1	cup (6 ounces) semisweet chocolate chips
1	cup coarsely chopped walnuts
1	cup coarsely chopped pecans

In a microwave or heavy saucepan, melt butter and the chocolate squares; cool. In a bowl, beat eggs until foamy; gradually add sugar. Dissolve the coffee granules in water. Add the coffee, vanilla and cooled chocolate mixture to egg mixture. Combine the flour, salt and baking powder; gradually add to the egg mixture. Stir in chocolate chips and nuts.

Drop by 1/3 cupfuls 4 in. apart onto ungreased baking sheets. Bake at 350° for 15-17 minutes or until firm. Cool for 4 minutes before removing to wire racks.

editor's note: 1/4 cup flour is the correct amount.

Marie Macy ✳
Fort Collins, Colorado
The combination of different kinds of chocolate makes these cookies irresistible. Friends and family are delighted to have a "big" cookie to enjoy.

＊ Denise DeJong, Pittsburgh, Pennsylvania
This is a cookie you will want to make again and again. I like to take it to church get-togethers and family reunions. It's very delicious...crispy on the outside and chewy on the inside.

white chocolate chip hazelnut cookies

yield 3 dozen

1-1/4	cups whole hazelnuts, toasted, *divided*
9	tablespoons butter, softened, *divided*
1/2	cup sugar
1/2	cup packed brown sugar
1	egg
1	teaspoon vanilla extract
1-1/2	cups all-purpose flour
1/2	teaspoon baking soda
1/2	teaspoon salt
1	cup white *or* vanilla chips

Coarsely chop 1/2 cup hazelnuts; set aside. Melt 2 tablespoons butter. In a food processor, combine melted butter and remaining hazelnuts. Cover and process until the mixture forms a crumbly paste; set aside.

In a large bowl, cream the remaining butter. Beat in the sugars. Add egg and vanilla; beat until light and fluffy. Beat in ground hazelnut mixture until blended. Combine the flour, baking soda and salt; add to batter and mix just until combined. Stir in chips and chopped hazelnuts.

Drop by rounded tablespoonfuls 2 in. apart onto greased baking sheets. Bake at 350° for 10-12 minutes or until lightly browned. Remove to wire racks to cool.

oatmeal s'more cookies

yield about 6 dozen

＊ Carmen Rae
New Haven, Indiana
I can't count how many times I have made these cookies—they are our favorites. I love to bake all kinds of goodies with my two daughters, and my husband loves to sample the treats.

1/2	cup butter, softened
1/2	cup shortening
1	cup packed brown sugar
1/2	cup sugar
2	eggs
1-1/2	teaspoons vanilla extract
3	cups all-purpose flour
1	teaspoon baking soda
1/4	teaspoon salt
1-1/2	cups old-fashioned oats
1	cup (6 ounces) semisweet chocolate chips
1	cup miniature marshmallows

In a large bowl, cream the butter, shortening and sugars until light and fluffy. Add eggs, one at a time, beating well after each addition. Beat in vanilla. Combine flour, baking soda and salt; gradually add to creamed mixture and mix well. Stir in oats, chocolate chips and marshmallows.

Drop by heaping teaspoonfuls 2 in. apart onto greased baking sheets. Bake at 350° for 9-11 minutes or until golden brown. Cool for 1-2 minutes before removing from pans to wire racks to cool completely.

Margaret Wilson, Hemet, California ✳

Chopped maraschino cherries and vanilla chips make a great color and flavor combination in these sweet treats. They're a nice change from chocolate chip cookies that use semisweet chocolate and nuts.

vanilla chip cherry cookies

yield 4-1/2 dozen

1	cup butter, softened
3/4	cup sugar
3/4	cup packed brown sugar
2	eggs
1/4	teaspoon almond extract
2-1/4	cups all-purpose flour
1	teaspoon baking soda
1/2	teaspoon salt
1	package (16 ounces) vanilla *or* white chips
1	jar (10 ounces) maraschino cherries, drained and chopped

In a large bowl, cream butter and sugars until light and fluffy. Add eggs, one at a time, beating well after each addition. Beat in almond extract. Combine the flour, baking soda and salt; gradually add to the creamed mixture and mix well. Stir in chips and cherries.

Drop by rounded tablespoonfuls 2 in. apart onto ungreased baking sheets. Bake at 350° for 10-12 minutes or until lightly browned. Remove to wire racks to cool.

Diane Neth, Menno, South Dakota ✳

Crazy about chocolate chips? This chewy cookie has plenty, not to mention lots of heart-healthy oatmeal. Your family will come back to the cookie jar again and again, so this big batch is perfect.

chocolate chip oatmeal cookies

yield about 7 dozen

1	cup butter, softened
3/4	cup sugar
3/4	cup packed brown sugar
2	eggs
1	teaspoon vanilla extract
3	cups quick-cooking oats
1-1/2	cups all-purpose flour
1	package (3.4 ounces) instant vanilla pudding mix
1	teaspoon baking soda
1	teaspoon salt
2	cups (12 ounces) semisweet chocolate chips
1	cup chopped nuts

In a large bowl, cream butter and sugars until light and fluffy. Beat in eggs and vanilla. Combine the oats, flour, pudding mix, baking soda and salt; gradually add to creamed mixture and mix well. Stir in chocolate chips and nuts.

Drop by rounded teaspoonfuls 2 in. apart onto ungreased baking sheets. Bake at 375° for 10-12 minutes or until lightly browned. Remove to wire racks.

Teri Rasey-Bolf, Cadillac, Michigan
These cookies are the next best thing to a good old-fashioned malted milk shake. With malted milk powder, chocolate syrup plus chocolate chips and chunks, these are the best cookies I've ever tasted.

chocolate malted cookies

yield about 1-1/2 dozen

1	cup butter-flavored shortening
1-1/4	cups packed brown sugar
1/2	cup malted milk powder
2	tablespoons chocolate syrup
1	tablespoon vanilla extract
1	egg
2	cups all-purpose flour
1	teaspoon baking soda
1/2	teaspoon salt
1-1/2	cups semisweet chocolate chunks
1	cup milk chocolate chips

In a large bowl, beat the shortening, brown sugar, malted milk powder, chocolate syrup and vanilla for 2 minutes. Add egg. Combine the flour, baking soda and salt; gradually add to creamed mixture, mixing well after each addition. Stir in the chocolate chunks and chips.

Roll into 2-in. balls; place 3 in. apart on ungreased baking sheets. Bake at 375° for 12-14 minutes or until golden brown. Cool for 2 minutes before removing to a wire rack.

Lois Bowman, Swanton, Maryland
I bake these terrific peanut butter cookies often. My grandchildren can't wait to dig into the cookie jar.

peanut butter maple cookies

yield about 5 dozen

1	cup butter, softened
1/2	cup peanut butter
1	cup sugar
1	cup packed brown sugar
2	eggs
1	tablespoon maple syrup
2	teaspoons vanilla extract
2	cups all-purpose flour
3/4	cup quick-cooking oats
1-1/2	teaspoons baking powder
1	teaspoon baking soda
1	teaspoon salt
1	package (10 ounces) peanut butter chips

In a large bowl, cream the butter, peanut butter and sugars. Add the eggs, one at a time, beating well after each addition. Beat in syrup and vanilla. Combine the flour, oats, baking powder, baking soda and salt; add to the creamed mixture and mix well. Stir in peanut butter chips.

Drop by heaping tablespoonfuls 2 in. apart onto ungreased baking sheets. Bake at 325° for 15-18 minutes or until golden brown. Cool for 1 minute before removing to wire racks.

editor's note: Reduced-fat or generic brands of peanut butter are not recommended for this recipe.

Debbie Johnson, New Bloomfield, Missouri ✳

I contribute this quick-and-easy treat to every bake sale our two daughters are involved in. Everyone seems to love the great-tasting combination of yummy chocolate and marshmallows on a homemade peanut butter cookie crust.

cookie pizza

yield 10-12 servings

1/2	**cup butter, softened**
1/2	**cup peanut butter**
1/2	**cup sugar**
1/2	**cup packed brown sugar**
1	**egg**
1/2	**teaspoon vanilla extract**
1-1/2	**cups all-purpose flour**
2	**cups miniature marshmallows**
1	**cup (6 ounces) semisweet chocolate chips**

In a large bowl, cream butter, peanut butter and sugars. Beat in egg and vanilla. Stir in flour until blended.

Spread the dough onto a greased 12-in. pizza pan. Bake at 375° for 12 minutes. Sprinkle with the marshmallows and chocolate chips. Bake 5-6 minutes longer or until lightly browned.

editor's note: Reduced-fat or generic brands of peanut butter are not recommended for this recipe.

chewy peanut butter crisps

yield 3-1/2 dozen

1	**cup peanut butter**
1	**cup sugar**
1/2	**cup evaporated milk**
4	**teaspoons cornstarch**
1/2	**cup semisweet chocolate chips**

In a large bowl, combine peanut butter and sugar. Stir in milk and cornstarch until smooth. Add chocolate chips.

Drop by heaping teaspoonfuls 2 in. apart onto ungreased baking sheets. Bake at 350° for 12-15 minutes or until golden brown. Remove to wire racks to cool.

editor's note: This recipe does not use flour. Reduced-fat or generic brands of peanut butter are not recommended for this recipe.

Lucy Garrett ✳
Cedartown, Georgia
This flourless cookies successfully combine a chewy inside and crispy outside. Plus, chocolate and peanut butter are a classic combination that's hard to beat. It uses only five ingredients and take just minutes to mix up.

BAKING

mixing it up — Drop cookie dough is usually so thick that it can be dropped from a spoon and requires no shaping. If while you are mixing the dough the mixer begins to strain, use a wooden spoon to stir in the last of the flour or all of the chips, nuts and dried fruit.

❋ Johna Nilson, Vista, California

My son especially likes testing—or should I say consuming—these chunky cookies! They're packed with yummy ingredients, including granola, nuts, vanilla chips and dried cranberries.

iced pumpkin cookies

yield 3 dozen

1	**cup butter, softened**
1/2	**cup sugar**
1/2	**cup packed brown sugar**
1	**egg**
1	**cup canned pumpkin**
1	**cup all-purpose flour**
1	**cup whole wheat flour**
1-1/2	**teaspoons ground cinnamon**
1	**teaspoon baking powder**
1	**teaspoon ground ginger**
1/2	**teaspoon salt**
1/2	**teaspoon baking soda**
1/2	**teaspoon ground nutmeg**
1/4	**teaspoon ground cloves**
1	**cup granola without raisins**
1	**cup chopped walnuts**

1	**cup vanilla *or* white chips**
1	**cup dried cranberries**

ICING:

1/4	**cup butter, softened**
2	**cups confectioners' sugar**
3	**tablespoons milk**

In a large bowl, cream butter and sugars until light and fluffy. Beat in egg and pumpkin. Combine the flours, cinnamon, baking powder, ginger, salt, baking soda, nutmeg and cloves; gradually add to creamed mixture and mix well. Stir in the granola, walnuts, chips and cranberries.

Drop by tablespoonfuls 2 in. apart onto greased baking sheets. Bake at 350° for 15-18 minutes or until lightly browned. Remove to wire racks to cool.

In a small bowl, combine icing ingredients until smooth. Spread over cooled cookies. Store in the refrigerator.

Ian Badeer, Hickman, Nebraska ✳

As simple as it may seem, the key to baking is to follow directions. Once I learned that, I began to modify recipes, which is how I created these chewy peanut butter cookies with swirled chips.

chippy peanut butter cookies

yield about 4 dozen

1	**cup butter, softened**
1	**cup creamy peanut butter**
1	**cup sugar**
1	**cup packed brown sugar**
2	**eggs**
1	**teaspoon vanilla extract**
2-1/4	**cups all-purpose flour**
2	**teaspoons baking soda**
1/4	**teaspoon salt**
1	**package (10 ounces) swirled milk chocolate and peanut butter chips**

In a large bowl, cream butter, peanut butter and sugars until light and fluffy. Add eggs, one at a time, beating well after each addition. Beat in vanilla. Combine the flour, baking soda and salt; gradually add to creamed mixture and mix well. Stir in chips.

Drop dough by rounded tablespoonfuls onto ungreased baking sheets. Bake at 350° for 12-15 minutes or until golden brown. Cool for 2 minutes before removing to wire racks.

editor's note: This recipe was tested with Nestle swirled milk chocolate and peanut butter chips. Reduced-fat or generic brands of peanut butter are not recommended for this recipe.

chunky mocha cookies

yield about 6 dozen

1	**cup butter-flavored shortening**	1	**cup chopped pecans**
3/4	**cup sugar**	1	**cup (6 ounces) semisweet chocolate chips**
1/2	**cup packed brown sugar**	3/4	**cup raisins**
2	**eggs**	3/4	**cup flaked coconut**
2	**tablespoons milk**		
1	**tablespoon instant coffee granules**		
1	**teaspoon vanilla extract**		
2-1/3	**cups all-purpose flour**		
2	**tablespoons baking cocoa**		
1	**teaspoon baking soda**		
1/2	**teaspoon salt**		

In a large bowl, cream shortening and sugars. Beat in eggs, milk, coffee granules and vanilla. Combine the flour, cocoa, baking soda and salt; add to the creamed mixture and mix well. Stir in pecans, chips, raisins and coconut.

Drop by rounded tablespoonfuls 2 in. apart onto ungreased baking sheets. Bake at 375° for 10-12 minutes. Remove to wire racks to cool.

Janet Sparks ✳
Shirley, Indiana

My Home Economics Club has a cookie exchange every Christmas. These cookies flavored with a hint of coffee are always a big hit.

❋ Monna Lu Bauer, Lexington, Kentucky

If you and your family like sweet-and-salty treats, these cookies are perfect. They quickly bake to a crispy, golden brown, and then they disappear even faster!

potato chip cookies

yield 4 dozen

1	cup butter-flavored shortening
3/4	cup sugar
3/4	cup packed brown sugar
2	eggs
2	cups all-purpose flour
1	teaspoon baking soda
2	cups crushed potato chips
1	cup butterscotch chips

In a large bowl, cream shortening and sugars until light and fluffy. Beat in eggs. Combine flour and baking soda; gradually add to creamed mixture and mix well. Stir in potato chips and butterscotch chips.

Drop by tablespoonfuls 2 in. apart onto ungreased baking sheets. Bake at 375° for 10-12 minutes or until golden brown. Cool for 1 minute before removing to wire racks.

❋ Diane Selich, Vassar, Michigan

With chocolate chips and coconut in the batter and a rich, pecan-coconut frosting, these cookies will remind you of German chocolate cake. A drizzle of chocolate tops them off in a festive way.

coconut pecan cookies

yield 6-1/2 dozen

1	egg, lightly beaten
1	can (5 ounces) evaporated milk
2/3	cup sugar
1/4	cup butter, cubed
1-1/4	cups flaked coconut
1/2	cup chopped pecans

COOKIE DOUGH:

1	cup butter, softened
3/4	cup sugar
3/4	cup packed brown sugar
2	eggs
1	teaspoon vanilla extract
2-1/4	cups all-purpose flour
1	teaspoon baking soda
1	teaspoon salt
4	cups (24 ounces) semisweet chocolate chips, *divided*
1/4	cup flaked coconut

For frosting, in a large saucepan, combine the egg, milk, sugar and butter. Cook and stir over medium-low heat for 10-12 minutes or until slightly thickened and mixture reaches 160° or is thick enough to coat the back of a metal spoon. Stir in coconut and pecans. Set aside.

In a large bowl, cream butter and sugars until light and fluffy. Add eggs, one at a time, beating well after each addition. Beat in vanilla. Combine the flour, baking soda and salt; gradually add to creamed mixture and mix well. Stir in 2 cups chips and coconut.

Drop by tablespoonfuls 2 in. apart onto ungreased baking sheets. Bake at 350° for 8-10 minutes or until lightly browned. Cool for 10 minutes before removing to wire racks to cool completely.

In a microwave, melt the remaining chocolate chips; stir until smooth. Spread frosting over cooled cookies; drizzle with melted chocolate.

Susan Henry, Bullhead City, Arizona ✳

My mom liked to add different spices to traditional recipes and create unexpected tastes. In my opinion, molasses and cinnamon make these cookies stand out.

oatmeal chip cookies

yield about 1-1/2 dozen

1/2	cup shortening
1	cup sugar
1	tablespoon molasses
1	egg
1	teaspoon vanilla extract
1	cup all-purpose flour
1	cup quick-cooking oats
1	teaspoon baking soda
1	teaspoon ground cinnamon
1/2	teaspoon salt
1	cup (6 ounces) semisweet chocolate chips

In a large bowl, cream shortening and sugar until light and fluffy. Beat in the molasses, egg and vanilla. Combine the flour, oats, baking soda, cinnamon and salt; gradually add to creamed mixture and mix well. Stir in the chocolate chips.

Roll into 1-1/2-in. balls. Place 2 in. apart on greased baking sheets. Bake at 350° for 8-10 minutes or until golden brown. Cool for 5 minutes before removing cookies from pans to wire racks.

Patricia Schroedl, Jefferson, Wisconsin ✳

This recipe combines several of my favorites flavors—peanut butter, butterscotch and chocolate—in one monster cookie. Before baking, press a few extra M&M's on top for added color.

monster cookies

yield about 2-1/2 dozen

1	cup peanut butter
1/2	cup butter, softened
1-1/4	cups packed brown sugar
1	cup sugar
3	eggs
2	teaspoons baking soda
1	teaspoon vanilla extract
4	cups quick-cooking oats
1	cup M&M's
1	cup butterscotch chips
1	cup salted peanuts
2	cups all-purpose flour

In a large bowl, cream peanut butter, butter and sugars. Add eggs, one at a time, beating well after each addition. Add baking soda and vanilla. Add oats, M&M's, butterscotch chips and peanuts; let stand for 10 minutes. Stir in flour (the dough will be crumbly).

Shape 1/4 cupfuls into balls. Place on greased baking sheets, about nine cookies on each sheet. Gently flatten cookies. Bake at 325° for 15-18 minutes or until edges are lightly browned. Remove to wire racks to cool.

editor's note: Reduced-fat or generic brands of peanut butter are not recommended for this recipe.

✳ Kathy Zielicke, Fond du Lac, Wisconsin
If you have a craving for cookies and you want them now, these yummy strips take just a few minutes to make from start to finish. Nothing could be quicker!

cookie sticks

yield about 3 dozen

1/2	cup vegetable oil
1/2	cup sugar
1/2	cup packed brown sugar
1	egg
1	teaspoon vanilla extract
1-1/2	cups all-purpose flour
1/2	teaspoon baking soda
1/2	teaspoon salt
1	cup (6 ounces) semisweet chocolate chips
1/2	cup chopped walnuts, optional

In a bowl, combine the oil, sugars, egg and vanilla. Combine the flour, baking soda and salt; gradually add to sugar mixture. Divide dough in half.

On a greased baking sheet, shape each portion into a 15-in. x 3-in. rectangle about 3 in. apart. Sprinkle chocolate chips and nuts if desired over dough; press lightly.

Bake at 375° for 6-7 minutes. (Bake for 8-9 minutes for crispier cookies.) Cool for 5 minutes. Cut with a serrated knife into 1-in. strips; remove to wire racks to cool.

✳ Betty Holzinger, West Olive, Michigan
Putting chocolate chips in these refrigerator cookies make them deliciously different. This treat is welcome at my house.

chocolate chip icebox cookies

yield 20 cookies

3	tablespoons butter, softened
2	tablespoons shortening
1/4	cup sugar
1/4	cup packed brown sugar
1	egg yolk
1/2	teaspoon vanilla extract
2/3	cup all-purpose flour
1/4	teaspoon baking soda
1/4	teaspoon salt
1/4	cup miniature semisweet chocolate chips
1/4	cup finely chopped pecans

In a small bowl, cream the butter, shortening and sugars. Beat in egg yolk and vanilla; mix well. Combine the flour, baking soda and salt; gradually add to creamed mixture and mix well. Stir in chips and pecans. Shape into a 9-in. roll; wrap in plastic wrap. Chill overnight.

Unwrap and cut into 1/4-in. slices. Place 2 in. apart on ungreased baking sheets. Bake at 375° for 8-10 minutes or until edges are golden brown. Cool for 2 minutes before removing to wire racks.

Tina Sawchuk, Ardmore, Alberta ✳
My husband and I live on a mixed farm with our daughter and son. Among my favorite hobbies are baking and gardening. These soft chocolaty cookies can be easily altered to make several different varieties.

sour cream chocolate cookies

yield about 3 dozen

1/2	cup butter, softened
3/4	cup sugar
1/2	cup packed brown sugar
1	egg
1/2	cup sour cream
1	teaspoon vanilla extract
1-3/4	cups all-purpose flour
1/2	cup baking cocoa
1	teaspoon baking powder
1/2	teaspoon baking soda
1/4	teaspoon salt
1	cup (6 ounces) semisweet chocolate chips
1/2	cup vanilla *or* white chips

In a large bowl, cream butter and sugars. Beat in the egg, sour cream and vanilla. Combine dry ingredients; gradually add to the creamed mixture. Stir in chips.

Drop by rounded tablespoonfuls 2 in. apart onto greased baking sheets. Bake at 350° for 12-15 minutes or until set. Cool for 2 minutes before removing to wire racks.

grandma's wheat germ cookies

yield 4 dozen

1	cup packed brown sugar
1/2	cup canola oil
2	eggs, lightly beaten
1/2	cup unsweetened applesauce
1-1/2	cups all-purpose flour
1-1/2	cups toasted wheat germ
1	cup quick-cooking oats
2	teaspoons baking powder
1	teaspoon salt
1	cup (6 ounces) miniature chocolate chips
1/2	cup chopped walnuts *or* pecans

In a large bowl, beat brown sugar and oil until blended. Beat in the eggs, then applesauce. Combine the flour, wheat germ, oats, baking powder and salt; gradually add to brown sugar mixture and mix well. Stir in chocolate chips and walnuts.

Drop by rounded teaspoonfuls 2 in. apart onto baking sheets coated with cooking spray. Flatten slightly with a glass bottom coated with cooking spray.

Bake at 350° for 10-12 minutes or until edges are lightly browned and cookies are set. Cool for 1 minute before removing to wire racks.

Pam Voigt ✳
Clear Lake, Minnesota
I lightened up an oatmeal chocolate chip cookie by adding wheat germ, eliminating butter and using applesauce. The result is healthier and tasty.

✳ Sybil Brown, Highland, California

Each Christmas, I make about 600 cookies to share with family and friends. The holidays wouldn't be the same without several batches of these goodies. The pecans, maraschino cherries and semisweet chips make a great flavor combination.

cherry chocolate nut cookies

yield 5 dozen

1/2	cup butter, softened
1/2	cup sugar
1/2	cup packed brown sugar
1	egg
1/4	cup milk
1	teaspoon vanilla extract
2	cups all-purpose flour
1	teaspoon baking powder
1/2	teaspoon salt
1/4	teaspoon baking soda
1	cup (6 ounces) semisweet chocolate chips
3/4	cup chopped maraschino cherries
3/4	cup chopped pecans

In a large bowl, cream butter and sugars. Beat in the egg, milk and vanilla. Combine the flour, baking powder, salt and baking soda; gradually add to the creamed mixture. Stir in the remaining ingredients.

Drop by tablespoonfuls 2 in. apart onto greased baking sheets. Bake at 375° for 10-12 minutes or until golden brown. Remove to wire racks to cool.

vanilla chip maple cookies

yield about 7 dozen

✳ Debra Hogenson
Brewster, Minnesota

These cookies have a distinct maple flavor and stay moist and soft, although they're never in my cookie jar for long!

1	cup shortening
1/2	cup butter, softened
2	cups packed brown sugar
2	eggs
1	teaspoon vanilla extract
1	teaspoon maple flavoring
3	cups all-purpose flour
2	teaspoons baking soda
2	cups vanilla *or* white chips
1/2	cup chopped pecans

FROSTING:

1/4	cup butter, softened
4	cups confectioners' sugar
1	teaspoon maple flavoring
4	to 6 tablespoons milk
3-1/2	cups pecan halves

In a large bowl, cream the shortening, butter and brown sugar. Add eggs, one at a time, beating well after each addition. Beat in vanilla and maple flavoring. Combine the flour and baking soda; gradually add to creamed mixture. Stir in vanilla chips and pecans.

Drop by rounded tablespoonfuls 2 in. apart onto ungreased baking sheets. Bake at 350° for 8-10 minutes or until golden brown. Cool for 2 minutes before removing to wire racks.

In a large bowl, cream the butter and confectioners' sugar. Beat in maple flavoring and enough milk to achieve spreading consistency. Frost cooled cookies. Top each cookie with a pecan half.

Karen Wissing, Vashon, Washington ✳
These pretty mint-green drops are dotted with chocolate chips. My kids always want them for Christmas.

minty meringue drops

yield about 2-1/2 dozen

2	egg whites
1/4	teaspoon cream of tartar
3/4	cup sugar
1/8	teaspoon vanilla extract
2	to 6 drops green food coloring, optional
1	package (10 ounces) mint chocolate chips

Lightly grease baking sheets or line with parchment paper; set aside. In a small bowl, beat egg whites until foamy. Add cream of tartar, beating until soft peaks form. Gradually beat in sugar, 1 tablespoon at a time, until stiff peaks form. Beat in vanilla and food coloring if desired. Fold in the chocolate chips.

Drop by rounded tablespoonfuls 2 in. apart onto prepared baking sheets. Bake at 250° for 30-35 minutes or until dry to the touch. Remove to wire racks to cool. Store in an airtight container.

editor's note: If mint chocolate chips are not available, place 2 cups (12 ounces) semisweet chocolate chips and 1/4 teaspoon peppermint extract in a plastic bag; seal and toss to coat. Allow the chips to stand for 24-48 hours.

Faith Jensen, Meridian, Idaho ✳
With the classic combination of chocolate and peanut butter, it's no surprise these are my family's favorite cookies.

peanut butter cup cookies

yield 7-1/2 dozen

1	cup butter, softened
2/3	cup peanut butter
1	cup sugar
1	cup packed brown sugar
2	eggs
2	teaspoons vanilla extract
2-1/4	cups all-purpose flour
1	teaspoon baking soda
1/2	teaspoon salt
2	cups (12 ounces) semisweet chocolate chips
2	cups chopped peanut butter cups (about six 1.6-ounce packages)

In a large bowl, cream butter, peanut butter and sugars. Add eggs, one at a time, beating well after each addition. Beat in vanilla. Combine flour, baking soda and salt; gradually add to the creamed mixture. Stir in the chocolate chips and peanut butter cups.

Drop by rounded tablespoonfuls 2 in. apart onto ungreased baking sheets. Bake at 350° for 10-12 minutes or until edges are lightly browned. Cool for 2 minutes before removing to wire racks.

editor's note: Reduced-fat or generic brands of peanut butter are not recommended for this recipe.

❋ Ellen Ball, Ilion, New York
Butterscotch has always been my favorite flavor, so when I found this recipe loaded with butterscotch chips and dates, I knew it was a winner. The warm golden tones and crispy crust make it a very nice cookie for autumn.

butterscotch date cookies
yield 2 dozen

1/2	cup shortening
1	cup packed brown sugar
1	egg
1/2	teaspoon vanilla extract
1/2	cup sour cream
2	cups all-purpose flour
1/2	teaspoon baking powder
1/2	teaspoon baking soda
1	cup butterscotch chips
1	cup chopped dates

In a large bowl, cream shortening and sugar until light and fluffy. Beat in egg and vanilla. Add sour cream; beat just until combined. Combine the flour, baking powder and baking soda; gradually add to creamed mixture and mix well. Stir in butterscotch chips and dates.

Drop by tablespoonfuls 2 in. apart onto greased baking sheets. Bake at 425° for 8-12 minutes or until lightly browned and set. Remove to wire racks.

❋ Judy Mabrey, Myrtle Beach, South Carolina
I like to share these treats with the neighborhood children who ring my doorbell on Halloween. Since they are so large, they also make impressive gifts at Christmas.

monster chip cookies
yield about 3 dozen

1	cup shortening
1/2	cup butter, softened
1-1/3	cups sugar
1	cup packed brown sugar
4	eggs
3	teaspoons vanilla extract
1	teaspoon lemon juice
3	cups all-purpose flour
1/2	cup quick-cooking oats
2	teaspoons baking soda
1-1/2	teaspoons salt
1	teaspoon ground cinnamon
4	cups (24 ounces) semisweet chocolate chips
2	cups chopped nuts

In a large bowl, cream shortening, butter and sugars until light and fluffy. Add eggs, one at a time, beating well after each. Beat in vanilla and lemon juice. Combine the dry ingredients; add to creamed mixture and mix well. Stir in chips and nuts. Refrigerate for 8 hours or overnight.

Drop by 1/4 cupfuls 3 in. apart onto lightly greased baking sheet. Bake at 350° for 14-16 minutes or until lightly browned and center is set. Cool for 2 minutes before removing to wire racks.

Liz Probelski, Port Washington, Wisconsin
Even though this recipe makes a large batch, these mild pistachio-flavored cookies disappear in a wink. The chocolate drizzle makes them look extra-special.

pistachio thumbprints

yield about 7 dozen

1	cup butter, softened
1/3	cup confectioners' sugar
1	egg
1	teaspoon vanilla extract
3/4	teaspoon almond extract
2	cups all-purpose flour
1	package (3.4 ounces) instant pistachio pudding mix
1/2	cup miniature chocolate chips
2	cups finely chopped pecans

FILLING:

2	tablespoons butter, softened
2	cups confectioners' sugar
1	teaspoon vanilla extract
2	to 3 tablespoons milk

GLAZE:

1/2	cup semisweet chocolate chips
2	teaspoons shortening

In a large bowl, cream butter and sugar until smooth. Add egg and extracts; mix well. Combine flour and pudding mix; add to the creamed mixture. Stir in chocolate chips.

Roll into 1-in. balls; roll in nuts. Place 2 in. apart on greased baking sheets; make a thumbprint in center of cookie. Bake at 350° for 10-12 minutes. Remove to a wire rack to cool.

For filling, cream butter, sugar, vanilla and milk. Spoon into center of cooled cookies.

For glaze, if desired, melt chocolate chips with shortening; drizzle over cookies. Let stand until set.

full-of-chips cookies

yield about 4 dozen

1	cup butter-flavored shortening
3/4	cup sugar
3/4	cup packed brown sugar
2	eggs
1	teaspoon vanilla extract
2-1/4	cups all-purpose flour
1	teaspoon baking soda
3/4	teaspoon salt
1/3	cup *each* semisweet chocolate chips, peanut butter chips, butterscotch chips and vanilla *or* white chips
1/3	cup milk chocolate M&M's
1/3	cup Reese's pieces candy

In a large bowl, cream shortening and sugars until light and fluffy. Add eggs, one at a time, beating well after each addition. Beat in vanilla. Combine the flour, baking soda and salt; gradually add to creamed mixture and mix well. Stir in chips and candy.

Drop by rounded tablespoonfuls 2 in. apart onto ungreased baking sheets. Bake at 375° for 7-9 minutes or until lightly browned around edges. Remove to wire racks to cool.

Dolores Hartford
Troy, Pennsylvania
Loaded with four kinds of chips and two types of colorful candy, these sweet treats are sure to become a favorite of kids of all ages.

✳ Elaine Anderson, New Galilee, Pennsylvania
I love to bake cookies more than anything else. And it's such a pleasure to serve these delicious treats to neighbors and family. My four daughters are eager to help with mixing, measuring and stirring!

chocolate chunk cookies

yield 3 dozen

6	squares (1 ounce *each*) white baking chocolate, *divided*
1	cup butter, softened
1/2	cup sugar
1/2	cup packed brown sugar
2	eggs
2	teaspoons vanilla extract
2-1/2	cups all-purpose flour
1	teaspoon baking soda
1/4	teaspoon salt
1	package (11-1/2 ounces) semisweet chocolate chunks *or* 2 cups semisweet chocolate chips

In a microwave, melt three squares of white chocolate at 70% power for 1 minute; stir. Microwave at additional 10- to 20-second intervals, stirring until smooth; cool.

In a large bowl, cream butter and sugars until light and fluffy. Add eggs, one at a time, beating well after each addition. Beat in melted chocolate and vanilla. Combine the flour, baking soda and salt; gradually add to the creamed mixture and mix well. Stir in semisweet chocolate chunks.

Drop by tablespoonfuls onto ungreased baking sheets. Bake at 375° for 10-12 minutes or until golden brown. Cool for 1 minute before removing to wire racks.

In a microwave, melt remaining white chocolate at 70% power for 1 minute; stir. Microwave at additional 10- to 20-second intervals, stirring until smooth; drizzle over cookies. Cookies may be frozen for up to 3 months.

✳ Maurane Ramsey
Fort Wayne, Indiana
My daughter loves the subtle coffee flavor in these soft cookies. The recipe makes plenty so you can share them with friends.

coffee chip cookies

yield 3-1/2 dozen

1	cup shortening
2	cups packed brown sugar
2	eggs
1	cup boiling water
2	tablespoons instant coffee granules
4	cups all-purpose flour
2	teaspoons baking powder
1	teaspoon baking soda
4	cups (24 ounces) semisweet chocolate chips

In a mixing bowl, cream shortening and brown sugar. Add eggs, one at a time, beating well after each addition. Combine water and coffee; set aside. Combine the flour, baking powder and baking soda; add to creamed mixture alternately with coffee. Stir in the chocolate chips. Refrigerate for 1 hour.

Drop dough by rounded tablespoonfuls 2 in. apart onto greased baking sheets. Bake at 350° for 10-12 minutes or until golden around the edges. Remove to wire racks to cool.

Sharon Hedstrom, Minnetonka, Minnesota ✳

With peanut butter, oats and five kinds of chips, these cookies make a hearty snack that appeals to kids of all ages. I sometimes double the recipe to share with friends and neighbors.

five-chip cookies

yield 4-1/2 dozen

1	cup butter, softened
1	cup peanut butter
1	cup sugar
2/3	cup packed brown sugar
2	eggs
1	teaspoon vanilla extract
2	cups all-purpose flour
1	cup old-fashioned oats
2	teaspoons baking soda
1/2	teaspoon salt
2/3	cup *each* milk chocolate chips, semisweet chocolate chips, peanut butter chips, vanilla chips and butterscotch chips

In a large bowl, cream the butter, peanut butter and sugars until light and fluffy. Add eggs, one at a time, beating well after each addition. Beat in vanilla. Combine the flour, oats, baking soda and salt; gradually add to the creamed mixture and mix well. Stir in chips.

Drop by rounded tablespoonfuls 2 in. apart onto ungreased baking sheets. Bake at 350° for 10-12 minutes or until lightly browned. Cool for 1 minute before removing to wire racks.

editor's note: Reduced-fat or generic brands of peanut butter are not recommended for this recipe.

Diane Hixon, Niceville, Florida ✳

The cocoa in the batter gives these treats a double dose of chocolate. They disappear fast from my cookie jar.

double chocolate chip cookies

yield 3-4 dozen

1	cup butter, softened
1	cup sugar
1/2	cup packed dark brown sugar
1	egg
1	teaspoon vanilla extract
1/3	cup baking cocoa
2	tablespoons milk
1-3/4	cups all-purpose flour
1/4	teaspoon baking powder
1	cup chopped walnuts
1	cup (6 ounces) semisweet chocolate chips

In a large bowl, cream the butter, sugars until light and fluffy. Beat in egg and vanilla. Add the cocoa and milk. Combine the flour and baking powder; fold into the creamed mixture with walnuts and chocolate chips.

Roll teaspoonfuls of dough into balls; place 2 in. apart on ungreased baking sheets. Bake at 350° for 10-12 minutes. Cool for 5 minutes before removing to wire racks.

※ Janis Gruca, Mokena, Illinois

Where I work, we often bring in goodies for special occasions. When co-workers hear I've baked these melt-in-your-mouth cookies, they make a special trip to my floor to sample these crisp, buttery treats.

chocolate chip butter cookies

yield about 4 dozen

1	**cup butter**
1/2	**teaspoon vanilla extract**
2	**cups all-purpose flour**
1	**cup confectioners' sugar**
1	**cup miniature semisweet chocolate chips**

In a microwave or heavy saucepan, melt butter; stir in vanilla. Cool completely. In a large bowl, combine flour and sugar; stir in butter mixture and chocolate chips (mixture will be crumbly).

Roll dough into 1-in. balls. Place 2 in. apart on ungreased baking sheets; flatten slightly. Bake at 375° for 12 minutes or until edges begin to brown. Remove to wire racks to cool.

※ Taste of Home Test Kitchen

Not fond of biscotti? Try this moister version that's especially good with a hot cup of coffee. It has a rich, chocolaty taste, plus a sweet chocolate drizzle on top.

double chocolate biscotti

yield about 1 dozen

2	**eggs**
1	**teaspoon vanilla extract**
1/4	**teaspoon almond extract**
1/2	**cup sugar**
1	**cup all-purpose flour**
1/2	**cup finely chopped pecans**
1/4	**cup baking cocoa**
1/4	**teaspoon salt**
1/2	**cup miniature semisweet chocolate chips**

ICING:

1-1/2	**teaspoons miniature semisweet chocolate chips**
3	**teaspoons fat-free milk**
1/2	**cup confectioners' sugar**
1/8	**teaspoon vanilla extract**

In a large bowl, beat the eggs and extracts. Beat in sugar. Combine the flour, pecans, cocoa and salt; gradually add to egg mixture. Stir in chocolate chips.

On a baking sheet coated with cooking spray, shape dough into a 14-in. x 3-in. rectangle. Bake at 350° for 20-25 minutes or until lightly browned. Cool for 5 minutes.

Transfer to a cutting board; cut with a serrated knife into 1-in. slices. Place cut side down on baking sheets coated with cooking spray. Bake for 15-20 minutes or until firm. Remove to wire racks to cool.

For icing, melt chocolate chips. Stir in milk, confectioners' sugar and vanilla. Drizzle over cookies; let stand until set.

These chewy oatmeal cookies are full of butterscotch chips and raisins. Every so often I add a half cup of chopped pecans to a batch for something different.

Victoria Zmarzley-Hahn, Northhampton, Pennsylvania ✳

butterscotch raisin cookies

yield 3-1/2 dozen

1	cup butter, softened
3/4	cup packed brown sugar
1/4	cup sugar
2	eggs
3	cups quick-cooking oats
1-1/2	cups all-purpose flour
1	package (3.4 ounces) instant butterscotch pudding mix
1	teaspoon baking soda
1	cup raisins
1/2	cup butterscotch chips

In a large bowl, cream butter and sugars. Add eggs; beat well. Combine the oats, flour, dry pudding mix and baking soda; gradually add to the creamed mixture. Stir in the raisins and butterscotch chips (dough will be stiff).

Drop by tablespoonfuls 2 in. apart onto ungreased baking sheets. Bake at 375° for 9-11 minutes or until lightly browned. Remove to wire racks to cool.

crisp 'n' chewy cookies

yield 7 dozen

1-1/4	cups butter-flavored shortening
3/4	cup sugar
3/4	cup packed brown sugar
1	egg
3	tablespoons maple syrup
1	teaspoon vanilla extract
3	cups quick-cooking oats
1-3/4	cups all-purpose flour
1	teaspoon baking soda
1	teaspoon salt
3/4	cup semisweet chocolate chips
2	Butterfinger candy bars (2.1 ounces *each*), chopped

In a large bowl, cream shortening and sugars. Beat in egg, syrup and vanilla. Combine oats, flour, baking soda and salt; gradually add to the creamed mixture. Stir in chocolate chips and candy bars.

Roll dough into 1-in. balls. Place 2 in. apart on ungreased baking sheets. Bake at 375° for 7-9 minutes or until golden brown. Remove to wire racks to cool completely.

Kristen Snyder ✳
Sugar Land, Texas
Knowing I'm a cookie lover, my mother-in-law sent me this recipe years ago. Many folks have told me these are the best. I think the Butterfinger candy bars make them extra-special.

BAKING
tip

breaking up candy bars — To quickly break up the Butterfinger candy bars, place them in a resealable plastic bag and pound with a meat mallet. Or, break into quarters, place in a mini food processor and pulse until broken into pieces. The pieces should be a little bigger than the chocolate chips.

✳ Jackie Ruckwardt, Cottage Grove, Oregon
These large, gourmet cookies are my most-requested recipe. Loaded with coconut and chocolate chips and dipped in white candy coating, they are truly a chocolate-lover's delight.

jumbo chocolate chip cookies

yield about 2 dozen

1	cup butter, softened
1	cup sugar
1	cup packed brown sugar
2	eggs
2	teaspoons vanilla extract
2-1/2	cups all-purpose flour
1	teaspoon baking soda
1	teaspoon baking powder
1	teaspoon salt
2-2/3	cups flaked coconut
1	cup (6 ounces) semisweet chocolate chips
1/2	cup milk chocolate chips
5	ounces white candy coating, chopped, optional

In a large bowl, cream butter and sugars until light and fluffy. Add eggs, one at a time, beating well after each addition. Beat in vanilla. Combine the flour, baking soda, baking powder and salt; gradually add to the creamed mixture and mix well. Stir in the coconut and chips. Shape 3 tablespoonfuls of dough into a ball; repeat with remaining dough.

Place balls 3 in. apart on ungreased baking sheets. Bake at 350° for 12-18 minutes or until lightly browned. Remove to wire racks to cool.

In a microwave, melt candy coating if desired; stir until smooth. Dip one end of cooled cookies in candy coating. Allow excess to drip off. Place on waxed paper; let stand until set.

chocolate chip crispies

✳ Stephanie DiGiovanni
Wakefield, Massachusetts
In this recipe from a cousin, potato chips add crunch while oats make them chewy. It's a fun twist to traditional chocolate chip cookies.

yield about 8 dozen

1	cup butter, softened
1	cup vegetable oil
1	cup sugar
1	cup packed brown sugar
1	egg
1	teaspoon vanilla extract
3-1/2	cups all-purpose flour
1	cup quick-cooking oats
1	teaspoon baking soda
1	teaspoon cream of tartar
1/2	teaspoon salt
1	tablespoon milk
1	teaspoon white vinegar
2	cups (12 ounces) semisweet chocolate chips
1	cup crushed potato chips

In a large bowl, beat butter, oil and sugars. Beat in egg and vanilla. Combine the flour, oats, baking soda, cream of tartar and salt; gradually add to the sugar mixture. Combine the milk and vinegar; add to the sugar mixture. Stir in the chocolate chips and potato chips.

Drop by tablespoonfuls 2 in. apart onto ungreased baking sheets. Bake at 350° for 12-15 minutes or until golden brown. Remove to wire racks to cool.

Mary Ann Mariotti, Plainfield, Illinois ✳

Packed with fruit, nuts and vanilla chips, these goodies are sure to please. If you prefer, replace the dried cherries with dried cranberries or apricots.

cherry pecan dreams
yield about 3 dozen

1	cup butter, softened
1/2	cup sugar
1/2	cup packed brown sugar
1	egg
1	tablespoon grated orange peel
2-1/4	cups all-purpose flour
1	teaspoon baking soda
1/2	teaspoon salt
2	cups vanilla *or* white chips
1	cup dried cherries, coarsely chopped
1	cup chopped pecans

In a large bowl, cream butter and sugars until light and fluffy. Beat in egg and orange peel. Combine the flour, baking soda and salt; gradually add to creamed mixture and mix well. Fold in the chips, cherries and pecans.

Drop by rounded tablespoonfuls 2 in. apart onto greased baking sheets. Bake at 350° for 10-12 minutes or until edges are golden brown. Cool for 2 minutes before removing to wire racks to cool.

Laura Bankard, Manchester, Maryland ✳

Here is a delicious twist on traditional chocolate chip cookies. They're great for coconut lovers, who will be delighted with the texture of the coconut and the added flavor of the coconut extract. My whole family agrees this recipe is a winner.

coconut chocolate chip cookies
yield about 1-1/4 dozen

1/2	cup butter, softened
3/4	cup sugar
1	egg
1/2	teaspoon coconut extract
1	cup plus 2 tablespoons all-purpose flour
1/2	teaspoon baking soda
1/2	teaspoon salt
1	cup (6 ounces) semisweet chocolate chips
1/2	cup flaked coconut

In a small bowl, cream butter and sugar. Beat in egg and coconut extract; mix well. Combine the flour, baking soda and salt; add to the creamed mixture. Stir in chocolate chips and coconut.

Drop by rounded tablespoonfuls 2 in. apart onto ungreased baking sheets. Bake at 375° for 11-13 minutes or until golden brown. Remove to wire racks to cool.

easy drop cookies

chocolate macadamia macaroons, p. 72

Drop cookies are some of

the simplest to make—just mix, drop and bake. Best of all, these effortless cookies can be baked up in a variety of flavors. They can be jazzed up with a swipe of frosting, a sprinkling of colored sugar or even a coating of chocolate!

white chocolate pumpkin dreams, p. 77

cherry oatmeal cookies, p. 92

✳ Linda Robinson, New Braunfels, Texas

Our family of chocolate lovers gets triply excited when these cookies come out of the oven. They have the texture and taste of fudge brownies, and the chocolate drizzle make them look so tempting.

triple-chocolate brownie cookies

yield 6 dozen

4	**squares (1 ounce *each*) unsweetened chocolate**
3/4	**cup butter, cubed**
4	**eggs**
2	**cups sugar**
1-1/2	**cups all-purpose flour**
1/2	**cup baking cocoa**
2	**teaspoons baking powder**
1/2	**teaspoon salt**
2	**cups (12 ounces) semisweet chocolate chips, *divided***
2	**teaspoons shortening**

In a microwave, melt chocolate and butter; stir until smooth. Cool slightly. In a large bowl, beat eggs and sugar. Stir in chocolate mixture. Combine the flour, cocoa, baking powder and salt; gradually add to chocolate mixture. Stir in 1-1/2 cups chocolate chips. Cover and refrigerate for 2 hours or until easy to handle.

Drop by tablespoonfuls 2 in. apart onto greased baking sheets. Bake at 350° for 7-9 minutes or until edges are set and tops are slightly cracked. Cool for 2 minutes before removing from pans to wire racks to cool completely.

In a microwave, melt remaining chips and shortening; stir until smooth. Drizzle over cookies. Let stand for 30 minutes or until chocolate is set. Store in an airtight container.

Pamela Alexander, Prosser, Washington ✳
These cinnamon-spiced oatmeal cookies get wonderful bursts of flavor from cherries and chocolate chips.

cherry chocolate chip cookies

yield about 3-1/2 dozen

1	cup dried cherries, chopped
1/3	cup hot water
6	tablespoons shortening
6	tablespoons butter, softened
1-1/2	cups packed brown sugar
1/2	cup sugar
2	eggs
3	teaspoons grated orange peel
1-1/2	teaspoons vanilla extract
3	cups quick-cooking oats
1-3/4	cups all-purpose flour
3/4	teaspoon baking soda
3/4	teaspoon ground cinnamon
1/2	teaspoon salt
1	cup (6 ounces) semisweet chocolate chips

In a small bowl, soak cherries in hot water for at least 10 minutes.

Meanwhile, in a large bowl, cream the shortening, butter and sugars until light and fluffy. Beat in the eggs, orange peel and vanilla. Combine the oats, flour, baking soda, cinnamon and salt; gradually add to creamed mixture and mix well. Stir in the chocolate chip and cherries with liquid.

Drop by rounded tablespoonfuls 2 in. apart onto ungreased baking sheets. Bake at 350° for 12-14 minutes or until edges are lightly browned. Cool for 1 minute before removing from pans to wire racks.

chewy german chocolate cookies

yield about 5 dozen

3	packages (4 ounces *each*) German sweet chocolate, chopped
2	tablespoons shortening
1	teaspoon instant coffee granules
3	eggs
1-1/4	cups sugar
1	teaspoon vanilla extract
1	cup all-purpose flour
1/2	teaspoon baking powder
1/2	teaspoon salt
1/2	cup chopped pecans
55	to 60 pecan halves

In a microwave, melt chocolate and shortening; stir until smooth. Stir in coffee granules; cool and set aside. In a large bowl, beat eggs and sugar until light and lemon-colored. Beat in the cooled chocolate and vanilla. Combine the flour, baking powder and salt; add to chocolate mixture and mix well (dough will be soft). Stir in chopped pecans. Cover and refrigerate for 30 minutes or until easy to handle.

Drop by rounded teaspoonfuls 2 in. apart onto greased baking sheets. Place a pecan half in the center of each. Bake at 350° for 9-10 minutes or until set. Cool for 1 minute before removing to wire racks.

Darlene Brenden ✳ Salem, Oregon
When I want a cookie that's chewy, this is the recipe I reach for. Coffee granules help create just the right amount of mocha flavor.

❋ Betty Thompson, La Porte, Texas
Grated lemon peel in the batter and on the icing of these soft, cake-like cookies gives them their fresh citrus flavor. This makes about three dozen of the tender treats.

honey lemon cookies
yield about 3 dozen

7	tablespoons butter, softened
1/2	cup sugar
1	egg
1-3/4	cups all-purpose flour
1	teaspoon baking powder
1/2	teaspoon salt
1/3	cup honey
1/4	cup plain yogurt
2	teaspoons grated lemon peel
1/2	teaspoon lemon extract

ICING:

1	cup confectioners' sugar
2	tablespoons lemon juice
2	teaspoons grated lemon peel

In a small bowl, cream butter and sugar. Beat in egg. Combine the flour, baking powder and salt. Combine the honey, yogurt, lemon peel and lemon extract. Add dry ingredients to creamed mixture alternately with the honey mixture.

Drop by tablespoonfuls 2 in. apart onto greased baking sheets. Bake at 350° for 10-12 minutes or until golden brown. Remove cookies to the wire racks.

In a small bowl, combine the confectioners' sugar and lemon juice until smooth. Brush over the warm cookies; sprinkle with lemon peel.

❋ Charlotte Mains, Cuyahoga Falls, Ohio
Brazil nuts may be an unusual ingredient for a cookie recipe, but the flavor is absolutely outstanding. The recipe for these rich, buttery cookies came from my mother and goes back more than 70 years.

brazil nut cookies
yield about 4-1/2 dozen

1	cup butter, softened
1	cup sugar
2	eggs
1-1/2	teaspoons vanilla extract
2-1/4	cups all-purpose flour
1/2	teaspoon baking soda
1/4	teaspoon salt
2	cups chopped Brazil nuts
1/2	cup flaked coconut

In a large bowl, cream butter and sugar until light and fluffy. Add eggs, one at a time, beating well after each addition. Beat in vanilla. Combine the flour, baking soda and salt; gradually add to creamed mixture and mix well. Stir in nuts and coconut.

Drop by tablespoonfuls 3 in. apart onto ungreased baking sheets. Bake at 350° for 10-12 minutes or until bottom of cookies are lightly browned. Remove to wire racks.

Sharon Crider, St. Robert, Missouri ✳

This delicious fruit- and nut-packed cookie recipe was my mother's, and it has been one of my favorites for many years.

vanilla-glazed apple cookies

yield about 4 dozen

1/2	cup shortening
1-1/3	cups packed brown sugar
1	egg
1/4	cup milk
2	cups all-purpose flour
1	teaspoon baking soda
1	teaspoon ground nutmeg
1	teaspoon ground cinnamon
1/2	teaspoon ground cloves
1	cup chopped walnuts
1	cup finely diced peeled apple
1	cup raisins

VANILLA GLAZE:

1-1/2	cups confectioners' sugar
1	tablespoon butter, melted
1/2	teaspoon vanilla extract
1/8	teaspoon salt
2	to 4 teaspoons milk

In a large bowl, cream shortening and brown sugar until light and fluffy. Beat in egg and milk. Combine the flour, baking soda, nutmeg, cinnamon and cloves; gradually add to the creamed mixture. Stir in the walnuts, apple and raisins.

Drop by rounded tablespoonfuls 2 in. apart onto ungreased baking sheets. Bake at 400° for 8-10 minutes or until edges begin to brown. Remove to wire racks.

In a small bowl, combine the confectioners' sugar, butter, vanilla, salt and enough milk to achieve drizzling consistency. Drizzle over warm cookies.

apple peanut butter cookies

yield about 2-1/2 dozen

1/2	cup shortening
1/2	cup chunky peanut butter
1/2	cup sugar
1/2	cup packed brown sugar
1	egg
1/2	teaspoon vanilla extract
1-1/2	cups all-purpose flour
1/2	teaspoon baking soda
1/2	teaspoon salt
1/2	teaspoon ground cinnamon
1/2	cup grated peeled apple

In a large bowl, cream the shortening, peanut butter and sugars until light and fluffy. Beat in egg and vanilla. Combine the dry ingredients; gradually add to creamed mixture and mix well. Stir in apple.

Drop by rounded tablespoonfuls 2 in. apart onto greased baking sheets. Bake at 375° for 10-12 minutes or until golden brown. Cool for 5 minutes before removing to wire racks.

editor's note: Reduced-fat or generic brands of peanut butter are not recommended for this recipe.

Marjorie Benson ✳
New Castle, Pennsylvania
These spiced peanut butter cookies are great for fall gatherings. They're crisp on the outside and soft on the inside.

* Judy Clark, Elkhart, Indiana
With a tall glass of ice-cold milk, a couple of cherry cookies really hit the spot for dessert or as a snack. The coconut and bits of cherries provide a fun look and texture.

cheery cherry cookies

yield 4 dozen

1	cup packed brown sugar
3/4	cup butter, softened
1	egg
2	tablespoons milk
1	teaspoon vanilla extract
2	cups all-purpose flour
1/2	teaspoon salt
1/2	teaspoon baking soda
1/2	cup maraschino cherries, well drained and chopped
1/2	cup chopped pecans
1/2	cup flaked coconut

In a large bowl, cream brown sugar and butter until light and fluffy. Beat in the egg, milk and vanilla. Combine flour, salt and baking soda; gradually add to creamed mixture. Fold in the cherries, pecans and coconut.

Drop by teaspoonfuls onto ungreased baking sheets. Bake at 375° for 10-12 minutes or until golden brown. Remove to wire racks to cool.

* Beverly Albrecht
Beatrice, Nebraska
Topped with creamy chocolate ribbons, these meringues are rich-tasting but feather-light. You'll think you're biting into a decadent dessert that's off-limits, but it's not.

crispy cereal meringues

yield about 5 dozen

4	egg whites
1/4	teaspoon cream of tartar
1/4	teaspoon salt
1	cup sugar
2	cups chocolate-flavored crisp rice cereal
1/4	cup semisweet chocolate chips
1/2	teaspoon vegetable shortening

In a large bowl, beat egg whites, cream of tartar and salt until soft peaks form. Gradually add sugar, 1 tablespoon at a time, until stiff peaks form, about 6 minutes. Fold in cereal.

Drop by rounded teaspoonfuls 1 in. apart onto baking sheets coated with cooking spray. Bake at 300° for 35-40 minutes or until firm to the touch. Remove to wire racks to cool.

In a microwave or heavy saucepan, melt the chocolate chips with the shortening. Transfer to a small resealable plastic bag; cut a small hole in the corner of bag. Drizzle melted chocolate over meringues. Place on waxed paper to set.

These chewy little cookies have a yummy coconut and almond flavor. Our home economists whipped them up in no time using only five ingredients.

crunchy macaroons

yield 2 dozen

1-1/2	cups crisp rice cereal
1-1/4	cups flaked coconut
2	egg whites
3	tablespoons sugar
1/8	teaspoon almond extract

In a small bowl, combine all ingredients. With damp fingers, shape into 1-1/2-in. mounds on parchment paper-lined baking sheets.

Bake at 300° for 20-25 minutes or until edges are lightly browned. Remove from pans to wire racks to cool.

Jeanne Matteson, South Dayton, New York ✳

My husband and I just built a new house in a small rural community in western New York. The aroma of these soft, delicious cookies in our oven has made our new house smell like home.

frosted ginger cookies

yield about 6 dozen

1-1/2	cups butter
1	cup sugar
1	cup packed brown sugar
2	eggs
1/2	cup molasses
2	teaspoons vanilla extract
4-1/2	cups all-purpose flour
1	tablespoon ground ginger
2	teaspoons *each* baking soda and ground cinnamon
1/2	teaspoon *each* salt and ground cloves

FROSTING:

1/3	cup packed brown sugar
1/4	cup milk
2	tablespoons butter
2	cups confectioners' sugar
1/2	teaspoon vanilla extract

Dash salt

In a large bowl, cream butter and sugars until light and fluffy. Add the eggs, one at a time, beating well after each addition. Stir in molasses and vanilla; mix well. Combine dry ingredients; gradually add to creamed mixture.

Drop by tablespoonfuls 2 in. apart onto ungreased baking sheets. Bake at 325° for 12-15 minutes or until cookies spring back when touched lightly (do not overbake). Remove to wire racks to cool completely.

For frosting, in a medium saucepan, bring brown sugar, milk and butter to a boil; boil for 1 minute, stirring constantly. Remove from the heat (mixture will look curdled at first). Cool for 3 minutes before adding confectioners' sugar, vanilla and salt; mix well. Frost the cooled cookies.

✳ Taste of Home Test Kitchen
This soft and chewy low-carb cookie recipe calls for canola oil instead of butter to reduce the saturated fat. It's hard to eat just one since they're so delicious.

chocolate peanut butter drops

yield 4 dozen

1	cup chunky peanut butter
1/4	cup canola oil
3/4	cup packed brown sugar
1/2	cup sugar
2	eggs
1	tablespoon vanilla extract
1	cup all-purpose flour
1/3	cup baking cocoa
1	teaspoon baking soda
1/2	teaspoon salt
1/2	cup miniature chocolate chips

In a large bowl, beat the peanut butter, oil and sugars until blended. Beat in eggs and vanilla. Combine the flour, cocoa, baking soda and salt; gradually add to peanut butter mixture just until blended (dough will be sticky). Stir in chocolate chips.

Drop by rounded teaspoonfuls 2 in. apart on ungreased baking sheets. Flatten slightly with a glass.

Bake at 350° for 8-10 minutes or until set and tops are cracked. Cool for 2 minutes before removing to wire racks.

✳ Heather Breen, Chicago, Illinois
These tasty oatmeal cookies are crunchy on the outside, chewy on the inside and dotted with dried cranberries.

cranberry oat cookies

yield 2-1/2 dozen

1/2	cup plus 2 tablespoons packed brown sugar
1/4	cup sugar
1/3	cup canola oil
1	egg
1	tablespoon fat-free milk
3/4	teaspoon vanilla extract
1-1/4	cups quick-cooking oats
3/4	cup plus 2 tablespoons all-purpose flour
1/2	teaspoon baking soda
1/2	teaspoon salt
1/2	cup dried cranberries

In a large bowl, combine sugars and oil until blended. Beat in the egg, milk and vanilla. Combine the oats, flour, baking soda and salt; gradually add to sugar mixture and mix well. Stir in cranberries.

Drop by tablespoonfuls 2 in. apart onto baking sheets coated with cooking spray. Bake at 375° for 10-12 minutes or until lightly browned. Remove to wire racks.

Lois Furcron, Coudersport, Pennsylvania ✳
This recipe originated with my grandmother. My mom also made these cookies. I too baked them for my family, then my daughters made them, and now their daughters are making them—a true legacy I'm happy to share.

chewy ginger drop cookies

yield about 2-1/2 dozen

1/2	**cup shortening**
1/2	**cup sugar**
2	**cups all-purpose flour**
1/2	**teaspoon baking soda**
1/2	**teaspoon ground ginger**
1/4	**teaspoon salt**
1/2	**cup molasses**
1/4	**cup water**

Additional sugar

In a large bowl, cream shortening and sugar until light and fluffy. Combine the flour, baking soda, ginger and salt. Combine molasses and water. Add dry ingredients to the creamed mixture alternately with molasses mixture.

Drop by rounded teaspoonfuls 2 in. apart onto greased baking sheets. Sprinkle with sugar. Bake at 350° for 13-15 minutes or until edges are set. Remove to wire racks to cool.

fudge-topped orange cookies

yield 2 dozen

3/4	**cup butter, softened**
1	**cup sugar**
1	**egg**
2	**egg yolks**
2	**teaspoons grated orange peel**
1-1/2	**teaspoons orange extract**
2	**cups all-purpose flour**
1	**teaspoon ground ginger**
1/2	**teaspoon baking soda**

TOPPING:

1	**jar (7 ounces) marshmallow creme**
3/4	**cup sugar**
1/3	**cup evaporated milk**
2	**tablespoons butter**
1/8	**teaspoon salt**
1	**cup (6 ounces) semisweet chocolate chips**
1/2	**teaspoon vanilla extract**

In a large bowl, cream butter and sugar until light and fluffy. Beat in the egg, egg yolks, orange peel and extract. Combine the flour, ginger and baking soda; gradually add to creamed mixture and mix well.

Drop by rounded tablespoonfuls 2 in. apart onto ungreased baking sheets. Bake at 300° for 21-23 minutes or until golden brown. Remove to wire racks to cool.

In a large saucepan, combine the marshmallow creme, sugar, milk, butter and salt. Bring to a rolling boil over medium heat; boil for 5 minutes, stirring constantly. Remove from the heat. Add chocolate chips and vanilla; stir until chips are melted. Spread over tops of cookies.

Lisa Evans ✳
Rileyville, Virginia
Cookies and fudge are two classic sweets around the holidays, so one day I decided to combine them. The chocolate marshmallow topping works well on a variety of cookies.

＊ Jack Horst, Westfield, New York

The next time you're craving peanut butter cookies, try this variation with oats and Grape-Nuts. I think it's even better than the regular cookies, which I like a lot.

peanut butter crunch cookies

yield 2-1/2 dozen

1/4	cup butter, softened
1/4	cup creamy peanut butter
1/4	cup sugar
1/4	cup packed brown sugar
1	egg
1/4	teaspoon vanilla extract
1/2	cup all-purpose flour
1/4	cup quick-cooking oats
1/4	teaspoon baking soda
1/8	teaspoon salt
1/4	cup Grape-Nuts

In a large bowl, cream the butter, peanut butter and sugars until light and fluffy. Beat in egg and vanilla. Combine the flour, oats, baking soda and salt; gradually add to the creamed mixture and mix well. Stir in the Grape-Nuts.

Drop by rounded teaspoonfuls 3 in. apart onto ungreased baking sheets. Flatten slightly with a fork dipped in flour. Bake at 350° for 9-12 minutes or until lightly browned. Cool for 5 minutes before removing from pans to wire racks to cool.

editor's note: Reduced-fat or generic brands of peanut butter are not recommended for this recipe.

apple-oat breakfast treats

yield 10 servings

＊ Dolores Kastello
Waukesha, Wisconsin

Our three grandsons gobble up these soft, chewy oatmeal cookies at breakfast with some yogurt and a glass of juice. If you don't have pie filling handy, use jam to make the cookie's fruity topping.

3/4	cup butter, softened
3/4	cup packed brown sugar
2	eggs
1	teaspoon vanilla extract
2-1/2	cups old-fashioned oats
3/4	cup all-purpose flour
1/2	cup nonfat dry milk powder
1	teaspoon salt
1/2	teaspoon baking powder
1/2	teaspoon ground cinnamon
1	to 1-1/4 cups apple pie filling

In a large bowl, cream butter and brown sugar. Add the eggs and vanilla. Combine the oats, flour, milk powder, salt, baking powder and cinnamon; add to the creamed mixture and mix well.

Drop by 1/4 cupfuls 6 in. apart onto ungreased baking sheets. Flatten into 3-in. circles. Make a slight indentation in the center of each; top with a rounded tablespoonful of pie filling.

Bake at 350° for 16-20 minutes or until edges are lightly browned. Cool for 5 minutes before removing to wire racks.

Pat Woolley, Jackson Center, Ohio ✳

These soft cookies are definitely a comforting, old-fashioned variety everyone will enjoy.

lemon poppy seed cookies

yield 3-1/2 dozen

1/2	cup poppy seed filling
2	teaspoons lemon juice
1	cup butter, softened
1-1/2	cups sugar
3	egg yolks
1	tablespoon grated lemon peel
2	teaspoons lemon extract
1	teaspoon vanilla extract
3-1/2	cups all-purpose flour
2	teaspoons baking powder
1-1/4	teaspoons baking soda
3/4	cup buttermilk

FROSTING:

3	cups confectioners' sugar
2	tablespoons butter, softened
1/4	cup milk
2	teaspoons lemon extract
1	teaspoon grated lemon peel

Poppy seeds, optional

In a small bowl, combine the poppy seed filling and lemon juice; set aside. In a large bowl, cream the butter and sugar until light and fluffy. Beat in the egg yolks, lemon peel and extracts. Combine the flour, baking powder and baking soda; add to creamed mixture alternately with buttermilk, beating well after each addition.

Drop by tablespoonfuls 2 in. apart onto greased baking sheets. Using the end of a wooden spoon handle, make an indentation about 1/2 in. deep in the center of each.

Fill with about 1/2 teaspoon of poppy seed filling. Top with a teaspoonful of dough. Bake at 350° for 14-16 minutes or until edges are golden brown. Remove to wire racks to cool.

For frosting, in a small bowl, beat the confectioners' sugar, butter, milk, extract and lemon peel until smooth. Spread over cookies. Sprinkle with poppy seeds if desired.

✳ Becky Baldwin, Annville, Pennsylvania
I created this recipe for a party my friend had for National Pig Day, which is March 1st. They were not only a big hit at the party, but also at my son's school parties.

cute pig cookies

yield 6 dozen

1	cup butter, softened
1-1/2	cups sugar
2	eggs
1	cup (8 ounces) sour cream
1	teaspoon vanilla extract
3	cups all-purpose flour
1	teaspoon baking powder
1/2	teaspoon salt

FROSTING/DECORATING:

1/2	cup butter
4	cups confectioners' sugar
2	teaspoons vanilla extract
6	tablespoons milk
3	to 4 drops red food coloring

Pink sugar wafer cookies

| 36 | large marshmallows, halved |

Reese's candy bar sprinkles

In a large bowl, cream butter and sugar until light and fluffy. Add eggs, sour cream and vanilla; mix well. Combine dry ingredients; add to creamed mixture and mix well.

Drop by tablespoonfuls 2 in. apart onto ungreased baking sheets. Bake at 375° for 10-12 minutes or until edges are lightly browned. Remove to wire racks to cool completely.

Melt butter. Add the sugar, vanilla, milk and food coloring; mix until smooth. Frost the cookies. Cut the sugar wafers into triangles; place two pieces on each cookie for ears. With a toothpick, poke two holes in each marshmallow half for nostrils; press light brown candy bar sprinkles into holes. Place nose on cookies. Add dark brown candy bar sprinkles for eyes.

butter meltaways

yield about 4 dozen

✳ Sue Call
Beech Grove, Indiana
Add variety to this recipe by substituting lemon flavoring for the vanilla plus a teaspoon of lemon peel.

1/2	cup butter, softened
1/2	cup canola oil
1/2	cup sugar
1/2	cup confectioners' sugar
1	egg
1/2	teaspoon vanilla extract
2-1/4	cups all-purpose flour
1/2	teaspoon baking soda
1/2	teaspoon cream of tartar

Additional sugar

In a large bowl, cream butter, oil and sugars until light and fluffy. Add egg and vanilla. Combine flour, baking soda and cream of tartar; gradually add to the creamed mixture. Chill for several hours or overnight.

Drop by rounded teaspoonfuls 2 in. apart onto ungreased baking sheets. Flatten with a fork dipped in flour; sprinkle with additional sugar. Bake at 350° for 13-15 minutes or until lightly browned. Remove to wire racks to cool.

Irene McDade, Cumberland, Rhode Island ✳
These colossal cookies taste best when golden around the edges and moist and chewy in the center.

giant cherry oatmeal cookies

yield 1 dozen

1/2	cup shortening
1/2	cup butter, softened
3/4	cup packed brown sugar
1/2	cup sugar
2	eggs
1	teaspoon vanilla extract
2-1/2	cups old-fashioned oats
1-1/3	cups all-purpose flour
2	teaspoons apple pie spice
1/2	teaspoon baking powder
1/4	teaspoon baking soda
1/4	teaspoon salt
1-1/2	cups dried cherries, chopped
1/2	to 1 teaspoon grated orange peel

In a large bowl, cream shortening, butter and sugars until light and fluffy. Beat in the eggs and vanilla. Combine the oats, flour, apple pie spice, baking powder, baking soda and salt; gradually add to the creamed mixture. Stir in cherries and orange peel.

Drop by 1/3 cupfuls onto an ungreased baking sheet. Press to form a 4-in. circle. Bake at 375° for 9-12 minutes or until golden brown. Let stand for 1 minute before removing to wire racks to cool.

Shirley Brazel, Coos Bay, Oregon ✳
I've been making these cookies for more than 25 years. These cookies have a crisp edge, soft center and subtle lemon flavor. Choose colored sugar to tailor them to any occasion.

drop sugar cookies

yield about 3-1/2 dozen

2	eggs
3/4	cup sugar
2/3	cup canola oil
2	teaspoons vanilla extract
1	teaspoon grated lemon peel
2	cups all-purpose flour
2	teaspoons baking powder
1/2	teaspoon salt

Additional sugar *or* colored sugar

In a large bowl, beat eggs, sugar, oil, vanilla and lemon peel until blended. Combine the flour, baking powder and salt; gradually beat into egg mixture.

Drop by rounded teaspoonfuls 2 in. apart onto greased baking sheets. Flatten with a glass dipped in sugar. Bake at 350° for 8-10 minutes or until edges are lightly browned. Cool for 1-2 minutes before removing to wire racks.

✳ Karen Nienaber, Erskine, Minnesota

My five children love maple and brown sugar oatmeal, so I decided to add those ingredients to my oatmeal cookies. The first time I made them, they vanished in just a few days!

maple raisin oatmeal cookies

yield 6 dozen

1	cup butter, softened
1	cup packed brown sugar
1/2	cup sugar
2	eggs
1	teaspoon maple flavoring
1-1/2	cups all-purpose flour
1	teaspoon baking soda
1	teaspoon ground cinnamon
1/2	teaspoon salt
3	cups quick-cooking oats
1	cup raisins

In a large bowl, cream the butter and sugars until light and fluffy. Add eggs, one at a time, beating well after each addition. Beat in maple flavoring. Combine the flour, baking soda, cinnamon and salt; gradually add to the creamed mixture. Stir in oats and raisins.

Drop by rounded teaspoonfuls 2 in. apart onto ungreased baking sheets. Bake at 350° for 10-12 minutes or until golden brown. Remove to wire racks to cool.

✳ Joylyn Trickel, Greendale, Wisconsin

These macaroons have got a great homemade feel to them. The chocolate and coconut combination make them a very rich treat that everyone seems to love.

white chocolate macaroons

yield 5 dozen

5	egg whites
1/2	teaspoon vanilla extract
1-1/3	cups sugar
5-1/4	cups flaked coconut, toasted, *divided*
3/4	cup ground almonds
6	squares (1 ounce *each*) white baking chocolate, coarsely chopped

Place egg whites in a large bowl; let stand at room temperature for 30 minutes. Add vanilla; beat on medium speed until soft peaks form. Gradually beat in sugar, about 2 tablespoons at a time, on high until stiff glossy peaks form and sugar is dissolved. Gradually fold in 4 cups coconut and nuts, about 1/2 cup at a time.

Drop by rounded tablespoonfuls 2 in. apart onto parchment-lined baking sheets. Bake at 275° for 25 minutes or until firm to the touch. Remove to wire racks to cool completely.

In a microwave-safe bowl, melt chocolate; stir until smooth. Spoon 1/4 teaspoon white chocolate on each cookie; sprinkle each with 1 teaspoon coconut. Place on waxed paper-lined baking sheets. Refrigerate for 1 hour or until chocolate is set. Store in an airtight container.

Beth Brown, Naples, Florida
This recipe can be changed to suit your sweet tooth. Try adding almond or mint extract.

fudgy no-bake cookies

yield 1 dozen

1	cup sugar
2	tablespoons baking cocoa
1/4	cup butter
1/4	cup milk
1	cup quick-cooking oats
1/4	cup flaked coconut
2	tablespoons peanut butter
1/2	teaspoon vanilla extract

In a saucepan, combine sugar and cocoa; add butter and milk. Cook and stir over medium heat until mixture comes to a boil; boil for 1 minute. Remove from the heat; stir in oats, coconut, peanut butter and vanilla.

Let stand until the mixture mounds when dropped by tablespoonfuls onto waxed paper. Let stand until set.

editor's note: Reduced-fat or generic brands of peanut butter are not recommended for this recipe.

frosted cashew drops

yield about 4 dozen

1/2	cup butter, softened
1	cup packed brown sugar
1/2	cup sour cream
1	egg
1	teaspoon vanilla extract
1-3/4	cups all-purpose flour
1	teaspoon baking powder
1/2	teaspoon baking soda
1/4	teaspoon salt
1	cup salted cashews, chopped and toasted

FROSTING:

1/4	cup butter, cubed
2	cups confectioners' sugar
2	to 3 tablespoons milk

In a large bowl, cream butter and brown sugar until light and fluffy; beat in the sour cream, egg and vanilla. Combine the flour, baking powder, baking soda and salt; gradually add to creamed mixture and mix well. Stir in the cashews.

Drop by rounded tablespoonfuls onto greased baking sheets. Bake at 375° for 8-10 minutes or until lightly browned. Remove to wire racks to cool completely.

For frosting, in a heavy saucepan, cook butter over medium heat for 7-9 minutes or until golden brown. Whisk in the confectioners' sugar and enough milk to achieve a smooth consistency. Spread over cooled cookies.

Lois McGrady
Hillsville, Virginia
If your family likes the taste of cashews, they will love these caramel-flavored cookies. I think they make a nice nutty addition to any holiday cookie platter, but they always disappear quickly no matter what time of year I serve them.

✳ June Quinn, Kalamazoo, Michigan
On busy days, I appreciate this fast-to-fix drop sugar cookie. Top each cookie with your favorite flavor of jam or jelly.

jelly-topped sugar cookies
yield about 3-1/2 dozen

3/4	cup sugar
3/4	cup canola oil
2	eggs
2	teaspoons vanilla extract
1	teaspoon lemon extract
1	teaspoon grated lemon peel
2	cups all-purpose flour
2	teaspoons baking powder
1/2	teaspoon salt
1/2	cup jam *or* jelly

In a large bowl, beat sugar and oil until blended. Beat in the eggs, extracts and lemon peel. Combine flour, baking powder and salt; gradually add to sugar mixture and mix well.

Drop by rounded tablespoonfuls 2 in. apart onto ungreased baking sheets. Coat bottom of a glass with cooking spray, then dip in sugar. Flatten cookies with prepared glass, redipping in sugar as needed.

Place 1/4 teaspoon jelly in the center of each cookie. Bake at 400° for 8-10 minutes or until set. Remove to wire racks to cool.

✳ Darlene Brenden, Salem, Oregon
I love coconut, chocolate and macadamia nuts, so in my effort to come up with the taste of my favorite candy bar, Almond Joy, I created this recipe. To make them more like a candy bar, I dipped the bottoms into chocolate.

chocolate macadamia macaroons
yield 1-1/2 dozen

2	cups flaked coconut
1/2	cup finely chopped macadamia nuts
1/3	cup sugar
3	tablespoons baking cocoa
2	tablespoons all-purpose flour
	Pinch salt
2	egg whites, beaten
1	tablespoon light corn syrup
1	teaspoon vanilla extract
4	squares (1 ounce *each*) semisweet chocolate

In a large bowl, combine the coconut, macadamia nuts, sugar, cocoa, flour and salt. Add the egg whites, corn syrup and vanilla and mix well.

Drop by rounded tablespoonfuls onto greased baking sheets. Bake at 325° for 15-20 minutes or until set and dry to the touch. Cool for 5 minutes before removing from pans to wire racks to cool completely.

In a microwave, melt chocolate; stir until smooth. Dip the bottom of each cookie in chocolate; allow excess to drip off. Place on waxed paper; let stand until set.

Elizabeth Hunter, Prosperity, South Carolina ✳
I got this recipe from my mother-in-law back in 1949, and my grown daughter asked me to share it with her.

no-bake fudgy oat cookies
yield about 3 dozen

2-1/4	**cups quick-cooking oats**
1	**cup flaked coconut**
1/2	**cup milk**
1/4	**cup butter**
2	**cups sugar**
1/2	**cup baking cocoa**
1	**teaspoon vanilla extract**

In a large bowl, combine oats and coconut; set aside. In a saucepan, combine milk and butter. Stir in sugar and cocoa; mix well. Bring to a boil. Add oat mixture; cook for 1 minute, stirring constantly. Remove from the heat; stir in vanilla.

Drop by rounded tablespoonfuls 1 in. apart onto waxed paper. Let stand until set.

root beer cookies
yield about 6 dozen

1	**cup butter, softened**
2	**cups packed brown sugar**
2	**eggs**
1	**cup buttermilk**
3/4	**teaspoon root beer concentrate** *or* **extract**
4	**cups all-purpose flour**
1	**teaspoon baking soda**
1	**teaspoon salt**
1-1/2	**cups chopped pecans**

FROSTING:

3-1/2	**cups confectioners' sugar**
3/4	**cup butter, softened**
3	**tablespoons water**
1-1/4	**teaspoons root beer concentrate** *or* **extract**

In a large bowl, cream butter and brown sugar until light and fluffy. Add eggs, one at a time, beating well after each addition. Beat in the buttermilk and root beer concentrate. Combine the flour, baking soda and salt; gradually add to the creamed mixture. Stir in the pecans.

Drop by tablespoonfuls 3 in. apart onto ungreased baking sheets. Bake at 375° for 10-12 minutes or until lightly browned. Remove to wire racks to cool.

In a large bowl, combine frosting ingredients; beat until smooth. Frost cooled cookies.

Violette Bawden ✳
West Valley City, Utah
Since it's too difficult to take along root beer floats on a picnic, pack these cookies instead! I've found the flavor is even better the next day. The hard part is convincing my family to wait that long before sampling them.

BAKING
tip

uniform drop cookies — An ice cream scoop is the perfect utensil for making uniformly sized drop cookies. A 1-tablespoon-size scoop will give a standard-size 2-inch cookie. Just scoop the dough, even off the top with a flat-edge metal spatula and release the dough onto the baking sheet.

* Rachel Greenawalt Keller, Roanoke, Virginia

Quick-cooking oats, oat bran, oat flour and whole wheat flour lend nutrition to these tasty cookies. They call for convenient canned peaches, so you can enjoy their fruit flavor any time of year.

peach oat cookies

yield 5 dozen

1/3	cup butter, softened
1/2	cup sugar
1/2	cup packed brown sugar
2	eggs
1-1/2	teaspoons vanilla extract
1/2	cup *each* all-purpose flour, whole wheat flour and oat flour
2	teaspoons baking powder
1	teaspoon salt
2-1/2	cups quick-cooking oats
1/2	cup oat bran
1-1/2	cups drained canned sliced peaches in extra-light syrup, chopped
1	cup raisins

In a large bowl, cream butter and sugars until light and fluffy. Add eggs, one at a time, beating well after each addition. Beat in vanilla. Combine the flours, baking powder and salt; gradually add to creamed mixture and mix well. Stir in oats and oat bran just until combined. Stir in peaches and raisins.

Drop by rounded tablespoonfuls onto baking sheets coated with cooking spray. Bake at 350° for 9-13 minutes or until edges are lightly browned. Remove to a wire rack to cool.

* Joyce Pierce
Caledonia, Michigan
Buttery, rich and delicious, Almond Sandies are my husband's favorite cookie. These are very popular wherever I take them, and they always disappear quickly.

almond sandies

yield about 4 dozen

1	cup butter, softened
1	cup sugar
1	teaspoon almond extract
1-3/4	cups all-purpose flour
1/2	teaspoon baking soda
1/4	teaspoon baking powder
1/4	teaspoon salt
1/2	cup slivered almonds

In a large bowl, cream butter and sugar until light and fluffy. Add extract; mix well. Combine flour, baking soda, baking powder and salt; gradually add to creamed mixture. Fold in almonds.

Drop dough by rounded teaspoonfuls onto ungreased baking sheets. Bake at 300° for 22-24 minutes or until lightly browned. Cool for 1-2 minutes before removing to wire racks.

BAKING tip

make your favorite sandies — Are almonds not your favorite nut? You can vary the Almond Sandies recipe above to suit your and your family's tastes. Simply replace the almond extract with vanilla extract and replace the slivered almonds with a 1/2 cup of chopped pecans, cashews, macadamia nuts or even pistachios.

Sheree Gilpin, Lehighton, Pennsylvania ✳

My aunt made these frosted cookies one year for Christmas, and my husband ate about a dozen. Since he liked them so much, I asked for the recipe and have made them often.

chocolate maple cookies

yield 4 dozen

1-1/4	cups shortening
1-1/2	cups packed brown sugar
5	eggs
1	teaspoon vanilla extract
1/2	teaspoon maple flavoring
2-1/2	cups all-purpose flour
3/4	teaspoon baking soda
1/2	teaspoon salt

FROSTING:

2	squares (1 ounce *each*) semisweet chocolate
1	tablespoon butter
1-1/2	cups confectioners' sugar
1/4	cup milk

In a large bowl, cream shortening and brown sugar until light and fluffy. Add eggs, one at a time, beating well after each addition. Beat in vanilla and maple flavoring. Combine the flour, baking soda and salt; gradually add to the creamed mixture and mix well.

Drop by teaspoonfuls 2 in. apart onto greased baking sheets. Bake at 350° for 8-10 minutes or until edges begin to brown. Remove to wire racks to cool.

For frosting, in a microwave, melt chocolate and butter; stir until smooth. Stir in confectioners' sugar and milk until smooth. Spread over cooled cookies.

chewy coconut cookies

yield about 5-1/2 dozen

3/4	cup butter-flavored shortening
1/2	cup peanut butter
1	cup sugar
1	cup packed brown sugar
3	eggs
1/2	cup mashed ripe banana
1	teaspoon vanilla extract
1/2	teaspoon almond extract
2-1/2	cups all-purpose flour
1	teaspoon baking soda
1	teaspoon salt
1/2	teaspoon baking powder
1	cup flaked coconut

In a large bowl, cream the shortening, peanut butter and sugars until light and fluffy. Add eggs, one at a time, beating well after each addition. Beat in the banana and extracts. Combine the flour, baking soda, salt and baking powder; gradually add to creamed mixture. Stir in coconut.

Drop by heaping teaspoonfuls 2 in. apart onto lightly greased baking sheets. Bake at 350° for 12-14 minutes or until edges are lightly browned. Remove to wire racks.

Nick Robeson ✳
Casper, Wyoming
I wanted to invent my own recipe, so I sat down with my mom and came up with a cookie I thought I would like to eat. The result is this treat that is crisp outside, moist and chewy inside, and mildly flavored with peanut butter.

 Melinda Leonowitz, Birdsboro, Pennsylvania

This treasured recipe is from a favorite aunt. Her soft, rich cookies have a yummy apricot flavor, but you could substitute strawberry, pineapple or raspberry preserves if you prefer.

apricot cream cheese drops

yield 3 dozen

1/2	cup butter, softened
1	package (3 ounces) cream cheese, softened
1/2	cup apricot preserves
1/4	cup packed brown sugar
1	tablespoon milk
1-1/4	cups all-purpose flour
1-1/2	teaspoons baking powder
1-1/2	teaspoons ground cinnamon
1/4	teaspoon salt

FROSTING:

1	cup confectioners' sugar
1/4	cup apricot preserves
1	tablespoon butter, softened
1	to 2 teaspoons milk

Ground nuts *or* flaked coconut

In a large bowl, beat the butter, cream cheese, apricot preserves, brown sugar and milk until blended. Combine the flour, baking powder, cinnamon and salt; gradually add to cream cheese mixture and mix well.

Drop by teaspoonfuls onto ungreased baking sheets. Bake at 350° for 8-10 minutes or until lightly browned. Remove to wire racks to cool.

For frosting, in a small bowl, combine the confectioners' sugar, apricot preserves, butter and enough milk to achieve desired consistency. Spread over the cooled cookies. Sprinkle with nuts or coconut.

Jean Kleckner, Seattle, Washington

If you like pumpkin pie, you'll love these delicious pumpkin cookies dotted with white chocolate chips and chopped pecans. Drizzled with a brown sugar icing, they're irresistible.

white chocolate pumpkin dreams

yield about 4-1/2 dozen

1	cup butter, softened
1/2	cup sugar
1/2	cup packed brown sugar
1	egg
2	teaspoons vanilla extract
1	cup canned pumpkin
2	cups all-purpose flour
3-1/2	teaspoons pumpkin pie spice
1	teaspoon baking powder
1	teaspoon baking soda
1/4	teaspoon salt
1	package (11 ounces) vanilla *or* white chips
1	cup chopped pecans

PENUCHE FROSTING:

1/2	cup packed brown sugar
3	tablespoons butter
1/4	cup milk
1-1/2	to 2 cups confectioners' sugar

In a large bowl, cream butter and sugars until light and fluffy. Beat in the egg, vanilla and pumpkin. Combine dry ingredients; gradually add to the creamed mixture and mix well. Stir in chips and pecans.

Drop by rounded teaspoonfuls 2 in. apart onto ungreased baking sheets. Bake at 350° for 12-14 minutes or until firm. Remove to wire racks to cool completely.

For frosting, combine brown sugar and butter in a small saucepan. Bring to a boil; cook over medium heat for 1 minute or until slightly thickened. Cool for 10 minutes. Add milk; beat until smooth. Beat in enough confectioners' sugar to reach desired consistency. Spread over cooled cookies.

cherry date cookies

yield 4-1/2 dozen

2-1/4	cups graham cracker crumbs (about 27 squares)
1	can (14 ounces) sweetened condensed milk
2	cups chopped dates
2	cups chopped walnuts
27	red *or* green maraschino cherries, halved

In a bowl, combine cracker crumbs and milk; let stand for 10 minutes. Stir in dates and walnuts (mixture will be very thick).

Drop by tablespoonfuls 2 in. apart onto greased baking sheets. Top each with a cherry half. Bake at 350° for 10-15 minutes or until set and edges are lightly browned. Cool for 1 minute before removing to wire racks to cool.

Charlotte Moore
Parkersburg, West Virginia
You can fix these chewy, old-fashioned drop cookies with just five ingredients. I received this recipe from a friend more than 40 years ago and have made these cookies every Christmas since.

* Michelle Nabe, Tonawanda, New York

My grandmother always made these cookies for us for Christmas, and now I have inherited that task. With rich cream cheese in the dough and the sugary almond topping, a batch doesn't last long at our house!

lemon oatmeal cookies

yield 4-1/2 dozen

1	cup butter-flavored shortening
1	package (3 ounces) cream cheese, softened
1-1/4	cups sugar
1	egg yolk
2	teaspoons grated lemon peel
1	teaspoon lemon extract
1-1/3	cups all-purpose flour
1-1/3	cups quick-cooking oats
1/2	teaspoon salt

TOPPING:

1	egg
1	egg white
Sugar	
1/2	cup sliced almonds

In a large bowl, cream the shortening, cream cheese and sugar until light and fluffy. Beat in the egg yolk, lemon peel and extract. Combine the flour, oats and salt; gradually add to creamed mixture and mix well.

Drop by heaping teaspoonfuls 2 in. apart onto greased baking sheets. Beat egg and egg white; brush over dough. Sprinkle with sugar; top with almonds.

Bake at 350° for 10-12 minutes or until edges are lightly browned. Remove to wire racks.

* Bethel Walters, Willow River, Minnesota

My mother shared the recipe for these soft spice cookies. I just love to eat them for a mid-afternoon snack.

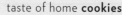

ginger drop cookies

yield about 5-1/2 dozen

1	cup shortening
1	cup packed brown sugar
1	cup molasses
2	eggs
4	cups all-purpose flour
2	teaspoons baking soda
2	teaspoons ground cinnamon
2	teaspoons ground ginger
1	teaspoon salt
1/2	cup water

In a large bowl, cream shortening and brown sugar until light and fluffy. Add molasses and eggs; mix well. Combine the dry ingredients; add to the creamed mixture alternately with water. Cover and refrigerate for at least 8 hours.

Drop dough by tablespoonfuls 2 in. apart onto greased baking sheets. Bake at 350° for 10-12 minutes or until lightly browned. Remove to wire racks to cool.

Shirley Steele, San Jose, California

Our state has an abundance of apricots and walnuts, and they are delicious in this cookie, which also includes chocolate chips.

apricot chip cookies

yield about 3 dozen

1/4	cup butter, softened
1/4	cup shortening
1/3	cup sugar
1/3	cup packed brown sugar
1	egg
1/2	teaspoon vanilla extract
1	cup all-purpose flour
1/2	teaspoon salt
1/2	teaspoon baking soda
2/3	cup chopped dried apricots
1/2	cup semisweet chocolate chips
1/2	cup chopped walnuts

In a large bowl, cream the butter, shortening and sugars until light and fluffy. Beat in egg and vanilla. Combine the flour, salt and baking soda; gradually add to the creamed mixture. Stir in apricots, chocolate chips and walnuts.

Drop by tablespoonfuls 2 in. apart onto ungreased baking sheets. Bake at 375° for 8-10 minutes or until golden brown. Remove to wire racks to cool.

whole wheat cookies

yield about 4 dozen

1/2	cup butter, softened
1/2	cup peanut butter
1/2	cup honey
1	egg
1	teaspoon vanilla extract
1	cup whole wheat flour
1/2	cup nonfat dry milk powder
1/2	cup toasted wheat germ
1	teaspoon baking soda

In a large bowl, cream the butter, peanut butter and honey. Beat in egg and vanilla. Combine the dry ingredients; gradually add to creamed mixture and mix well. Cover and refrigerate for 30 minutes.

Drop by teaspoonfuls 2 in. apart onto ungreased baking sheets. Flatten with a fork dipped in sugar.

Bake at 350° for 8-10 minutes or until golden brown. Cool for 1 minute before removing to wire racks to cool completely.

editor's note: Reduced-fat or generic brands of peanut butter are not recommended for this recipe.

Bertie Carter
Tahlequah, Oklahoma
These soft, old-fashioned cookies are quite flavorful. With the goodness of wheat gern, they make a wholesome snack.

* Blanche Whytsell, Arnoldsburg, Wyoming

It's a snap to stir up these soft frosted cookies. With their big apple-and-spice flavor and abundance of nuts, you'll have a hard time eating just one.

apple spice drops
yield about 3-1/2 dozen

1/2	cup butter, softened
2/3	cup sugar
2/3	cup packed brown sugar
1	egg
1/4	cup apple juice
2	cups all-purpose flour
1	teaspoon ground cinnamon
1/2	teaspoon baking soda
1/2	teaspoon ground nutmeg
1	cup finely chopped peeled tart apple
1	cup chopped walnuts

FROSTING:

1/4	cup butter, softened
3	cups confectioners' sugar
1	teaspoon vanilla extract
3	to 4 tablespoons apple juice

In a large bowl, cream butter and sugars until light and fluffy. Beat in egg and apple juice. Combine the dry ingredients; gradually add to the creamed mixture. Fold in apple and walnuts.

Drop by teaspoonfuls 2 in. apart onto greased baking sheets. Bake at 375° for 12-14 minutes or until golden brown. Remove to wire racks to cool completely.

For frosting, cream butter, sugar, vanilla and enough apple juice to achieve spreading consistency. Frost cooled cookies.

cranberry chip cookies
yield 9 dozen

* Jo Ann McCarthy
Canton, Massachusetts

I received these delightful cookies for Christmas a few years ago. I was watching my diet, but I couldn't stay away from them! The tart cranberries blend beautifully with the sweet chocolate and vanilla chips.

1/2	cup butter, softened
1/2	cup shortening
3/4	sugar
3/4	cup packed brown sugar
2	eggs
1	teaspoon vanilla extract
2-1/4	cups all-purpose flour
1	teaspoon baking soda
1/2	teaspoon salt
1	cup semisweet chocolate chips
1	cup vanilla or white chips
1	cup dried cranberries
1	cup chopped pecans

In a large bowl, cream butter, shortening and sugars until light and fluffy. Add eggs, one at a time, beating well after each addition. Beat in vanilla. Combine flour, baking soda and salt; gradually add to the creamed mixture. Stir in the chips, cranberries and pecans.

Drop by tablespoonfuls 2 in. apart onto ungreased baking sheets. Bake at 375° for 9-11 minutes or until golden brown. Cool for 2 minutes before removing to wire racks.

These cookie pops from our home economists are a great way to liven up a Halloween party. Kids love their yummy taste and cute jack-o'-lantern faces.

pumpkin cookie pops

yield 2-1/2 dozen

1/2	cup butter, softened
3/4	cup packed brown sugar
1/2	cup sugar
1	egg
1	teaspoon vanilla extract
1	cup canned pumpkin
2-1/2	cups all-purpose flour
1	teaspoon baking powder
1	teaspoon baking soda
1	teaspoon ground cinnamon
30	Popsicle sticks
1/3	cup green gumdrops, quartered lengthwise

ICING:

4	cups confectioners' sugar
1/4	cup water

Orange, black, purple, green and red paste *or* gel food coloring

In a large bowl, cream butter and sugars until light and fluffy. Beat in egg and vanilla. Beat in pumpkin. Combine the flour, baking powder, baking soda and cinnamon; gradually add to creamed mixture (dough will be soft).

Drop by rounded tablespoonfuls 2 in. apart onto greased or parchment paper-lined baking sheets. Insert Popsicle sticks into dough. Insert a gumdrop piece into the top of each for the pumpkin stem.

Bake at 350° for 14-16 minutes or until set and lightly browned around the edges. Remove to wire racks to cool.

For icing, in a large bowl, combine confectioners' sugar and water until smooth. Remove 1/2 cup to another bowl; cover and set aside. Stir orange food coloring into remaining icing. Spread or pipe over cookies. Let stand for 30 minutes or until icing is set and dry.

Tint reserved icing with colors of your choice; use colored icing to create jack-o'-lantern faces.

coconut caramel oat cookies

yield 4-1/2 dozen

1/2	cup butter
1/2	cup milk
1	cup sugar
1	teaspoon vanilla extract
1/2	teaspoon salt
25	caramels
3	cups quick-cooking oats
1	cup flaked coconut

In a heavy saucepan, bring butter and milk to a boil; add sugar, vanilla and salt. Cook for 1 minute. Add caramels and stir until melted, about 4 minutes. Stir in oats and coconut.

Drop by heaping tablespoonfuls onto waxed paper. Let stand at room temperature until set.

Tammy Schroeder ✳
Aitkin, Minnesota
When I was a little girl, my grandmother and I used to whip up this no-bake snack to munch on while playing rummy.

※ Loretta Patterson, Mentor, Ohio
These old-fashioned, cake-like cookies are sweet and buttery. They pair well with a glass of milk or a cup of hot coffee.

frosted brown sugar cookies

yield about 2 dozen

1/2	cup butter, softened
1	cup packed brown sugar
1	egg
1/2	cup sour cream
1-3/4	cups all-purpose flour
1/2	teaspoon baking soda
1/4	teaspoon salt

BROWN SUGAR FROSTING:

1/4	cup butter
1/2	cup packed brown sugar
2	tablespoons milk
1	cup confectioners' sugar

In a small bowl, cream butter and brown sugar until light and fluffy. Beat in egg and sour cream. Combine the flour, baking soda and salt; gradually add to creamed mixture and mix well.

Drop by tablespoonfuls 2 in. apart onto greased baking sheets. Bake at 375° for 9-11 minutes or until golden brown. Remove to wire racks to cool completely.

For frosting, in a small saucepan, melt butter over low heat; add brown sugar. Cook and stir for 2 minutes. Gradually add the milk. Bring to a boil, stirring constantly. Remove from the heat. Stir in confectioners' sugar. Cool for 20-30 minutes. Frost cooled cookies.

out-on-the-range cookies

yield 4-1/2 dozen

※ Sharon Weaver
Orlando, Florida
I bake these cookies for our two nephews when they make their annual trip to visit us. They love them because they combine the best of chocolate chip, oatmeal and peanut butter cookies into one treat.

3/4	cup shortening
1-1/4	cups packed brown sugar
1	cup sugar
2	eggs
1	cup peanut butter
1	teaspoon vanilla extract
1-3/4	cups all-purpose flour
1	cup quick-cooking oats
2	teaspoons baking soda
1/2	teaspoon salt
1	cup (6 ounces) semisweet chocolate chips

In a large bowl, cream shortening and sugars until light and fluffy. Add eggs, one at a time, beating well after each addition. Beat in peanut butter and vanilla. Combine the flour, oats, baking soda and salt; gradually add to the creamed mixture and mix well. Stir in chips.

Drop by rounded tablespoonfuls 2 in. apart onto greased baking sheets. Bake at 325° for 12-14 minutes or until golden brown. Remove to wire racks to cool.

Elaine Scott, Lafayette, Indiana ✳

I like the sudden hit of sweetness when you bite into the white chocolate in these cookies. It really complements the tart flavor from the rhubarb and cranberries.

rhubarb cranberry cookies

yield about 5-1/2 dozen

1	cup butter, softened
1	cup packed brown sugar
1/2	cup sugar
2	eggs
1	teaspoon vanilla extract
1-1/2	cups all-purpose flour
1	teaspoon baking soda
1/2	teaspoon salt
1/2	teaspoon ground cinnamon
2-1/2	cups old-fashioned oats
1-1/2	cups diced frozen rhubarb
1	cup vanilla *or* white chips
1	cup dried cranberries
4	squares (1 ounce *each*) white baking chocolate

In a large bowl, cream the butter and sugars until light and fluffy. Beat in eggs and vanilla. Combine the flour, baking soda, salt and cinnamon; gradually add to creamed mixture and mix well. Stir in the oats, rhubarb, chips and cranberries.

Drop by tablespoonfuls 2 in. apart onto parchment paper-lined baking sheets. Bake at 350° for 10-12 minutes or until set. Remove to wire racks to cool.

In a microwave, melt the white chocolate at 70% power for 1 minute; stir. Microwave at additional 10- to 20-second intervals, stirring until smooth. Drizzle over cookies; let stand until set. Store in an airtight container.

Lucille Dent, Galesburg, Michigan ✳

The prunes in this recipe are finely chopped so no one will need to know they appear in these crisp, lightly sweet cookies.

prune-pecan cookies

yield 2 dozen

1	egg
7	pitted dried prunes *or* plums
1/2	cup sugar
1	cup all-purpose flour
1/2	teaspoon baking soda

Dash salt

24	pecan halves

In a blender, puree egg and prunes until finely chopped. Pour into a bowl. Add sugar. Combine the flour, baking soda and salt; add to prune mixture and mix well.

Drop by rounded teaspoonfuls onto greased baking sheets. Top each cookie with a pecan half. Bake at 350° for 13-15 minutes or until golden brown. Remove to wire racks to cool.

✳ Pauline Bondy, Grand Forks, North Dakota
I won a blue ribbon at our local fair for these tender cookies. They're so pretty with the filling peeking through the dough. When not just any cookie will do, try making these and watch the smiles appear.

rhubarb-filled cookies
yield about 4-1/2 dozen

1	cup butter, softened
1	cup sugar
1	cup packed brown sugar
4	eggs
4-1/2	cups all-purpose flour
1	teaspoon baking soda
1	teaspoon salt

FILLING:

3-1/2	cups chopped fresh *or* frozen rhubarb, thawed
1-1/2	cups sugar
6	tablespoons water, *divided*
1/4	cup cornstarch
1	teaspoon vanilla extract

In a large bowl, cream the butter and sugars. Add the eggs, one at a time, beating well after each addition. Combine the flour, baking soda and salt; gradually add to creamed mixture and mix well (dough will be sticky).

For filling, combine rhubarb, sugar and 2 tablespoons water in a large saucepan. Bring to a boil. Reduce heat; simmer, uncovered, for 10 minutes or until thickened, stirring frequently. Combine cornstarch and remaining water until smooth; stir into rhubarb mixture. Bring to a boil; cook and stir for 2 minutes or until thickened. Remove from the heat; stir in vanilla.

Drop dough by tablespoonfuls 2 in. apart onto ungreased baking sheets. Using the end of a wooden spoon handle, make an indentation in the center of each cookie; fill with a rounded teaspoon of filling. Top with 1/2 teaspoon of dough, allowing some filling to show. Bake at 375° for 8-10 minutes or until lightly browned. Remove to wire racks to cool.

✳ Doris Barb
El Dorado, Kansas
These cake-like cookies are flavorful and firm enough to pack in brown-bag lunches or take on picnics.

date drops
yield about 6 dozen

1/2	cup butter, softened
3/4	cup packed brown sugar
2	eggs
1/4	cup milk
1/2	teaspoon vanilla extract
1-1/2	cups all-purpose flour
1	teaspoon baking powder
1/4	teaspoon salt
1	cup quick-cooking oats
1	cup chopped dates
1/2	cup chopped walnuts

In a large bowl, cream the butter and brown sugar. Beat in eggs, milk and vanilla. Combine flour, baking powder and salt; gradually add to creamed mixture and mix well. Stir in oats, dates and nuts.

Drop by rounded teaspoonfuls 1 in. apart onto greased baking sheets. Bake at 350° for 12-15 minutes or until edges are lightly browned and tops are firm to the touch. Remove to wire racks to cool.

Tammie Young, Mattoon, Illinois ✳
I remember my dad making a big batch of these citrus cookies when I was growing up. They're very moist.

frosted orange cookies

yield about 4 dozen

2	medium navel oranges
1/2	cup butter-flavored shortening
1	cup sugar
1/2	cup milk
2	cups all-purpose flour
1	teaspoon baking powder
1/2	teaspoon baking soda
1/2	teaspoon salt
2-1/2	cups confectioners' sugar
1	tablespoon butter, melted

With a sharp paring knife, score each orange into quarters; remove peel. Use knife to remove white pith from the peel and the fruit; discard. Quarter oranges and place in a blender. Add peel; cover and process until smooth (mixture should measure 3/4 cup).

In a large bowl, cream the shortening and sugar until light and fluffy. Beat in the milk and 6 tablespoons orange mixture. Combine the flour, baking powder, baking soda and salt; add to creamed mixture until blended.

Drop by rounded teaspoonfuls 2 in. apart onto greased baking sheets. Bake at 350° for 10-13 minutes or until set and edges are lightly browned. Remove to wire racks to cool.

For frosting, in a small mixing bowl, combine confectioners' sugar, butter and enough of the remaining orange mixture to achieve spreading consistency. Frost cookies.

butter wafers

yield about 2-1/2 dozen

1	cup butter, softened
1/3	cup confectioners' sugar
1	cup all-purpose flour
2/3	cup cornstarch
Colored sugar, optional	

In a large bowl, cream butter and confectioners' sugar. Combine flour and cornstarch; add to creamed mixture and mix well.

Drop by rounded tablespoonfuls 3 in. apart onto ungreased baking sheets (cookies will spread). Sprinkle with colored sugar if desired. Bake at 325° for 12-15 minutes or until edges are lightly browned and tops are set. Cool for 2 minutes before carefully removing to wire racks.

Evelyn Starr ✳
Raymond, Washington
These crisp drop cookies are great for folks who don't like their treats too sweet and who don't want to fuss with rolling out the dough. Just beat together four ingredients, and you are on your way to a delicious treat.

✳ Anne Revers, Omaha, Nebraska
Since chocolate-mint is my favorite flavor combination, I sometimes eat these dainty shortbread-like treats by the dozen. But I manage to save some for guests because they make my cookie trays look so elegant.

chocolate mint dreams

yield 4 dozen

3/4	cup butter, softened
1	cup confectioners' sugar
2	squares (1 ounce *each*) unsweetened chocolate, melted and cooled
1/4	teaspoon peppermint extract
1-1/2	cups all-purpose flour
1	cup miniature semisweet chocolate chips

ICING:

2	tablespoons butter, softened
1	cup confectioners' sugar
1/4	teaspoon peppermint extract
1	to 2 drops green food coloring
1	to 2 tablespoons milk

DRIZZLE:

1/2	cup semisweet chocolate chips
1/2	teaspoon shortening

In a large bowl, cream butter and confectioners' sugar until light and fluffy. Beat in chocolate and mint extract. Gradually add flour and mix well. Stir in chocolate chips. (Dough will be soft.)

Drop by tablespoonfuls 2 in. apart on ungreased baking sheets. Bake at 375° for 6-8 minutes or until firm. Cool for 2 minutes before removing to wire racks to cool completely.

Meanwhile, combine the butter, confectioners' sugar, extract, food coloring and enough milk to reach desired consistency; spread over cooled cookies. Let set. In a microwave, melt chocolate chips and shortening; stir until smooth. Drizzle over cookies.

✳ Cindy Colley
Othello, Washington
These cookies have coconut, walnuts and oats to make them a satisfying snack no matter what time of day. They're a hit with everyone who tries them.

toasted coconut cookies

yield about 5 dozen

1/2	cup butter, softened
1/2	cup shortening
3/4	cup sugar
3/4	cup packed brown sugar
2	eggs
2	teaspoons vanilla extract
2	cups all-purpose flour
1	teaspoon baking powder
1	teaspoon baking soda
3/4	teaspoon salt
1-1/2	cups quick-cooking oats
1-1/2	cups flaked coconut, toasted
3/4	cup chopped walnuts, toasted

In a large bowl, cream butter, shortening and sugars until light and fluffy. Add eggs and vanilla; beat well. Combine flour, baking powder, baking soda and salt; gradually add to creamed mixture. Fold in oats, coconut and nuts.

Drop by tablespoonfuls onto greased baking sheets. Bake at 375° for 10-11 minutes or until golden brown. Cool 2-3 minutes before removing to wire racks.

Dorothy Hawkins, Springhill, Florida ✳

My mother used to bake these mouthwatering cookies for an after-school treat. These cookies stay moist and fresh for a long time, or the dough can be stored in the refrigerator for several days so you can bake as you need them.

apple butter cookies
yield about 2-1/2 dozen

1/4   cup butter, softened
1   cup packed brown sugar
1   egg
1/2   cup quick-cooking oats
1/2   cup apple butter
1   cup all-purpose flour
1/2   teaspoon baking soda
1/2   teaspoon baking powder
1/2   teaspoon salt
2   tablespoons milk
1/2   cup chopped nuts
1/2   cup raisins

In a small bowl, cream butter and sugar until light and fluffy. Beat in egg, oats and apple butter. Combine dry ingredients; gradually add to creamed mixture along with the milk; beat until blended. Stir in nuts and raisins. Cover and refrigerate until easy to handle.

Drop by teaspoonfuls 2 in. apart onto lightly greased baking sheets. Bake at 350° for 15 minutes or until set. Remove to wire racks.

macadamia almond delights
yield 4 dozen

2/3   cup butter, softened
2/3   cup shortening
1   cup sugar
1   cup packed brown sugar
2   eggs
2   teaspoons vanilla extract
1   cup almond paste
3   cups plus 3 tablespoons all-purpose flour
1   teaspoon baking soda
1   teaspoon salt
1-1/2   cups macadamia nuts, chopped
1   package (11 ounces) vanilla *or* white chips

In a large bowl, cream the butter, shortening and sugars until light and fluffy. Add eggs, one at a time, beating well after each addition. Beat in vanilla and almond paste. Combine the flour, baking soda and salt; gradually add to the creamed mixture and mix well. Stir in the nuts and chips.

Drop by heaping tablespoonfuls 2 in. apart onto ungreased baking sheets. Bake at 350° for 12-15 minutes or until lightly browned. Remove to wire racks to cool.

Ethel Marshall ✳
Salem, Oregon
A few years ago, I decided to liven up my basic chocolate chip cookie recipe by adding macadamia nuts, white chocolate chips and almond paste. Since the scrumptious results got such rave reviews from my 26 grandchildren, we've designated this version a "keeper."

✳ Jane Darling , Simi Valley, California
The recipe for these comforting "cookie pillows" originated with my mother. The tender treats are jazzed up with thick frosting and a sprinkling of chopped walnuts.

mom's buttermilk cookies

yield 3 dozen

1/2	cup butter, softened
1	cup sugar
1	egg
1	teaspoon vanilla extract
2-1/2	cups all-purpose flour
1/2	teaspoon baking soda
1/2	teaspoon salt
1/2	cup buttermilk

FROSTING:

3	tablespoons butter, softened
3-1/2	cups confectioners' sugar
1/4	cup milk
1	teaspoon vanilla extract
1/2	cup finely chopped walnuts, optional

In a large bowl, cream butter and sugar until light and fluffy. Beat in egg and vanilla. Combine flour, baking soda and salt; add to the creamed mixture alternately with buttermilk and mix well.

Drop by rounded tablespoonfuls 2 in. apart onto greased baking sheets. Bake at 375° for 10-12 minutes or until edges are lightly browned. Remove to wire racks to cool.

For frosting, combine butter, sugar, milk and vanilla in a large bowl; beat until smooth. Frost cookies; sprinkle with walnuts if desired.

Denise and George Hymel, Gramercy, Louisiana ✳
These old-fashioned, mildly sweet cookies are dotted with walnuts and raisins. We like them soft right from the oven. Later, they crisp up and are perfect for dunking.

molasses raisin cookies

yield about 3-1/2 dozen

3/4	**cup shortening**
1	**cup packed brown sugar**
1/4	**cup molasses**
2	**eggs**
2-1/4	**cups all-purpose flour**
1	**teaspoon baking soda**
1	**teaspoon ground ginger**
1	**teaspoon ground cinnamon**
1/2	**teaspoon ground cloves**
1/2	**teaspoon salt**
1/2	**cup raisins**
1/2	**cup chopped walnuts**

In a large bowl, cream shortening and brown sugar until light and fluffy. Beat in molasses. Add eggs, one at a time, beating well after each addition. Combine the flour, baking soda, spices and salt; gradually add to creamed mixture. Stir in raisins and nuts.

Drop by rounded tablespoonfuls 2 in. apart onto greased baking sheets. Bake at 375° for 8-10 minutes or until the edges are lightly browned. Remove to wire racks to cool.

Pat Oviatt, Zimmerman, Minnesota ✳
I've had this recipe for years. It's economical to make, yet results in a delicious cookie.

chocolate waffle cookies

yield about 1-1/2 dozen

1/4	**cup butter, softened**
6	**tablespoons sugar**
1	**egg**
1/2	**teaspoon vanilla extract**
1	**square (1 ounce) unsweetened chocolate, melted**
1/2	**cup all-purpose flour**
	Confectioners' sugar

In a large bowl, cream butter and sugar until light and fluffy. Beat in egg and vanilla. Blend in chocolate. Add flour; mix well.

Drop dough by rounded teaspoonfuls 1 in. apart onto a preheated waffle iron. Bake for 1 minute. Remove to wire racks to cool. Dust with confectioners' sugar.

Carol Birkemeier, Nashville, Indiana

I like to think these oatmeal treats are better for you than the standard chocolate chip cookies. Our three sons just can't get enough of them. And they have no idea I've made the cookies healthier.

cranberry oat yummies

yield 3 dozen

1/2	cup butter, melted
1/2	cup sugar
1	cup packed brown sugar
1	egg
1/4	cup egg substitute
2	tablespoons corn syrup
1-1/2	teaspoons vanilla extract
3	cups quick-cooking oats
1	cup all-purpose flour
1	teaspoon baking soda
1	teaspoon ground cinnamon
1/2	teaspoon baking powder
1/2	teaspoon salt
1/8	teaspoon ground nutmeg
1	cup dried cranberries

In a large bowl, beat butter and sugars. Add egg, egg substitute, corn syrup and vanilla; mix well. Combine the oats, flour, baking soda, cinnamon, baking powder, salt and nutmeg; gradually add to egg mixture. Stir in cranberries.

Drop by heaping tablespoonfuls 2 in. apart onto ungreased baking sheets. Bake at 375° for 8-10 minutes or until golden brown. Cool for 2 minutes before removing to wire racks.

Geraldine Larkin, San Antonio, Texas

A friend gave me this recipe many years ago, and they're fabulous. I love the aroma of these cookies as they're baking.

oatmeal raisin cookies

yield 5 dozen

1	cup shortening
1	cup sugar
1	cup packed brown sugar
2	eggs
1	teaspoon vanilla extract
3	cups old-fashioned oats
1-1/2	cups all-purpose flour
1	teaspoon baking soda
1	teaspoon salt
1/2	cup chopped walnuts
1/2	cup golden raisins

In a large bowl, cream shortening and sugars until light and fluffy. Beat in eggs and vanilla. Combine the oats, flour, baking soda and salt; gradually add to creamed mixture and mix well. Stir in walnuts and raisins.

Drop by tablespoonfuls 2 in. apart onto ungreased baking sheets. Bake at 375° for 10-12 minutes or until golden brown. Remove to wire racks to cool.

Dottie LaPierre, Woburn, Massachusetts ✳

These sweet and tart cookies are a special treat. And, since they use pantry items, they are easy on your grocery budget.

sugar 'n' spice cookies

yield about 4-1/2 dozen

3/4	cup shortening
1	cup sugar
1	egg
1/4	cup molasses
2	cups all-purpose flour
1	teaspoon baking soda
1-1/2	teaspoons ground ginger
1	teaspoon ground cinnamon
3/4	teaspoon ground cloves
1/2	teaspoon salt

LEMON FROSTING:

3	tablespoons butter, softened
2	cups confectioners' sugar
1	teaspoon grated lemon peel
3	to 4 tablespoons lemon juice

In a large bowl, cream shortening and sugar until light and fluffy. Add egg; mix well. Beat in molasses. Combine dry ingredients; add to creamed mixture and mix well.

Drop by rounded teaspoonfuls 2 in. apart onto greased baking sheets. Bake at 350° for 8-10 minutes. Remove to wire racks to cool.

For frosting, cream the butter, sugar and lemon peel in a mixing bowl. Gradually add enough of the lemon juice to achieve a spreading consistency. Frost cookies.

almond sugar cookies

yield 5 dozen

2	cups butter-flavored shortening
1	cup sugar
1	cup packed brown sugar
2	eggs
1	teaspoon vanilla extract
1	teaspoon almond extract
4	cups all-purpose flour
2	teaspoons baking soda
2	teaspoons cream of tartar

Additional sugar *or* **colored sugar**

In a large bowl, cream the shortening and sugars until light and fluffy. Add eggs, one at a time, beating well after each addition. Beat in extracts. Combine the flour, baking soda and cream of tartar; gradually add to creamed mixture and mix well.

Drop by tablespoonfuls 2 in. apart onto ungreased baking sheets. Flatten with a glass dipped in sugar. Bake at 350° for 10-12 minutes or until lightly browned. Remove to wire racks to cool.

Linda Holt ✳
Wichita Falls, Texas
We made these crisp cookies often when I worked in the lunchroom at our daughters' grade school. The almond flavor makes them unique.

* Betty Huddleston, Liberty, Indiana
I like to make these old-fashioned treats with raspberry chips, but cherry-flavored chips also work well to add color and sweetness. These cookies stack nicely for packing.

cherry oatmeal cookies
yield about 4 dozen

1	cup butter, softened
1	cup packed brown sugar
1/2	cup sugar
2	eggs
1	teaspoon vanilla extract
3	cups old-fashioned oats
1-1/2	cups all-purpose flour
1	teaspoon baking soda
1	teaspoon ground cinnamon
1/2	teaspoon salt
1	package (10 ounces) cherry chips
1/2	cup chopped walnuts

In a large bowl, cream butter and sugars until light and fluffy. Beat in eggs and vanilla. Combine the oats, flour, baking soda, cinnamon and salt; gradually add to creamed mixture and mix well. Stir in chips and walnuts.

Drop by tablespoonfuls 3 in. apart onto ungreased baking sheets. Bake at 350° for 11-13 minutes or until lightly browned. Cool for 2 minutes before removing to wire racks.

* June Russell
Green Cove Springs, Florida

Years ago, I was eager to enter a recipe contest I'd read about. I went to my pantry and threw together these nutty cookies. Although they didn't win, they've been a hit with my family and friends ever since!

pecan grahams
yield about 4-1/2 dozen

1/2	cup shortening
1/2	cup sugar
1/2	cup packed brown sugar
1	egg
1	cup all-purpose flour
1/2	teaspoon baking powder
1/2	teaspoon baking soda
1/4	teaspoon salt
1	cup graham cracker crumbs
1	cup ground pecans
54	to 60 pecan halves

In a large bowl, cream shortening and sugars until light and fluffy. Add egg and mix well. Combine flour, baking powder, baking soda and salt; add to the creamed mixture. Stir in cracker crumbs and ground pecans; mix well.

Drop by rounded teaspoonfuls 2 in. apart onto ungreased baking sheets. Place a pecan half in the center of each cookie; press down lightly. Bake at 350° for 9-11 minutes or until lightly browned. Cool for 2 minutes before removing to wire racks.

Shirley Kidd , New London, Minnesota ✳

I started making these treats after tasting a batch my friend whipped up. I immediately requested the recipe and have been baking them by the dozens ever since.

frosted cranberry drop cookies

yield about 5 dozen

1/2	cup butter, softened
1	cup sugar
3/4	cup packed brown sugar
1/4	cup milk
1	egg
2	tablespoons orange juice
3	cups all-purpose flour
1	teaspoon baking powder
1/2	teaspoon salt
1/4	teaspoon baking soda
2-1/2	cups chopped fresh *or* frozen cranberries
1	cup chopped walnuts

FROSTING:

1/3	cup butter
2	cups confectioners' sugar
1-1/2	teaspoons vanilla extract
2	to 4 tablespoons hot water

In a large bowl, cream butter and sugars. Add milk, egg and orange juice; mix well. Combine the flour, baking powder, salt and baking soda; add to the creamed mixture and mix well. Stir in cranberries and nuts.

Drop by tablespoonfuls 2 in. apart onto greased baking sheets. Bake at 350° for 12-15 minutes or until golden brown. Remove to wire racks to cool completely.

For frosting, heat the butter in a saucepan over low heat until golden brown, about 5 minutes. Cool for 2 minutes; transfer to a small bowl. Add sugar and vanilla. Beat in water, 1 tablespoon at a time, until frosting reaches desired consistency. Frost the cooled cookies.

※ Rollin Barkeim, Trempealeau, Wisconsin
These cookies are soft and chewy with the old-fashioned goodness of oatmeal and peanut butter. I take them to work and on camping trips since they travel very well.

peanut butter oatmeal cookies

yield 5 dozen

3	egg whites
1	cup packed brown sugar
1	cup reduced-fat peanut butter
1/2	cup unsweetened applesauce
1/4	cup honey
2	teaspoons vanilla extract
3	cups quick-cooking oats
1	cup all-purpose flour
1	cup nonfat dry milk powder
2	teaspoons baking soda

In a large bowl, beat egg whites and brown sugar. Beat in peanut butter, applesauce, honey and vanilla. Combine the oats, flour, milk powder and baking soda; gradually add to peanut butter mixture, beating until combined.

Drop by tablespoonfuls 2 in. apart onto baking sheets coated with cooking spray. Bake at 350° for 8-10 minutes or until golden brown. Remove to wire racks to cool.

※ Iona Hamilton
Rocky Ford, Colorado
Everyone who has tried these cookies says they're the best they've ever eaten. I'm sure the addition of the pudding mix makes all the difference. Try instant chocolate pudding mix for a nice change.

chewy chocolate chip cookies

yield 9-1/2 dozen

1	cup butter, softened
3/4	cup packed brown sugar
1/4	cup sugar
1	package (3.4 ounces) instant vanilla pudding mix
2	eggs
1	teaspoon vanilla extract
2-1/4	cups all-purpose flour
1	teaspoon baking soda
2	cups (12 ounces) semisweet chocolate chips
1	cup finely chopped walnuts

In a large bowl, cream butter, sugars and pudding mix. Add eggs, one at a time, beating well after each addition. Beat in vanilla. Combine flour and baking soda; gradually add to creamed mixture. Stir in chocolate chips and walnuts (dough will be stiff).

Drop by rounded teaspoonfuls 2 in. apart onto ungreased baking sheets. Bake at 350° for 8-10 minutes or until lightly browned. Remove to wire racks to cool.

editor's note: One 3.9-ounce package of instant chocolate pudding mix may be substituted for the vanilla pudding mix.

BAKING
tip

creaming butter — To cream butter, it should be soft enough that a table knife will glide through it. The easiest way to soften butter is to let it stand at room temperature. When warming in the microwave, take care not to melt the butter...as melted butter will not cream properly and will adversely affect baking.

Chantal Cornwall, Prince Rupert, British Columbia ✳
When I make these yummy treats with my young grandson, Ben, I use an extra-big bowl to prevent the flour and other ingredients from flying all over. He enjoys making these cookies.

double chocolate cookies

yield about 9 dozen

1-1/4	cups butter, softened
2	cups sugar
2	eggs
2	teaspoons vanilla extract
2	cups all-purpose flour
3/4	cup baking cocoa
1	teaspoon baking soda
1/2	teaspoon salt
2	cups (12 ounces) semisweet chocolate chips

In a large bowl, cream butter and sugar until smooth. Beat in eggs and vanilla. Combine the flour, cocoa, baking soda and salt; gradually add to creamed mixture and mix well. Stir in chocolate chips.

Drop by rounded teaspoonfuls 2 in. apart onto greased baking sheets. Bake at 350° for 8-10 minutes or until set. Cool for 2 minutes; remove to wire racks to cool completely.

rosemary honey cookies

yield about 4 dozen

1/2	cup shortening
1/4	cup butter, softened
3/4	cup sugar
1	egg
1/4	cup honey
1	tablespoon lemon juice
2	cups all-purpose flour
2	teaspoons dried rosemary, crushed
1	teaspoon baking soda
1/2	teaspoon salt
1/2	teaspoon ground cinnamon
1/4	teaspoon ground nutmeg

In a large bowl, cream shortening, butter and sugar until light and fluffy. Beat in egg, honey and lemon juice. Combine dry ingredients; add to creamed mixture.

Drop by teaspoonfuls 2 in. apart onto greased baking sheets. Bake at 325° for 12-14 minutes or until lightly browned. Remove to wire racks to cool.

Audrey Thibodeau ✳
Mesa, Arizona
You'll be delighted with this unusual cookie's wonderful flavor. Rosemary combined with cinnamon and nutmeg make this cookie unique from other spice cookies.

✳ Patricia Crawford, Garland, Texas
Most everyone who comes to our home asks for my "famous" apricot cookies. They are really good, and I try not to eat them all myself! If you like apricots, I recommend you make two batches for starters.

apricot-nut drop cookies

yield 4-1/2 dozen

3/4	cup butter-flavored shortening
1-1/4	cups packed brown sugar
1	egg
2	tablespoons milk
1	teaspoon vanilla extract
1-3/4	cups all-purpose flour
1	teaspoon baking powder
3/4	teaspoon baking soda
1/2	teaspoon salt
1	cup chopped dried apricots
1	cup chopped pecans

In a large bowl, cream shortening and brown sugar. Beat in egg, milk and vanilla. Combine dry ingredients; gradually add to creamed mixture. Stir in apricots and pecans.

Drop by rounded tablespoonfuls 3 in. apart onto ungreased baking sheets. Bake at 375° for 10-13 minutes or until light golden brown. Cool for 2 minutes before removing to wire racks.

✳ Karen Ann Bland
Gove, Kansas
I live in the "Sunflower State," and these crisp cookies feature my state's bounty, sunflower seeds. It takes just minutes to mix up a batch of these tasty cookies.

crisp sunflower cookies

yield 5 dozen

3/4	cup shortening
1	cup sugar
1	cup packed brown sugar
2	eggs
1	teaspoon vanilla extract
2	cups all-purpose flour
1	teaspoon baking soda
1/2	teaspoon baking powder
1/2	teaspoon salt
2	cups quick-cooking oats
1	cup flaked coconut
1	cup salted sunflower seeds

In a large bowl, cream shortening and sugars until light and fluffy. Add eggs and vanilla; mix well. Combine flour, baking soda, baking powder and salt; add to creamed mixture and mix well. Stir in oats, coconut and sunflower seeds.

Drop by teaspoonfuls 2 in. apart onto greased baking sheets. Bake at 350° for 12-15 minutes or until golden brown. Remove to wire racks to cool completely.

Reba Legrand, Jericho, Vermont ✳
My husband, Bob, and I have a small sugaring operation with Bob's father. I love to bake with our syrup.

chewy maple cookies

yield 3 dozen

1/2	cup shortening
1	cup packed brown sugar
1	egg
1/2	cup pure maple syrup
1/2	teaspoon vanilla extract *or* maple flavoring
1-1/2	cups all-purpose flour
2	teaspoons baking powder
1/2	teaspoon salt
1	cup flaked coconut

In a large bowl, cream shortening and brown sugar until light and fluffy. Beat in the egg, syrup and vanilla until well mixed. Combine flour, baking powder and salt; add to the creamed mixture. Stir in coconut.

Drop by tablespoonfuls 2 in. apart onto greased baking sheets. Bake at 375° for 12-15 minutes or until lightly browned. Remove to wire racks to cool completely.

Nancy Grace, San Diego, California ✳
These cookies are great for fancy occasions but easy enough to make as a snack. My grandma was an avid baker, known in her neighborhood as the "cookie lady." With 18 nieces and nephews, I'm carrying on her tradition.

chocolate meringues

yield about 2-1/2 dozen

2	egg whites
1/2	teaspoon white vinegar
1/4	teaspoon cream of tartar
1/8	teaspoon salt
1/2	cup sugar
1/2	teaspoon vanilla *or* almond extract
1	cup (6 ounces) semisweet chocolate chips
1/2	cup flaked coconut
1/4	cup chopped almonds

In a large bowl, beat the egg whites, vinegar, cream of tartar and salt until soft peaks form. Add sugar, 1 tablespoon at a time, beating until stiff peaks form, about 5 minutes. Beat in the vanilla.

Meanwhile, in a microwave, melt chocolate chips and stir until smooth. Fold into egg white mixture; fold in coconut and almonds.

Drop by tablespoonfuls 2 in. apart onto lightly greased baking sheets. Bake at 350° for 10-11 minutes or until firm. Remove to wire racks to cool. Store in an airtight container.

timeless slice & bake

icebox honey cookies, p. 122

If you need to manage your

kitchen tasks but still want to make cookies, these treats can be mixed up ahead of time! Just wrap up the logs of dough, then stash them in the refrigerator for up to a week before cutting into slices, baking and enjoying.

chewy almond cookies, p. 106

delicate mint thins, p. 102

✳ Taste of Home Test Kitchen

When you want something fun and festive to make with the grandkids, try these cookies. The grandkids can help sprinkle on the jimmies just before baking. Once baked, these buttery, melt-in-your-mouth cookies will keep for a week.

versatile slice 'n' bake cookies

yield 4-1/2 dozen

1	**cup butter, softened**
1	**cup sugar**
1/4	**teaspoon vanilla extract**
1-3/4	**cups all-purpose flour**
3/4	**teaspoon baking soda**
1/4	**teaspoon salt**
2	**tablespoons chopped mixed candied fruit, optional**

Nonpareils, jimmies, melted semisweet chocolate chips and chopped nuts, optional

In a small bowl, cream butter and sugar until light and fluffy. Beat in vanilla. Combine the flour, baking soda and salt; gradually add to creamed mixture and mix well.

Divide into three portions. If desired, add candied fruit to one portion. Shape each into a 5-in. roll; place in a freezer bag. Seal and freeze for up to 3 months.

to use frozen dough: Remove from the freezer 1 hour before baking. Unwrap and cut into 1/4-in. slices. Place 2 in. apart on baking sheets coated with cooking spray. Sprinkle with nonpareils and jimmies if desired.

Bake at 350° for 12-14 minutes or until set. Remove to wire racks to cool. Frost with melted chocolate chips and sprinkle with nuts if desired.

Ruth Glick, New Holland, Pennsylvania ✳
My aunt baked these cookies as part of my wedding day dinner. Everyone was impressed with their eye-catching appeal, rich flavor and attractive flair.

cream cheese-filled cookies

yield about 2-1/2 dozen

1/3	**cup butter, softened**
1/3	**cup shortening**
3/4	**cup sugar**
1	**egg**
1	**teaspoon vanilla extract**
1-3/4	**cups all-purpose flour**
1	**teaspoon baking powder**
1/2	**teaspoon salt**

FILLING:

2	**packages (3 ounces *each*) cream cheese, softened**
1-1/2	**cups confectioners' sugar**
2	**tablespoons all-purpose flour**
1	**teaspoon vanilla extract**
1	**drop yellow food coloring, optional**

TOPPING:

3/4	**cup semisweet chocolate chips**
3	**tablespoons butter**

In a large bowl, cream the butter, shortening and sugar. Beat in egg and vanilla. Combine the flour, baking powder and salt; gradually add to the creamed mixture. Shape into two 12-in. rolls; wrap each in plastic wrap. Refrigerate for 4 hours or overnight.

Unwrap and cut into 1-in. slices. Place 1 in. apart on greased baking sheet. Bake at 375° for 10-12 minutes or until lightly browned. Immediately make an indentation in the center of each cookie using the end of a wooden spoon handle. Remove to wire racks to cool.

In a large bowl, combine the filling ingredients; mix well. Place 2 teaspoonfuls in the center of each cookie. Let stand until set. In a heavy saucepan or microwave, melt chocolate chips and butter; stir until smooth. Drizzle over cookies. Store in the refrigerator.

sesame coconut cookies

yield 10 dozen

2	**cups butter, softened**
1-1/2	**cups sugar**
1	**teaspoon vanilla extract**
3	**cups all-purpose flour**
1/2	**teaspoon salt**
2	**cups flaked coconut**
1	**cup sesame seeds**
1/2	**cup finely chopped almonds**

In a large bowl, cream butter and sugar until light and fluffy. Beat in vanilla. Combine flour and salt; gradually add to creamed mixture. Stir in the coconut, sesame seeds and almonds. Shape into three 10-in. rolls; wrap each in plastic wrap. Refrigerate for 1-2 hours or until firm.

Unwrap dough and cut into 1/4-in. slices. Place 1 in. apart on ungreased baking sheets. Bake at 300° for 25-30 minutes or until lightly browned. Cool for 2 minutes before removing to wire racks.

Roberta Myers ✳
Elwood, Indiana
Even folks who normally pass on coconut treats can't resist these crisp butter cookies. They make a nice accompaniment to a hot cup of coffee or tea.

❋ Kristine McDaniel, Kettering, Ohio

When I was newly married, I needed something fancy to impress my relatives at a reunion and came up with these cookies. I got many compliments on their subtle flavor.

delicate mint thins

yield about 4-1/2 dozen

1/2	cup butter, softened
1/2	cup sugar
1	egg yolk
1/2	teaspoon vanilla extract
1-1/2	cups all-purpose flour
1-1/2	teaspoons baking powder
1/8	teaspoon salt
3	tablespoons milk
1	cup fresh mint, finely chopped
1-2/3	cups semisweet chocolate chips
1	tablespoon shortening

In a large bowl, cream butter and sugar. Beat in egg yolk and vanilla. Combine dry ingredients; add to creamed mixture alternately with milk, mixing well after each addition. Stir in mint. Shape into two 8-in. rolls; wrap each in plastic wrap. Chill for 2 hours or until firm.

Unwrap and cut into 1/4-in. slices. Place 1 in. apart on greased baking sheets. Bake at 350° for 8-12 minutes or until edges are golden. Remove to wire racks to cool.

In a microwave, melt chocolate chips and shortening; stir until smooth. Dip each cookie halfway; allowing excess to drip off. Place on waxed paper; let stand until set.

❋ Kathy Kittell, Lenexa, Kansas

During the hectic holiday season, you'll appreciate the ease of these irresistible butter cookies. It's wonderful to pull the two-tone dough from the freezer and bake a festive batch in no time.

two-tone butter cookies

yield about 5 dozen

1	cup butter, softened
1	cup confectioners' sugar
1	teaspoon vanilla extract
2	cups all-purpose flour

Red and green liquid *or* paste food coloring

Red colored sugar, optional

In a large bowl, cream butter and sugar. Beat in vanilla. Add flour; mix well. Divide dough in half; with food coloring, tint half the dough red and half green. Shape each portion into an 8-in. log; wrap each in plastic wrap. Chill for at least 1 hour.

Unwrap and cut each log in half lengthwise. Press red and green halves together. Tightly wrap each roll in plastic wrap; freeze for up to 6 months.

to prepare cookies: Let dough stand at room temperature for 15 minutes. Cut into 1/4-in. slices; place 2 in. apart on ungreased baking sheets. Sprinkle with colored sugar if desired. Bake at 350° for 12-14 minutes or until set. Cool on wire racks.

Donna Grace, Clancy, Montana ✳

My granddaughter nicknamed my mother "Cookie Grandma" because she made such wonderful cookies. Mom made these delicious crisp and chewy cookies every Christmas.

date swirls cookies

yield 4 dozen

FILLING:

2	cups chopped dates
1	cup water
1	cup sugar
1	cup chopped nuts
2	teaspoons lemon juice

DOUGH:

1	cup butter, softened
1	cup packed brown sugar
1	cup sugar
3	eggs
1	teaspoon lemon extract
4	cups all-purpose flour
1	teaspoon salt
3/4	teaspoon baking soda

In a saucepan, combine filling ingredients. Cook over medium-low heat, stirring constantly, until mixture becomes stiff, about 15-20 minutes. Chill.

For dough, in a large bowl, cream butter and sugars. Add eggs, one at a time, beating well after each addition. Add extract. Combine the flour, salt and baking soda; gradually add to creamed mixture and mix well. Cover and refrigerate for at least 1 hour.

On a lightly floured surface, roll out half of the dough to a 12-in. x 9-in. rectangle, about 1/4 in. thick. Spread with half of the filling. Roll up jelly-roll style, starting with the long side. Repeat with remaining dough and filling. Wrap with plastic wrap; refrigerate overnight.

Unwrap and cut rolls into 1/4-in. slices. Place 2 in. apart on greased baking sheets. Bake at 375° for 8-10 minutes or until lightly browned. Remove to wire racks to cool.

coconut shortbread

yield 5 dozen

2	cups butter, softened
1	cup sugar
2	teaspoons vanilla extract
4	cups all-purpose flour
1/2	cup flaked coconut

Confectioners' sugar

In a large bowl, cream butter, sugar until light and fluffy. Beat in vanilla. Gradually add flour and mix well. Stir in coconut. Shape into two 8-in. rolls; wrap each in plastic wrap. Refrigerate for 4 hours or until firm.

Unwrap and cut into 1/4-in. slices. Place 1 in. apart on ungreased baking sheets.

Bake at 350° for 12-15 minutes or until edges are lightly browned. Dip both sides of cookies in confectioners' sugar while warm. Cool on wire racks.

Nancy Siefert ✳
Wauwatosa, Wisconsin

My niece makes this shortbread for special occasions. My family enjoys the rich flavor of these cookies so much, I bake them all year long.

⁎ Jill Heatwole, Pittsville, Maryland

My mom used to make these cookies every Christmas, and I still love them. They are so colorful, and you can get two kinds of cookies from one dough! They're perfect for including in gift boxes.

pinwheels and checkerboards

yield 6 dozen pinwheel and 4 dozen checkerboard cookies

1-1/4	cups butter, softened
1	cup packed brown sugar
1/2	cup sugar
2	eggs
1/4	teaspoon vanilla extract
4	cups all-purpose flour
1	teaspoon baking powder
1	teaspoon salt
1/4	teaspoon baking soda

Red and green gel food coloring

1	square (1 ounce) unsweetened chocolate, melted and cooled

In a large bowl, cream butter and sugars until light and fluffy. Beat in eggs and vanilla. Combine the flour, baking powder, salt and baking soda; gradually add to creamed mixture and mix well.

Divide dough into fourths. Tint one portion red and one portion green. Stir chocolate into another portion. Wrap chocolate and plain portions in plastic wrap; chill for 1 hour or until easy to handle.

For pinwheel cookies, divide red and green portions in half. Roll out each portion between waxed paper into a 9-in. x 6-in. rectangle. Refrigerate for 30 minutes.

Remove waxed paper. Place one green rectangle over a red rectangle. Roll up tightly jelly-roll style, starting with a long side; wrap in plastic wrap. Repeat. Refrigerate for 2 hours or until firm.

For checkerboard cookies, divide plain and chocolate portions in half. Roll out each portion between waxed paper into a 6-in. x 4-in. rectangle. Cut each rectangle lengthwise into eight 1/2-in. strips.

Stack the strips in groups of four, alternating plain and chocolate strips and forming eight separate stacks. Form a four-stack block by alternating chocolate-topped and plain-topped stacks. Repeat. Press together gently. Wrap in plastic. Chill for at least 2 hours.

Unwrap and cut pinwheel and checkerboard dough into 1/4-in. slices. Place 1 in. apart on ungreased baking sheets. Bake at 375° for 9-11 minutes or until set. Remove to wire racks to cool completely.

BAKING tip

slicing refrigerator cookie dough — To make the dough easier to slice, use nuts and fruits that are finely chopped. If the nuts and fruit are too large, the cookie dough may break apart when sliced. Use a thin sharp knife to slice through the dough. After each slice, rotate the dough to avoid have one side that's flat.

Sharon Nichols, Brookings, South Dakota ✳

There's just the right accent of anise in these crisp old-fashioned cookies. They are great with a hot cup of coffee.

anise icebox cookies

yield about 5-1/2 dozen

1	cup butter, softened
1	cup sugar
1	cup packed brown sugar
1	egg
2-1/2	cups all-purpose flour
1	teaspoon baking soda
1/2	teaspoon salt
1/2	teaspoon ground cinnamon
1/2	teaspoon ground cloves
1/2	cup finely chopped pecans
1	tablespoon aniseed

In a large bowl, cream butter and sugars until light and fluffy. Beat in egg. Combine the flour, baking soda, salt, cinnamon and cloves; gradually add to creamed mixture and mix well. Stir in pecans and aniseed.

Shape into two 10-in. rolls; wrap each in plastic wrap. Refrigerate for 4 hours.

Unwrap; cut 1/4 in. off the ends of each roll. Cut dough into 1/4-in. slices. Place 2 in. apart on ungreased baking sheets. Bake at 375° for 8-10 minutes or until golden brown. Remove to wire racks to cool.

Eileen Milacek, Waukomis, Oklahoma ✳

When I anticipate a busy day during the holiday season, I make this cookie dough the night before. The next day, I can just slice and bake. The make-ahead feature of this recipe makes it a perfect cookie for me.

jeweled coconut crisps

yield about 5 dozen

1	cup butter, softened
1	cup sugar
2	tablespoons milk
1-1/2	teaspoons vanilla extract
2-1/2	cups all-purpose flour
3/4	cup finely chopped red and green candied cherries
3/4	cup finely chopped pecans
1	cup flaked coconut

In a large bowl, cream butter and sugar until light and fluffy. Beat in milk and vanilla. Gradually add flour and mix well. Stir in cherries and pecans.

Shape into two 8-in. logs. Sprinkle the coconut over waxed paper; place each log on waxed paper and roll in coconut. Wrap in plastic wrap. Refrigerate for 4 hours or until firm.

Unwrap dough and cut into 1/4-in. slices. Place 2 in. apart on ungreased baking sheets. Bake at 375° for 10-12 minutes or until edges are lightly browned. Remove to wire racks to cool.

✳ Betty Speth, Vincennes, Indiana
These old-fashioned cookies are requested by my grandchildren. The unbaked cookie dough can be frozen (well wrapped) for up to 1 year. When ready to bake, let stand at room temperature for 15-30 minutes. Then just slice and bake.

chewy almond cookies

yield 4-1/2 dozen

3	tablespoons butter, softened
1	cup packed brown sugar
1	egg
1/4	teaspoon vanilla extract
1/4	teaspoon almond extract
1-1/2	cups all-purpose flour
1/4	teaspoon baking soda
1/4	teaspoon ground cinnamon
1/2	cup sliced almonds

In a large bowl, beat butter and brown sugar until crumbly. Add egg and extracts; mix well. Combine flour, baking soda and cinnamon; gradually add to the butter mixture and mix well. Shape into two 6-in. rolls; wrap each in plastic wrap. Refrigerate overnight.

Unwrap; cut into 1/4-in. slices. Place 2 in. apart on greased baking sheets. Sprinkle with almonds. Bake at 350° for 7-10 minutes or until lightly browned. Cool for 2-3 minutes before removing to wire racks.

crisp pecan rounds

yield about 3-1/2 dozen

✳ Denise DeJong
Pittsburgh, Pennsylvania
I adapted an old recipe to produce these lightly sweet cookies. They have a wonderful cinnamon and nutmeg flavor that makes them a favorite at our house.

1-1/2	cups all-purpose flour
1/4	cup packed brown sugar
2	tablespoons sugar
1/2	teaspoon salt
1/4	teaspoon ground cinnamon
1/4	teaspoon ground nutmeg
2/3	cup cold butter
2	tablespoons maple syrup
1/2	cup chopped pecans
GLAZE:	
1	egg yolk
1	teaspoon water
TOPPING:	
1-1/2	teaspoons sugar
1/2	teaspoon ground cinnamon

In a large bowl, combine the first six ingredients. Cut in butter until mixture resembles coarse crumbs. Stir in syrup. Add pecans. Shape into a 12-in. roll; wrap in plastic wrap. Refrigerate for 4 hours or until firm.

Unwrap and cut into 1/4-in. slices. Place 1 in. apart on ungreased baking sheets.

For glaze, beat egg yolk and water. For topping, combine sugar and cinnamon. Brush glaze over cookies and sprinkle with cinnamon-sugar.

Bake at 325° for 20-25 minutes or until golden brown. Remove to wire racks to cool.

Mary Schmidt, Eau Claire, Wisconsin ✳

My mother-in-law baked these cookies in the 1930s for her two sons, and later for her grandchildren. Now I make them for my grandchildren and great-grandchildren.

coconut oatmeal crispies

yield 4 dozen

1	cup butter-flavored shortening
1	cup sugar
1	cup packed brown sugar
2	eggs
1	teaspoon vanilla extract
2	cups quick-cooking oats
1-1/2	cups all-purpose flour
1	cup flaked coconut
1	teaspoon baking soda
1	teaspoon salt

In a large bowl, cream shortening and sugars until light and fluffy. Add eggs, one at a time, beating well after each addition. Beat in vanilla. Combine the oats, flour, coconut, baking soda and salt; gradually add to creamed mixture and mix well. Shape into two 6-in. rolls; wrap each roll in plastic wrap. Refrigerate for 1 hour or until firm.

Unwrap dough and cut into 1/4-in. slices. Place 2 in. apart on ungreased baking sheets. Bake at 350° for 8-10 minutes or until golden brown. Remove to wire racks to cool.

chocolate coconut neapolitans

yield 5-1/2 dozen

1	cup butter, softened
1-1/2	cups sugar
1	egg
1	teaspoon vanilla extract
2-1/2	cups all-purpose flour
1-1/2	teaspoons baking powder
1/2	teaspoon salt
1	teaspoon almond extract
4	drops red food coloring
1/2	cup flaked coconut, finely chopped
4-1/2	teaspoons chocolate syrup
1/2	cup semisweet chocolate chips
1-1/2	teaspoons shortening

Line a 9-in. x 5-in. x 3-in. loaf pan with waxed paper; set aside. In a large bowl, cream butter and sugar. Beat in egg and vanilla. Combine the flour, baking powder and salt; gradually add to creamed mixture and mix well.

Divide dough into thirds. Add almond extract and red food coloring to one portion; spread evenly into prepared pan. Add coconut to second portion; spread evenly over first layer. Add chocolate syrup to third portion; spread over second layer. Cover with foil; freeze for 4 hours or overnight.

Unwrap loaf and cut in half lengthwise. Cut each portion widthwise into 1/4-in. slices. Place 2 in. apart on ungreased baking sheets. Bake at 350° for 12-14 minutes or until edges are lightly browned. Remove to wire racks to cool.

In a microwave, melt chocolate chips and shortening; stir until smooth. Dip one end of each cookie into chocolate. Place on wire racks until set.

Lena Marie Brownell ✳ Rockland, Massachusetts

These yummy striped cookies with a chocolaty twist are easy and fun to make, but they do need some time in the freezer. The red layer has an almond flavor, the middle layer has bits of coconut and the brown layer is flavored with chocolate syrup.

* Cheri Booth, Gering, Nebraska
These crispy cookies with a chewy coconut center travel really well. They always arrive unbroken when I send them to my son.

coconut chocolate slices

yield about 4 dozen

1	package (3 ounces) cream cheese, softened
1/3	cup sugar
1	teaspoon vanilla extract
1	cup flaked coconut
1/2	cup finely chopped nuts

COOKIE DOUGH:

6	tablespoons butter, softened
1	cup confectioners' sugar
1	egg
2	squares (1 ounce *each*) semisweet chocolate, melted and cooled
1	teaspoon vanilla extract
1-1/2	cups all-purpose flour
1/2	teaspoon baking soda
1/2	teaspoon salt

In a small bowl, beat the cream cheese, sugar and vanilla until smooth. Stir in coconut and nuts. Refrigerate until easy to handle.

In a large bowl, cream butter and confectioners' sugar. Beat in the egg, chocolate and vanilla. Combine the flour, baking soda and salt; gradually add to creamed mixture and mix well. Refrigerate for 30 minutes or until easy to handle.

Roll dough between waxed paper into a 14-in. x 4-1/2-in. rectangle. Remove top piece of waxed paper. Shape coconut filling into a 14-in. roll; place on dough, 1 in. from a long side. Roll dough around filling and seal edges. Wrap in plastic wrap. Refrigerate for 2-3 hours or overnight.

Unwrap and cut into 1/4-in. slices. Place 2 in. apart on greased baking sheets. Bake at 350° for 8-10 minutes or until set. Cool for 1 minute before removing to wire racks.

* Mrs. Robert Nelson, Des Moines, Iowa
The crushed peppermint candy adds a fun twist to these simple slice-and-bake sugar cookies.

peppermint cookies

yield about 6 dozen

1	cup shortening
1/2	cup sugar
1/2	cup packed brown sugar
2	eggs
1-1/2	teaspoons vanilla extract
2-3/4	cups all-purpose flour
1	teaspoon salt
1/2	teaspoon baking soda
1/2	cup crushed peppermint candies

In a large bowl, cream shortening and sugars. Add eggs, one at a time, beating well. Beat in vanilla. Combine dry ingredients; gradually add to the creamed mixture. Stir in crushed candies. Shape into a 15-in. roll; wrap in plastic wrap. Chill for 4 hours or until firm.

Unwrap and cut into 1/8-in. slices. Place 2 in. apart on ungreased baking sheets. Bake at 375° for 6-8 minutes or until edges begin to brown. Remove to wire racks to cool.

Karlyne Moreau, Yakima, Washington ✳

Three ribbons of flavor—cherry, chocolate and poppy seed—combine into one tender, Neapolitan-style cookie. My mom made these when we were kids. They are so good.

ribbon icebox cookies

yield 20 cookies

- 1/2   cup shortening
- 2/3   cup sugar
- 2   tablespoons beaten egg
- 1/2   teaspoon vanilla extract
- 1-1/4 cups all-purpose flour
- 3/4   teaspoon baking powder
- 1/4   teaspoon salt
- 2   tablespoons red candied cherries, chopped
- 1/2   square (1/2 ounce) unsweetened chocolate, melted
- 2   teaspoons poppy seeds

Line a 5-in. x 3-in. x 2-in. loaf pan with waxed paper; set aside. In a small bowl, cream shortening and sugar until light and fluffy. Beat in egg and vanilla. Combine the flour, baking powder and salt; gradually add to creamed mixture and mix well.

Divide dough into thirds. Add cherries to one portion; spread evenly into prepared pan. Add melted chocolate to second portion; spread evenly over first layer. Add poppy seeds to third portion; spread over second layer. Cover with plastic wrap; refrigerate overnight.

Remove from pan, unwrap and cut into 1/4-in. slices. Place 1 in. apart on ungreased baking sheets. Bake at 375° for 8-9 minutes or until lightly browned. Cool for 1 minute before removing to wire racks.

three-nut cherry slices

yield 7 dozen

- 1-1/2 cups butter, softened
- 1   cup packed brown sugar
- 1/4   cup milk
- 1   teaspoon vanilla extract
- 3-1/2 cups all-purpose flour
- 1   teaspoon ground cinnamon
- 1/2   teaspoon baking soda
- 1/2   teaspoon salt
- 1/2   pound red candied cherries, chopped
- 1/4   cup *each* chopped walnuts, Brazil nuts and hazelnuts

In a large bowl, cream butter and brown sugar until light and fluffy; beat in milk and vanilla. Combine the flour, cinnamon, baking soda and salt; gradually add to the creamed mixture and mix well. Stir in the cherries and nuts.

Shape into three 10-in. rolls; wrap each in plastic wrap. Chill for 4 hours overnight.

Unwrap and cut into 1/4-in. slices. Place 2 in. apart on ungreased baking sheets. Bake at 350° for 10-12 minutes or until golden brown. Remove to wire racks to cool.

Sue Megonigle ✳
Greendale, Wisconsin
The men in my family like this refrigerator cookie, so I always keep the dough on hand. I'm happy to make a batch for them—it's so easy.

✳ Sue Ann Benham, Valparaiso, Indiana

When I made these rich butter cookies for a neighborhood event, one neighbor thought they were so attractive that she kept one in her freezer for the longest time so she could show it to friends and relatives.

watermelon slice cookies

yield about 3 dozen

3/4	cup butter, softened
3/4	cup sugar
1	egg
1/2	teaspoon almond extract
2	cups all-purpose flour
1/4	teaspoon baking powder
1/8	teaspoon salt

Red and green gel food coloring

1/3	cup raisins
1	teaspoon sesame seeds

In a large bowl, cream butter and sugar. Beat in egg and extract. Combine flour, baking powder and salt; gradually add to creamed mixture. Set aside 1 cup of dough. Tint remaining dough red and shape into a 3-1/2-in.-long log. Wrap in plastic wrap. Tint 1/3 cup of the reserved dough green; wrap in plastic wrap. Wrap remaining plain dough in a plastic bag. Refrigerate for 2 hours or until firm.

On a lightly floured surface, roll plain dough into an 8-1/2-in. x 3-1/2-in. rectangle. Place red dough log on the end of a short side of the rectangle; roll up. Roll green dough into a 10-in. x 3-1/2-in. rectangle. Place red and white log on the end of a short side on green dough; roll up. Wrap in plastic wrap; refrigerate overnight.

Unwrap and cut into 3/16-in. slices (just less than 1/4 in.). Place 2 in. apart on ungreased baking sheets. Cut raisins into small pieces. Lightly press raisin bits and sesame seeds into red dough to resemble watermelon seeds. Bake at 350° for 9-11 minutes or until firm. Immediately cut the cookies in half. Remove to wire racks to cool.

strawberry-nut pinwheel cookies

yield: 4 dozen

✳ Ruth Gillmore
Alden, New York

All the "cookie monsters" I know love these treats. They make a great after-school snack. I enjoy the cookies because they're easy to roll up, cut and bake. The strawberry-walnut filling is very tasty!

1/2	cup butter, softened
1	cup sugar
1	egg
1	teaspoon vanilla extract
2	cups all-purpose flour
1	teaspoon baking powder
1/2	cup strawberry jam
1	cup chopped walnut

In a large bowl, cream butter and sugar. Add egg and vanilla; mix well. Combine flour and baking powder; gradually add to creamed mixture. On a lightly floured surface, roll dough into a 14-in. x 10-in. rectangle. Spread jam to within 1/2 in. of edges. Sprinkle nuts over jam. Roll up jelly-roll style, starting with a long side; wrap in plastic wrap. Refrigerate for at least 3 hours or overnight.

Unwrap and cut into 1/4-in. slices. Place 1 in. apart on greased baking sheets. Bake at 375° for 10-12 minutes or until lightly browned. Remove to wire racks to cool.

Eilene Bogar, Minier, Illinois ✳

My daughters and I have been "fairly" successful competitors at county fairs and baking contests for years. This is one of those tasty winning recipes. It's easy to make, so don't hesitate to bake up a winner, too!

brown sugar icebox cookies

yield about 3-1/2 dozen

1/2	cup butter, softened
1	cup packed brown sugar
1	egg
1	teaspoon vanilla extract
1-3/4	cups all-purpose flour
1/2	teaspoon baking soda
1/4	teaspoon salt
2/3	cup chopped pecans *or* flaked coconut

In a large mixing bowl, cream the butter and sugar until light and fluffy. Beat in egg and vanilla. Combine the flour, baking soda and salt; gradually add to cream mixture. Fold in pecans or coconut (dough will be sticky). Shape into two rolls; wrap each in plastic wrap. Refrigerate for 4 hours or overnight.

Unwrap and cut into 1/4-in. slices. Place 2 in. apart on ungreased baking sheets. Bake at 375° for 7 to 10 minutes or until set. Remove to wire racks to cool.

lemon pecan slices

yield about 7 dozen

1	cup butter, softened
3/4	cup packed brown sugar
1/2	cup sugar
2	eggs
1-1/2	teaspoons vanilla extract
1	tablespoon grated lemon peel
3	cups all-purpose flour
1-1/2	teaspoons baking powder
3/4	teaspoon salt

TOPPING:

3/4	cup finely chopped pecans
1/4	cup sugar

LEMON GLAZE:

1-1/4	cups confectioners' sugar
5	teaspoons lemon juice
1	drop yellow food coloring, optional

In a large bowl, cream the butter and sugars. Separate one egg; refrigerate egg white. Add the egg yolk, second egg, vanilla and lemon peel to creamed mixture; mix well. Combine the flour, baking powder and salt; gradually beat into creamed mixture. Shape into three 7-in. rolls; wrap each in plastic wrap. Refrigerate for 2 hours or until firm.

Unwrap logs. Lightly beat reserved egg white. Combine pecans and sugar. Brush each log with egg white, then roll in pecan mixture; press firmly into dough.

Cut into 1/4-in. slices. Place 2 in. apart on ungreased baking sheets. Bake at 400° for 6-7 minutes or until very lightly browned. Remove to wire racks to cool. Combine glaze ingredients; drizzle over cookies.

Melissa Branning ✳ Fontana, Wisconsin

These attractive morsels are my daughter's favorite. The lemon glaze pairs well with the delicate nut-topped cookie.

✳ Beverly Duncan, Lakeville, Ohio
This old-fashioned recipe has been in my family for years. It's also delicious with miniature chocolate chips or coconut in place of the toffee bits. You can also switch the pecans to your favorite nut.

butterscotch cookies

yield about 1-1/2 dozen

2	tablespoons butter, softened
2	tablespoons shortening
1	cup packed brown sugar
1	egg
1	teaspoon vanilla extract
1-1/2	cups all-purpose flour
3/4	teaspoon baking soda
3/4	teaspoon cream of tartar
1/4	teaspoon salt
1/4	cup English toffee bits *or* almond brickle chips
1/4	cup finely chopped pecans

In a large bowl, cream the butter, shortening and brown sugar until light and fluffy. Beat in egg and vanilla. Combine the flour, baking soda, cream of tartar and salt; gradually add to creamed mixture. Stir in toffee bits and pecans. Shape into a 10-in. roll; wrap in plastic wrap. Refrigerate for 4 hours or until firm.

Unwrap dough and cut into 1/2-in. slices. Place 2 in. apart on baking sheets coated with cooking spray. Bake at 375° for 9-11 minutes or until lightly browned. Cool for 1-2 minutes before removing from pans to wire racks.

chocolate icebox pinwheels

✳ Nancy Arevalo
Brookfield, Wisconsin
Chocolate and vanilla provide a delightful contrast in flavor and appearance in these buttery refrigerator cookies.

yield about 3 dozen

3/4	cup butter, softened
3/4	cup sugar
1	egg yolk
1/2	teaspoon vanilla extract
1-3/4	cups all-purpose flour
1-1/2	teaspoons baking powder
1/2	teaspoon salt
1	square (1 ounce) semisweet chocolate, melted
3	tablespoons milk, warmed

In a large bowl, cream butter and sugar until light and fluffy. Beat in egg yolk and vanilla. Combine the flour, baking powder and salt; gradually add to creamed mixture and mix well.

Divide dough in half. Add melted chocolate to one portion; mix well. Refrigerate until chilled.

Divide each portion of dough into fourths; shape each into a 5-in. log. Flatten into triangular-shaped logs. Brush long sides with milk. Assemble one large roll by alternating two chocolate and two plain logs. Repeat. Wrap in plastic wrap. Chill for 4 hours or until firm.

Unwrap each roll; cut into 1/4-in. slices. Place 2 in. apart on lightly greased baking sheets. Bake at 375° for 8-10 minutes or until set. Remove from pans to wire racks.

Eleanor Senske, Rock Island, Illinois ✳

I like to serve these spiced treats with a dollop of lemon sherbet to make a simple, but elegant dessert.

ginger thins

yield 3-1/2 dozen

6	**tablespoons butter, softened**
1/2	**cup plus 2 tablespoons sugar, *divided***
2	**tablespoons molasses**
1	**tablespoon cold strong brewed coffee**
1-1/4	**cups all-purpose flour**
3/4	**teaspoon ground ginger**
1/2	**teaspoon baking soda**
1/2	**teaspoon ground cinnamon**
1/4	**teaspoon ground cloves**
1/8	**teaspoon salt**

In a large bowl, cream butter and 1/2 cup sugar; set the remaining sugar aside. Add molasses and coffee to creamed mixture; mix well. Combine the remaining ingredients; add to creamed mixture. Mix well (dough will be soft). Cover and freeze for 15 minutes. Shape into a 7-in. roll; flatten to 1-in. thickness. Wrap in plastic wrap. Freeze for 8 hours or overnight.

Unwrap and cut into 1/8-in. slices; place 2 in. apart on parchment paper-lined baking sheets. Sprinkle with reserved sugar. Bake at 350° for 8-10 minutes or until firm. Remove to wire racks to cool.

Taste of Home Test Kitchen ✳

Get a head start on these buttery Halloween cookies by shaping and chilling the homemade dough ahead of time. When you're ready, just slice and bake the tricolor treats.

candy corn cookies

yield about 5 dozen

1-1/2	**cups butter, softened**
1-1/2	**cups sugar**
1/2	**teaspoon vanilla extract**
3	**cups all-purpose flour**
1	**teaspoon baking soda**
1/2	**teaspoon salt**

Yellow and orange paste food coloring

In a large bowl, cream butter and sugar until light and fluffy. Beat in vanilla. Combine flour, baking soda and salt; gradually add to creamed mixture and mix well.

Divide dough in half. Tint one portion yellow. Divide remaining dough into two-thirds and one-third portions. Color the larger portion orange; leave smaller portion white.

Shape each portion of dough into two 8-in. logs. Flatten top and push sides in at a slight angle. Place orange logs on yellow logs; push the sides in at a slight angle. Top with white logs; form a rounded top. Wrap in plastic wrap. Chill for 4 hours or until firm.

Unwrap and cut into 1/2-in. slices. Place 2 in. apart on ungreased baking sheets. Bake at 350° for 10-12 minutes or until set. Remove to wire racks to cool.

✳ Esther Thys, Belle Plaine, Iowa
I love the rich, buttery flavor these crisp cookies get from pecans and brown sugar. Once the dough is in the refrigerator, I can have freshly baked cookies in just minutes. For a gathering or when company drops in, I'm prepared with a tasty treat.

butterscotch pecan slices

yield 4 dozen

6	tablespoons butter, softened
2/3	cup packed brown sugar
1	egg
1/2	teaspoon vanilla extract
1-1/4	cups all-purpose flour
1/2	teaspoon baking powder
1/4	teaspoon salt
3/4	cup finely chopped pecans, *divided*

In a large bowl, cream the butter and brown sugar until light and fluffy. Beat in egg and vanilla. Combine flour, baking powder and salt; gradually add to the creamed mixture and mix well. Stir in 1/2 cup pecans. Shape into two 7-in. rolls; wrap each in plastic wrap. Refrigerate for 2 hours or until firm.

Unwrap and cut into 1/4-in. slices. Place 2 in. apart on ungreased baking sheets. Sprinkle with remaining nuts; press gently. Bake at 350° for 10-12 minutes or until edges begin to brown. Remove to wire racks to cool.

peanut chocolate whirls

yield about 3 dozen

✳ Joanne Woloschuk
Yorkton, Saskatchewan
The sensational combination of chocolate and peanut butter is irresistible in these tender swirled cookies. My daughters and I have such fun making and sharing these yummy snacks.

1/2	cup shortening
1/2	cup creamy peanut butter
1	cup sugar
1	egg
2	tablespoons milk
1	teaspoon vanilla extract
1-1/4	cups all-purpose flour
1/2	teaspoon baking soda
1/2	teaspoon salt
1	cup (6 ounces) semisweet chocolate chips

In a large bowl, cream the shortening, peanut butter and sugar until light and fluffy. Beat in the egg, milk and vanilla. Combine the flour, baking soda and salt; gradually add to creamed mixture and mix well.

Cover and refrigerate for 1 hour or until easy to handle. Turn onto a lightly floured surface; roll into a 16-in. x 12-in. rectangle.

In a microwave, melt chocolate chips; stir until smooth. Cool slightly. Spread over dough to within 1/2 in. of edges. Tightly roll up jelly-roll style, starting with a short side. Wrap in plastic wrap. Refrigerate for up to 30 minutes.

Unwrap and cut into 1/4-in. slices with a serrated knife. Place 1 in. apart on ungreased baking sheets. Bake at 350° for 8-10 minutes or until lightly browned. Remove to wire racks to cool completely.

Deb Perry, Bluffton, Indiana ✳

With the combination of cranberries, cherries, orange zest and cinnamon, these festive cookies are as fragrant as they are flavorful.

cherry cranberry pinwheels

yield 4-1/2 to 5 dozen

1-1/2	cups dried cranberries
1	jar (10 ounces) cherry spreadable fruit
1/4	cup water
1/2	teaspoon ground cinnamon

DOUGH:

1/4	cup butter, softened
1-1/4	cups sugar
3	egg whites
3	tablespoons canola oil
2	tablespoons fat-free milk
2	teaspoons vanilla extract
1-1/2	teaspoons grated orange peel
3-1/3	cups all-purpose flour
3/4	teaspoon baking powder
1/2	teaspoon ground cinnamon
1/8	teaspoon baking soda

For filling, combine the first four ingredients in a small saucepan. Cook and stir over medium heat for 8 minutes or until liquid is absorbed and cranberries are softened. Remove from the heat; cool slightly. Transfer to a blender; cover and process until smooth. Transfer to a bowl; cover and refrigerate until chilled.

For dough, in a large bowl, beat butter and sugar for 2 minutes or until crumbly. Beat in the egg whites, oil, milk, vanilla and orange peel. Combine the flour, baking powder, cinnamon and baking soda; gradually add to sugar mixture and mix well.

Divide dough in half. On a floured surface, roll one portion of dough into a 14-in. x 9-in. rectangle. Spread with half of the filling. Roll up jelly-roll style, starting with a long side. Repeat with remaining dough and filling. Wrap each roll in plastic wrap; chill for at least 4 hours.

Unwrap dough; cut into 1/2-in. slices. Place 2 in. apart on baking sheets coated with cooking spray. Bake at 375° for 10-12 minutes or until bottoms are lightly browned (do not overbake). Remove to wire racks to cool.

✳ Kathi Peters, Chilliwack, British Columbia

I like to keep some of this dough in the freezer at all times since it's so handy to slice, bake and serve at a moment's notice. These wholesome cookies are super with a cup of coffee—in fact, we occasionally grab a few for breakfast when we're in a hurry.

rolled oat cookies

yield: 3-1/2 dozen

1	cup butter, softened
1	cup packed brown sugar
1/4	cup water
1	teaspoon vanilla extract
3	cups quick-cooking oats
1-1/4	cups all-purpose flour
1	teaspoon salt
1/4	teaspoon baking soda

In a large bowl, cream butter and sugar. Add the water and vanilla; mix well. Combine the dry ingredients; add to creamed mixture and mix well. Chill for 30 minutes. Shape into two 1-1/2-in.-diameter rolls; wrap each in plastic wrap. Refrigerate for 2 hours or until firm.

Unwrap and cut into 1/2-in. slices. Place 2 in. apart on greased baking sheets. Bake at 375° for 12 minutes or until lightly browned. Remove to wire racks to cool.

✳ Terri Lins, San Diego, California

In Mexico, these rich cookies are called "Little Wedding Cakes" and are usually served with hot chocolate. Since moving close to Mexico from the Midwest, I've enjoyed trying authentic recipes.

pastelitos de boda

yield about 3 dozen

3/4	cup butter, softened
1/2	cup confectioners' sugar
2	teaspoons vanilla extract
2	cups sifted all-purpose flour
1/4	teaspoon salt
1	cup finely chopped walnuts
1/4	cup heavy whipping cream

Additional confectioners' sugar

In a large bowl, cream butter and sugar; add vanilla. Combine the flour, salt and nuts; gradually add to creamed mixture. Add cream; knead lightly. Shape into a 2-1/2-in.-diameter roll. Wrap in plastic wrap. Refrigerate for several hours or overnight.

Unwrap and cut into 1/4-in. slices. Place 2 in. apart on ungreased baking sheets. Bake at 375° for 15 minutes or until delicately browned around edges. Remove to wire racks. While warm, roll in additional confectioners' sugar.

Pat Habiger, Spearville, Kansas ✳

A number of years ago, I won first prize in a recipe contest with these yummy swirl cookies. The taste of raspberries and walnuts really comes through in each bite, and they're so much fun to make!

raspberry nut pinwheels

yield about 3-1/2 dozen

1/2	cup butter, softened
1	cup sugar
1	egg
1	teaspoon vanilla extract
2	cups all-purpose flour
1	teaspoon baking powder
1/4	cup seedless raspberry jam
3/4	cup finely chopped walnuts

In a large bowl, cream butter and sugar until light and fluffy. Beat in egg and vanilla. Combine flour and baking powder; gradually add to creamed mixture and mix well.

Roll out dough between waxed paper into a 12-in. square. Remove top piece of waxed paper. Spread dough with jam and sprinkle with nuts. Roll up tightly jelly-roll style; wrap in plastic wrap. Chill for 2 hours or until firm.

Unwrap dough and cut into 1/4-in. slices. Place 2 in. apart on ungreased baking sheets. Bake at 375° for 9-12 minutes or until edges are lightly browned. Remove to wire racks to cool.

honey spice cookies

yield 12-1/2 dozen

2	cups honey
2	cups sugar
3	eggs
7-1/2	cups all-purpose flour
3	teaspoons baking soda
3	teaspoons ground cinnamon
1	teaspoon salt
1	teaspoon ground allspice
1	teaspoon ground cloves
2	cups confectioners' sugar
3	tablespoon fat-free milk

In a large bowl, beat honey and sugar. Add the eggs, one at a time, beating well after each addition. Combine the flour, baking soda, cinnamon, salt, allspice and cloves; gradually add to honey mixture. Shape dough into five 10-in. rolls; wrap each in plastic wrap. Refrigerate for 2 hours or until firm.

Unwrap and cut into 1/4-in. slices. Place 2 in. apart on baking sheets coated with cooking spray. Combine confectioners' sugar and milk; lightly brush over cookies. Bake at 350° for 8-10 minutes or until lightly browned. Remove to wire racks to cool.

Joan Gerber ✳
Bluffton, Indiana

With four children, I bake a lot of cookies. These nicely seasoned sweets are a favorite of my family. When I bake them up they go fast—it's a good thing the recipe makes a lot.

✳ Patricia Kile, Greentown, Pennsylvania
My husband's grandfather was always intrigued with how the swirls got in these very tasty cookies!

chocolate pinwheels

yield 9 dozen

1/2	cup butter, softened
1	cup sugar
1/4	cup packed brown sugar
1	egg
1-1/2	teaspoons vanilla extract
2	cups all-purpose flour
1	teaspoon baking powder

Dash salt

FILLING:

2	cups (12 ounces) semisweet chocolate chips
2	tablespoons butter
1/4	teaspoon vanilla extract

Dash salt

In a large bowl, cream butter and sugars. Add egg and vanilla; beat until light and fluffy. Combine dry ingredients; beat into creamed mixture. Divide dough in half; place each half between two sheets of waxed paper. Roll into 12-in. x 10-in. rectangles. Chill until almost firm, about 30 minutes.

In a saucepan over low heat, melt chips and butter. Add vanilla and salt; mix well. Spread over dough. Carefully and tightly roll up jelly-roll style, starting with a long side. Wrap each in plastic wrap. Refrigerate for 2 hours or until firm.

Cut rolls into 1/8-in. slices with a sharp thin knife; place on greased or parchment-lined baking sheets. Bake at 350° for 7-10 minutes or until lightly browned. Remove to wire racks to cool.

lemon meltaways

yield about 5 dozen

✳ Mary Houchin
Lebanon, Illinois
Both the cookie and the frosting are sparked with lemon in these melt-in-your-mouth goodies.

3/4	cup butter, softened
1/3	cup confectioners' sugar
1	teaspoon lemon juice
1-1/4	cups all-purpose flour
1/2	cup cornstarch

FROSTING:

1/4	cup butter, softened
3/4	cup confectioners' sugar
1	teaspoon lemon juice
1	teaspoon grated lemon peel
1	to 3 drops yellow food coloring, optional

In a large bowl, cream butter and confectioners' sugar until light and fluffy; beat in lemon juice. Combine the flour and cornstarch; gradually add to the creamed mixture and mix well. Shape into two 8-in. rolls; wrap each roll in plastic wrap. Refrigerate for 2 hours or until firm.

Unwrap and cut into 1/4-in. slices. Place 2 in. apart on ungreased baking sheets. Bake at 350° for 8-12 minutes or until the cookies are firm to the touch. Remove to wire racks to cool.

For frosting, in a small bowl, beat the butter and confectioners' sugar until smooth. Stir in the lemon juice, lemon peel and food coloring if desired. Frost cooled cookies.

Gloria McKenzie, Panama City, Florida ✳
These buttery mint treats practically melt in your mouth. Plus, bright food coloring gives them a lively look for wintertime parties.

peppermint candy cookies

yield about 4 dozen

1-1/4	cups butter, softened
3/4	cup confectioners' sugar
1/2	teaspoon peppermint extract
2-1/2	cups all-purpose flour
1/2	teaspoon salt

Green and red paste *or* gel food coloring

In a large bowl, cream butter and sugar. Beat in extract. Add the flour and salt; mix well. Divide dough into fourths. Tint one portion green and one red; leave the remaining portions plain.

Divide each portion into thirds; shape each into a 6-in. log. Flatten into triangular logs, bending the top of one point slightly (to give finished cookies a pinwheel effect; fig. 1). Assemble one large roll by alternating three green and three plain logs; fig. 2. Wrap in plastic wrap. Repeat with the red and the remaining plain dough. Refrigerate for 4 hours or until firm.

Unwrap and cut into 1/4-in. slices. Place 2 in. apart on ungreased baking sheets. Bake at 375° for 8-10 minutes or until edges are golden brown. Cool for 1 minute before removing to wire racks. Cut 6-in.-square pieces of cellophane or plastic wrap to wrap each cookie; twist ends securely or tie with a ribbon.

fig. 1

fig. 2

mom's coconut cookies

yield 4-1/2 dozen

1/2	cup butter, softened
1	cup sugar
1/4	cup packed brown sugar
1	egg
1-1/2	teaspoons vanilla extract
2	cups all-purpose flour
1-1/2	teaspoons baking powder
1/8	teaspoon salt
1	cup flaked coconut

In a large bowl, cream butter and sugars. Beat in egg and vanilla. Combine the flour, baking powder and salt; gradually add to the creamed mixture. Stir in coconut. Shape into two 3-1/2-in. rolls; wrap each in plastic wrap. Refrigerate for 2 hours or until firm.

Unwrap and cut into 1/8-in. slices. Place 2 in. apart on ungreased baking sheets. Bake at 425° for 5-7 minutes or until lightly browned. Remove to wire racks to cool.

Shirley Secrest ✳
Mattoon, Illinois
Mom worked hard to keep us fed during the Depression, and there was never a day we went hungry. These cookies could always be found in the cookie jar. They are still a favorite today.

✳ Ruth Ann Stelfox, Raymond, Alberta

These treats are perfect for folks who like both chocolate and vanilla cookies because it gives them the best of both worlds. They're an appealing addition to any cookie tray, and they're usually the first to disappear.

double delights

yield about 15 dozen

CHOCOLATE DOUGH:

1	cup butter, softened
1-1/2	cups sugar
2	eggs
2	teaspoons vanilla extract
2	cups all-purpose flour
2/3	cup baking cocoa
3/4	teaspoon baking soda
1/2	teaspoon salt
1	cup coarsely chopped pecans
5	squares (1 ounce *each*) white baking chocolate, cut into chunks

VANILLA DOUGH:

1	cup butter, softened
1-1/2	cups sugar
2	eggs
2	teaspoons vanilla extract
2-3/4	cups all-purpose flour
2	teaspoons cream of tartar
1	teaspoon baking soda
1/2	teaspoon salt
1	cup coarsely chopped pecans
1	package (4 ounces) German sweet chocolate, cut into chunks

For chocolate dough, in a large bowl, cream butter and sugar until light and fluffy. Beat in eggs and vanilla. Combine the flour, cocoa, baking soda and salt; gradually add to creamed mixture and mix well. Stir in pecans and white chocolate.

For vanilla dough, in another large bowl, cream butter and sugar until light and fluffy. Beat in eggs and vanilla. Combine the flour, cream of tartar, baking soda and salt; gradually add to creamed mixture and mix well. Stir in pecans and German chocolate. Cover and refrigerate both doughs for 2 hours.

Divide both doughs in half. Shape each portion into a 12-in. roll; wrap in plastic wrap. Refrigerate for 3 hours or until firm.

Unwrap and cut each roll in half lengthwise. Place a chocolate half and vanilla half together, pressing to form a log; wrap in plastic wrap. Refrigerate for 1 hour or until the dough holds together when cut.

Using a serrated knife, cut into 1/4-in. slices. Place 2 in. apart on greased baking sheets. Bake at 350° for 8-10 minutes or until set. Remove to wire racks to cool.

Patty Courtney, Jonesboro, Texas

The maraschino cherries add colorful flecks to these sweet treats. It's so handy to keep a roll or two of the dough in the fridge, so I can bake a batch whenever I want.

cherry icebox cookies

yield about 6 dozen

1	cup butter, softened
1	cup sugar
1/4	cup packed brown sugar
1	egg
1	teaspoon vanilla extract
3-1/4	cups all-purpose flour
1/2	teaspoon baking soda
1/2	teaspoon ground cinnamon
1/4	teaspoon cream of tartar
1/4	cup maraschino cherry juice
4-1/2	teaspoons lemon juice
1/2	cup chopped walnuts
1/2	cup chopped maraschino cherries

In a large bowl, cream butter and sugars until light and fluffy. Beat in egg and vanilla. Combine dry ingredients; gradually add to creamed mixture. Beat in cherry and lemon juices. Stir in nuts and cherries.

Shape into four 12-in. rolls; wrap each in plastic wrap. Refrigerate for 4 hours or until firm.

Unwrap and cut into 1/4-in. slices. Place 2 in. apart on ungreased baking sheets. Bake at 375° for 8-10 minutes or until the edges begin to brown. Remove to wire racks to cool.

peanut butter pinwheels

yield about 4 dozen

1/2	cup shortening
1/2	cup creamy peanut butter
1	cup sugar
1	egg
2	tablespoons milk
1-1/4	cups all-purpose flour
1/2	teaspoon baking soda
1/2	teaspoon salt
1	cup (6 ounces) semisweet chocolate chips

In a large bowl, cream shortening, peanut butter and sugar. Beat in egg and milk. Combine the flour, baking soda and salt; gradually add to creamed mixture. Roll out between waxed paper into a 12-in. x 10-in. rectangle. Melt chocolate chips; cool slightly. Spread over dough to within 1/2 in. of edges. Roll up tightly jelly-roll style, starting with a long side; wrap in plastic wrap. Refrigerate for 20-30 minutes or until easy to handle.

Unwrap and cut into 1/2-in. slices. Place 1 in. apart on greased baking sheets. Bake at 375° for 10-12 minutes or until edges are lightly browned. Remove to wire racks to cool.

editor's note: Reduced-fat or generic brands of peanut butter are not recommended for this recipe.

Kandy Dick
Junction, Texas
Chocolate is swirled through these tasty peanut butter cookies. So you get two delicious tastes in one bite— chocolate and peanut butter.

*Kristi Gleason, Flower Mound, Texas
Grandma Wruble always had a batch of these cookies in the cookie jar and another roll in the refrigerator ready to slice and bake. Their honey and lemon flavor is delicious.

icebox honey cookies

yield 8 dozen

1-1/2	cups shortening
2	cups packed brown sugar
2	eggs
1/2	cup honey
1	teaspoon lemon extract
4-1/2	cups all-purpose flour
2	teaspoons baking soda
2	teaspoons baking powder
1	teaspoon salt
1	teaspoon ground cinnamon

In a large bowl, cream shortening and brown sugar until light and fluffy. Add eggs, one at a time, beating well after each addition. Beat in honey and extract. Combine the remaining ingredients; gradually add to creamed mixture and mix well.

Shape into two 12-in. rolls; wrap each in plastic wrap. Refrigerate for 2 hours or until firm.

Unwrap and cut into 1/4-in. slices. Place 1 in. apart on ungreased baking sheets. Bake at 325° for 12-14 minutes or until golden brown. Remove to wire racks to cool.

*Marcia Hostetter
Canton, New York
My mother-in-law shared the recipe for these old-fashioned cookies. Swirls of raspberry jam give them a yummy twist.

raspberry swirls

yield 8 dozen

1	cup butter, softened
2	cups sugar
2	eggs
1	teaspoon vanilla extract
1/2	teaspoon lemon extract
3-3/4	cups all-purpose flour
2	teaspoons baking powder
1	teaspoon salt
1	jar (12 ounces) seedless raspberry jam
1	cup flaked coconut
1/2	cup chopped pecans

In a large bowl, cream butter and sugar. Add the eggs and extracts; mix well. Combine flour, baking powder and salt; add to creamed mixture and mix well. Cover and chill for at least 2 hours.

Divide dough in half. On a lightly floured surface, roll each half into a 12-in. x 9-in. rectangle. Combine jam, coconut and pecans; spread over rectangles. Carefully roll up rectangle jelly-roll style, starting with a long side; wrap in plastic wrap. Chill overnight or freeze for 2-3 hours.

Unwrap and cut dough into 1/4-in. slices; place 1-1/2 in. apart on parchment-lined baking sheets. Bake at 375° for 10-12 minutes or until lightly browned. Remove to wire racks to cool completely.

Maria Regakis, Somerville, Massachusetts ✳
When you bite into one of these yummy cookies, you'll never guess it's low in fat.

peanut butter cookies

yield 2 dozen

3	tablespoons butter
2	tablespoons reduced-fat peanut butter
1/2	cup packed brown sugar
1/4	cup sugar
1	egg white
1	teaspoon vanilla extract
1	cup all-purpose flour
1/4	teaspoon baking soda
1/8	teaspoon salt

In a large bowl, cream the butter, peanut butter and sugars until light and fluffy. Add egg white; beat until blended. Beat in vanilla. Combine the flour, baking soda and salt; gradually add to the creamed mixture and mix well. Shape into an 8-in. roll; wrap in plastic wrap. Freeze for 2 hours or until firm.

Unwrap and cut into slices, about 1/4 in. thick. Place 2 in. apart on baking sheets coated with cooking spray. Flatten with a fork. Bake at 350° for 6-8 minutes for chewy cookies or 8-10 minutes for crisp cookies. Cool for 1-2 minutes before removing to wire racks.

chocolate peppermint pinwheels

yield about 4 dozen

1	cup shortening
1-1/2	cups sugar
2	eggs
2	tablespoons milk
2	teaspoons peppermint extract
2-1/2	cups all-purpose flour
1/2	teaspoon salt
1/2	teaspoon baking powder
2	squares (1 ounce *each*) unsweetened chocolate, melted

In a large bowl, cream shortening and sugar. Add egg, milk and extract; mix well. Combine the flour, salt and baking powder; gradually add to creamed mixture. Divide dough in half. Add the chocolate to one portion; mix well. Roll each portion between waxed paper into a rectangle about 1/2 in. thick. Remove top sheet of waxed paper; place plain dough over chocolate dough. Roll up jelly-roll style, starting with a long side. Wrap in each plastic warp. Refrigerate for 2 hours or until firm.

Unwrap and cut into 1/4-in. slices. Place 2 in. apart on greased baking sheets. Bake at 375° for 8-10 minutes or until lightly browned. Remove to wire racks to cool.

Ellen Johnson ✳
Hampton, Virginia
My cookie-loving family is never satisfied with just one batch of these minty pinwheels, so I automatically double the recipe each time I bake them. Even then the cookie tin is quickly emptied.

shaped sensations

browned-butter sandwich spritz, p. 150

Dig into cookie making by

forming dough into balls, logs, crescents, cups and other fanciful, fun shapes that will surely delight your family and friends. These delectable treats may take a bit longer to make but the yummy results will be well worth it!

apricot coconut treasures, p. 155

angel wings, p. 136

✳ Jennifer Moran, Elizabethtown, Kentucky

With their chocolate-dipped bottoms, peanut butter thumbprint filling and pretty chocolate drizzle on top, these cookies are fancy and fun! The recipe is from my mother.

peanut butter delights

yield about 5 dozen

1/2	cup shortening
1/2	cup butter, softened
1/2	cup creamy peanut butter
1-1/2	cups sugar, *divided*
1	cup packed brown sugar
2	eggs
3	cups all-purpose flour
3/4	teaspoon baking soda
1/2	teaspoon salt

FILLING:

1/2	cup creamy peanut butter
4	ounces cream cheese, softened
1/4	cup sugar
1	egg yolk
1/2	teaspoon vanilla extract
2-1/2	cups milk chocolate chips

TOPPING:

1	tablespoon butter
1-1/2	cups confectioners' sugar
6	tablespoons baking cocoa
3	tablespoons water
1/4	teaspoon vanilla extract

In a large bowl, cream the shortening, butter, peanut butter, 1 cup sugar and brown sugar. Add eggs, one at a time, beating well after each addition. Combine the flour, baking soda and salt; gradually add to creamed mixture.

Roll into 1-1/2-in. balls; roll in remaining sugar. Place 2 in. apart on ungreased baking sheets. Using the end of a wooden spoon handle, make an indentation in the center of each ball.

In a small bowl, beat peanut butter and cream cheese until smooth. Beat in the sugar, egg yolk and vanilla. Spoon about 3/4 teaspoon of filling into each indentation. Bake at 350° for 12-15 minutes or until firm to the touch. Remove to wire racks to cool.

Melt the chocolate chips; stir until smooth. Dip bottoms of cookies in chocolate; shake off excess. Place chocolate side up on waxed paper-lined baking sheets. Refrigerate until set.

For topping, melt butter in a saucepan. Whisk in confectioners' sugar and cocoa. Gradually add water, whisking until smooth. Stir in vanilla. Drizzle over tops of cookies. Chill until chocolate is set. Store in an airtight container in the refrigerator.

editor's note: Reduced-fat or generic brands of peanut butter are not recommended for this recipe.

Rhonda Berstad, Melfort, Saskatchewan ✳
Everyone had a "hay day" when our daughter, Naomi got married. Naomi's grandmother, who made these tender cookies for 48 years, fixed them in the shape of hearts for the wedding. Make the cookies ahead and freeze until serving.

braided sweetheart cookies

yield 2 dozen

1	cup butter, softened
1-1/2	cups confectioners' sugar
1	egg
1/2	teaspoon vanilla extract
2-1/2	cups all-purpose flour
1/2	teaspoon baking powder
1/2	teaspoon salt
6	to 8 drops red food coloring

In a large bowl, cream the butter and sugar. Beat in egg and vanilla. Combine the flour, baking powder and salt; gradually add the to creamed mixture.

Divide dough in half; tint one portion pink, leaving the remaining portion white. Wrap each portion in plastic wrap; refrigerate for 4 hours or overnight.

For each cookie, shape a 1-in. ball of each color into an 8-in. rope. Place a pink and white rope side-by-side; press together gently and twist. Place 2 in. apart on ungreased baking sheets; shape into a heart and pinch ends to seal. Bake at 350° for 8-11 minutes or until edges are lightly browned. Remove to wire racks to cool.

butterscotch snickerdoodles

yield 8 dozen

1	cup butter, softened
1/3	cup canola oil
1-1/4	cups sugar
1/3	cup confectioners' sugar
2	eggs
3	tablespoons plain yogurt
1-1/2	teaspoons almond extract
1/8	teaspoon lemon extract
3-1/2	cups all-purpose flour
1	cup whole wheat flour
1	teaspoon cream of tartar
1	teaspoon baking soda
1/2	teaspoon salt
1	cup butterscotch chips
1/2	cup chopped almonds

Additional sugar

In a large bowl, beat the butter, oil and sugars. Add eggs, one at a time, beating well after each addition. Add yogurt and extracts. Combine the flours, cream of tartar, baking soda and salt; gradually add to the butter mixture. Stir in the butterscotch chips and chopped almonds.

Roll into 1-in. balls, then roll in sugar. Place 2 in. apart on ungreased baking sheets. Flatten with a fork dipped in sugar. Bake at 350° for 12-15 minutes or until lightly browned. Remove to wire racks to cool.

Nancy Radenbaugh ✳
White Lake, Michigan
This recipe is a combination of the traditional Snickerdoodle recipe and my mother's best spritz recipe. Everyone raves about this combination.

✳ Taste of Home Test Kitchen
Get ready to pour yourself a cup of tea because you won't be able to resist sampling one of these cookies. Almonds add taste and texture to the simple strips that are dressed up with raspberry pie filling.

raspberry almond strips

yield 16 cookies

1/2	**tube refrigerated sugar cookie dough, softened**
1/3	**cup all-purpose flour**
1/4	**cup finely chopped almonds**
3	**tablespoons raspberry filling**
1/4	**cup confectioners' sugar**
1-1/2	**teaspoons milk**
1/8	**teaspoon almond extract**

In a small bowl, beat the cookie dough, flour and almonds until combined. Roll into a 13-1/2-in. x 2-in. rectangle on an ungreased baking sheet.

Using the end of a wooden spoon handle, make a 1/4-in.-deep indentation lengthwise down the center of rectangle. Bake at 350° for 5 minutes.

Spoon raspberry filling into indentation. Bake 8-10 minutes longer or until lightly browned. Cool for 2 minutes. Remove to a cutting board; cut into 3/4-in. slices. Place on a wire rack.

In a small bowl, combine the confectioners' sugar, milk and extract until smooth. Drizzle over warm cookies.

✳ Ozela Haynes, Emerson, Arkansas
Serve up these crispy snacks for a super party appetizer, or just keep a batch on hand to nibble anytime.

pecan cheddar crisps

yield about 2 dozen

1/2	**cup butter, softened**
1/2	**cup finely shredded cheddar cheese**
1	**cup all-purpose flour**
1/4	**teaspoon paprika**
1/4	**teaspoon salt**
1/2	**cup pecan halves**

In a large bowl, beat the butter and cheese until blended. Combine the flour, paprika and salt; add to creamed mixture.

Shape dough into 1-in. balls. Place 2 in. apart on ungreased baking sheets. Top each with a pecan; press down to flatten. Bake at 350° for 15-20 minutes or until golden brown. Remove to wire rack to cool.

Amber Sumner, Congress, Arizona ✳

Daintily drizzled with white chocolate, these eye-catching biscotti are loaded with chocolate chips and crunchy almonds. They look lovely in a holiday gift basket with an assortment of hot chocolate and teas.

brownie biscotti

yield 3 dozen

- 1/2 **cup butter, melted**
- 3 **eggs**
- 2 **teaspoons vanilla extract**
- 2-1/2 **cups all-purpose flour**
- 1-1/3 **cups sugar**
- 3/4 **cup baking cocoa**
- 2 **teaspoons baking powder**
- 1/2 **teaspoon baking soda**
- 1 **cup unblanched almonds, toasted and coarsely chopped**
- 1/2 **cup miniature semisweet chocolate chips**

DRIZZLE:
- 1/2 **cup vanilla *or* white chips**
- 1-1/2 **teaspoons shortening**

In a large bowl, combine the butter, eggs and vanilla until well blended. Combine the flour, sugar, cocoa, baking powder and baking soda; gradually add to butter mixture just until combined (dough will be crumbly).

Turn dough onto a lightly floured surface; knead in almonds and chocolate chips. Divide dough in half. On an ungreased baking sheet, shape each portion into a 12-in. x 3-in. log, leaving 3 in. between the logs.

Bake at 325° for 30-35 minutes or until set and tops are cracked. Cool for 15 minutes. Carefully transfer to a cutting board; cut diagonally with a serrated knife into 1/2-in. slices. Place cut side down on ungreased baking sheets. Bake for 20-25 minutes or until firm and dry. Remove to wire racks to cool.

For drizzle, in a microwave-safe bowl, melt vanilla chips and shortening; stir until smooth. Drizzle over biscotti.

no-bake cookie balls

yield 5 dozen

- 1 **cup (6 ounces) semisweet chocolate chips**
- 3 **cups confectioners' sugar**
- 1-3/4 **cups crushed vanilla wafers (about 55 wafers)**
- 1 **cup chopped walnuts, toasted**
- 1/3 **cup orange juice**
- 3 **tablespoons light corn syrup**

Additional confectioners' sugar

In a large microwave-safe bowl, melt the chocolate chips; stir until smooth. Stir in the confectioners' sugar, vanilla wafers, walnuts, orange juice and corn syrup.

Roll into 1-in. balls; roll in additional confectioners' sugar. Store in an airtight container.

Carmeletta Dailey ✳
Winfield, Texas
These quick bites are great when you're short on time or don't want to turn on the oven. I make them a day or two ahead to let the flavors blend.

✳ Ruth Gilhousen, Knoxdale, Pennsylvania
Traditionally, I bake these for Christmas. A cross between sweet breads and cookies, they're also something that I have been asked to make for weddings.

apricot cheese crescents

yield 4-1/2 dozen

2	cups all-purpose flour
1/2	teaspoon salt
1	cup cold butter
1	cup (8 ounces) small-curd cottage cheese

FILLING:

1	package (6 ounces) dried apricots
1/2	cup water
1/2	cup sugar

TOPPING:

3/4	cup finely chopped almonds
1/2	cup sugar
1	egg white, lightly beaten

In a large bowl, combine flour and salt; cut in butter until crumbly. Add cottage cheese; mix well. Shape into 1-in. balls. Cover and refrigerate several hours or overnight.

For the filling, combine dried apricots and water in a saucepan. Cover and simmer for 20 minutes. Cool for 10 minutes. Pour into a blender; cover and process on high speed until smooth. Transfer to a bowl; stir in the sugar. Cover and refrigerate.

For topping, combine almonds and sugar; set aside. On a floured surface, roll the balls into 2-1/2-in. circles. Spoon about 1 teaspoon of filling onto each. Fold dough over filling and pinch edges to seal. Place on greased baking sheets. Brush tops with egg white; sprinkle with almond mixture. Bake at 375° for 12-15 minutes or until lightly browned. Remove to wire racks to cool.

favorite molasses cookies

yield 6 dozen

✳ Marjorie Jenkins
Lees Summit, Missouri
Clove and ginger spice these chewy molasses cookies. One bite and you'll know why they are my favorite.

3/4	cup butter, softened
1	cup sugar
1/4	cup molasses
1	egg
2	cups all-purpose flour
2	teaspoons baking powder
1/2	teaspoon baking soda
1	teaspoon ground cinnamon
1/2	teaspoon ground cloves
1/2	teaspoon ground ginger

In a large bowl, cream butter and sugar until light and fluffy. Beat in molasses and egg. Combine dry ingredients; gradually add to creamed mixture. Cover and refrigerate for 1 hour or until firm.

Roll into 1-in. balls. Place 2 in. apart on greased baking sheets. Press flat with a glass dipped in sugar. Bake at 375° for 8-10 minutes or until lightly browned. Remove to wire racks to cool.

Betty Ferrell, Jasper, Georgia ✳

These cookies are easy to make and taste so good. They're very crisp and light, perfect with milk or coffee.

crispy butter cookies

yield about 4 dozen

1	cup butter, softened
1-1/2	cups confectioners' sugar
2	egg whites
1	teaspoon vanilla extract
2-1/2	cups all-purpose flour
1/2	teaspoon baking powder
1/2	teaspoon baking soda

Sugar

In a large bowl, cream butter and confectioners' sugar until light and fluffy. Beat in egg whites and vanilla. Combine the flour, baking powder and baking soda; gradually add to the creamed mixture and mix well.

Roll into 1-1/2-in. balls, then roll in sugar. Place 2 in. apart on greased baking sheets. Flatten with a fork. Bake at 350° for 12-14 minutes or until edges are lightly browned. Remove to wire racks to cool.

Patricia Grall, Hortonville, Wisconsin ✳

A cookie exchange introduced me to these fancy peanut butter treats. They're eye-catching for the holidays and bake sales.

chocolate-dipped peanut logs

yield about 8-1/2 dozen

1	cup creamy peanut butter
1/2	cup butter, softened
1/2	cup shortening
1	cup sugar
1	cup packed brown sugar
2	eggs
2-1/2	cups all-purpose flour
1-1/2	teaspoons baking soda
1	teaspoon baking powder
1/4	teaspoon salt
8	ounces dark chocolate candy coating
2/3	cup ground salted peanuts

In a large bowl, cream the peanut butter, butter, shortening and sugars until light and fluffy. Add eggs, one at a time, beating well after each addition. Combine the dry ingredients; gradually add to the creamed mixture and mix well.

Shape into 2-in. logs. Place 2 in. apart on ungreased baking sheets. Bake at 350° for 8-10 minutes or until lightly browned. Remove to wire racks to cool.

In a microwave, melt candy coating; stir until smooth. Dip one end of each cookie into coating; allow excess to drip of. Dip into peanuts. Place on waxed paper to set.

editor's note: Reduced-fat or generic brands of peanut butter are not recommended for this recipe.

Are you looking for a quick way to dress up an ordinary cookie mix? Try this idea from our home economists. The frosting can be used on a variety of cookies, including sugar and chocolate chip.

frosted peanut butter cookies

yield about 2 dozen

1	package (17-1/2 ounces) peanut butter cookie mix
2	cups confectioners' sugar
1/4	cup baking cocoa
1/4	cup hot water
1	teaspoon vanilla extract

Sliced almonds *or* **pecan halves**

In a large bowl, prepare the cookie dough mix according to package directions. Shape into 1-in. balls. Place 2 in. apart on ungreased baking sheets.

Bake at 375° for 8-10 minutes or until edges are golden brown. Cool for 1 minute before removing to wire racks.

For frosting, in a bowl, combine the confectioners' sugar, cocoa, water and vanilla. Spread over cookies; top with nuts.

✳ Ellen Marie Byler, Munfordville, Kentucky

Red raspberry preserves add a festive flair to these tender coconut cookies. Perfect for potlucks and cookie exchanges, these shaped cookies never last long when I make them for my husband and two sons.

jeweled coconut drops

yield about 3-1/2 dozen

1/3	cup butter, softened
1	package (3 ounces) cream cheese, softened
3/4	cup sugar
1	egg yolk
2	teaspoons orange juice
1	teaspoon almond extract
1-1/4	cups all-purpose flour
1-1/2	teaspoons baking powder
1/4	teaspoon salt
3-3/4	cups flaked coconut, *divided*
1	cup seedless raspberry preserves, warmed

In a large bowl, cream the butter, cream cheese and sugar until light and fluffy. Beat in egg yolk, orange juice and almond extract. Combine the flour, baking powder and salt; gradually add to creamed mixture and mix well. Stir in 3 cups of coconut. Refrigerate for 30 minutes or until easy to handle.

Shape dough into 2-in. balls; roll in remaining coconut. Place 2 in. apart on ungreased baking sheets. Using the end of a wooden spoon handle, make an indentation in the center of each ball.

Bake at 350° for 8-10 minutes or until lightly browned. Remove to wire racks to cool. Fill each cookie with preserves.

Anna Brydl, Tobias, Nebraska ✳
My family loves these big old-fashioned cookies. They're crisp, yet still chewy in the center, and the cinnamon makes them a little different from typical oatmeal cookies.

cinnamon oatmeal cookies

yield 4 dozen

1	cup butter, softened
1	cup sugar
1	cup packed brown sugar
2	eggs
1	teaspoon vanilla extract
1-1/2	cups all-purpose flour
1	teaspoon baking soda
1	teaspoon ground cinnamon
1/2	teaspoon baking powder
1/2	teaspoon salt
3	cups quick-cooking oats

In a large bowl, cream butter and sugars until light and fluffy. Beat in eggs and vanilla. Combine the flour, baking soda, cinnamon, baking powder and salt; gradually add to creamed mixture and mix well. Stir in oats.

Shape into 1-1/2-in. balls. Place 2 in. apart on ungreased baking sheets. Bake at 350° for 10-12 minutes or until golden brown. Cool for 1 minute before removing to wire racks.

caramel tassies

yield 4 dozen

1	cup butter, softened
2	packages (3 ounces *each*) cream cheese, softened
2	cups all-purpose flour

FILLING:

1	package (14 ounces) caramels
1/4	cup plus 3 tablespoons evaporated milk

FROSTING:

2	tablespoons shortening
2	tablespoons butter, softened
1	cup confectioners' sugar
1	tablespoon evaporated milk

In a large bowl, cream butter and cream cheese until light and fluffy. Gradually add flour and mix well. Cover and refrigerate for 1 hour or until easy to handle.

Roll dough into 1-in. balls; press onto the bottom and up the sides of ungreased miniature muffin cups. Prick bottoms with a fork. Bake at 375° for 15-17 minutes or until golden brown. Cool for 5 minutes before removing from pans to wire racks.

In a large heavy saucepan over low heat, melt caramels with milk. Remove from the heat; cool slightly. Transfer to a heavy-duty resealable plastic bag; cut a small hole in a corner of the bag. Pipe filling into pastry cups. Cool to room temperature.

For frosting, in a small bowl, beat shortening and butter until smooth. Gradually beat in confectioners' sugar and milk until fluffy. Pipe onto filling. Store in the refrigerator.

Jane Bricker ✳
Scottdale, Pennsylvania
Buttery cookie cups with a smooth caramel filling make a nice addition to a Christmas dessert tray. These sweet treats are one of my personal favorites as well as for my entire family.

Looking for a little something special to bake up for the holidays? Try these elegant mocha-frosted cookies. They're wonderful with coffee and make an eye-catching addition to any cookie platter.

mocha cookie pretzels

yield 4 dozen

1/2	cup butter, softened
1/2	cup sugar
1	egg
2	squares (1 ounce *each*) unsweetened chocolate, melted and cooled
1	teaspoon vanilla extract
2	cups cake flour
1/4	teaspoon salt

GLAZE:

1	cup (6 ounces) semisweet chocolate chips
1	teaspoon shortening
1	teaspoon light corn syrup
1	cup confectioners' sugar
3	to 5 tablespoons hot brewed coffee
2	squares (1 ounce *each*) white baking chocolate, chopped

Green colored sugar, optional

In a large bowl, cream butter and sugar until light and fluffy. Beat in egg. Beat in melted chocolate and vanilla. Combine flour and salt; gradually add to the creamed mixture and mix well. Cover and refrigerate for 1 hour or until dough is easy to handle.

Divide dough into fourths; divide each portion into 12 pieces. Shape each piece into a 6 in. rope; twist into a pretzel shape. Place 1 in. apart onto lightly greased baking sheets. Bake at 400° for 7-9 minutes or until set. Remove to wire racks to cool.

For glaze, in a microwave, melt the semisweet chips, shortening and corn syrup; stir until smooth. Stir in confectioners' sugar and enough coffee to achieve a glaze consistency. Dip cookies in glaze; allow excess to drip off. Place on waxed paper until set.

In a microwave, melt white chocolate over 30% power; stir until smooth. Drizzle over cookies. Decorate with green sugar if desired; let stand until set.

mexican wedding cakes

yield about 6 dozen

✳ Sarita Johnston
San Antonio, Texas

As part of a Mexican tradition, I tucked these tender cookies into small gift boxes for the guests at my sister's wedding. Most folks ate them up before they got home!

2	cups butter, softened
1	cup confectioners' sugar
4	cups all-purpose flour
1	teaspoon vanilla extract
1	cup finely chopped pecans

Additional confectioners' sugar

In a large bowl, cream butter and sugar. Gradually add flour; mix well. Beat in vanilla. Stir in pecans.

Shape tablespoonfuls into 2-in. crescents. Place 2 in. apart on ungreased baking sheets. Bake at 350° for 12-15 minutes or until lightly browned. Roll warm cookies in confectioners' sugar; cool on wire racks.

Brenda Bawdon, Alpena, South Dakota ✳
These cute cookie pops are a big hit at bake sales. I sell them for $1 a piece and they disappear! The bright and cheery faces catch the kids' eyes, making them surefire sellers.

smiling sugar cookies

yield about 2 dozen

1/2	**cup butter, softened**
1/2	**cup sugar**
1/2	**cup packed brown sugar**
1	**egg**
1/3	**cup milk**
2	**teaspoons vanilla extract**
3	**cups all-purpose flour**
2	**teaspoons cream of tartar**
1	**teaspoon baking soda**
1/2	**teaspoon salt**

About 24 Popsicle sticks

1	**cup vanilla frosting**

Red, blue and green paste food coloring
Assorted small candies

In a large bowl, cream the butter and sugars until light and fluffy. Beat in the egg, milk and vanilla. Combine the flour, cream of tartar, baking soda and salt; gradually add to creamed mixture and mix well. Roll dough into 1-1/2-in. balls; insert a Popsicle stick in the center of each.

Place 2 in. apart on lightly greased baking sheets; flatten slightly. Bake at 375° for 8-10 minutes or until lightly browned. Remove to wire racks to cool.

Divide frosting among three bowls; tint as desired. Place each color of frosting in a resealable plastic bag; cut a small hole in a corner of bag. Pipe hair and mouths onto cookies; use a dab of frosting to attach small candies for eyes. Let dry for at least 30 minutes.

Anna Mary Knier, Mount Joy, Pennsylvania ✳
This is a nice change from the usual peanut butter cookie. Children like to help with this recipe by unwrapping the kisses.

oatmeal kiss cookies

yield 6 dozen

1/2	**cup butter, softened**
1/2	**cup shortening**
1	**cup sugar**
1	**cup packed brown sugar**
2	**eggs**
2	**cups all-purpose flour**
1	**teaspoon baking soda**
1	**teaspoon salt**
2-1/4	**cups quick-cooking oats**
1	**cup chopped nuts**
72	**milk chocolate kisses**

In a large bowl, cream the butter, shortening and sugars until light and fluffy. Add eggs, one at a time, beating well after each addition. Combine the flour, baking soda and salt; gradually add to creamed mixture and mix well. Stir in oats and nuts. Roll into 1-in. balls. Place 2 in. apart on ungreased baking sheets.

Bake at 375° for 10-12 minutes or until lightly browned. Immediately press a chocolate kiss in the center of each cookie. Remove to wire racks to cool.

 R. Lane, Tenafly, New Jersey

The shape of these delicate cookies reminds me of angel wings. They are a favorite at my house for the holidays. They also make a pretty presentation on a cookie tray.

angel wings

yield about 3 dozen

1	**cup cold butter, cubed**
1-1/2	**cups all-purpose flour**
1/2	**cup sour cream**
10	**tablespoons sugar,** *divided*
1	**tablespoon ground cinnamon,** *divided*

Colored sugar, optional

In a bowl, cut butter into flour until the mixture resembles coarse crumbs. Stir in the sour cream. Turn onto a lightly floured surface; knead 6-8 times or until mixture holds together. Shape into four balls; flatten slightly. Wrap in plastic wrap; refrigerate for 4 hours or overnight.

Unwrap one ball. Sprinkle 2 tablespoons sugar on waxed paper; coat all sides of ball with sugar. Roll into a 12-in. x 5-in. rectangle between two sheets of waxed paper. Remove top sheet of waxed paper. Sprinkle dough with 3/4 teaspoon cinnamon. Lightly mark a line down the center of dough, making two 6-in. x 5-in. rectangles. Starting with a short side, roll up jelly-roll style to center mark; peel waxed paper away while rolling. Repeat with other side. Wrap; freeze for 30 minutes. Repeat with remaining dough balls.

Place remaining sugar or place colored sugar if desired on waxed paper. Cut rolls into 1/2-in. slices; dip each side into sugar. Place 2 in. apart on ungreased baking sheets. Bake at 375° for 12 minutes or until golden brown. Turn cookies; bake for 5-8 minutes. Remove to wire racks.

These cute cookies created by our home economists are a great addition to your table when entertaining at Easter. Enlist the kids to help shape the bunnies.

meringue bunnies

yield 1 dozen

2	egg whites
1/8	teaspoon cream of tartar
1/2	cup sugar
1/4	cup pink candy coating disks
36	heart-shaped red decorating sprinkles

In a large bowl, beat the egg whites and cream of tartar on medium speed until soft peaks form. Gradually add sugar, 1 tablespoon at a time, beating on high until stiff peaks form.

Transfer to a pastry or plastic bag; cut a small hole in a corner of the bag. On parchment-lined baking sheets, pipe the meringue into 4-3/4-in. bunny shapes. Bake at 225° for 1-1/2 hours or until firm. Remove to wire racks to cool completely.

In a microwave or heavy saucepan, melt candy coating, stirring until smooth. Place in a pastry or plastic bag. Pipe ears, whiskers and mouths on bunnies. Attach hearts for eyes and nose with melted candy coating.

chocolate mint crisps

yield 6-1/2 dozen

1-1/2	cups packed brown sugar
3/4	cup butter, cubed
2	tablespoons plus 1-1/2 teaspoons water
2	cups (12 ounces) semisweet chocolate chips
2	eggs
2-1/2	cups all-purpose flour
1-1/4	teaspoons baking soda
1/2	teaspoon salt
3	packages (4.67 ounces *each*) mint Andes candies

In a heavy saucepan, cook and stir the brown sugar, butter and water over low heat until butter is melted and mixture is smooth. Remove from the heat; stir in chocolate chips until melted. Transfer to a bowl. Let stand for 10 minutes.

With mixer on high speed, add the eggs one at a time, beating well after each addition. Combine the flour, baking soda and salt; add to the chocolate mixture, beating on low until blended. Cover and refrigerate for 8 hours or overnight.

Roll dough into 1-in. balls. Place the balls 3 in. apart on lightly greased baking sheets. Bake at 350° for 11-13 minutes or until edges are set and the tops are puffed and cracked (cookies will become crisp after cooling). Immediately top each cookie with a mint. Let stand for 1-2 minutes; spread over cookie. Remove to wire racks; let stand until chocolate is set and cookies are cooled.

Karen Ann Bland ✳
Gove, Kansas

If you like chocolate and mint, you can't help but love these yummy, crispy cookies with their creamy icing. We always make them for the holidays .

Light and flaky, these delicate fruit-filled cookies have the look of petite and elegant pastries. They're yummy made with raspberry or apricot filling and served with a pot of tea.

raspberry treasures

yield 2 dozen

1/2	cup butter, softened
1	package (3 ounces) cream cheese, softened
1	teaspoon vanilla extract
1	cup all-purpose flour
1/8	teaspoon salt
1/2	cup raspberry cake and pastry filling
1	egg
1	teaspoon water

In a large bowl, cream butter and cream cheese until light and fluffy. Beat in vanilla. Combine flour and salt; add to the creamed mixture and mix well. Divide dough in half; wrap each in plastic wrap. Refrigerate for 1 hour or until dough is easy to handle.

On a lightly floured surface, roll out dough to 1/8-in. thickness. Cut with a lightly floured 3-in. round cookie cutter. Place 1 teaspoon raspberry filling in the center of each. Bring three edges together over filling, overlapping slightly (a small amount of filling will show); pinch edges gently. In a small bowl, beat egg and water; brush over dough.

Place 1 in. apart on ungreased baking sheets. Bake at 375° for 10-12 minutes or until golden brown. Cool for 1 minute before removing to wire racks.

editor's note: This recipe was tested with Solo brand cake and pastry filling. Look for it in the baking aisle.

✳ Jennifer Branum
O'Fallen, Illinois

I set out these cookies as we open our gifts on Christmas Eve. Before long, the plate is empty and I'm being asked to refill it! The cinnamon-sugar coating adds a special touch to these cookies.

cinnamon almond crescents

yield about 3-1/2 dozen

1	cup butter, softened
1/3	cup sugar
1/2	teaspoon vanilla extract
1-2/3	cups all-purpose flour
1/2	cup finely ground blanched almonds

TOPPING:

1/2	cup sugar
1/2	teaspoon ground cinnamon

In a large bowl, cream butter and sugar until light and fluffy. Beat in vanilla. Combine the flour and almonds; gradually add to the creamed mixture.

Roll into 1-in. balls; shape into crescents. Place 2 in. apart on lightly greased baking sheets. Bake at 350° for 10-12 minutes or until set (do not brown). Combine the sugar and cinnamon in a small bowl. Roll the warm cookies in cinnamon-sugar; cool on wire racks.

Kristen Proulx, Canton, New York
I made these cookies as part of a circus theme for my son's birthday party. To shape the Peanut Cookies, just flatten each dough log with a fork, then pinch in the center before baking.

peanut cookies

yield about 5-1/2 dozen

1	cup butter, softened
1	cup creamy peanut butter
1	cup sugar
1	cup packed brown sugar
2	eggs
1	teaspoon vanilla extract
2-1/2	cups all-purpose flour
1	teaspoon baking powder
1	teaspoon baking soda

Additional sugar

In a large bowl, cream butter, peanut butter and sugars until light and fluffy. Add eggs, one at a time, beating well after each addition. Beat in vanilla. Combine the flour, baking powder and baking soda; gradually add to creamed mixture. Refrigerate for 1 hour.

Roll dough into 1-in. balls; roll in sugar. Shape into logs. Place 2 in. apart on ungreased baking sheets. Flatten with a fork. Pinch center to form peanut shape. Bake at 375° for 7-10 minutes or until golden brown. Cool for 2 minutes before removing to wire racks.

editor's note: Reduced-fat or generic brands of peanut butter are not recommended for this recipe.

frosted cocoa cookies

yield 3-1/2 dozen

1	cup shortening
2	cups sugar
4	eggs
2	teaspoons vanilla extract
3-1/2	cups all-purpose flour
1	cup baking cocoa
2	teaspoons baking soda
1	teaspoon salt

FROSTING:

3	cups confectioners' sugar
1/3	cup baking cocoa
1/3	cup butter, softened
1/4	teaspoon almond extract
3	to 4 tablespoons milk

In a large bowl, cream shortening and sugar until light and fluffy. Add eggs, one at a time, beating well after each addition. Beat in vanilla. Combine the flour, cocoa, baking soda and salt; gradually add to creamed mixture.

Roll into 1-1/2-in. balls. Place 2 in. apart on ungreased baking sheets. Bake at 350° for 13-16 minutes or until set. Remove to wire racks to cool completely.

For frosting, in a large bowl, combine the confectioners' sugar, cocoa, butter and extract. Add enough milk to achieve spreading consistency. Frost cooled cookies.

Diane Moran
Rhame, North Dakota
Almond flavor in the chocolate frosting accents these soft cookies nicely. My husband and two sons gobble them up quickly! They also make a nice take-along to potlucks.

※ Kathy Aldrich, Webster, New York
These cookies are unbelievable! They're easy to make, look elegant and are absolutely delicious with almond, raspberry and chocolate flavors.

almond kiss cookies

yield 40 cookies

1/2	cup butter, softened
1/2	cup sugar
1/2	cup packed brown sugar
1	egg
1	teaspoon almond extract
2	cups all-purpose flour
1	teaspoon baking soda
1/4	teaspoon salt

Additional sugar

40	milk chocolate kisses with almonds

GLAZE:

1	cup confectioners' sugar
1	tablespoon milk
4	teaspoons raspberry jam
1/4	teaspoon almond extract

In a large bowl, cream butter and sugars. Beat in egg and extract. Combine the flour, baking soda and salt; gradually add to creamed mixture. Cover and chill for 1 hour or until easy to handle.

Roll dough into 1-in. balls, then roll in additional sugar. Place 2 in. apart on ungreased baking sheets. Bake at 325° for 13-15 minutes or until golden brown. Immediately press a chocolate kiss into the center of each cookie. Remove to wire racks to cool. Combine glaze ingredients; drizzle over cooled cookies.

※ Sharon Crider, St. Robert, Missouri
These crisp shortbread-like cookies are wonderful with a cup of coffee. They're delectable yet so easy to make with only four ingredients.

butter pecan cookies

yield about 2 dozen

3/4	cup butter, softened
1	package (3.4 ounces) instant butterscotch pudding mix
1-1/4	cups all-purpose flour
1/2	cup chopped pecans

In a small bowl, beat butter and pudding mix until smooth. Gradually beat in flour. Fold in pecans. Roll into 1-1/2-in. balls.

Place 2 in. apart on greased baking sheets; flatten to 1/2 in. with a greased glass. Bake at 375° for 10-13 minutes or until light golden brown. Remove from pans to wire racks.

A hint of orange and a sprinkling of spices lend old-fashioned goodness to these delightful treats. The logs are dipped in melted chocolate and sprinkled with nuts for a special look.

dipped spice cookies

yield about 3-1/2 dozen

1/2   tube refrigerated sugar cookie dough, softened
1/2   cup all-purpose flour
1/4   cup packed brown sugar
1   tablespoon orange juice
3/4   teaspoon ground cinnamon
1/2   teaspoon ground ginger
1/2   teaspoon grated orange peel
1/2   cup semisweet chocolate chips
4   teaspoons shortening
1/4   cup finely chopped walnuts

In a large bowl, beat the cookie dough, flour, brown sugar, orange juice, cinnamon, ginger and orange peel until combined. Shape teaspoonfuls of dough into 2-in. logs. Place 2 in. apart on ungreased baking sheets.

Bake at 350° for 8-10 minutes or until edges are golden brown. Remove to wire racks to cool.

In a microwave-safe bowl, melt chocolate chips and shortening; stir until smooth. Dip one end of each cookie into melted chocolate, allowing excess to drip off; sprinkle with walnuts. Place on waxed paper; let stand until set.

caramel-filled chocolate cookies

yield about 5 dozen

1   cup butter, softened
1   cup plus 1 tablespoon sugar, *divided*
1   cup packed brown sugar
2   eggs
1   teaspoon vanilla extract
2-1/2   cups all-purpose flour
3/4   cup baking cocoa
1   teaspoon baking soda
1-1/4   cups chopped pecans, *divided*
1   package (13 ounces) Rolo candies
4   squares (1 ounce *each*) white baking chocolate

In a large bowl, cream butter, 1 cup sugar and brown sugar until light and fluffy. Add the eggs, one at a time, beating well after each addition. Beat in vanilla. Combine the flour, cocoa and baking soda; gradually add to the creamed mixture, beating just until combined. Stir in 1/2 cup pecans.

Shape a tablespoonful of dough around each candy, forming a ball. In a small bowl, combine the remaining sugar and pecans; dip each cookie halfway. Place nut side up 2 in. apart on greased baking sheets.

Bake at 375° for 7-10 minutes or until tops are slightly cracked. Cool for 3 minutes before removing to wire racks to cool completely.

In a microwave, melt white chocolate at 70% power for 1 minute; stir. Microwave at additional 10- to 20-second intervals, stirring until smooth. Drizzle over cookies.

Deb Walsh ✳
Cabery, Illinois
These yummy chocolate cookies have a tasty caramel surprise inside. With pecans on top and a contrasting white chocolate drizzle, they're almost too pretty to eat!

✳ Emily Barrett, Wyoming, Pennsylvania
If you like the taste of coconut and chocolate, you can't help but love these fancy cookies.

chocolate-dipped coconut snowballs

yield about 5-1/2 dozen

1/3	cup butter, softened
2/3	cup packed brown sugar
1	egg
1/2	teaspoon vanilla extract
1-1/3	cups all-purpose flour
1/4	teaspoon baking powder
1/4	teaspoon baking soda
1/4	teaspoon salt
1	package (4 ounces) German sweet chocolate, finely chopped
1/2	cup flaked coconut
1/2	cup finely chopped pecans, toasted

TOPPING:

12	squares (1 ounce *each*) semisweet chocolate, coarsely chopped
4	teaspoons shortening
2-1/2	cups flaked coconut, toasted

In a large bowl, cream butter and brown sugar until light and fluffy. Beat in egg and vanilla. Combine the flour, baking powder, baking soda and salt; gradually add to creamed mixture and mix well. Stir in the German sweet chocolate, coconut and pecans.

Roll into 3/4-in. balls. Place 2 in. apart on ungreased baking sheets. Bake at 350° for 10-12 minutes or until edges are browned. Remove to wire racks to cool.

In a microwave, melt semisweet chocolate and shortening; stir until smooth. Dip tops of cookies into chocolate mixture; allow excess to drip off. Place on waxed paper-lined baking sheets; sprinkle with toasted coconut. Chill for 1 hour or until firm.

Jeanette Ray, Lindenhurst, Illinois

I dream of one day owning a cookie shop. Until then, I'll delight friends and family with my homemade concoctions. These cookies are like pecan sandies, but I've added a touch of delicious chocolate.

fudge-filled sandies

yield 4 dozen

1	**cup butter, softened**
3/4	**cup confectioners' sugar**
1	**teaspoon vanilla extract**
2	**cups all-purpose flour**
1	**cup finely chopped pecans**

Additional confectioners' sugar

FILLING:

3/4	**cup semisweet chocolate chips**
2	**tablespoons light corn syrup**
1	**tablespoon water**
1	**tablespoon shortening**

In a large bowl, cream butter and confectioners' sugar until light and fluffy. Beat in vanilla. Combine flour and pecans; gradually add to creamed mixture and mix well.

Roll into 1-in. balls. Place 1 in. apart on ungreased baking sheets. Using the end of a wooden spoon handle, make an indentation in the center of each.

Bake at 325° for 18-20 minutes or until lightly browned. Roll warm cookies in additional confectioners' sugar; cool on wire racks.

In a microwave, melt chocolate chips; stir until smooth. Stir in the corn syrup, water and shortening. Spoon or pipe into cooled cookies.

chocolate puddles

yield about 5 dozen

1	**cup butter, softened**
1	**cup sugar**
1	**cup packed brown sugar**
2	**eggs**
2	**teaspoons vanilla extract**
3	**cups all-purpose flour**
3/4	**cup baking cocoa**
1	**teaspoon baking soda**

FILLING:

1	**cup vanilla** *or* **white chips**
1/2	**cup plus 2 tablespoons sweetened condensed milk**
3/4	**cup coarsely chopped mixed nuts**

In a large bowl, cream butter and sugars. Add the eggs, one at a time. Beat in vanilla. Combine flour, cocoa and baking soda; gradually add to creamed mixture. Cover and chill for 2 hours or until dough is stiff.

Melt chips with milk in a heavy saucepan over low heat; stir constantly. Stir in nuts. Cover and chill for 1 hour or until easy to handle.

Roll cookie dough into 1-1/4-in. balls. Place 2 in. apart on lightly greased baking sheets. Using the end of a wooden spoon handle, make an indentation in the center; smooth any cracks. Roll filling into 1/2-in. balls; gently push one into each cookie. Bake at 375° for 8-10 minutes or until cookies are set. Remove to wire racks to cool.

Kathie Griffin
Antelope, California
The variations on this original recipe are almost endless. For a great twist, use peanut butter chips and peanuts for the vanilla chips and mixed nuts.

Looking for a lighter alternative to traditional Christmas cookies? Try these pretty jam-filled thumbprints. The melt-in-your-mouth treats have a buttery taste and get a nice crunch from chopped pecans.

thumbprint cookies

yield 2-1/2 dozen

6	tablespoons butter, softened
1/2	cup sugar
1	egg
2	tablespoons canola oil
1	teaspoon vanilla extract
1/4	teaspoon butter flavoring *or* almond extract
1-1/2	cups all-purpose flour
1/4	cup cornstarch
1	teaspoon baking powder
1/4	teaspoon salt
1	egg white
1/3	cup chopped pecans
7-1/2	teaspoons assorted jams

In a large bowl, cream butter and sugar. Beat in egg. Beat in oil, vanilla and butter flavoring. Combine the flour, cornstarch, baking powder and salt; stir into creamed mixture.

Roll into 1-in. balls. In a small bowl, lightly beat egg white. Dip each ball halfway into egg white, then into pecans. Place nut side up 2 in. apart on baking sheets coated with cooking spray. Using the end of a wooden spoon handle, make an indentation in the center of each. Bake at 350° for 8-10 minutes or until the edges are lightly browned. Remove to wire racks. Fill each cookie with 1/4 teaspoon jam; let cool.

cream filberts

yield about 5 dozen

※ Deanna Richter
Elmore, Minnesota

These cookies remind me of "mothball candy" I used to buy with dimes Grandma gave me. The fillbert, which is another name for hazelnut, is a nice crunchy surprise in the middle of the cookie.

1	cup shortening
3/4	cup sugar
1	egg
1	teaspoon vanilla extract
2-1/2	cups all-purpose flour
1/2	teaspoon baking powder
1/8	teaspoon salt
3/4	cup whole filberts *or* hazelnuts

GLAZE:

2	cups confectioners' sugar
3	tablespoons water
2	teaspoons vanilla extract

Granulated sugar

In a large bowl, cream shortening and sugar. Add egg and vanilla; mix well. Combine the dry ingredients and add to creamed mixture.

Roll heaping teaspoonfuls into balls; press a filbert into each and reshape so dough covers nut. Place on ungreased baking sheets. Bake at 375° for 12-15 minutes or until lightly browned. Remove to wire racks to cool completely.

Combine the confectioners' sugar, water and vanilla. Dip entire top of cookies into glaze, then roll in sugar.

Kay Curtis, Guthrie, Oklahoma ✳
Eeeek! The whimsical mice I made evoked shrieks of delight from the kids at our party. Peanut-half "ears" and the licorice "tails" transformed these peanut butter cookies into country critters.

farm mouse cookies

yield 4 dozen

1	cup creamy peanut butter
1/2	cup butter, softened
1/2	cup sugar
1/2	cup packed brown sugar
1	egg
1	teaspoon vanilla extract
1-1/2	cups all-purpose flour
1/2	teaspoon baking soda

Peanut halves
Black shoestring licorice, cut into
  2-1/2-inch pieces

In a large bowl, cream peanut butter, butter and sugars. Beat in egg and vanilla. Combine flour and baking soda; gradually add to creamed mixture. Cover and chill dough for 1 hour or overnight.

Roll into 1-in. balls. Dash one end, forming a teardrop shape. Place 2 in. apart on ungreased baking sheets; press to flatten. For ears, press two peanuts into each cookie near the pointed end. Using a toothpick, make a 1/2-in.-deep hole for the tail in the end opposite the ears. Bake at 350° for 8-10 minutes or until golden. While cookies are warm, insert licorice for tails. Cool on wire racks.

editor's note: Reduced-fat or generic brands of peanut butter are not recommended for this recipe.

peanut crescents

yield about 3 dozen

1	cup butter, softened
1/3	cup sugar
1	tablespoon water
1	teaspoon vanilla extract
2	cups all-purpose flour
1/2	cup finely chopped salted peanuts

Confectioners' sugar

In a small bowl, cream the butter and sugar until light and fluffy. Beat in water and vanilla. Gradually add flour. Stir in peanuts. Cover and refrigerate for 1 hour or until easy to handle.

Shape rounded tablespoonfuls of the dough into 2-1/2-in. crescents. Place 2 in. apart on ungreased baking sheets. Bake at 350° for 15-18 minutes or until set (do not brown).

Roll warm cookies in confectioners' sugar; cool completely on wire racks. Roll cooled cookies again in confectioners' sugar.

Kay Brantley ✳
Shaver Lake, California
I've been making these festive crescents for 30 years. They freeze well and look pretty served on Christmas dishes.

*Elisa Lochridge, Tigard, Oregon
Chocolate and nuts are enjoyed very much in our household, and these cookies are no exception. I also hand them out at our Bible study, and everyone enjoy them.

hazelnut chocolate cookies
yield 2 dozen

1/2	cup butter, softened
6	tablespoons sugar
1	teaspoon vanilla extract
3/4	cup cake flour
1/4	cup baking cocoa
3/4	cup ground hazelnuts
24	whole hazelnuts, toasted and peeled

Confectioners' sugar

In a small bowl, cream butter and sugar until light and fluffy. Beat in vanilla. Combine flour and cocoa; gradually add to creamed mixture and mix well. Stir in ground hazelnuts.

Roll into 1-in. balls. Press one whole hazelnut into each. Place 2 in. apart on ungreased baking sheets.

Bake at 325° for 15-19 minutes or until firm to the touch. Let stand for 2 minutes before removing from pans to wire racks to cool completely. Sprinkle with confectioners' sugar.

*Paula Zsiray, Logan, Utah
When my daughter, Jennifer, was 15 years old, she created this recipe as a way to combine two of her favorite flavors.

chocolate gingersnaps
yield 3 dozen

1/2	cup butter, softened
1/2	cup packed dark brown sugar
1/4	cup molasses
1	tablespoon water
2	teaspoons minced fresh gingerroot
1-1/2	cups all-purpose flour
1	tablespoon baking cocoa
1-1/4	teaspoons ground ginger
1	teaspoon baking soda
1	teaspoon ground cinnamon
1/4	teaspoon ground nutmeg
1/4	teaspoon ground cloves
7	squares (1 ounce *each*) semisweet chocolate, chopped
1/4	cup sugar

In a large bowl, cream butter and brown sugar until light and fluffy. Beat in the molasses, water and gingerroot. Combine the flour, cocoa, ginger, baking soda, cinnamon, nutmeg and cloves; gradually add to creamed mixture and mix well. Stir in chocolate. Cover and refrigerate for 2 hours or until easy to handle.

Shape dough into 1-in. balls; roll in sugar. Place 2 in. apart on greased baking sheets.

Bake at 350° for 10-12 minutes or until tops begin to crack. Cool for 2 minutes before removing to wire racks.

Susan Schuller, Brainerd, Minnesota ✳

These cheery cookie cubs, served at my teddy bear picnic, will delight "kids" of all ages! I like to make fun foods but don't care to spend a whole lot of time fussing. So the idea of using candy for the bears' features was right up my alley.

beary cute cookies

yield 2-1/2 dozen

3/4	**cup shortening**
1/2	**cup sugar**
1/2	**cup packed brown sugar**
1	**egg**
1	**teaspoon vanilla extract**
2	**cups all-purpose flour**
1	**teaspoon salt**
1/2	**teaspoon baking soda**

Additional sugar

30	**miniature milk chocolate kisses**
60	**miniature M&M baking bits**

In a large bowl, cream shortening and sugars. Beat in egg and vanilla; mix well. Combine the flour, salt and baking soda; gradually add to creamed mixture and mix well (dough will be crumbly).

Set aside about 1/2 cup of dough for ears. Shape remaining dough into 1-in. balls; roll in additional sugar. Place 3 in. apart on ungreased baking sheets. Flatten to about 1/2-in. thickness. Roll the reserved dough into 1/2-in. balls; roll in the sugar. Place two smaller balls about 1 in. apart touching each flattened ball (do not flatten smaller balls).

Bake at 375° for 10-12 minutes or until set and edges are lightly browned. Remove from oven; immediately press one kiss and two baking bits into each cookie for nose and eyes. Cool for 5 minutes before removing to wire racks.

crispy oat cookies

yield 8 dozen

1	**cup butter, softened**
1	**cup canola oil**
1-1/3	**cups sugar, *divided***
1	**egg**
1	**teaspoon vanilla extract**
3-1/2	**cups all-purpose flour**
1	**teaspoon baking soda**
1	**teaspoon cream of tartar**
1	**teaspoon salt**
1	**cup crisp rice cereal**
1	**cup quick-cooking oats**
1	**cup flaked coconut**
1	**cup chopped walnuts**

In a large bowl, beat the butter, oil and 1 cup sugar. Beat in egg and vanilla. Combine flour, baking soda, cream of tartar and salt; gradually add to the butter mixture. Stir in the cereal, oats, coconut and nuts.

Roll dough into 1-in. balls; roll in some of the remaining sugar. Place 2 in. apart on ungreased baking sheets. Flatten with a glass dipped in remaining sugar. Bake at 350° for 10-12 minutes or until lightly browned. Remove to wire racks to cool.

Stephanie Malszycki ✳
Ft. Myers, Florida
These tasty oat cookies have added crunch from the crisp rice cereal and walnuts. Send them for a classroom party or share them with friends.

✳ Laurie Knoke, DeKalb, Illinois

We enjoyed these rich, buttery cookies at a bed-and-breakfast in Galena, Illinois, and the hostess was kind enough to share her simple recipe. The pretty nut-topped treats are so special, you could give a home-baked batch as a gift.

scandinavian pecan cookies

yield 4-5 dozen

1	**cup butter, softened**
3/4	**cup packed brown sugar**
1	**egg**, *separated*
2	**cups all-purpose flour**
1/2	**cup finely chopped pecans**

In a large bowl, cream butter, brown sugar and egg yolk. Gradually add flour.

Roll into 1-in. balls. In a small bowl, beat egg white. Dip balls in egg white, then roll in pecans. Place 2 in. apart on ungreased baking sheets; flatten slightly. Bake at 375° for 8-12 minutes or until edges are lightly browned. Remove to wire racks to cool.

✳ Barbara Hart
Hickory, North Carolina

My five brothers and I started cooking at an early age. Being successful in the kitchen is easy with tried-and-true recipes like this one. I hope you like it as much as I do.

chocolate-covered cherry cookies

yield about 2-1/2 dozen

1/2	**cup butter, softened**
1	**cup sugar**
1	**egg**
1-1/2	**teaspoons vanilla extract**
1-1/2	**cups all-purpose flour**
1/2	**cup baking cocoa**
1/2	**teaspoon salt**, *divided*
1/4	**teaspoon baking powder**
1/4	**teaspoon baking soda**
1	**jar (10 ounces) maraschino cherries**
1	**cup (6 ounces) semisweet chocolate chips**
1/2	**cup sweetened condensed milk**

In a large bowl, cream the butter and sugar. Add egg and vanilla; mix well. Combine the flour, cocoa, 1/4 teaspoon salt, baking powder and baking soda; gradually add to the creamed mixture.

Drain cherries, reserving 1-1/2 teaspoons juice. Pat cherries dry. Shape 1 tablespoon of dough around each cherry. Place cookies 2 in. apart on ungreased baking sheets. Bake at 350° for 8-10 minutes or until set. Remove to wire racks to cool.

For frosting, in a saucepan, heat chocolate chips and milk until chips are melted; stir until smooth. Remove from the heat. Add reserved cherry juice and remaining salt. Frost cookies.

BAKING tip

shaped cookie know-how — Shaped cookie dough is easier to handle if it is first chilled in the refrigerator. The heat from your hands can soften the butter in the dough, making it harder to shape, so work quickly. Dust hands lightly with flour to prevent dough from sticking while shaping it.

Mrs. Walter Max, Wabasha, Minnesota

I serve these lovely cookies to guests. They freeze well so you can keep some in the freezer and always have a tasty treat to offer unexpected company.

special chocolate treats

yield about 3-1/2 dozen

3/4	cup butter, softened
3/4	cup packed brown sugar
1-1/2	teaspoons vanilla extract
1/2	teaspoon salt
1-3/4	cups all-purpose flour

FILLING/GLAZE:

1	cup (6 ounces) semisweet chocolate chips
1	tablespoon shortening
2/3	cup finely chopped pecans
1/2	cup sweetened condensed milk
1	teaspoon vanilla extract
1/8	teaspoon salt
1	tablespoon light corn syrup
1	teaspoon water

In a large bowl, cream butter and sugar until fluffy. Beat in vanilla and salt. Add flour; mix well. Cover and refrigerate.

For filling, melt the chocolate chips and shortening in a microwave or heavy saucepan; stir until smooth. Remove from the heat; set aside 1/4 cup for glaze. To remaining chocolate, add pecans, milk, vanilla and salt; blend well. Cover and refrigerate until cool, about 15 minutes.

Place a 16-in. x 12-in. piece of foil in a greased baking sheet; lightly sprinkle with flour. Divide dough in half; place one portion on foil. Roll into a 14-in. x 5-in. rectangle. Spread half of the filling lengthwise on half of the dough to within 1/2 in. of edges. Using the foil, fold the dough over filling; seal edges. Repeat with the remaining dough and filling. Bake at 350° for 15-20 minutes or until golden brown. Cool on a wire rack for 10 minutes.

For glaze, warm reserved chocolate; stir in corn syrup and water. Spread over cookies. Cool completely. Cut cookies widthwise into 3/4-in. strips.

*✳ Deirdre Cox, Milwaukee, Wisconsin
A heavenly sweet maple filling makes these scrumptious spritz cookies a little different. You can count on them to come out buttery and tender. If you don't want to make sandwich cookies, just serve them plain for a melt-in-your-mouth treat.

browned-butter sandwich spritz

yield about 3 dozen

1	**cup plus 2 tablespoons butter, cubed**
1-1/4	**cups confectioners' sugar,** *divided*
1	**egg**
1	**egg yolk**
2	**teaspoons vanilla extract**
2-1/4	**cups all-purpose flour**
1/2	**teaspoon salt**
1/2	**cup maple syrup**

In a small heavy saucepan, cook and stir butter over medium heat for 8-10 minutes or until golden brown. Transfer to a small bowl; refrigerate until firm, about 1 hour.

Set aside 2 tablespoons browned butter for filling. In a large bowl, beat 1/2 cup confectioners' sugar and remaining browned butter until smooth. Beat in the egg, yolk and vanilla. Combine flour and salt; gradually add to creamed mixture and mix well.

Using a cookie press fitted with the disk of your choice, press dough 2 in. apart onto parchment paper-lined baking sheets. Bake at 375° for 8-9 minutes or until set (do not brown). Remove to wire racks to cool.

In a small heavy saucepan, bring syrup to a boil. Cool slightly. Whisk in remaining confectioners' sugar until smooth. Beat reserved browned butter until light and fluffy. Beat in syrup mixture until smooth.

Spread 1 teaspoon of filling over the bottom of half of the cookies. Top with remaining cookies.

*✳ Elaine Anderson
Aliquippa, Pennsylvania
My husband loves these cookies. They have an old-fashioned flavor that goes well with a cup of tea. Plus, they're simple to put together.

buttery almond cookies

yield about 4 dozen

1	**cup butter, softened**
1	**cup confectioners' sugar,** *divided*
2	**cups all-purpose flour**
1	**teaspoon vanilla extract**
3/4	**cup chopped almonds**

In a large bowl, cream butter and 1/2 cup confectioners' sugar until light and fluffy. Add flour and vanilla; mix well. Stir in almonds.

Shape into 1-in. balls. Place 2 in. apart on ungreased baking sheets. Bake at 350° for 13-16 minutes or until bottoms are golden brown and cookies are set. Cool for 1-2 minutes before removing to wire racks. Roll in remaining confectioners' sugar.

Ruth Griggs, South Hill, Virginia ✳
These cookies are favorites of my nephews, who love the creamy frosting.

butter cookies

yield about 6-1/2 dozen

1	**cup butter, softened**
3/4	**cup sugar**
1	**egg**
1/2	**teaspoon vanilla extract**
2-1/2	**cups all-purpose flour**
1	**teaspoon baking powder**
1/4	**teaspoon salt**

FROSTING:

1/2	**cup butter, softened**
4	**cups confectioners' sugar**
1	**teaspoon vanilla extract**
3	**to 4 tablespoons milk**

Red food coloring, optional

In a large bowl, cream butter and sugar. Add egg and vanilla; mix well. Combine the flour, baking powder and salt; add to creamed mixture and mix well.

Place the dough in a cookie press fitted with a heart plate; press dough 2 in. apart on ungreased baking sheets. Bake at 375° for 6-8 minutes or until set (do not brown). Remove to wire racks to cool.

Beat butter, sugar and vanilla until smooth. Blend in enough milk until frosting achieves desired spreading consistency. Add food coloring to a portion or all of the frosting if desired. Frost cookies.

Eleanor Senske, Rock Island, Illinois ✳
A touch of coffee gives these cookies a mocha flavor. The corn syrup makes them chewy.

chocolate cappuccino cookies

yield 3-1/2 dozen

1	**tablespoon instant coffee granules**
1	**tablespoon hot water**
1	**egg white**
3/4	**cup plus 1 tablespoon sugar,** *divided*
1/4	**cup canola oil**
2	**tablespoons corn syrup**
2	**teaspoons corn syrup**
2	**teaspoons vanilla extract**
1-1/4	**cups all-purpose flour**
1/2	**cup baking cocoa**
1/4	**teaspoon salt**

In a small bowl, dissolve coffee granules in hot water. In a large bowl, combine the egg white, 3/4 cup sugar, canola oil, corn syrup, vanilla and coffee; beat until well blended. Combine the flour, cocoa and salt; gradually add to coffee mixture.

Roll into 1-in. balls. Place the balls 2 in. apart on ungreased baking sheets. Flatten to 1/4-in. thickness with a glass dipped in the remaining sugar. Bake at 350° for 5-7 minutes or until center is set. Remove to wire racks to cool. Store in an airtight container.

✳ Jim Ries, Milwaukee, Wisconsin

Every Christmas for over 30 years, I have rolled, cut, shaped and baked batches of cookies for family and friends. These melt-in-your-mouth morsels with a dollop of chocolate in the center are among my favorites.

chocolate pecan thumbprints
yield about 1-1/2 dozen

1/2	cup plus 1 tablespoon butter, softened, *divided*
1/4	cup packed brown sugar
1	egg yolk
1	teaspoon vanilla extract
1	cup all-purpose flour
1	egg white, lightly beaten
3/4	cup finely chopped pecans
3/4	cup semisweet chocolate chips

In a large bowl, cream 1/2 cup butter and brown sugar. Beat in egg yolk and vanilla. Gradually add flour; mix well. Cover and refrigerate for 2 hours or until easy to handle.

Roll dough into 1-in. balls. Dip in egg white, then coat with pecans. Place 2 in. apart on greased baking sheets. Using the end of a wooden spoon handle, make a 1/2-in. indentation in the center of each ball. Bake at 325° for 10 minutes. Press again into indentations with the spoon handle. Bake 10-15 minutes longer or until pecans are golden brown. Remove to wire racks to cool.

In a microwave or heavy saucepan, melt the chocolate chips and remaining butter, stirring until smooth. Spoon into cooled cookies.

Joy Corie, Ruston, Louisiana ✳

Any cookie tray will be perked up with the addition of these pretty tarts. If you don't have miniature tart pans, use miniature muffin pans instead.

tassies

yield 2 dozen

PASTRY:

- 1 **package (3 ounces) cream cheese, softened**
- 1/2 **cup butter**
- 1 **cup all-purpose flour**

FILLING:

- 3/4 **cup packed brown sugar**
- 1 **tablespoon butter, softened**
- 1 **egg**
- 1 **teaspoon vanilla extract**

Dash salt

- 2/3 **cup finely chopped pecans, *divided***

Maraschino cherries, halved, optional

For pastry, blend cream cheese and butter until smooth; stir in flour. Cover and refrigerate for about 1 hour.

Roll dough into twenty-four 1 in. balls. Place in ungreased miniature muffin tins or small cookie tarts; press the dough against bottom and sides to form shell. Set aside.

In a bowl, beat brown sugar, butter and egg until combined. Add vanilla, salt and half the pecans; spoon into pastry. Top with remaining pecans. Bake at 375° for 20 minutes, or until filling is set and pastry is light golden brown. Cool and remove from pans. Top each with a maraschino half if desired.

low-cal molasses cookies

yield 5 dozen

- 1/2 **cup canola oil**
- 1/4 **cup molasses**
- 1/4 **cup plus 2 tablespoons sugar, *divided***
- 1 **egg**
- 2 **cups all-purpose flour**
- 2 **teaspoons baking soda**
- 1 **teaspoon ground cinnamon**
- 1/2 **teaspoon ground ginger**
- 1/4 **teaspoon ground cloves**

In a large bowl, beat oil, molasses, 1/4 cup sugar and egg. Combine flour, baking soda, cinnamon, ginger and cloves; add to molasses mixture and mix well. Cover and refrigerate for at least 2 hours.

Shape into 1-in. balls; roll in remaining sugar. Place 2 in. apart on ungreased baking sheets. Bake at 375° for 10-12 minutes or until cookies are set and surface cracks. Remove to wire racks to cool.

Kim Marie Van Rheenen Mendota, Illinois ✳

Whenever we want a super snack, I bake up a batch of these lighter, yummy molasses cookies. Underneath the pretty crackled tops are soft, chewy centers.

✳ Sharon Allen, Allentown, Pennsylvania
At our house, it wouldn't be Christmas without these delicious Pennsylvania Dutch cookies that are known locally as "kiffels."

walnut horn cookies

yield about 8 dozen

1	pound butter, softened
2	packages (one 8 ounces, one 3 ounces) cream cheese, softened
4	egg yolks
4-1/4	cups all-purpose flour

FILLING:

4	cups ground walnuts (about 1 pound)
5-3/4	cups confectioners' sugar, *divided*
4	egg whites
1/2	teaspoon vanilla extract
1/2	teaspoon almond extract

In a large bowl, combine butter, cream cheese, egg yolks and flour; beat until smooth.

Roll into 1-in. balls; place in a container with waxed paper separating each layer. Cover and refrigerate overnight.

For filling, combine walnuts and 3-3/4 cups sugar (the mixture will be dry). In a small bowl, beat egg whites until soft peaks form; fold into nut mixture. Add extracts and a few drops of water if necessary until filling reaches a spreading consistency. Place remaining sugar in a bowl; roll cream cheese balls in sugar until completely covered. Place a few balls at a time between two sheets of waxed paper. Roll balls into 2-1/2-in. circles. Gently spread about 2 teaspoons of filling over each. Roll up.

Place seam side down 2 in. apart on ungreased baking sheets. Curve the ends slightly. Bake at 350° for 20 minutes or until lightly browned.

honey-peanut butter cookies

yield 5 dozen

✳ Lucile H. Proctor
Panguitch, Utah
When my husband wants a treat, he requests these chewy cookies. The honey adds sweetness and a subtle flavor to the peanut butter cookies.

1/2	cup shortening
1	cup creamy peanut butter
1	cup honey
2	eggs, lightly beaten
3	cups all-purpose flour
1	cup sugar
1-1/2	teaspoons baking soda
1	teaspoon baking powder
1/2	teaspoon salt

In a large bowl, beat shortening, peanut butter and honey. Add eggs; mix well. Combine flour, sugar, baking soda, baking powder and salt; add to peanut butter mixture and mix well.

Roll into 1- to 1-1/2-in. balls. Place 2 in. apart on ungreased baking sheets. Flatten with a fork dipped in flour. Bake at 350° for 8-10 minutes or until set. Remove to wire racks to cool.

editor's note: Reduced-fat or generic brands of peanut butter are not recommended for this recipe.

Helen Keber, Oshkosh, Wisconsin ✳

These elegant, filled cookies are some of my favorites for Christmas time. Serve them at a bridal shower or spring brunch, too.

apricot coconut treasures
yield 2-1/2 dozen

1	cup butter, softened
1	cup (8 ounces) sour cream
2	cups all-purpose flour
1/2	teaspoon salt
1/2	cup flaked coconut
1/2	cup apricot preserves
1/4	cup chopped walnuts

In a large bowl, cream butter and sour cream until light and fluffy. Combine flour and salt; gradually add to creamed mixture and mix well. Divide dough into fourths; wrap in plastic wrap. Chill for 4 hours or until easy to handle.

In a small bowl, combine the coconut, preserves and walnuts; set aside. On a lightly floured surface, roll out each portion of dough to 1/8-in. thickness.

Cut into 2-1/2-in. squares; spread each with a rounded teaspoonful of coconut mixture. Carefully fold one corner over filling. Moisten opposite corner with water and fold over first corner; seal.

Place 1-1/2 in. apart on ungreased baking sheets. Bake at 350° for 18-20 minutes or until lightly browned. Remove to wire racks to cool.

Melissa Vannoy, Childress, Texas ✳

This is my favorite recipe for bake sales and bazaars. Each delightfully sweet chocolate cookie has a fun caramel surprise in the middle, thanks to Rolo candy. Dipped in pecans before baking, they look so nice that they sell in a hurry.

chocolate caramel cookies
yield about 5 dozen

1	cup butter, softened
1	cup plus 1 tablespoon sugar, *divided*
1	cup packed brown sugar
2	eggs
2	teaspoons vanilla extract
2-1/2	cups all-purpose flour
3/4	cup baking cocoa
1	teaspoon baking soda
1	cup chopped pecans, *divided*
1	package (13 ounces) Rolo candies

In a large bowl, cream butter, 1 cup sugar and brown sugar. Add eggs and vanilla; mix well. Combine flour, cocoa and baking soda; add to the creamed mixture and beat just until combined. Stir in 1/2 cup pecans.

Shape dough by tablespoonfuls around each candy. In a small bowl, combine remaining pecans and sugar; dip each cookie halfway into the nut mixture. Place each with nut side up on ungreased baking sheets.

Bake at 375° for 7-10 minutes or until top is slightly cracked. Cool for 3 minutes before removing to wire racks.

✳ Leah Gallington, Corona, California

These cookies were created when I made an error and used regular sugar for the confectioners' sugar called for in the original recipe. I didn't notice the error until I tasted one and thought it was even better than the original!

frosted snowmen

yield 6 dozen

1-1/2	cups butter, softened
2-1/4	cups sugar
1	egg
3	teaspoons vanilla extract
3-3/4	cups all-purpose flour
1/2	teaspoon baking powder
1	can (16 ounces) vanilla frosting
72	pretzel sticks

Red and blue decorating icing

In a large bowl, cream the butter and sugar. Gradually beat in the egg and vanilla. Combine the flour and baking powder; add to the creamed mixture. Roll dough into 1-in., 5/8-in. and 1/4-in. balls.

For each snowman, place one of each size ball 1/4 in. apart on ungreased baking sheets; place snowmen 2 in. apart. Break pretzel sticks in half; press into sides of middle ball.

Bake at 375° for 10-12 minutes or until bottoms are lightly browned. Cool 1 minute before removing to wire racks.

Frost cooled cookies. Decorate with blue icing for eyes, mouth and buttons, and red for nose and scarf.

✳ Mary L. Steiner, West Bend, Wisconsin

These melt-in-your-mouth morsels are sure to be a hit at your house. Cardamom, almond extract and walnuts enhance the flavor of these delicate cookies.

cardamom cookies

yield 6 dozen

2	cups butter, softened
2-1/2	cups confectioners' sugar, *divided*
1-1/2	teaspoons almond extract
3-3/4	cups all-purpose flour
1	cup finely chopped walnuts
1	teaspoon ground cardamom
1/8	teaspoon salt

In a large bowl, cream butter and 1-1/2 cups confectioners' sugar until smooth. Beat in extract. Combine flour, walnuts, cardamom and salt; gradually add to creamed mixture.

Roll into 1-in. balls. Place 2 in. apart on ungreased baking sheets. Bake at 350° for 15-17 minutes or until edges are golden. Roll warm cookies in remaining confectioners' sugar. Remove to wire racks to cool.

Kimberly Santoro, Stuart, Florida
This family favorite was handed down to me by my mother, and everyone who tastes the flaky, chocolate-filled strips asks for the recipe. They're delicious!

fudge-filled dessert strips

yield 3 dozen

- 1 **cup butter, softened**
- 1 **package (8 ounces) cream cheese, softened**
- 2 **cups all-purpose flour**
- 2 **cups (12 ounces) semisweet chocolate chips**
- 1 **can (14 ounces) sweetened condensed milk**
- 2 **cups chopped walnuts**

Confectioners' sugar, optional

In a large bowl, cream butter and cream cheese until fluffy. Gradually add the flour and mix well.

Turn onto lightly floured surface; knead until smooth, about 3 minutes. Divide dough into fourths; cover and refrigerate for 1-2 hours or until easy to handle.

In a microwave, melt chocolate chips and milk; stir until smooth. Stir in the walnuts. Cool to room temperature.

Roll out each portion of dough onto an ungreased baking sheet into an 11-in. x 6-1/2-in. rectangle. Spread 3/4 cup chocolate filling down the center of each rectangle. Fold long sides to the center; press to seal all edges. Turn over so the seam sides are down.

Bake at 350° for 27-32 minutes or until lightly browned. Remove to wire racks to cool. Cut into 1/2-in. slices. Dust with confectioners' sugar if desired.

coffee bonbons

yield 5 dozen

- 1 **cup butter, softened**
- 3/4 **cup confectioners' sugar**
- 1/2 **teaspoon vanilla extract**
- 1 **tablespoon instant coffee granules**
- 1-3/4 **cups all-purpose flour**

CHOCOLATE GLAZE:
- 1 **tablespoon butter**
- 1/2 **ounce unsweetened chocolate**
- 1 **cup confectioners' sugar**
- 2 **tablespoons milk**

In a large bowl, cream butter and sugar until light and fluffy. Add vanilla. Combine coffee and flour; stir into creamed mixture and mix well. Cover and refrigerate until easy to handle.

Roll into 3/4-in. balls. Place 2 in. apart on ungreased baking sheets. Bake at 350° for 18-20 minutes or until set. Remove to wire racks.

Meanwhile, for glaze, melt butter and chocolate together. Add melted mixture to the sugar along with milk; beat until smooth. Frost the cookies while still warm.

Leitzel Malzahn
Fox Point, Wisconsin
When I first sampled this unique cookie, I decided it was the best cookie I'd ever tasted! The coffee flavor and chocolate icing make it a delightful treat at buffets and church socials.

※ Phyllis Schmalz, Kansas City, Kansas
These whimsical ghosts are perfect for Halloween, but I often skip the food coloring and pipe the meringue into cookies instead. With just 15 calories, each little treat can be enjoyed guilt-free!

"boo"-rrific kisses

yield 2-1/2 dozen

2	egg whites
1/2	teaspoon vanilla extract
1/4	teaspoon almond extract
1/8	teaspoon cider vinegar
1/2	cup sugar

Orange food coloring, optional

1-1/2	teaspoons miniature semisweet chocolate chips

Place egg whites in a small bowl; let stand at room temperature for 30 minutes. Add extracts and vinegar; beat on medium speed until soft peaks form. Gradually beat in sugar, 1 tablespoon at a time, on high until stiff glossy peaks form and sugar is dissolved, about 6 minutes. Beat in food coloring if desired.

Cut a small hole in the corner of a pastry or plastic bag; insert a #10 round pastry tip. Fill bag with egg white mixture. Pipe 1-1/2-in.-diameter ghosts onto parchment paper-lined baking sheets. Add two chips on each for eyes.

Bake at 250° for 40-45 minutes or until set and dry. Turn oven off; leave cookies in oven for 1 hour. Carefully remove from parchment paper. Store in an airtight container.

peppermint snowballs

yield about 4 dozen

*※ Judith Scholovich
Waukesha, Wisconsin*
You'll smile in delight when you taste the surprise peppermint filling in these cookies. Topped with crushed peppermint candy, they make a great treat when served with hot cocoa.

1	cup butter, softened
1/2	cup confectioners' sugar
1	teaspoon vanilla extract
2-1/2	cups all-purpose flour

FILLING:

2	tablespoons cream cheese, softened
1	tablespoon milk
1/2	cup confectioners' sugar
2	tablespoons finely crushed peppermint candy *or* candy canes
1	drop red food coloring

TOPPING:

1/4	cup confectioners' sugar
6	tablespoons finely crushed peppermint candy *or* candy canes

In a large bowl, cream butter and sugar; add vanilla. Stir in flour; knead until mixed well. Reserve 1/2 cup of dough; shape remaining dough into 1-in. balls.

For filling, combine cream cheese and milk in a small bowl. Stir in sugar, candy and food coloring; mix well. Make a deep well in the center of each ball; fill with 1/4 teaspoon filling. Use reserved dough to cover filling. Reshape if necessary into smooth balls.

Place 2 in. apart on ungreased baking sheets. Bake at 350° for 12-14 minutes. Combine topping ingredients; roll cookies in mixture while still warm. Cool on wire racks.

Mary Ann Ludwig, Edwardsville, Illinois ✳

These cute cookie bites always get a recipe request. They make special holiday gifts and freeze well, too.

eggnog thumbprints

yield 4 dozen

2/3	**cup butter, softened**
1/2	**cup sugar**
2	**eggs,** *separated*
1	**teaspoon vanilla extract**
1-1/2	**cups all-purpose flour**
1/4	**teaspoon salt**
1/8	**teaspoon ground nutmeg**
1	**cup finely chopped walnuts**

FILLING:

1/4	**cup butter, softened**
1	**cup confectioners' sugar**
1/4	**teaspoon rum extract**
1	**to 2 teaspoons milk**
1	**to 2 drops yellow food coloring, optional**

In a large bowl, cream the butter and sugar until light and fluffy. Beat in egg yolks and vanilla. Gradually stir in the flour, salt and nutmeg and mix well. Cover and refrigerate for 1 hour or until firm.

In a small bowl, whisk egg whites until foamy. Shape dough into 1-in. balls; dip in egg whites, then roll in walnuts. Place 2 in. apart on baking sheets coated with cooking spray.

Using a wooden spoon handle, make a 1/2-in. indentation in the center of each ball. Bake at 350° for 10-12 minutes or until center is set. Carefully remove from pans to wire racks to cool.

For filling, combine the butter, confectioners' sugar, extract and enough milk to achieve a spreading consistency. Tint with food coloring if desired. Pipe about 1/2 teaspoon into each cookie.

cookie cutter delights

chocolate heart cookies, p. 164

These fun-to-make cookies

can be stylized to reflect any holiday, season or occasion. Just let your creativity loose as you decorate them. Or, simply frost them, adding a sprinkle of colored sugar for a quick finish.

smooth sailing sugar cookies, p. 168

strawberry wedding bell cookies, p. 177

✳ Taste of Home Test Kitchen

A hint of pumpkin pie spice in the homemade dough gives a mild taste twist to these crunchy sugar cookies. Canned frosting tinted with food coloring decorates the beach towel treats.

beach blanket sugar cookies

yield 1 dozen

1/2	**cup butter, softened**
2/3	**cup sugar**
1	**egg**
1-3/4	**cups all-purpose flour**
1	**teaspoon baking powder**
1/4	**teaspoon pumpkin pie spice**
1	**can (16 ounces) vanilla frosting**

Gel *or* **liquid food coloring**

In a large bowl, cream the butter and sugar until light and fluffy. Beat in egg. Combine the flour, baking powder and pumpkin pie spice; gradually add to creamed mixture and mix well. Cover and refrigerate for 1 hour or until easy to handle.

Divide dough in half. On a lightly floured surface, roll each portion into a 15-in. x 8-in. rectangle. Cut in half lengthwise; cut widthwise into thirds, forming six strips. Place 1 in. apart on ungreased baking sheets. Bend slightly if desired to form curves in cookies.

Bake at 350° for 10-13 minutes or until edges are lightly browned. Remove to wire racks to cool. Tint frosting with food coloring; decorate cookies as desired.

BAKING

tip

rolling out cookie dough — Roll out only a portion of the dough at a time and keep the rest of the dough refrigerated. Roll out from the center to the edge and check for thickness with a ruler. If the thickness of the dough is uneven, it will bake unevenly and the thinner areas may burn before the thicker ones are baked.

Krissy Fossmeyer, Huntley, Illinois ✳

I make these cookie pops often during the year. In the spring, I cut them into flower shapes and insert the pops into a block of foam fitted into a basket or bowl. They make a great centerpiece or hostess gift.

almond-butter cookie bouquet

yield about 2-1/2 dozen

1-1/4	cups butter, softened
1-3/4	cups confectioners' sugar
2	ounces almond paste
1	egg
1/4	cup milk
1	teaspoon vanilla extract
4	cups all-purpose flour
1/2	teaspoon salt

Wooden skewers or lollipop sticks

ICING:

1	cup confectioners' sugar
4	teaspoons evaporated milk

Food coloring of your choice

In a large bowl, cream butter and confectioners' sugar until light and fluffy; add almond paste. Beat in the egg, milk and vanilla. Combine flour and salt; gradually add to creamed mixture and mix well. Cover and refrigerate for 1 hour.

On a lightly floured surface, roll out dough to 1/4-in. thickness. Cut out with floured 3-in. cookie cutters. Place 1 in. apart on ungreased baking sheets. Insert skewers or sticks. Bake at 375° for 7-8 minutes or until firm. Let stand for 2 minutes before removing to wire racks to cool completely.

In a bowl, whisk confectioners' sugar and milk. Divide into small bowls; tint with food coloring. Gently spread icing over cooled cookies. Decorate with other colors of icing if desired.

Edna Hoffman, Hebron, Indiana ✳

A handy cookie cutter shapes these sensational sweets. With a hint of mint flavor, they're especially yummy.

shamrock cookies

yield 3 dozen

1	cup shortening
1	cup confectioners' sugar
1	egg
1	teaspoon peppermint extract
2-1/2	cups all-purpose flour
1	teaspoon salt

Green paste food coloring

Green colored sugar, optional

In a large bowl, cream the shortening and confectioners' sugar until light and fluffy. Beat in the egg and extract. Add flour and salt; mix well. Tint with food coloring; mix well. Cover and chill for 1 hour or until easy to handle.

On a lightly floured surface, roll dough to 1/4-in. thickness. Cut with a floured 2-in. shamrock cookie cutter.

Place 1 in. apart on ungreased baking sheets. Sprinkle with colored sugar if desired. Bake at 375° for 10-12 minutes or until edges are lightly browned. Cool for 1 minute before removing to wire racks.

✳ TerryAnn Moore, Oaklyn, New Jersey
For a dramatic presentation, I dust dessert plates with cocoa powder and drizzle on a bit of melted raspberry fruit spread. I place a couple of these melt-in-your-mouth cookies in the center, along with raspberries, lemon zest and a sprig of mint.

chocolate heart cookies

yield about 2 dozen

1	cup butter, softened
1/2	cup sugar
1	teaspoon vanilla extract
2	cups all-purpose flour
1/4	cup baking cocoa
1	cup vanilla *or* white chips
2	tablespoons shortening, *divided*
1/2	cup semisweet chocolate chips

In a small bowl, cream butter and sugar until light and fluffy. Beat in vanilla. Combine the flour and cocoa; gradually add to creamed mixture and mix well.

On a lightly floured surface, roll out dough to 1/4-in. thickness. Cut with a 3-in. heart-shaped cookie cutter. Place 2 in. apart on ungreased baking sheets.

Bake at 375° for 8-10 minutes or until firm. Remove to wire racks to cool.

In a microwave, melt vanilla chips and 1 tablespoon shortening at 70% power for 1 minute; stir. Microwave at additional 10- to 20-second intervals, stirring until smooth.

Dip both sides of cookies into melted mixture; allow excess to drip off. Place on waxed paper; let stand until set.

In a microwave, melt the chocolate chips and remaining shortening; stir until smooth. Drizzle over the cookies. Place on wire racks to dry.

✳ Dixie Terry, Marion, Illinois
You'll be remembered for these cookies when you serve them for a morning coffee or at a gathering. Melted chips drizzled on top these easy-to-do cookies make them look fancy.

coffee shortbread

yield about 5 dozen

1	cup butter, softened
1/2	cup packed brown sugar
1/4	cup sugar
2	tablespoons instant coffee granules
2	cups all-purpose flour
1/4	teaspoon salt
1/2	cup semisweet chocolate chips, melted
1/2	cup vanilla *or* white chips, melted

In a large bowl, cream butter, sugars and coffee granules. Gradually beat in flour and salt.

On a lightly floured surface, roll the dough to 1/4-in. thickness. Cut with floured 2-in. to 3-in. cookie cutters.

Place 2 in. apart on ungreased baking sheets. Bake at 300° for 20-22 minutes or until set. Remove to wire racks to cool. Drizzle with melted chips.

Marlene Jackson, Kingsburg, California ✳
These soft cookies make a comforting evening snack. They have a delicious, delicate flavor and cake-like texture.

sour cream cutout cookies

yield about 3-1/2 dozen

1	**cup butter, softened**
1-1/2	**cups sugar**
3	**eggs**
1	**cup (8 ounces) sour cream**
2	**teaspoons vanilla extract**
3-1/2	**cups all-purpose flour**
2	**teaspoons baking powder**
1	**teaspoon baking soda**

FROSTING:

1/3	**cup butter, softened**
2	**cups confectioners' sugar**
2	**to 3 tablespoons milk**
1-1/2	**teaspoons vanilla extract**
1/4	**teaspoon salt**

In a large bowl, cream butter and sugar. Beat in eggs. Add sour cream and vanilla; mix well. Combine flour, baking powder and baking soda; add to the creamed mixture and mix well. Cover and refrigerate for at least 2 hours or overnight.

On a heavily floured surface, roll the dough to 1/4-in. thickness. Cut with a floured 3-in. cutter.

Place 2 in. apart on lightly greased baking sheets. Bake at 350° for 10-12 minutes or until cookie springs back when lightly touched. Remove to wire racks to cool. Combine all the frosting ingredients; beat until smooth. Spread over cooled cookies.

apple cutout sugar cookies

yield 4 dozen

1	**cup butter, softened**
1-1/2	**cups confectioners' sugar**
1	**egg**
1-1/2	**teaspoons vanilla extract**
2-1/4	**cups all-purpose flour**
1	**teaspoon baking soda**
1	**teaspoon cream of tartar**

FROSTING:

2	**cups confectioners' sugar**
1/4	**cup light corn syrup**
2	**tablespoons water**

Red and green food coloring

In a large bowl, cream the butter and sugar until light and fluffy. Beat in egg and vanilla. Combine flour, baking soda and cream of tartar. Add to creamed mixture and mix well. Cover and refrigerate dough for 2-3 hours or until easy to handle.

On a lightly floured surface, roll dough into 1/4-in. thickness. Cut with a floured apple-shaped cookie cutter.

Place 2 in. apart on greased baking sheets. Bake at 375° for 7-8 minutes or until lightly browned. Remove to wire racks to cool.

For frosting, combine sugar, corn syrup and water in a small bowl. Transfer three-fourths of the frosting into another bowl; add red food coloring for apples. Add green food coloring to remaining frosting for stems. Frost cookies. Allow to sit overnight for frosting to set.

Marlys Benning ✳
Wellsburg, Iowa
Not only are these pretty cookies fun to serve, but they bake up delicate and flaky and taste wonderful. Even the dough is a treat to work with— it's so easy to roll out and cut.

* Michelle Duncan, Callaway, Florida
When the military relocated our family, my children had never lived near the beach before. I came up with this special treat with a beach theme—it made our move more fun!

sand dollar cookies

yield 9 cookies

3/4	cup butter, softened
1/3	cup confectioners' sugar
4-1/2	teaspoons sugar
2	teaspoons almond extract
1-1/3	cups all-purpose flour
1/4	teaspoon salt
1	egg, lightly beaten

Slivered almonds and cinnamon-sugar

In a large bowl, cream butter and sugars until light and fluffy. Beat in extract. Combine the flour and salt; gradually add to creamed mixture and mix well. Cover and refrigerate for 1 hour or until easy to handle.

Roll dough between waxed paper to 1/8-in. thickness. Cut with a floured 3-1/2-in. round cookie cutter. Using a floured spatula, place 1 in. apart on ungreased baking sheets. Brush with egg. Decorate with almonds and sprinkle with cinnamon-sugar.

Bake at 325° for 12-16 minutes or until edges begin to brown. Cool for 2 minutes before removing to wire racks.

* Ilona Barron
Ontonagon, Michigan
When my sister was hosting an exchange student from Finland, she served these cookies I'd made to her guest. The young lady instantly recognized what they were. So I know they're still being made in our ancestors' country!

finnish pinwheels

yield about 7 dozen

FILLING:

1/2	pound pitted dried plums, chopped
1/2	pound pitted dates, chopped
1	cup boiling water
2	tablespoons sugar
1	tablespoon butter

PASTRY:

3	cups all-purpose flour
1	cup sugar
2	teaspoons baking powder
1/2	teaspoon salt
1	cup butter
1	egg, beaten
3	tablespoons cream
1	teaspoon vanilla extract

In a saucepan, combine plums, dates, water and sugar. Cook over low heat, stirring constantly, until thickened. Remove from the heat and stir in butter. Cool.

Meanwhile, in a large bowl, sift together flour, sugar, baking powder and salt. Cut in butter as for a pie pastry. Blend in egg, cream and vanilla. Form into two balls.

On a floured surface, roll one portion to 1/8-in. thickness. Cut into 2-in. squares. Place 2 in. apart on ungreased baking sheets. Make 1-in. slits in corners. Place 1/2 teaspoon filling in the center of each square. Bring every other corner up into center to form a pinwheel and press lightly. Repeat with remaining dough and filling. Bake at 325° for 12 minutes or until the points are light golden brown. Remove to wire racks to cool.

Shannon Wade, Kansas City, Kansas ✳

For a jungle or animal theme party, these striped cookies are a lot of fun. They are real eye-catchers. I started with a horse cookie cutter and got exotic!

zebra butter cookies

yield 1-1/2 dozen

- 1-1/4 **cups butter, softened**
- 1 **cup sugar**
- 2/3 **cup confectioners' sugar**
- 1 **egg**
- 1 **teaspoon vanilla extract**
- 3 **cups all-purpose flour**
- 1/4 **teaspoon salt**
- 1/4 **cup baking cocoa**

In a large bowl, cream butter and sugars until light and fluffy. Beat in egg and vanilla. Combine flour and salt; gradually add to the creamed mixture and mix well.

Divide the dough in half. Add the cocoa to one half and mix well. Roll each half between waxed paper into a 9-in. square. Cut both squares into three 3-in. strips. Cut the strips in half lengthwise to make six 4-1/2-in. x 3-in. rectangles.

Place one cream-colored rectangle on a large piece of plastic wrap; top with a chocolate rectangle. Repeat layers twice. Wrap in plastic wrap and refrigerate for 2 hours. Unwrap and cut widthwise into eighteen 1/4-in. slices.

Cut each slice with a horse-shaped cookie cutter dipped in flour. Place 1 in. apart on ungreased baking sheets. Bake at 375° for 8-10 minutes or until edges are lightly golden. Let stand for 2 minutes before removing to wire racks to cool.

Marilyn Wheeler, Ellijay, Georgia ✳

These are our favorite sugar cookies. They're one of the homemade treats I love to bake for friends and neighbors. Cut the dough for these crisp cookies into heart shapes or form into letters to spell out sweet nothings.

for-my-love sugar cookies

yield about 5-1/2 dozen

- 3/4 **cup shortening**
- 1-1/2 **cups sugar**
- 2 **eggs**
- 1 **teaspoon orange extract**
- 3 **cups self-rising flour**
- **Colored sugar, optional**

In a large bowl, cream shortening and sugar until light and fluffy. Beat in eggs and extract. Gradually add flour and mix well. Cover and refrigerate for 1 hour or until easy to handle.

On a floured surface, roll out dough to 1/4-in. thickness. Cut with lightly floured 2-in. cookie cutters. Sprinkle with colored sugar if desired.

Place 1 in. apart on ungreased baking sheets. Bake at 375° for 6-8 minutes or until lightly browned. Remove to wire racks to cool.

editor's note: As a substitute for each cup of self-rising flour, place 1-1/2 teaspoons baking powder and 1/2 teaspoon salt in a measuring cup. Add all-purpose flour to measure 1 cup.

※ Martha Conaway, Pataskala, Ohio

With a fresh breeze, my longtime-favorite sugar cookie recipe got under way on a new track. I cut out sailboats and frisky fish, frosting them brightly for the nautical gathering. My guests ate their limit!

smooth sailing sugar cookies

yield about 4 dozen

1	**cup butter, softened**
3/4	**cup sugar**
1	**egg**
2	**tablespoons milk**
1-1/2	**teaspoons vanilla extract**
3	**cups all-purpose flour**
1	**teaspoon baking powder**
1/2	**teaspoon salt**

FROSTING:

1	**cup confectioners' sugar**
1/2	**teaspoon vanilla *or* almond extract**
1/4	**teaspoon salt**
1	**to 2 tablespoons milk**

Food coloring, optional

In a large bowl, cream butter and sugar. Add egg, milk and vanilla. Combine flour, baking powder and salt; gradually add to creamed mixture. Cover and refrigerate for 1 hour or until easy to handle.

On a lightly floured surface, roll dough to 1/8-in. thickness. Cut with floured cookie cutters of your choice.

Place 2 in. apart on greased baking sheets. Bake at 375° for 5-8 minutes or until lightly browned. Remove to wire racks to cool.

In a large bowl, combine sugar, extract, salt and enough milk to achieve spreading consistency. Add food coloring if desired. Frost cookies; decorate as desired.

Mari Lynn Van Ginkle, Sandia Park, New Mexico

Here in New Mexico, these cookies are known as "bizcochitos," which means "small biscuit." There are many variations of the recipe, which has been passed down through the generations. The cookies are enjoyed on special celebrations.

anise butter cookies

yield 5 dozen

2	**cups butter, softened**
1-3/4	**cups sugar**, *divided*
2	**eggs**
1/4	**cup orange juice concentrate**
4	**teaspoons aniseed, crushed**
6	**cups all-purpose flour**
3	**teaspoons baking powder**
1/2	**teaspoon salt**
1	**teaspoon ground cinnamon**

In a large bowl, cream the butter and 1-1/2 cups sugar until light and fluffy. Add eggs, one at a time, beating well after each addition. Beat in the orange juice concentrate and aniseed. Combine the flour, baking powder and salt; gradually add to creamed mixture and mix well.

On a lightly floured surface, roll out dough to 1/4-in. thickness. Cut with a floured 2-1/2-in. round cookie cutter. Place 1 in. apart on ungreased baking sheets.

Combine the cinnamon and remaining sugar; sprinkle over cookies. Bake at 350° for 12-15 minutes or until golden brown. Remove to wire racks to cool.

creamy frosted butter cutouts

yield 5-1/2 dozen

1/2	**cup butter, softened**
1	**cup sugar**
1	**egg**
1/2	**cup sour cream**
1	**teaspoon vanilla extract**
3-1/2	**cups all-purpose flour**
1	**teaspoon baking soda**
1/2	**teaspoon salt**

FROSTING:

1/4	**cup cold milk**
3	**tablespoons instant vanilla pudding mix**
1/4	**cup butter, softened**
2-1/2	**cups confectioners' sugar**
1	**teaspoon vanilla extract**

Food coloring, optional

In a large bowl, cream butter and sugar. Beat in egg, sour cream and vanilla. Combine flour, baking soda and salt; gradually add to creamed mixture. Cover and refrigerate for 1 hour or until easy to handle.

On a work surface sprinkled heavily with confectioners' sugar, roll dough to 1/8-in. thickness. Cut with floured 2-1/2-in. cookie cutters.

Place 1 in. apart on greased baking sheets. Bake at 375° for 8-10 minutes or until lightly browned. Immediately remove to wire racks to cool.

For frosting, combine milk and pudding mix until smooth; set aside. In a small bowl, cream butter. Beat in pudding mixture. Gradually add confectioners' sugar, vanilla and food coloring if desired; beat on high speed until light and fluffy. Frost cookies.

Stephanie McKinnon
West Valley City, Utah
With their soft tender insides, these cookies quickly disappear from the cookie jar. Vanilla pudding mix gives the frosting a velvety texture and fabulous flavor.

✳ Elaine Anderson, New Galilee, Pennsylvania

This recipe for heart-shaped cookies is one of the tastiest I've tried. Folks always "ooh" and "aah" over the buttery flavor combined with chocolate. These make great Valentine's Day gifts wrapped up in cellophane and ribbon.

cherry shortbread hearts

yield about 1-1/2 dozen

1-1/4	cups all-purpose flour
3	tablespoons sugar
1/2	cup cold butter
1/2	cup maraschino cherries, patted dry and finely chopped
1	tablespoon cold water
1/4	teaspoon almond extract
1	cup (6 ounces) semisweet chocolate chips
1	tablespoon shortening

In a large bowl, combine flour and sugar; cut in butter until crumbly. Stir in the cherries, water and extract until dough forms a ball.

On a lightly floured surface, roll dough to 1/4-in. thickness. Cut with a floured 2-1/2-in. heart-shaped cookie cutter. Place 1 in. apart on ungreased baking sheets.

Bake at 325° for 20-25 minutes or until edges are lightly browned. Remove to wire racks to cool.

In a microwave, melt chocolate chips and shortening; stir until smooth. Dip half of each cookie into chocolate; allow excess to drip off. Place on waxed paper until set.

✳ Elizabeth Turner, Lula, Georgia

These simple cookies are so crisp and buttery, it's hard to eat just one. I make this small batch for special occasions, but they're welcome anytime.

old-fashioned cutout cookies

yield about 1-1/2 dozen

1/4	cup butter, softened
3/4	cup sugar
1	egg
1	teaspoon milk
1/2	teaspoon vanilla extract
1-1/2	cups self-rising flour

Additional sugar

In a small bowl, cream butter and sugar until light and fluffy. Beat in the egg, milk and vanilla. Add flour and mix well.

On a lightly floured surface, roll out dough to 1/8-in. thickness. Cut with floured 3-in. cookie cutters. Sprinkle with additional sugar.

Place 1 in. apart on greased baking sheets. Reroll scraps if desired. Bake at 375° for 7-8 minutes or until edges are lightly browned. Remove to wire racks to cool.

editor's note: As a substitute for 1-1/2 cups self-rising flour, place 2-1/4 teaspoons baking powder and 3/4 teaspoon salt in a measuring cup. Add all-purpose flour to measure 1 cup. Combine with an additional 1/2 cup all-purpose flour.

Carolyn Hayes, Marion, Illinois ✳

I first made these crescent-shaped cream cheese cookies—traditionally called "rugalach"—for my Jewish son-in-law. We all loved their wonderful texture. The diced pears rolled up inside are a delightful surprise.

pear crescent cookies

yield 4 dozen

- 1 **cup butter, softened**
- 1 **package (8 ounces) cream cheese, softened**
- 2 **cups all-purpose flour**
- 1/8 **teaspoon salt**
- 1/4 **cup packed brown sugar**
- 2 **teaspoons ground cinnamon**
- 1/2 **cup diced peeled pears**
- 1/2 **cup finely chopped walnuts**
- 3/4 **cup confectioners' sugar**
- 2 **tablespoons milk**

In a large bowl, cream the butter and cream cheese until light and fluffy. Combine flour and salt; gradually add to creamed mixture and mix well. Cover and refrigerate for 2 hours or until easy to handle. Combine brown sugar and cinnamon; set aside.

Divide the dough into fourths. On a floured surface; roll out each portion into a 12-in. circle. Cut into 12 wedges. Place about 1/4 teaspoon cinnamon-sugar at the wide end of each wedge. Top wedges with 1/2 teaspoon each pears and walnuts.

Roll up, beginning at wide end. Place pointed side down 2 in. apart on ungreased baking sheets; curve ends to form a crescent.

Bake at 375° for 16-19 minutes or until lightly browned. Immediately remove to wire racks. Combine confectioners' sugar and milk; drizzle over cooled cookies.

easter sugar cookies

yield 4 dozen

- 1 **cup butter, softened**
- 1 **package (3 ounces) cream cheese, softened**
- 1 **cup sugar**
- 1 **egg yolk**
- 1/2 **teaspoon vanilla extract**
- 1/4 **teaspoon almond extract**
- 2-1/4 **cups all-purpose flour**
- 1/2 **teaspoon salt**
- 1/4 **teaspoon baking soda**
- **Tinted frosting *or* colored sugar**

In a large bowl, cream butter, cream cheese and sugar. Beat in egg yolk and extracts. Combine the flour, salt and baking soda; gradually add to creamed mixture. Cover and refrigerate for 3 hours or until easy to handle.

On a lightly floured surface, roll out dough to 1/8-in. thickness. Cut with a floured 2-1/2-in. egg- or chick-shaped cookie cutter.

Place 1 in. apart on ungreased baking sheets. Bake at 375° for 8-10 minutes or until edges begin to brown. Cool for 2 minutes before removing to wire racks. Decorate as desired.

Julie Brunette ✳
Green Bay, Wisconsin
Cream cheese contributes to the rich taste of these melt-in-your-mouth cookies. They have such nice flavor, you can skip the frosting and sprinkle them with colored sugar for a change.

✳ Jerri Moror, Rio Rancho, New Mexico

Mother prepared these soft cookies for holidays and special-occasion meals. My seven siblings and I gobbled them up as fast as she made them. I still can't resist the cinnamon-sugar coating.

anise cutout cookies

yield about 5 dozen

2	cups shortening
1-1/2	cups sugar, *divided*
2	eggs
2	teaspoons aniseed
6	cups all-purpose flour
1	tablespoon baking powder
1	teaspoon salt
1/4	cup apple juice
1	teaspoon ground cinnamon

In a large bowl, cream shortening and sugar until light and fluffy. Beat in eggs and aniseed. Combine the flour, baking powder and salt; add to the creamed mixture. Add apple juice and mix well.

On a floured surface, knead until well blended, about 4-5 minutes. Roll dough to 1/2-in. thickness. Cut into 2-in. shapes.

Place 2 in. apart on greased baking sheets. Bake at 375° for 12-16 minutes or until lightly browned. Combine cinnamon and remaining sugar; roll cookies in the mixture while still warm. Cool on wire racks.

✳ Edna Hall
Aitkin, Minnesota

Fans of oatmeal cookies will love this variation that combines oats, chocolate and coconut. These star-shaped cookies "shine" wherever I take them!

chocolate oatmeal stars

yield about 3 dozen

2/3	cup shortening
1	cup sugar
1	egg
1	teaspoon vanilla extract
1/2	teaspoon almond extract
1	cup (6 ounces) semisweet chocolate chips, melted
1	cup all-purpose flour
1	teaspoon salt
1/2	teaspoon baking soda
1	cup quick-cooking oats
1	cup flaked coconut, finely chopped

Colored sugar *or* nonpareils

In a large bowl, cream shortening and sugar. Beat in egg and extracts. Stir in melted chocolate chips. Combine the flour, salt and baking soda; gradually add to the creamed mixture. Stir in oats and coconut. Cover and refrigerate for 2 hours or until easy to handle.

On a lightly floured surface, roll the dough to 1/8-in. thickness. Cut with a floured 3-in. star-shaped cookie cutter.

Place 1 in. apart on ungreased baking sheets. Sprinkle with colored sugar or nonpareils. Bake at 350° for 7-9 minutes or until firm. Remove to wire racks to cool.

The dough for these sweet treats can be mixed in a flash and is easy to roll and cut. Outlining each cookie with colored frosting highlights their fun shape.

little piggy sugar cookies

yield about 4 dozen

3/4	cup butter, softened
1	cup sugar
2	eggs
2	tablespoons milk
1/2	teaspoon almond extract
3-1/4	cups all-purpose flour
2	teaspoons baking powder

Tinted frosting

In a large bowl, cream the butter and sugar until light and fluffy. Beat in the eggs, milk and extract. Combine the flour and baking powder; gradually add to creamed mixture and mix well. Cover and refrigerate for 2-3 hours or until easy to handle.

On a lightly floured surface, roll out dough to 1/8-in. thickness. Cut out with a 3-in. pig-shaped cookie cutter dipped in flour. Place 1 in. apart on ungreased baking sheets.

Bake at 375° for 7-9 minutes or until edges begin to brown. Remove to wire racks to cool. Outline cutouts with tinted frosting.

cherry-filled cookies

yield about 3 dozen

1/2	cup shortening
1	cup packed brown sugar
1/2	cup sugar
2	eggs
1/4	cup buttermilk
1	teaspoon vanilla extract
3-1/2	cups all-purpose flour
1/2	teaspoon salt
1/2	teaspoon baking soda
1	can (21 ounces) cherry pie filling

In a large bowl, cream shortening and sugars. Add eggs, buttermilk and vanilla; mix well. Combine flour, salt and baking soda; gradually add to creamed mixture and mix well. Cover and refrigerate for 1 hour or until firm.

Divide dough in half. On a floured surface, roll each portion to 1/8-in. thickness. Cut with a floured 2-3/4-in. round cutter.

Place half of circles 2 in. apart on greased baking sheets; top each with a heaping teaspoon of pie filling. Cut holes in the center of remaining circles with a floured 1-in. round cutter; place over filled circles. Seal edges.

Bake at 375° for 10 minutes or until golden brown. Remove to wire racks to cool.

The luscious cherry filling peeking out of these rounds is just a hint of how scrumptious they are. Using a doughnut cutter to shape each cookie top really speeds up the cutting process.

BAKING

tip

cutting out cutouts — After the dough is rolled out, position the shapes from the cookie cutters as close together as possible to avoid having too many scraps. Save all the scraps and chill them in the refrigerator. Reroll all of the scraps just once since overhandling will cause the cookies to be tough.

❋ Debbie Hurlbert, Howard, Ohio
My husband's grandmother always had these cookies for him when he visited. Today, he enjoys them more than ever—and so I do.

frosted spice cookies

yield 5-6 dozen

1	cup butter, softened
1	cup sugar
1	cup molasses
1	egg
1	cup buttermilk
6	cups all-purpose flour
1	tablespoon baking powder
1	teaspoon baking soda
1	teaspoon ground cinnamon
1	teaspoon ground ginger
1/2	teaspoon salt
1	cup chopped walnuts
1	cup golden raisins
1	cup chopped dates

FROSTING:

3-3/4	cups confectioners' sugar
1/3	cup orange juice
2	tablespoons butter, melted

In a large bowl, cream butter and sugar until light and fluffy. Add molasses, egg and buttermilk; mix well. Combine the flour, baking powder, baking soda, cinnamon, ginger and salt; gradually add to creamed mixture. Stir in walnuts, raisins and dates. Cover and refrigerate for 2 hours until easy to handle.

On a floured surface, roll dough to 1/4-in. thickness. Cut with a floured 2-1/2-in.-round cookie cutter.

Place 2 in. apart on greased baking sheets. Bake at 350° for 12-15 minutes. Remove to wire racks to cool.

For frosting, beat all ingredients in a small bowl until smooth. Frost cookies.

crisp sugar cookies

yield about 4 dozen

❋ Josiah Hildenbrand
San Leandro, California

It takes just a handful of ingredients to stir up a batch of these crunchy cookies. Lemon extract lends a mild taste twist while colored sugar gives them their pretty look.

3/4	cup shortening
1	cup sugar
2	eggs
1/2	teaspoon lemon extract
2-1/2	cups all-purpose flour
1	teaspoon baking powder
1	teaspoon salt

Colored sugar

In a large bowl, cream shortening and sugar until light and fluffy. Beat in eggs and lemon extract. Combine the flour, baking powder and salt; gradually add to creamed mixture and mix well. Cover and refrigerate for at least 2 hours or until easy to handle.

On a floured surface, roll dough to 1/8-in. thickness. Cut with 2-1/2-in. cookie cutters. Place on greased baking sheets. Sprinkle with colored sugar.

Bake at 400° for 7-9 minutes or until lightly browned. Remove to wire racks to cool.

Sue Gronholz, Columbus, Wisconsin

The idea to hang Easter egg-shaped cookies from a tree came from hanging gingerbread cookies on a Christmas tree. Use the tree as a decoration, then at the end of the meal, serve the cookies for dessert.

decorated easter cookies

yield 7-8 dozen (2-1/2-inch cookies)

1	**cup butter, softened**
1	**cup sugar**
2	**eggs**
1/4	**cup cold water**
1	**teaspoon vanilla extract**
3-1/4	**cups all-purpose flour**
1	**teaspoon baking soda**
1/2	**teaspoon salt**

GLAZE:

2	**cups confectioners' sugar**
1/4	**cup water**
2	**tablespoons light corn syrup**

Food coloring

Decorator's gel

In a large bowl, cream butter and sugar. Add eggs, water and vanilla. Combine flour, baking soda and salt; gradually add to creamed mixture. Cover and refrigerate for several hours.

On a lightly floured surface, roll dough to 1/4-inch thickness. Cut with a floured egg-shaped cookie cutter (or cutters with other Easter themes such as chicks and rabbits). Make a hole with a plastic straw or toothpick in the top of at least 27 cookies.

Place cookies 2 in. apart on greased baking sheets. Bake at 350° for 8-10 minutes or until light golden brown. Remove to wire racks to cool completely.

For glaze, combine confectioners' sugar, water and corn syrup until smooth. Depending on how many colors are desired, divide glaze into several small bowls and tint with food coloring. Using a small brush and stirring glaze often, brush glaze on cookies (or leave some plain if desired). Allow glazed cookies to set for at least 1 hour.

Add designs with tinted glaze or decorator's gel, referring to photo above for ideas. Allow to set.

 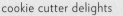

✳ Sharon Kotsovos, Coos Bay, Oregon

These sugar cookies are so yummy! They're even more popular when I decorate them to look like cute little ladybugs.

ladybug cookies

yield about 5 dozen

1	**cup butter, softened**
1	**cup canola oil**
1	**cup sugar**
1	**cup confectioners' sugar**
4	**eggs**
1	**teaspoon vanilla extract**
4-3/4	**cups all-purpose flour**
1	**teaspoon cream of tartar**
1	**teaspoon baking soda**

Red and black liquid food coloring

1	**cup (6 ounces) semisweet chocolate chips**
1/2	**cup vanilla chips or white chips**
1	**cup miniature semisweet chocolate chips**

In a large bowl, beat butter, oil and sugars until blended. Add two eggs, one at a time, beating well after each addition. Beat in vanilla. Combine the flour, cream of tartar and baking soda; gradu-ally add to creamed mixture and mix well. Cover and refrigerate for 2 hours or until easy to handle.

On a floured surface, roll out dough to 1/4-in. thickness. Cut with a floured 3-in. round cookie cutter. Place 1 in. apart on lightly greased baking sheets.

In a small bowl, beat remaining eggs. Add red food coloring; mix well. Brush over cutouts.

Bake at 375° for 8 minutes. With a small new paintbrush and black food coloring, paint two lines, forming wings.

Arrange four chocolate chips in a half circle on the top third of each cookie. Randomly place 16 chocolate chips on the lower part of the cookie for spots. Return to the oven for 1 minute or until chips are melted. Spread the four chips to form the head.

For eyes, position two white chips, pointed side down, over melted chocolate. Return to the oven for 1 minute or until slightly melted. Place one miniature chocolate chip in the center of each white chip. Remove to wire racks to cool completely.

Laurie Messer, Bonifay, Florida

To ring in a joyous occasion like a bridal shower or wedding, I'm often asked to make these festive cookies. You can use different flavors of jam to suit your tastes.

strawberry wedding bell cookies

yield about 5 dozen

1 **cup butter, softened**
1 **package (3 ounces) cream cheese, softened**
1/4 **cup sugar**
1 **teaspoon vanilla extract**
2 **cups all-purpose flour**
1/4 **teaspoon salt**
1/2 **cup strawberry jam**
Confectioners' sugar

In a large bowl, cream butter, cream cheese and sugar until light and fluffy. Beat in vanilla. Combine flour and salt; gradually add to the creamed mixture and mix well. Divide dough into fourths. Cover and refrigerate for 2 hours or until easy to handle.

On a lightly floured surface, roll out each piece of dough to 1/8-in. thickness. Cut with floured 2-in. round cookie cutters. Place 1 in. apart on ungreased baking sheets. Spoon 1/4 teaspoon jam in the center and spread to within 1/4 in. of edge of cookie.

Shape into a bell by folding edges of dough to meet over filling. Bake at 375° for 8-10 minutes or until lightly browned. Remove to wire racks to cool. Dust with confectioners' sugar.

cinnamon anise cookies

yield about 7 dozen

2 **cups shortening**
1 **cup plus 3 tablespoons sugar,** *divided*
2 **eggs**
1/2 **cup orange juice**
2 **teaspoons aniseed**
6 **cups all-purpose flour**
1 **tablespoon baking powder**
3/4 **teaspoon salt**
1/2 **teaspoon ground cinnamon**

In a large bowl, cream shortening and 1 cup sugar until light and fluffy. Beat in the eggs, orange juice and aniseed. Combine the flour, baking powder and salt; gradually add to creamed mixture and mix well.

Cover and refrigerate for 2 hours or until easy to handle. Combine cinnamon and remaining sugar; set aside.

On a lightly floured surface, roll the dough to 1/8-in. thickness. Cut with 2-1/2-in. cookie cutters dipped in flour. Place 1 in. apart on ungreased baking sheets. Sprinkle with cinnamon-sugar.

Bake at 375° for 8-10 minutes or until lightly browned. Remove to wire racks to cool.

Viola Ward
Fruita, Colorado
This recipe makes a big batch of Southwestern cookies that have a hint of anise and a sprinkling of cinnamon-sugar.

❉ Lisa Rupple, Keenesburg, Colorado
A gingerbread boy cookie cutter makes it a breeze to create these cute Halloween treats. Put the sweet skeletons out for your next ghost and goblin party and watch them disappear.

chocolate skeleton cookies

yield 3 dozen

1	**cup butter, softened**
1	**cup sugar**
1/2	**cup packed brown sugar**
1	**egg**
1	**teaspoon vanilla extract**
2-3/4	**cups all-purpose flour**
1/2	**cup baking cocoa**
1	**teaspoon baking soda**
1-1/2	**cups confectioners' sugar**
2	**tablespoons milk**

In a large bowl, cream butter and sugars until light and fluffy. Beat in egg and vanilla. Combine the flour, cocoa and baking soda; gradually add to creamed mixture. Cover and refrigerate for 1-2 hours or until easy to handle.

On a lightly floured surface, roll dough to 1/8-in. thickness. Cut with a floured 3-in. gingerbread boy cookie cutter. Place on greased baking sheets.

Bake at 375° for 7-8 minutes or until set. Cool for 1 minute before removing from pans to wire racks to cool completely.

For icing, in a small bowl, combine the confectioners' sugar and milk until smooth. Cut a small hole in the corner of a resealable plastic bag; fill with the icing. Pipe skeleton bones on cookies.

cottage cheese cookies

yield 4 dozen

❉ Linda Hobbs
Albion, New York
These delicate, puffy turnover cookies are sparked with raspberry and almond—delightful with afternoon tea.

2	**cups sifted all-purpose flour**
1	**cup cold butter**
1	**cup plus 2 tablespoons small-curd cottage cheese**

Raspberry jam
GLAZE:

1	**cup confectioners' sugar**
1/8	**teaspoon almond extract**

Milk

Place flour in a large bowl; cut in butter until crumbly. Blend in cottage cheese until mixture forms a ball. Cover and chill for 1 hour.

On a floured surface, roll dough to 1/8-in. thickness. Cut with a floured 3-in. round cutter. Place a level 1/4 teaspoon of jam in center of each cookie. Moisten edges and fold in half; seal tightly with a fork.

Place 2 in. apart on lightly greased baking sheets; prick tops with fork. Bake at 400° for 15 minutes or until lightly browned. Remove to wire racks to cool.

For glaze, combine sugar, extract and enough milk to make a thin spreading consistency; drizzle on cooled cookies.

Pat Thompson, Sun Prairie, Wisconsin ✳
Creating these tom treats is just as much fun as gobbling them up!

handprint turkey cookies

yield about 3 dozen

1/4	cup shortening
1/4	cup butter, softened
1	cup sugar
1	egg
1	teaspoon vanilla extract
2-2/3	cups all-purpose flour
1	teaspoon baking powder
1/2	teaspoon baking soda
1/2	teaspoon salt
1/4	teaspoon ground nutmeg
1/2	cup sour cream

GLAZE:

5	cups confectioners' sugar
3	to 4 tablespoons water
2-1/4	teaspoons light corn syrup
3/4	teaspoon vanilla extract

Red, yellow, orange, green and brown gel
food coloring

In a large bowl, cream shortening, butter and sugar. Beat in the egg and vanilla. Combine dry ingredients, then add to the creamed mixture alternately with sour cream. Cover and chill for 2 hours or until easy to handle.

Use a hand-shaped cookie cutter or trace a child's hand onto a piece of cardboard with pencil and cut out for a pattern.

On a well-floured surface, roll out dough to a 1/2-in. thickness. Either use a sharp knife to cut around the cardboard hand pattern in dough or use cookie cutter to cut out hand shapes. Place 2 in. apart on ungreased baking sheets. Bake at 425° for 7-9 minutes or until lightly browned. Remove to wire racks to cool.

In a large bowl, combine the glaze ingredients and beat until smooth. Set aside 1 teaspoon of white glaze for eyes. Place 1/4 cup of glaze into each of four bowls. Tint one red, one yellow, one orange and one green. Place 1 tablespoon of glaze in another bowl and tint dark brown. Tint the remaining glaze light brown.

Frost the palm and thumb of each cookie light brown. Frost each finger a different color, using red, yellow, orange and green. Place remaining yellow glaze in a pastry or plastic bag. Cut a small hole in the corner of bag. Pipe a beak on each thumb.

In the same way, use dark brown glaze to pipe a pupil in each eye and to pipe wings on each cookie. Use remaining red glaze to pipe wattles on each thumb. Let stand until set.

✳ Virginia Kroon, Roanoke Rapids, North Carolina

These cute cookies are great for any fall gathering. Melted chocolate and ground pecans give them their perfect look.

acorn cookies

yield about 3 dozen

1	cup butter, softened
1	cup sugar
1	egg
1/2	cup milk
1	teaspoon almond extract
1	teaspoon vanilla extract
3-1/2	cups all-purpose flour
1	teaspoon baking powder
1/2	teaspoon salt
2	cups (12 ounces) semisweet chocolate chips
1	cup ground pecans

In a large bowl, cream butter and sugar until light and fluffy. Beat in the egg, milk and extracts. Combine the flour, baking powder and salt; gradually add to creamed mixture and mix well. Cover and refrigerate for 4 hours or until easy to handle.

Divide the dough in half. On a lightly floured surface, roll out each portion to 1/4-in. thickness. Cut with 2-1/2-in. acorn cookie cutter. Place 1 in. apart on ungreased baking sheets.

Bake at 375° for 8-10 minutes or until edges are firm. Remove to wire racks to cool.

In a microwave, melt chocolate chips; stir until smooth. Spread chocolate over the stem and cap of each acorn, leaving about a 1/4-in. border. Sprinkle pecans over chocolate. Pipe remaining chocolate in a crisscross pattern over each acorn. Let stand until firm.

✳ Marcy Cella, L'Anse, Michigan

Sharing sweets has long been the way to show affection. I use these hearts to show my love on Valentine's Day.

frosted valentine cookies

yield 3-1/2-dozen

2	cups butter, softened
1	cup confectioners' sugar
4	cups all-purpose flour
2	cups quick-cooking oats
2	teaspoons vanilla extract
1/2	teaspoon almond extract
1/2	teaspoon salt
1/2	pound semisweet *or* milk chocolate confectionery coating, melted

Pink confectioners' sugar icing, optional

In a large bowl, cream butter and sugar. Add flour, oats, extracts and salt; mix well.

On a lightly floured surface, roll the dough to 1/4-in thickness. Cut with a floured 3-in. heart-shaped cookie cutter.

Place 2 in. apart on ungreased baking sheets. Bake at 350° for 12-15 minutes. While cookies are warm, spread melted chocolate on tops. Cool on wire racks. Using a pastry bag, decorate with pink confectioners' sugar icing if desired.

What could be better than

one cookie? Two fabulous cookies with a marvelous filling in between them. Sandwich cookies are delightfully different and are easy to assemble, too...just spread the filling on the bottom of one cookie and top with another.

linzer cookies, p. 190

walnut sandwich cookies, p. 201

✳ Eudora Delezenne, Port Huron, Michigan

When I was growing up, my mother and I created special Christmas memories in the kitchen preparing these cute, bite-size cookies. Vary the food coloring for holidays throughout the year.

tiny tim sandwich cookies

yield 5 dozen

1	cup sugar, *divided*
2	to 3 drops red food coloring
2	to 3 drops green food coloring
1/2	cup butter, softened
1/2	cup shortening
1/4	cup confectioners' sugar
1	teaspoon almond extract
2-1/3	cups all-purpose flour

FROSTING:

2	cups confectioners' sugar
3	tablespoons butter, softened
4-1/2	teaspoons heavy whipping cream
3/4	teaspoon almond extract

Red and green food coloring

In a small bowl, combine 1/2 cup sugar and red food coloring; set aside. In another small bowl, combine remaining sugar with green food coloring; set aside.

In a large bowl, cream the butter, shortening and confectioners' sugar until light and fluffy. Beat in extract. Gradually add flour and mix well. Shape into 1/2-in. balls.

Place 1 in. apart on ungreased baking sheets. Coat bottom of two glasses with cooking spray, then dip one in red sugar and the other in green sugar. Flatten cookies alternately with prepared glasses, redipping in sugar as needed.

Bake at 375° for 8-10 minutes or until edges are lightly browned. Remove to wire racks to cool completely.

For frosting, in a small bowl, combine the confectioners' sugar, butter, cream and extract. Tint half of the frosting red and the other half green. Frost the bottoms of half of the cookies; top with remaining cookies.

Carole Vogel, Allison Park, Pennsylvania ✳

I've made these cookies for years and like to give them out to family and friends. Ground pecans in the dough and a homemade lemon filling give them their special taste.

lemon curd cookies

yield 1-1/2 dozen

1	**cup butter, softened**
3/4	**cup sugar**
1	**egg**
1	**teaspoon lemon extract**
1	**teaspoon vanilla extract**
2-1/2	**cups all-purpose flour**
1/2	**teaspoon baking soda**
1/2	**teaspoon salt**
1	**cup ground pecans, toasted**

FILLING:

1-1/2	**cups sugar**
2	**tablespoons cornstarch**
1/8	**teaspoon salt**
1/2	**cup lemon juice**
4	**egg yolks, lightly beaten**
6	**tablespoons butter, cubed**
2	**teaspoons grated lemon peel**

Confectioners' sugar

In a large bowl, cream butter and sugar until light and fluffy. Beat in egg and extracts. Combine the flour, baking soda and salt; gradually add to creamed mixture and mix well. Stir in pecans.

Divide dough in half; shape into logs. Wrap each in plastic wrap. Refrigerate for 1-2 hours or until firm.

On a floured surface, roll each portion to 1/8-in. thickness. Cut with a floured 3-in. fluted round cookie cutter. With a floured 1/2-in. round cookie cutter, cut out the centers of half of the cookies. (Reroll small cutouts if desired.)

Place solid and cutout cookies 1 in. apart on ungreased baking sheets. Bake at 350° for 10-12 minutes or until lightly browned. Remove to wire racks to cool.

In a small saucepan, combine the sugar, cornstarch and salt. Stir in lemon juice until smooth. Cook and stir until slightly thickened and bubbly, about 2 minutes. Stir a small amount into egg yolks. Return all to the pan; bring to a gentle boil; stirring constantly. Cook and stir 2 minutes longer until mixture reaches 160° and coats the back of a metal spoon.

Remove from the heat; stir in butter and lemon peel. Pour into a bowl; cover surface with plastic wrap. Chill for 2-3 hours (mixture will be thick).

Spread 1 tablespoon of the filling on the bottoms of the solid cookies; place the cookies with cutout centers over the filling, pressing down lightly. Sprinkle with confectioners' sugar. Store in the refrigerator.

BAKING
tip

removing cookies from a baking sheet — If cookies crumble when you remove them from a baking sheet, let them cool for 1 to 2 minutes first. However, if they cool too long, they can become hard and can break when lifted. If this happens, return the baking sheet to the oven to warm the cookies slightly so they'll release more easily.

※ Jane Pearcy, Verona, Wisconsin
This specialty cookie takes a little extra effort, but the delectable results are well worth it. I bake these tender, jam-filled hearts when I need something fancy to serve for Valentine's Day or other special occasions.

linzer cookies

yield 3 dozen

1-1/4	cups butter, softened
1	cup sugar
2	eggs
3	cups all-purpose flour
1	tablespoon baking cocoa
1/2	teaspoon salt
1/4	teaspoon ground cinnamon
1/4	teaspoon ground nutmeg
1/8	teaspoon ground cloves
2	cups ground almonds

Raspberry jam
Confectioners' sugar

In a large bowl, cream the butter and sugar until light and fluffy. Add eggs, one at a time. Combine flour, cocoa, salt, cinnamon, nutmeg and cloves; gradually add to the creamed mixture and mix well. Stir in almonds. Cover and chill for 1 hour or until easy to handle.

On a lightly floured surface, roll dough to 1/8-in. thickness. Cut with a floured 3-in. heart-shaped or 2-1/2-in. round cookie cutter. Cut a 1-1/2-in. heart or circle from the center of half the cookies.

Place 2 in. apart on ungreased baking sheets. Bake at 350° for 10-12 minutes or until edges are golden brown. Remove to wire racks to cool completely.

Spread 1/2 teaspoon jam over the bottom of the solid cookies; place cutout cookies over jam. Sprinkle with confectioners' sugar.

dipped sandwich cookies

yield 2 dozen

※ Jane Delahoyde
Poughkeepsie, New York
With a lemon filling and chocolate coating, these buttery sandwich cookies are often requested at my house—particularly for special occasions.

1	cup butter, softened
1/2	cup sugar
1	egg yolk
1	teaspoon vanilla extract
2	cups all-purpose flour

LEMON FILLING:

1/2	cup butter, softened
2	cups confectioners' sugar
2	tablespoons lemon juice

DIPPING CHOCOLATE:

4	squares (1 ounce *each*) semisweet chocolate
2	tablespoons butter
1/2	cup finely chopped nuts

In a large bowl, cream butter and sugar. Beat in egg yolk and vanilla. Gradually add the flour.

Shape into 1-in. balls. Place 2 in. apart on ungreased baking sheets. With a glass dipped in sugar, flatten into 2-in. circles. Bake at 350° for 10-12 minutes or until firm. Remove to wire racks to cool.

Combine filling ingredients. Spread on the bottom of half of the cookies; top with remaining cookies. Melt chocolate and butter; stir until smooth. Dip each cookie halfway in chocolate, then in nuts. Place on waxed paper until set.

Abby Metzger, Larchwood, Iowa *

Capture the taste of campfire s'mores in your kitchen! Graham cracker crumbs added to chocolate chip cookie dough bring out the flavor of the fireside favorite.

s'more sandwich cookies

yield about 2 dozen

3/4	cup butter, softened
1/2	cup sugar
1/2	cup packed brown sugar
1	egg
2	tablespoons milk
1	teaspoon vanilla extract
1-1/4	cups all-purpose flour
1-1/4	cups graham cracker crumbs (about 20 squares)
1/2	teaspoon baking soda
1/4	teaspoon salt
1/8	teaspoon ground cinnamon
2	cups (12 ounces) semisweet chocolate chips
24	to 28 large marshmallows

In a large bowl, cream butter and sugars. Beat in egg, milk and vanilla. Combine flour, graham cracker crumbs, baking soda, salt and cinnamon; gradually add to creamed mixture. Stir in chocolate chips.

Drop by tablespoonfuls 2 in. apart onto ungreased baking sheets. Bake at 375° for 8-10 minutes or until golden brown. Remove to wire racks to cool completely.

Place four cookies bottom side up on a microwave-safe plate; top each with a marshmallow. Microwave, uncovered, on high for 10-15 seconds or until marshmallows begin to puff (do not overcook). Top each with another cookie. Repeat.

editor's note: This recipe was tested with a 1,100-watt microwave.

easter sugar sandwich cookies

yield 1-1/2 dozen sandwich cookies and 1-1/2 dozen small cutouts

1/2	cup shortening
1	cup sugar
2	eggs
1	teaspoon lemon extract
2-1/2	cups all-purpose flour
1/2	teaspoon salt
1/4	teaspoon baking soda
1/3	cup raspberry filling
1/3	cup apricot filling

In a large bowl, cream shortening and sugar. Beat in eggs and extract. Combine the flour, salt and baking soda; gradually add to creamed mixture and mix well. Cover and chill for 1 hour or until easy to handle.

Divide dough in half. On a lightly floured surface, roll out one portion to 1/8-in. thickness. Cut with a floured 2-1/2-in. round cookie cutter. Repeat with remaining dough. Using a small floured bunny- or chick-shaped cookie cutter, cut out the center of half of the cookies.

Place cookies and cutouts 1 in. apart on ungreased baking sheets. Bake at 350° for 8-10 minutes or until edges are very lightly browned. Remove to wire racks to cool.

Spread bottoms of the solid cookies with filling; place cookies with cutout centers over filling. Serve with cutouts.

Taste of Home Test Kitchen *
Using both raspberry and apricot filling lends beautiful color and great taste to these fruit-filled sugar cookies. Prepare them throughout the year by using different cookie cutter shapes.

✳ Maria Costello, Monroe, North Carolina
Who can resist soft chocolate sandwich cookies filled with a layer of fluffy white frosting? My family can't!

old-fashioned whoopie pies
yield 2 dozen

1/2	cup baking cocoa
1/2	cup hot water
1/2	cup shortening
1-1/2	cups sugar
2	eggs
1	teaspoon vanilla extract
2-2/3	cups all-purpose flour
1	teaspoon baking powder
1	teaspoon baking soda
1/4	teaspoon salt
1/2	cup buttermilk

FILLING:

3	tablespoons all-purpose flour
Dash salt	
1	cup milk
3/4	cup shortening
1-1/2	cups confectioners' sugar
2	teaspoons vanilla extract

In a small bowl, combine cocoa and water; mix well. Cool for 5 minutes. In a large bowl, cream shortening and sugar. Add cocoa mixture, eggs and vanilla; mix well. Combine dry ingredients. Add to creamed mixture alternately with buttermilk; mix well.

Drop by rounded tablespoonfuls 2 in. apart onto greased baking sheets. Flatten slightly with a spoon. Bake at 350° for 10-12 minutes or until firm to the touch. Remove to wire racks to cool completely.

In a saucepan, combine the flour and salt. Gradually whisk in milk until smooth; cook and stir over medium-high heat until thick, 5-7 minutes. Remove from heat. Cover and chill until completely cool.

In a small bowl, cream shortening, sugar and vanilla. Add chilled milk mixture; beat for 7 minutes or until fluffy. Spread filling on half of the cookies; top with remaining cookies. Store in the refrigerator.

lacy oat sandwich wafers
yield about 3-1/2 dozen

✳ Ruth Lee
Troy, Ontario
These cookies appear on my table for various special occasions. I'm often asked for the recipe, so I'm sure to have a few copies on hand.

2/3	cup butter
2	cups quick-cooking oats
1	cup sugar
2/3	cup all-purpose flour
1/4	cup milk
1/4	cup corn syrup
2	cups semisweet chocolate, milk chocolate, vanilla *or* white chips, melted

Line a baking sheet with parchment paper or foil; set aside. In a saucepan, melt butter over low heat. Remove from the heat. Stir in the oats, sugar, flour, milk and corn syrup; mix well.

Drop by teaspoonfuls 2 in. apart onto the prepared baking sheets. Bake at 375° for 8-10 minutes or until golden brown. Cool completely; peel cookies off paper or foil. Spread melted chocolate on the bottom of half of the cookies; top with remaining cookies.

Ingeborg Keith, Newark, Delaware ✳

From the first time I baked these cookies, they've been a delicious, lip-smacking success. Old-fashioned and attractive, they make the perfect holiday pastry.

fruit-filled spritz cookies

yield about 7-1/2 dozen

1-1/2	cups chopped dates
1	cup water
1/2	cup sugar
2	teaspoons orange juice
2	teaspoons grated orange peel
1	cup maraschino cherries, chopped
1/2	cup flaked coconut
1/2	cup ground nuts

DOUGH:

1	cup butter, softened
1	cup sugar
1/2	cup packed brown sugar
3	eggs
1/2	teaspoon almond extract
1/2	teaspoon vanilla extract
4	cups all-purpose flour
1/2	teaspoon baking soda
1/2	teaspoon salt

Confectioners' sugar

In a saucepan, combine the first five ingredients; bring to a boil, stirring constantly. Reduce heat; cook and stir for 8 minutes or until thickened. Cool completely. Stir in the cherries, coconut and nuts; set aside.

In a large bowl, cream butter and sugars until light and fluffy. Beat in eggs and extracts. Combine the flour, baking soda and salt; gradually add to creamed mixture.

Using a cookie press fitted with a bar disk, press a 12-in.-long strip of dough onto an ungreased baking sheet. Spread fruit filling over dough. Press another strip over filling. Cut into 1-in. pieces (there is no need to separate the pieces). Repeat with remaining dough and filling.

Bake at 375° for 12-15 minutes or until edges are golden. Recut into pieces if necessary. Remove to wire racks to cool. Dust with confectioners' sugar.

✳ Barbara Sessoyeff, Redwood Valley, California
These yummy Strawberry Sandwich Cookies are made with a nutty, tender cookie, and make a terrific indulgence.

strawberry sandwich cookies

yield 1-1/2 dozen

1	cup blanched almonds
3/4	cup butter, softened
1	cup confectioners' sugar, *divided*
1	egg
1/2	teaspoon almond extract
1-1/2	cups all-purpose flour
1/8	teaspoon salt
1	tablespoon lemon juice
3	tablespoons strawberry jam

In a food processor or blender, process almonds until ground; set aside. In a large bowl, cream butter and 1/2 cup sugar. Beat in egg and extract. Combine flour and salt; gradually add to creamed mixture. Stir in the ground almonds. Divide dough in half; cover and refrigerate for 2 hours or until easy to handle.

On a lightly floured surface, roll out each portion of the dough into a 12-in. x 9-in. rectangle. Cut lengthwise into three strips; cut each strip widthwise into six pieces. With a floured 3/4-in.-round cookie cutter, cut out a circle in the center of half of the pieces (discard circles).

Place 1 in. apart on ungreased baking sheets. Bake at 375° for 8-10 minutes or until golden brown. Remove to wire racks to cool.

For glaze, combine lemon juice and remaining sugar; thinly spread over whole cookies. Top with cutout cookies; fill center with 1/2 teaspoon jam.

chocolate mint cookies

✳ Christina Burbage
Spartanburg, South Carolina
My dad sandwiches mint patties between two chocolate cookies to create these chewy treats. Best of all, these cookies are easy and fun to make.

yield 32 sandwich cookies

1-1/4	cups butter, softened
2	cups sugar
2	eggs
2	teaspoons vanilla extract
2	cups all-purpose flour
3/4	cup baking cocoa
1	teaspoon baking soda
1/2	teaspoon salt
32	round thin chocolate-covered mint patties

In a large bowl, cream the butter and sugar. Add the eggs, one at a time, beating well after each addition. Beat in vanilla. Combine the flour, cocoa, baking soda and salt; gradually add to the creamed mixture, beating until mixture is well combined.

Drop by tablespoonfuls 2 in. apart onto ungreased baking sheets. Bake at 350° for 8-9 minutes or until puffy and tops are cracked. Invert half of the cookies onto wire racks. Immediately place a mint patty on each, then top with remaining cookies. Press lightly to seal. Cool.

These dazzling sandwich cookies are sure to be the star of your holiday dessert tray. A rich mixture of white chocolate and cream cheese forms the sweet yet simple filling.

star sandwich cookies

yield about 1 dozen

1/2	**tube refrigerated sugar cookie dough, softened**
1/3	**cup all-purpose flour**

Red sugars, nonpareils *or* sprinkles

1	**square (1 ounce) white baking chocolate**
2	**tablespoons cream cheese, softened**
1	**tablespoon butter, softened**
4	**drops red food coloring**
1/2	**cup confectioners' sugar**

In a small bowl, beat cookie dough and flour until combined. Roll out on a lightly floured surface to 1/8-in. thickness. Cut with a floured 2-3/4-in. star cookie cutter. Place 2 in. apart on ungreased baking sheets.

Decorate half of the cookies with sugars and nonpareils. Bake at 350° for 7-9 minutes or until edges are golden brown. Remove to wire racks to cool.

In a microwave, melt white chocolate; stir until smooth. Cool. In a small bowl, beat the cream cheese, butter and food coloring until fluffy. Gradually beat in confectioners' sugar and melted chocolate until smooth. Spread over the bottoms of plain cookies; top with decorated cookies. Store in the refrigerator.

sweet sandwich cookies

yield about 1-1/2 dozen

1	**cup butter, softened**
3/4	**cup packed brown sugar**
1	**egg yolk**
2	**cups all-purpose flour**
1/4	**teaspoon salt**

BROWNED BUTTER FILLING:

2	**tablespoons butter**
1-1/4	**cups confectioners' sugar**
1/2	**teaspoon vanilla extract**
4	**to 5 teaspoons milk**

In a large bowl, cream butter and brown sugar until light and fluffy. Beat in egg yolk. Combine flour and salt; gradually add to creamed mixture and mix well. Cover and refrigerate for 20 minutes.

Shape into 1-in. balls. Place 1-1/2 in. apart on ungreased baking sheets. Flatten with a fork, forming a crisscross pattern.

Bake at 325° for 8-10 minutes or until golden brown. Remove to wire racks to cool.

For filling, heat butter in a saucepan over medium heat until golden brown. Remove from the heat; stir in confectioners' sugar, vanilla and enough milk to achieve spreading consistency. Spread on the bottoms of half of the cookies; top with remaining cookies.

Pat Schar ✳
Zelienople, Pennsylvania
This caramel cookie is a past winner of our family's holiday bake-off. The tender brown sugar cookie and the rich browned butter frosting produce a yummy flavor combination. They are sweet and so special.

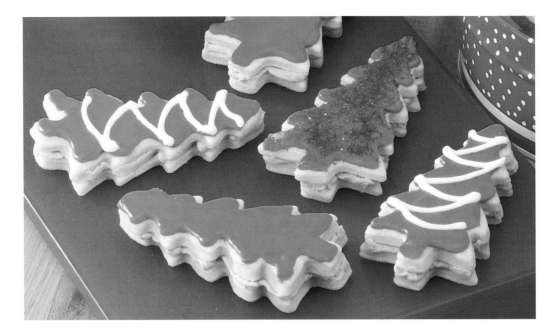

✳ Evelyn Moll, Tulsa, Oklahoma
A fluffy vanilla filling makes these cookies a big holiday favorite at our house. My family also likes their rich shortbread flavor.

evergreen sandwich cookies

yield about 2 dozen

1	**cup butter, softened**
2	**cups all-purpose flour**
1/3	**cup milk**
1/4	**teaspoon salt**

FILLING:

1/4	**cup shortening**
1/4	**cup butter, softened**
2	**cups confectioners' sugar**
4-1/2	**teaspoons milk**
1/2	**teaspoon vanilla extract**

Green paste food coloring

GLAZE:

1-1/3	**cups confectioners' sugar**
4	**teaspoons milk**

Green paste food coloring

Green colored sugar

In a large bowl, combine the butter, flour, milk and salt. Cover and refrigerate for 1-1/2 hours or until easy to handle.

Divide dough into thirds. On a floured surface, roll out each portion to 1/8-in. thickness. Cut with a floured 3-3/4-in. Christmas tree cookie cutter. Place on ungreased baking sheets. Prick each with a fork several times. Bake at 375° for 8-11 minutes or until set. Remove to wire racks.

For filling, in a small bowl, cream the shortening, butter and confectioners' sugar until light and fluffy. Beat in milk and vanilla until smooth. Tint with food coloring. Spread about one table-spoon of filling on the bottoms of half of the cookies; top with remaining cookies.

For glaze, combine confectioners' sugar and milk until smooth; set aside 1/4 cup. Stir food coloring into remaining glaze; spread a thin layer over cooled cookies. If desired, sprinkle tops of half of the cookies with colored sugar. Pipe garland onto half of the cookies with reserved glaze. Let stand until set.

Teresa Gaetzke, North Freedom, Wisconsin ✳
Store-bought ice cream treats can't hold a candle to homemade ones. This frozen dessert is fantastic.

peanut butter ice cream sandwiches

yield 16 servings

1/2	**cup shortening**
1/2	**cup creamy peanut butter**
3/4	**cup sugar,** *divided*
1/2	**cup packed brown sugar**
1	**egg**
1/2	**teaspoon vanilla extract**
1-1/2	**cups all-purpose flour**
1	**teaspoon baking soda**
1/2	**teaspoon salt**
12	**ounces dark chocolate candy coating, chopped**
1	**quart vanilla ice cream, softened**

In a large bowl, cream the shortening, peanut butter, 1/2 cup sugar and brown sugar until light and fluffy. Beat in egg and vanilla. Combine the flour, baking soda and salt; gradually add to creamed mixture and mix well.

Roll into 1-in. balls; roll in remaining sugar. Place 1 in. apart on ungreased baking sheets. Flatten with a fork, forming a crisscross pattern.

Bake at 350° for 9-11 minutes or until set (do not overbake). Remove to wire racks to cool completely.

In a microwave, melt candy coating; stir until smooth. Spread a heaping teaspoonful on the bottom of each cookie; place chocolate side up on waxed paper until set.

To make sandwiches, place 1/4 cup ice cream on the bottom of half of the cookies; top with remaining cookies. Wrap in plastic wrap; freeze.

berry-almond sandwich cookies

yield 3 dozen

1-1/2	**cups butter, softened**
1	**cup sugar**
1	**teaspoon vanilla extract**
2-3/4	**cups all-purpose flour**
1/2	**teaspoon salt**
2	**cups ground almonds**
3/4	**cup raspberry filling**

Edible glitter *or* **confectioners' sugar**

In a large bowl, cream butter and sugar until light and fluffy. Beat in vanilla. Combine the flour and salt; gradually add to creamed mixture and mix well. Stir in almonds.

On a heavily floured surface, roll out dough to 1/8-in. thickness. With floured 2-1/2-in. cookie cutters, cut into desired shapes.

Place 1 in. apart on ungreased baking sheets. Bake at 325° for 10-12 minutes or until edges begin to brown. Remove to wire racks to cool.

Spread 1 teaspoon raspberry filling on the bottoms of half of the cookies; top with remaining cookies. Sprinkle with edible glitter or confectioners' sugar.

editor's note: Edible glitter is available from Wilton Industries. Call 1-800/794-5866 or visit *www.wilton.com.*

Helga Schlape ✳
Florham Park, New Jersey
Almond shortbread cookies
cradle a delightful berry filling
for this Christmas cookie
favorite. They're unbeatable!

✳ Debbie Rode, Oxbow, Saskatchewan
Of all the cookies I've baked over the years, these have remained one of my all-time favorite. The dough is very easy to work with, and the result is eye-catching.

date-filled sandwich cookies

yield 3 dozen

1	cup butter, softened
2	cups packed brown sugar
2	eggs
2	teaspoons vanilla extract
3-1/2	cups all-purpose flour
1	teaspoon baking powder
1	teaspoon baking soda

FILLING:

2	cups chopped dates
3/4	cup sugar
3/4	cup water

In a large bowl, cream butter and brown sugar until light and fluffy. Add eggs, one at a time, beating well after each addition. Beat in vanilla.

Combine the flour, baking powder and baking soda; gradually add to creamed mixture and mix well. Refrigerate for 1 hour or until dough is easy to handle.

On a lightly floured surface, roll out dough to 1/8-in. thickness. Cut with a floured 2-1/2-in. cookie cutter. Place 1 in. apart on greased baking sheets. Bake at 350° for 10-12 minutes or until edges are lightly browned. Remove to wire racks to cool.

In a small saucepan, combine filling ingredients. Cook over medium heat for 3 minutes or until thickened and bubbly. Cool to room temperature. Spread on the bottoms of half of the cookies; top with remaining cookies.

oatmeal sandwich cookies

✳ Jan Woodall
Cadiz, Kentucky
These fun treats put a sweet fluffy filling between two chewy oatmeal cookies. They're perfect for snacking or for packing in lunch boxes.

yield about 4-1/2 dozen

1-1/2	cups shortening
2-2/3	cups packed brown sugar
4	eggs
2	teaspoons vanilla extract
2-1/4	cups all-purpose flour
2	teaspoons ground cinnamon
1-1/2	teaspoons baking soda
1	teaspoon salt
1/2	teaspoon ground nutmeg
4	cups old-fashioned oats

FILLING:

3/4	cup shortening
3	cups confectioners' sugar
1	jar (7 ounces) marshmallow creme
1	to 3 tablespoons milk

In a large bowl, cream shortening and brown sugar until light and fluffy. Add eggs, one at a time, beating well after each addition. Beat in the vanilla. Combine the flour, cinnamon, baking soda, salt and nutmeg; add to creamed mixture. Stir in oats.

Drop by rounded teaspoonfuls 2 in. apart onto lightly greased baking sheets. Bake at 350° for 10-12 minutes or until golden brown. Remove to wire racks to cool.

For filling, in a large bowl, beat the first three ingredients until blended. Add enough milk to achieve spreading consistency. Spread filling on the bottom of half of the cookies; top with remaining cookies.

Marilyn Blankschien, Clintonville, Wisconsin ✳
I like to use a cookie disk with an open center so the creamy mint filling peeks through. A chocolate drizzle on top is a flavorful finishing touch.

filled chocolate spritz

yield about 2 dozen

3/4	**cup semisweet chocolate chips**
1/4	**cup butter, cubed**
1/2	**cup packed brown sugar**
2	**eggs, lightly beaten**
1	**teaspoon vanilla extract**
1-1/2	**cups all-purpose flour**
1/8	**teaspoon baking soda**

PEPPERMINT FILLING:

1/4	**cup butter, softened**
3/4	**cup confectioners' sugar**
1	**tablespoon milk**
1/2	**teaspoon peppermint extract**
3	**to 4 drops green food coloring**

GLAZE:

2/3	**cup milk chocolate chips**
1	**teaspoon shortening**

In a large microwave-safe bowl, melt chocolate chips; stir until smooth. Stir in the butter, brown sugar, eggs and vanilla. Add flour and baking soda and mix well. Cover and refrigerate for 30 minutes or until easy to handle.

Using a cookie press fitted with the disk of your choice, press dough 2 in. apart onto ungreased baking sheets. Bake at 375° for 6-8 minutes or until set. Remove to wire racks to cool.

In a small bowl, combine filling ingredients; stir until smooth. Spread on the bottoms of half of the cookies; top with the remaining cookies.

In a microwave, melt milk chocolate chips and shortening; stir until smooth. Drizzle over cookies. Let stand until set.

※ Cheryl Johnson, Upper Marlboro, Maryland
I first tried these fun crispy cookies at a family picnic when I was a child. Packed with oats, cornflakes and coconut, they quickly became a "regular" at our house. Years later, I still make them for my own family.

chocolaty double crunchers

yield 2 dozen

1/2	cup butter, softened
1/2	cup sugar
1/2	cup packed brown sugar
1	egg
1/2	teaspoon vanilla extract
1	cup all-purpose flour
1/2	teaspoon baking soda
1/4	teaspoon salt
1	cup quick-cooking oats
1	cup crushed cornflakes
1/2	cup flaked coconut

FILLING:

2	packages (3 ounces *each*) cream cheese, softened
1-1/2	cups confectioners' sugar
2	cups (12 ounces) semisweet chocolate chips, melted

In a large bowl, cream butter and sugars. Beat in egg and vanilla. Combine flour, baking soda and salt; add to creamed mixture and mix well. Add oats, cornflakes and coconut.

Roll into 1-in. balls. Place 2 in. apart on greased baking sheets. Flatten with a glass dipped lightly in flour. Bake at 350° for 8-10 minutes or until lightly browned. Remove to wire racks to cool.

For filling, beat cream cheese and sugar until smooth. Add chocolate; mix well. Spread about 1 tablespoon on half of the cookies and top each with another cookie. Store in refrigerator.

※ Carol Steiner
Arrowwood, Alberta
A light lemon filling spread between flaky butter cookies makes these a perfect accompaniment to hot tea or coffee. They also make a delicious dessert.

lemon-cream sandwich cookies

yield 2 dozen

3/4	cup butter, softened
1/2	cup confectioners' sugar
2	teaspoons lemon extract
1-1/2	cups all-purpose flour
1/4	cup cornstarch

LEMON FILLING:

1/4	cup butter, softened
1-1/2	cups confectioners' sugar
2	tablespoons lemon juice
2	teaspoons grated lemon peel

In a large bowl, cream butter and sugar. Beat in extract. Combine flour and cornstarch; beat into creamed mixture. Divide into two balls; wrap in plastic wrap and chill for 1 hour.

On a lightly floured surface, roll out each portion of dough to 1/8-in. thickness. Cut out with a floured 2-in.-round cookie cutter.

Place 2 in. apart on ungreased baking sheets. Bake at 350° for 10-12 minutes or until edges are lightly browned. Remove to wire racks to cool completely.

For filling, in a bowl, cream butter and sugar. Beat in lemon juice and peel. Spread over the bottoms of half of the cookies; top with remaining cookies.

editor's note: This recipe does not use eggs.

Shirley Barker, Normal, Illinois ✳
These cookies are really easy to prepare. I've made this recipe many times over the years, and the cookies are always a hit.
The orange flavor is a refreshing change from typical fillings.

walnut sandwich cookies

yield 2 dozen

3/4	cup butter, softened
1	cup sugar
1	tablespoon water
1-1/2	cups all-purpose flour
1/2	teaspoon salt
3/4	cup ground walnuts

FILLING:

1	package (3 ounces) cream cheese, softened
1	tablespoon butter, softened
1-1/2	cups confectioners' sugar
1/2	teaspoon grated orange peel

In a large bowl, cream butter and sugar until light and fluffy. Beat in water. Combine the flour and salt; gradually add to creamed mixture and mix well. Stir in walnuts. Roll into 1-in. balls.

Place 1 in. apart on ungreased baking sheets. Coat bottom of a glass with cooking spray, then dip in sugar. Flatten cookies with prepared glass, redipping in sugar as needed.

Bake at 350° for 12-15 minutes or until edges are lightly browned. Cool for 2 minutes. Remove to wire racks; cool completely.

For filling, in a small bowl, beat cream cheese and butter until fluffy. Gradually add confectioners' sugar and orange peel; beat until smooth. Spread over the bottoms of half of the cookies; top with remaining cookies. Store in the refrigerator.

chocolate mint whoopie pies

yield 1-1/2 dozen

1/2	cup sugar
3	tablespoons canola oil
1	egg
1	cup all-purpose flour
1/4	cup baking cocoa
1/2	teaspoon baking soda
1/4	teaspoon salt
4	tablespoons fat-free milk, *divided*
2	tablespoons butter, softened
1-1/3	cups confectioners' sugar
1/8	teaspoon mint extract
4	drops green food coloring, optional

In a large bowl, beat sugar and oil until crumbly. Add egg; beat for 1 minute. Combine the flour, cocoa, baking soda and salt. Gradually beat into sugar mixture. Add 2 tablespoons milk and mix well. Roll dough into 36 balls.

Place 2 in. apart on baking sheets coated with cooking spray. Coat bottom of a glass with cooking spray, then dip in sugar. Flatten cookies with prepared glass, redipping in sugar as needed.

Bake at 425° for 5-6 minutes or until edges are set and tops are cracked. Cool for 2 minutes before removing to wire racks to cool.

In a small bowl, combine butter and confectioners' sugar until crumbly. Beat in extract, food coloring if desired and remaining milk. Spread on the bottoms of half of the cookies; top with remaining cookies.

Taste of Home Test Kitchen ✳
These cute sandwich cookies would be a pretty addition to any holiday goodie tray. The combination of chocolate and mint is simply irresistible.

✳ Phyllis Dietz, Westland, Michigan
These little sandwich cookies taste rich and buttery and have a lemon filling. The recipe has been in our family since the 1950s, when my mother got it from a French friend. Mom always made them at Christmas, and now my sister and I do.

lemon tea cookies

yield about 4-1/2 dozen

3/4	cup butter, softened
1/2	cup sugar
1	egg yolk
1/2	teaspoon vanilla extract
2	cups all-purpose flour
1/4	cup finely chopped walnuts

FILLING:

3	tablespoons butter, softened
4-1/2	teaspoons lemon juice
3/4	teaspoon grated orange peel
1-1/2	cups confectioners' sugar
2	drops yellow food coloring, optional

In a large bowl, cream butter and sugar until light and fluffy. Beat in the egg yolk and vanilla. Gradually add flour and mix well.

Shape into two 14-in. rolls; reshape each roll into a 14-in. x 1-1/8-in. x 1-1/8-in. block. Wrap each in plastic wrap. Refrigerate overnight.

Unwrap and cut into 1/4-in. slices. Place 2 in. apart on ungreased baking sheets. Sprinkle half of the cookies with nuts, gently pressing into dough.

Bake at 400° for 8-10 minutes or until golden brown around the edges. Remove to wire racks to cool.

In a small bowl, cream the butter, lemon juice and orange peel until fluffy. Gradually add confectioners' sugar until smooth. Tint yellow if desired. Spread about 1 teaspoon on bottoms of the plain cookies; place nut-topped cookies over filling.

cutout pumpkin sandwich cookies

yield 2 dozen

✳ Schelby Thompson
Winter Haven, Florida
Apricot preserves peek out of these buttery, tender sugar cookies. Make them throughout the year with a variety of fanciful cookie cutter shapes.

1	cup butter, softened
1-1/4	cups sugar, *divided*
2	eggs, *separated*
2-1/2	cups all-purpose flour
1/4	teaspoon salt

Confectioners' sugar

1/2	cup ground almonds
3/4	cup apricot preserves

In a large bowl, cream butter and 3/4 cup sugar until light and fluffy. Add egg yolks, one at a time, beating well after each addition. Combine flour and salt; gradually add to creamed mixture and mix well. Shape dough into a ball; chill for 1 hour or until firm.

On a surface dusted with confectioners' sugar, roll dough to 1/8-in. thickness; cut with a 3-in. pumpkin-shaped cookie cutter. Cut a 1-1/2-in. pumpkin from the center of half the cookies and remove (set aside small pumpkin cutouts to bake separately).

Place on greased baking sheets. Beat egg whites until frothy. Combine almonds and remaining sugar. Brush each cookie with egg whites; sprinkle with almond mixture. Bake at 350° for 6-8 minutes or until lightly browned. Remove immediately to wire racks to cool completely.

Spread 1-1/2 teaspoons of apricot preserves on the bottoms of the solid cookies; place cookies with cutout centers, almond side up, over filling.

Gaylene Anderson, Sandy, Utah ✳
These chocolaty cookies with a cool peppermint filling are simply delicious.

chocolate-mint creme cookies

yield 4 dozen

1-1/2	cups packed brown sugar
3/4	cup butter, cubed
2	tablespoons water
2	cups (12 ounces) semisweet chocolate chips
2	eggs
3	cups all-purpose flour
1-1/4	teaspoons baking soda
1	teaspoon salt

FILLING:

1/3	cup butter, softened
3	cups confectioners' sugar
3	to 4 tablespoons milk
1/8	teaspoon peppermint extract

Dash salt

In a small saucepan, combine the brown sugar, butter and water. Cook and stir over medium heat until sugar is dissolved. Remove from the heat; stir in the chocolate chips until melted and smooth. Transfer to a large bowl; cool slightly.

Add eggs, one at a time, beating well after each addition. Combine flour, baking soda and salt; gradually add to chocolate mixture and mix well.

Drop by rounded teaspoonfuls onto greased baking sheets. Bake at 350° for 8-10 minutes or until set. Remove to wire racks; flatten slightly. Cool completely.

Combine filling ingredients; spread on the bottoms of half of the cookies; top with remaining cookies. Store in the refrigerator.

✻ Audrey Groe, Lake Mills, Iowa

These crisp, flaky cookies are a wonderful way to show you care. The compliments you'll receive make them worth the effort.

cherry-filled heart cookies

yield about 4-1/2 dozen

1/2	**cup butter, softened**
1/2	**cup shortening**
1	**cup sugar**
1	**egg**
1/2	**cup milk**
1	**teaspoon vanilla extract**
3-1/2	**cups all-purpose flour**
2	**teaspoons baking powder**
1	**teaspoon baking soda**
1/2	**teaspoon salt**

FILLING:

1/2	**cup sugar**
4-1/2	**teaspoons cornstarch**
1/2	**cup orange juice**
1/4	**cup red maraschino cherry juice**
12	**red maraschino cherries, chopped**
1	**tablespoon butter**

Additional sugar

In a large bowl, cream the butter and shortening; gradually add sugar. Add the egg, milk and vanilla. Combine dry ingredients; gradually add to creamed mixture and mix well. Cover and chill for at least 2 hours.

Meanwhile, for filling, combine sugar and cornstarch in small saucepan. Add juices, cherries and butter. Bring to a boil; boil and stir for 1 minute. Chill.

On a lightly floured surface, roll dough to 1/8-in. thickness. Cut with a floured 2-1/2-in. heart-shaped cookie cutter.

Place half of the cookies 2 in. apart on greased baking sheets; spoon 1/2 teaspoon filling in the center of each. Use a 1-1/2-in. heart-shaped cutter to cut small hearts out of the other half of the cookies. (Bake small heart cutouts separately.) Place the remaining hearts over filled cookies; press edges together gently. Fill centers with additional filling if needed. Sprinkle with sugar.

Bake at 375° for 8-10 minutes or until lightly browned. Remove to wire racks to cool.

Celena Cantrell-Richardson, Eau Claire, Michigan *

These yummy cookies are an eye-catcher at any Halloween party. Or make them for a canine-themed birthday party for your favorite dog lover.

boneyard cookies

yield about 2-1/2 dozen

1	cup confectioners' sugar
1/2	cup cornstarch
1/2	cup cold butter
2	eggs
1	teaspoon almond extract
2	cups all-purpose flour
1/8	teaspoon salt
2	to 3 tablespoons seedless raspberry jam
16	to 18 squares (1 ounce *each*) white baking chocolate

In a small bowl, combine sugar and cornstarch. Cut in butter until mixture resembles coarse crumbs. Add eggs, one at a time, beating well after each addition. Beat in extract. Combine flour and salt; gradually add to sugar mixture and mix well. Shape dough into a ball; flatten into a disk. Wrap in plastic wrap; refrigerate for 30 minutes or until easy to handle.

On a lightly floured surface, roll dough to 1/8-in. thickness. Cut with a floured 3-1/2-in. bone-shaped cookie cutter. Place 1 in. apart on parchment paper-lined baking sheets. Bake at 350° for 8-10 minutes or until edges begin to brown. Remove to wire racks to cool.

On the bottoms of half the cookies, spread 1/8 to 1/4 teaspoon jam down the center; top with remaining cookies.

In a microwave, melt white chocolate at 70% power for 1 minute; stir. Heat at 10- to 20-second intervals, stirring until smooth.

Dip each cookie in chocolate, allowing excess to drip off. Place on waxed paper; let stand until set.

Julie Wellington, Youngstown, Ohio *

My husband loves peppermint patties, and our son is crazy for vanilla wafers. So I put the two together to make a fun cookie that looks just like a burger. Kids of all ages get a kick out of them.

hamburger cookies

yield 20 cookies

1/2	cup vanilla frosting
	Red and yellow paste *or* gel food coloring
40	vanilla wafers
20	peppermint patties
1	teaspoon corn syrup
1	teaspoon sesame seeds

Place 1/4 cup frosting in each of two small bowls. Tint one red and the other yellow. Frost the bottoms of 20 vanilla wafers yellow; top with a peppermint patty. Spread with red frosting. Brush tops of the remaining vanilla wafers with corn syrup; sprinkle with sesame seeds. Place over red frosting.

unbeatable brownies

peanut butter brownie bars, p. 228

Whether you crave moist,

fudgy brownies or comforting cake-like brownies...

classic chocolate treats or new taste twists...simple

frosted bars or elaborately decorated ones, you'll

discover the perfect brownie here!

raspberry truffle brownies, p. 214

marble brownies, p. 217

✳ Barbara Birk, St. George, Utah

I used candy sprinkles to dress up my tried-and-true Favorite Frosted Brownies for Valentine's Day. No matter what the occasion, everyone always agrees that they are so yummy!

favorite frosted brownies

yield 12-15 servings

1	**cup butter, softened**
2	**cups sugar**
4	**eggs**
2	**teaspoons vanilla extract**
1-3/4	**cups all-purpose flour**
6	**tablespoons baking cocoa**
1	**teaspoon baking powder**
1/4	**teaspoon salt**

FROSTING:

1/2	**cup butter, softened**
1/4	**cup evaporated milk**
1	**teaspoon vanilla extract**
2	**tablespoons baking cocoa**
3	**cups confectioners' sugar**

Decorating sprinkles, optional

In a large bowl, cream butter and sugar. Add eggs, one at a time, beating well after each addition. Beat in vanilla. Combine the flour, cocoa, baking powder and salt; gradually add to creamed mixture and mix well.

Spread into a greased 13-in. x 9-in. baking pan. Bake at 350° for 25-30 minutes or until a toothpick inserted near the center comes out clean. Cool in pan on a wire rack.

For frosting, in a large bowl, beat the butter, milk and vanilla; add cocoa. Gradually beat in confectioners' sugar until smooth. Spread over cooled brownies. Decorate with sprinkles if desired. Cut into bars.

Karla Johnson, Tyler, Minnesota

The kids I baby-sit for love these moist chewy bars. There's plenty of peanut butter flavor plus a yummy chocolate frosting and a sprinkling of peanut butter chips.

peanut butter blondies

yield 2 dozen

3/4	cup creamy peanut butter
2/3	cup butter, softened
1	cup packed brown sugar
1/2	cup sugar
2	eggs
1	teaspoon vanilla extract
1-3/4	cups all-purpose flour
1	teaspoon baking powder
1/3	cup milk
1	cup peanut butter chips

FROSTING:

1/4	cup butter, softened
1/4	cup baking cocoa
2	tablespoons milk
1	tablespoon light corn syrup
1	teaspoon vanilla extract
1-1/2	cups confectioners' sugar
1/3	cup peanut butter chips

In a large bowl, cream the peanut butter, butter and sugars until light and fluffy. Beat in eggs and vanilla. Combine the flour and baking powder; add to creamed mixture alternately with milk, beating well after each addition. Stir in chips.

Spread into a greased 13-in. x 9-in. baking pan. Bake at 325° for 35-40 minutes or until a toothpick inserted near the center comes out clean (do not overbake). Cool on a wire rack.

For frosting, in a small bowl, combine the butter, cocoa, milk, corn syrup and vanilla. Gradually add confectioners' sugar; beat until smooth. Frost brownies. Sprinkle with chips. Cut into bars.

praline brownies

yield 16 brownies

1/2	cup packed dark brown sugar
3/4	cup butter, *divided*
2	tablespoons evaporated milk
1/2	cup coarsely chopped pecans
2	cups packed light brown sugar
2	eggs
1-1/2	cups all-purpose flour
1	teaspoon vanilla extract
1/2	teaspoon salt

In a saucepan, combine the dark brown sugar, 1/4 cup butter and milk. Stir over low heat just until butter is melted. Pour into an ungreased 8-in. square baking pan; sprinkle evenly with the pecans.

In a small bowl, cream light brown sugar and remaining butter; add eggs. Stir in flour, vanilla and salt until moistened. Spread over pecans.

Bake at 350° for 40-45 minutes or until brownies test done. Cool for 5 minutes before inverting on to a tray or serving plate. Cool slightly before cutting.

Mindy Weiser
Southport, North Carolina
I created these brownies as a tribute to that luscious candy, which is so popular in the Deep South.

※ Marianne Wolfe, Westlock, Alberta
This treat is in a book of good-but-easy recipes my sister compiled as a wedding present for me. She refers to them as "money-back-guaranteed" brownies.

treasured brownies

yield 1-1/2 dozen

1	cup butter, melted and cooled
3	eggs
1-1/2	teaspoons vanilla extract
1	cup all-purpose flour
1	cup sugar
1	cup packed brown sugar
3/4	cup baking cocoa
1-1/2	teaspoons baking powder
1	cup chopped nuts

ICING:

1/2	cup butter, softened
1-1/4	cups confectioners' sugar
2/3	cup baking cocoa
2	tablespoons milk
2	tablespoons hot brewed coffee
1	teaspoon vanilla extract

In a large bowl, combine the butter, eggs and vanilla. Combine the dry ingredients; gradually add to the butter mixture. Stir in the nuts (do not overmix).

Spread into a greased 13-in. x 9-in. baking pan. Bake at 350° for 25-30 minutes or until a toothpick inserted near the center comes out clean. Cool in pan on a wire rack.

Combine icing ingredients in a small bowl; beat until smooth. Spread over the cooled brownies. Cut into bars.

※ Diane Truver
Valencia, Pennsylvania
We have lots of great cooks in our clan, so adding to our collection of family recipes is a tradition. I came up with these moist, nut-covered brownies while doing my Christmas baking. Now everyone requests them.

fudgy walnut brownies

yield 1-1/2 dozen

3/4	cup butter
4	squares (1 ounce *each*) unsweetened chocolate
4	eggs
2	cups sugar
1	teaspoon vanilla extract
1	cup all-purpose flour

WALNUT CRUNCH TOPPING:

3/4	cup packed brown sugar
1/4	cup butter, cubed
2	eggs, lightly beaten
2	tablespoons all-purpose flour
1	teaspoon vanilla extract
4	cups chopped walnuts

In a microwave, melt butter and chocolate; stir until smooth. Cool slightly. In a bowl, beat eggs and sugar; stir in the vanilla and chocolate mixture. Stir in flour until well blended. Pour into a greased 13-in. x 9-in. baking pan; set aside.

For topping, in a saucepan, combine brown sugar and butter. Cook and stir over low heat until butter is melted. Stir in the eggs, flour and vanilla until well blended. Stir in nuts. Spread evenly over brownie batter.

Bake at 350° for 40-45 minutes or until a toothpick inserted near the center comes out with moist crumbs (do not overbake). Cool in pan on a wire rack. Cut into bars.

Elinor Townsend, North Grafton, Massachusetts ✳

I have to give my husband credit for this idea. Since we love chocolate and orange together, he suggested I come up with this recipe. Now they're not only his favorite, but also the whole family's.

double chocolate orange brownies

yield 2 dozen

3/4	**cup butter, cubed**
4	**squares (1 ounce** *each***) unsweetened chocolate**
3	**eggs**
2	**cups sugar**
1	**teaspoon orange extract**
1	**cup all-purpose flour**
1	**cup (6 ounces) semisweet chocolate chips**

Confectioners' sugar

In a microwave-safe bowl, melt butter and chocolate; stir until smooth. Cool slightly. In a large bowl, beat eggs and sugar. Stir in chocolate mixture. Beat in extract. Gradually add flour to chocolate mixture.

Pour into a greased 13-in. x 9-in. baking dish. Sprinkle with chocolate chips. Bake at 350° for 30-35 minutes or until a toothpick inserted near the center comes out clean.

Cool completely on a wire rack. Cut into squares. Just before serving, sprinkle with confectioners' sugar.

Darla Wester, Meriden, Iowa ✳

Our kids beg for this cute pumpkin brownie every year. To easily make the eye-catching treat, bake brownie batter in a pizza pan, spread with orange-tinted frosting and let the kids design a pumpkin stem and jack-o'-lantern face using candy.

great pumpkin brownie

yield 16-20 servings

1	**package fudge brownie mix (13-inch x 9-inch pan size)**
1	**can (16 ounces) vanilla frosting**

Orange paste food coloring

16	**green milk chocolate M&M's**
22	**yellow milk chocolate M&M's**
13	**orange milk chocolate M&M's**
8	**dark brown milk chocolate M&M's**
20	**pieces candy corn**

Prepare brownie batter according to package directions for fudge-like brownies. Spread on a greased 12-in. pizza pan to within 1 in. of edges.

Bake at 350° for 20-25 minutes or until a toothpick inserted near the center comes out clean. Cool on a wire rack.

Tint frosting orange; frost entire top of brownie. For stem, arrange green M&M's in a square pattern at top of pumpkin. For each eye, arrange 11 yellow M&M's in a triangle. For nose, arrange orange M&M's in a triangle. For mouth, place brown M&M's in a horizontal line; surround with candy corn, tips pointing out. Cut into squares to serve.

❋ Lori Risdal, Sioux City, Iowa

I wanted something special to take to a church potluck, so I invented these layered brownies topped with a mint-flavored mousse and bittersweet chocolate icing. They are great for St. Patrick's Day as well.

irish mint brownies

yield 2-1/2 dozen

1	cup butter, cubed
4	squares (1 ounce *each*) bittersweet chocolate, chopped
4	eggs
2	cups sugar
2	teaspoons vanilla extract
1-1/2	cups all-purpose flour
1	cup (6 ounces) double dark chocolate chips *or* semisweet chocolate chips
1/2	cup chopped walnuts

FILLING:

4	squares (1 ounce *each*) white baking chocolate, chopped
1/4	cup refrigerated Irish creme nondairy creamer
1	cup heavy whipping cream
15	mint Andes candies, chopped

ICING:

12	squares (1 ounce *each*) bittersweet chocolate, chopped
1	cup heavy whipping cream
2	tablespoons butter

Mint Andes candies, halved, optional

In a microwave, melt butter and bittersweet chocolate; stir until smooth. Cool slightly. In a large bowl, beat the eggs, sugar and vanilla. Stir in chocolate mixture. Gradually add flour until blended. Stir in chips and walnuts.

Spread into a greased 13-in. x 9-in. baking pan. Bake at 350° for 30-35 minutes or until a toothpick inserted near the center comes out clean (do not overbake). Cool on a wire rack.

In a microwave, melt white chocolate and creamer at 70% power for 1 minute; stir. Microwave at additional 10- to 20-second intervals, stirring until smooth. Transfer to a small bowl. Refrigerate for 30-40 minutes or until chilled.

In another small bowl, beat cream until soft peaks form; fold into white chocolate mixture. Beat on medium speed until stiff peaks form, about 4 minutes. Fold in chopped candies. Spread over brownies. Cover and refrigerate.

In a small saucepan, combine bittersweet chocolate and cream. Cook and stir over low heat until chocolate is melted and smooth; remove from the heat. Stir in butter until melted. Cool to room temperature. Carefully spread over filling. Cover and refrigerate for 1 hour or until icing is set. Cut into bars. Garnish with additional candies if desired. Store in the refrigerator.

BAKING

tip

keeping brownies — Cool brownies completely before storing. Most brownies can be stored in an airtight container at room temperature. For brownies baked in a square pan, simply slide the entire pan into a resealable plastic bag. Brownies that contain a pudding layer, cream cheese or other perishable ingredients should be stored in the refrigerator.

Diane Bridge, Clymer, Pennsylvania ✳

Looking for an ooey-gooey brownie that's delicious and different? This sweet recipe combines a shortbread-like crust and a brown sugar meringue with chocolate, coconut and nuts. These never last long!

meringue coconut brownies

yield 3 to 3-1/2 dozen

3/4	cup butter, softened
1-1/2	cups packed brown sugar, *divided*
1/2	cup sugar
3	eggs, *separated*
1	teaspoon vanilla extract
2	cups all-purpose flour
1	teaspoon baking powder
1/4	teaspoon baking soda
1/4	teaspoon salt
2	cups (12 ounces) semisweet chocolate chips
1	cup flaked coconut
3/4	cup chopped walnuts

In a large bowl, cream the butter, 1/2 cup brown sugar and sugar. Add egg yolks and vanilla. Beat on medium speed for 2 minutes. Combine the flour, baking powder, baking soda and salt; add to creamed mixture and mix well (batter will be thick). Spread into a greased 13-in. x 9-in. baking pan. Sprinkle with the chocolate chips, coconut and walnuts.

In another large bowl, beat the egg whites on medium speed until soft peaks form. Gradually beat in remaining brown sugar, 1 tablespoon at a time, beating on high until stiff peaks form. Spread over the top.

Bake at 350° for 30-35 minutes or until a toothpick inserted near the center comes out clean. Cool in pan on a wire rack. Cut into bars. Store in the refrigerator.

zucchini brownies

yield about 1-1/2 dozen

1	cup butter, softened
1-1/2	cups sugar
2	eggs
1/2	cup plain yogurt
1	teaspoon vanilla extract
2-1/2	cups all-purpose flour
1/4	cup baking cocoa
1	teaspoon baking soda
1/2	teaspoon salt
2	cups shredded zucchini
FROSTING:	
2/3	cup semisweet chocolate chips
1/2	cup creamy peanut butter

Allyson Wilkins ✳
Amherst, New Hampshire
A fast-to-fix peanut butter and chocolate frosting tops these moist brownies that are a sweet way to use up your green garden squash. We really like their cake-like texture.

In a large bowl, cream butter and sugar until light and fluffy. Add eggs, one at a time, beating well after each addition. Beat in yogurt and vanilla. Combine the flour, cocoa, baking soda and salt; gradually add to creamed mixture. Stir in zucchini.

Pour into a greased 13-in. x 9-in. baking pan. Bake at 350° for 35-40 minutes or until a toothpick inserted near the center comes out clean.

For frosting, in a small saucepan, combine chocolate chips and peanut butter. Cook and stir over low heat until smooth. Spread over warm brownies. Cool on a wire rack. Cut into bars.

✳ Agnes Ward, Stratford, Ontario
This is such a sophisticated dessert! Each rich, fudge-like brownie is bursting with fresh, plump red raspberries and topped with a dreamy, bittersweet ganache. It's true perfection for chocolate lovers of all ages!

raspberry truffle brownies

yield 1 dozen

6	squares (1 ounce *each*) bittersweet chocolate, chopped
1/2	cup butter, cubed
2	eggs
1	cup sugar
1	teaspoon vanilla extract
1	cup all-purpose flour
1/4	teaspoon baking soda
1/4	teaspoon salt
1	cup fresh raspberries

FROSTING:

6	squares (1 ounce *each*) bittersweet chocolate, chopped
3/4	cup heavy whipping cream
2	tablespoons seedless raspberry jam
1	teaspoon vanilla extract
12	fresh raspberries

In a microwave, melt chocolate and butter; stir until smooth. In a bowl, beat eggs, sugar and vanilla. Stir in chocolate mixture. Combine flour, baking soda and salt; gradually add to chocolate mixture. Gently fold in raspberries.

Spread into a greased 9-in. square baking pan. Bake at 350° for 25-30 minutes or until a toothpick inserted near the center comes out clean (do not overbake). Cool on a wire rack.

For frosting, in a microwave-safe bowl, combine the chocolate, cream and jam. Microwave at 50% power for 2-3 minutes or until smooth, stirring twice. Transfer to a small bowl; stir in vanilla. Place in a bowl of ice water; stir for 3-5 minutes. Beat on medium speed until soft peaks form.

Cut a small hole in a corner of a heavy-duty resealable plastic bag; insert #825 star tip. Fill with 1/2 cup frosting. Spread remaining frosting over brownies. Cut into 12 bars. Pipe a chocolate rosette in the center of each brownie; top with a raspberry. Cover and refrigerate for 30 minutes or until frosting is set. Refrigerate leftovers.

editor's note: This recipe was tested in a 1,100-watt microwave.

blonde brownie nut squares

yield 16 squares

✳ Edie Farm
Farmington, New Mexico
These moist bars get a small but satisfying crunch from pecans. They are a tasty change from traditional chocolate brownies.

1/4	cup butter, melted
1	cup packed brown sugar
1	egg
1	teaspoon vanilla extract
3/4	cup all-purpose flour
1	teaspoon baking powder
1/4	teaspoon salt
1/2	cup finely chopped pecans

In a mixing bowl, beat the butter, sugar, egg and vanilla. Combine the flour, baking powder and salt; gradually add to sugar mixture and mix well. Fold in nuts.

Spread in a greased 8-in. baking dish. Bake at 350° for 15-20 minutes or until a toothpick comes out clean. Cool in pan on a wire rack. Cut into squares.

Marjorie Hoyt, Center Conway, New Hampshire
I don't know where I got this recipe, but I've had it for over 30 years—it's written on an old yellowed piece of paper. Adding chocolate chips was my idea. When my children were in school, I found out they were selling these brownies to their friends!

simply fudgy brownies
yield 16 brownies

1/2	cup canola oil
1/4	cup baking cocoa
1	cup sugar
2	eggs
1	teaspoon vanilla extract
3/4	cup all-purpose flour
1/8	teaspoon salt
1/2	cup chopped walnuts
1/2	cup milk chocolate chips

In a small bowl, combine oil and cocoa until smooth; set aside. In a large bowl, beat sugar and eggs. Stir in vanilla and cocoa mixture. Combine flour and salt; gradually add to chocolate mixture just until moistened. Stir in the walnuts.

Pour into a greased 8-in. square baking pan; sprinkle with chocolate chips. Bake at 325° for 30 minutes or until a toothpick inserted near the center comes out clean. Cool completely on a wire rack.

dark chocolate butterscotch brownies
yield about 5 dozen

4	squares (1 ounce *each*) unsweetened chocolate
3/4	cup butter, cubed
2	cups sugar
3	egg whites
1-1/2	teaspoons vanilla extract
1	cup all-purpose flour
1	cup 60% cocoa bittersweet chocolate baking chips
1	cup butterscotch chips

GLAZE:

1	cup 60% cocoa bittersweet chocolate baking chips
1/4	cup butter, cubed

In a microwave, melt unsweetened chocolate and butter; stir until smooth. Cool slightly. In a large bowl, combine sugar and chocolate mixture. Stir in the egg whites and vanilla. Gradually add flour to chocolate mixture. Stir in chips.

Spread into a greased 13-in. x 9-in. baking pan. Bake at 350° for 25-30 minutes or until a toothpick inserted near the center comes out clean. Cool on a wire rack.

For glaze, in a microwave, melt chips and butter; stir until smooth. Immediately spread over brownies. Cool before cutting.

Kit Concilus
Meadville, Pennsylvania
My daughters and I love homemade brownies. We experimented with many recipes and finally came up with this family favorite. The rich, satiny frosting and the butterscotch chips are irresistible.

✳ Gloria Stange, Claresholm, Alberta

When our two grown children were at home, I baked these brownies often. These days, I make them for big occasions—everyone thinks that they're quite nice. As a bonus, they're a good way to use up leftover sour cream.

swiss chocolate brownies

yield about 3 dozen

1	cup water
1/2	cup butter
1-1/2	squares (1-1/2 ounces) unsweetened chocolate
2	cups all-purpose flour
2	cups sugar
1	teaspoon baking soda
1/2	teaspoon salt
2	eggs, lightly beaten
1/2	cup sour cream
1/2	teaspoon vanilla extract
1	cup chopped walnuts

ICING:

1/2	cup butter
1-1/2	squares (1-1/2 ounces) unsweetened chocolate
3	cups confectioners' sugar, *divided*
5	tablespoons milk
1	teaspoon vanilla extract

In a saucepan, bring water, butter and chocolate to a boil. Boil for 1 minute. Remove from the heat; cool. In a large bowl, combine flour, sugar, baking soda and salt. Add chocolate mixture and mix. Add eggs, sour cream and vanilla; mix. Fold in walnuts.

Pour into a greased 15-in. x 10-in. x 1-in. baking pan. Bake at 350° for 20-25 minutes or until brownies test done. Cool for 10 minutes.

For icing, melt butter and chocolate. Place in a large bowl; beat in 1-1/2 cups confectioners' sugar. Add milk, vanilla and remaining sugar; beat until smooth. Spread over the warm brownies. Cool completely. Cut into bars.

blond toffee brownies

✳ Mary Williams
Lancaster, California

Whenever my co-worker brought these to company bake sales, they sold in minutes. After getting the recipe from her, I was happy to discover how fast they could be thrown together.

yield 1-1/2 dozen

1/2	cup butter, softened
1	cup sugar
1/2	cup packed brown sugar
2	eggs
1	teaspoon vanilla extract
1-1/2	cups all-purpose flour
2	teaspoons baking powder
1/4	teaspoon salt
1	cup English toffee bits *or* almond brickle bits

In a large bowl, cream butter and sugars. Add eggs, one at a time, beating well after each addition. Beat in vanilla. Combine the flour, baking powder and salt; gradually add to creamed mixture. Stir in toffee bits.

Spread evenly into a greased 13-in. x 9-in. baking pan. Bake at 350° for 35-40 minutes or until a toothpick inserted near the center comes out clean. Cool in pan on a wire rack. Cut into bars.

Diana Coppernoll, Linden, North Carolina ✳

I like to bake and enjoy trying new recipes. The cream cheese topping in these delights quickly made them a favorite in my house.

marble brownies

yield 1 dozen

5	tablespoons butter
2	squares (1 ounce *each*) unsweetened chocolate
2/3	cup sugar
2	eggs
1	teaspoon vanilla extract
2/3	cup all-purpose flour
1/2	teaspoon baking powder

CHEESECAKE LAYER:

1	package (8 ounces) cream cheese
1/2	cup sugar
1	egg
1	teaspoon vanilla extract
1	cup (6 ounces) semisweet chocolate chips

In a large microwave-safe bowl, combine butter and chocolate. Cover and microwave on high for 30-60 seconds; stir until smooth. Beat in sugar, eggs and vanilla. Combine flour and baking powder; gradually add to chocolate mixture until blended. Spread into a greased microwave-safe 8-in. square dish; set aside.

In a large microwave-safe bowl, microwave cream cheese on high for 30-45 seconds or until softened; stir until smooth. Beat in sugar, egg and vanilla. Spoon over brownie batter; cut through batter with a knife to swirl. Sprinkle with chocolate chips.

Microwave, uncovered, at 70% power for 8-10 minutes or until a toothpick comes out clean. Cook on high for 1 minute longer. Remove to a wire rack to cool. Store in the refrigerator.

editor's note: This recipe was tested in a 1,100-watt microwave.

graham cracker brownies

yield 1-1/2 dozen

Cathy Guffey ✳
Towanda, Pennsylvania

I enjoy making these brownies for last-minute bake sales and family gathering alike. My grandmother first baked them nearly 50 years ago, and they're as popular today as they were then!

2	cups graham cracker crumbs (about 32 squares)
1	cup (6 ounces) semisweet chocolate chips
1	teaspoon baking powder
Dash salt	
1	can (14 ounces) sweetened condensed milk

In a large bowl, combine all ingredients. Spread into a greased 8-in. square baking dish.

Bake at 350° for 30-35 minutes or until a toothpick inserted near the center comes out clean. Cool on a wire rack.

✳ Patsy Burgin, Lebanon, Indiana

My husband and I have two sons and I sent these brownies to them regularly when they were in college. They used to hide a few from their roommates just so they could make sure there would be some left!

chocolate peanut butter brownies

yield about 5 dozen

2	squares (1 ounce *each*) unsweetened chocolate
1/2	cup butter
2	eggs
1	cup sugar
1/2	cup all-purpose flour

FILLING:

1-1/2	cups confectioners' sugar
1/2	cup creamy peanut butter
1/4	cup butter, softened
2	to 3 tablespoons half-and-half cream *or* milk

GLAZE:

1	square (1 ounce) semisweet baking chocolate
1	tablespoon butter

In a small saucepan, melt chocolate and butter over low heat; set aside. In a large bowl, beat eggs and sugar until light and pale colored. Add flour and melted chocolate; stir well.

Pour into a greased 9-in. square baking pan. Bake at 350° for 25 minutes or until the brownies test done. Cool in pan on a wire rack.

For filling, beat confectioners' sugar, peanut butter and butter in a small bowl. Stir in cream until mixture achieves spreading consistency. Spread over cooled brownies; cover and refrigerate until firm.

For glaze, melt chocolate and butter in a saucepan, stirring until smooth. Drizzle over the filling. Chill before cutting. Store in the refrigerator.

editor's note: Reduced-fat or generic brands of peanut butter are not recommended for this recipe.

Edith Amburn, Mount Airy, North Carolina ✳

I grew up on a farm, and even at a young age, I liked to help my mother in the kitchen, especially when it came to making desserts. When we're planning to serve refreshments at one of our social meetings, I'm often asked to make these brownies.

double frosted brownies

yield 3 dozen

4	eggs
1	cup canola oil
1-1/2	cups sugar
1/2	cup packed brown sugar
1/4	cup water
2	teaspoons vanilla extract
1-1/2	cups all-purpose flour
1/2	cup baking cocoa
1	teaspoon salt
1/2	cup chopped walnuts

FROSTING:

1	can (16 ounces) vanilla frosting
1	tablespoon rum extract

GLAZE:

1	cup (6 ounces) semisweet chocolate chips
1	tablespoon canola oil

In a large bowl, beat the eggs, oil, sugars, water and vanilla. Combine the flour, cocoa, salt and walnuts; stir into egg mixture until blended.

Pour into a greased 15-in. x 10-in. x 1-in. baking pan. Bake at 350° for 20-25 minutes or until center is set. Cool on a wire rack. Combine frosting and extract; spread over brownies. Chill for 30 minutes.

In a microwave, melt chocolate chips and oil; stir until smooth. Drizzle over frosting. Let stand until set before cutting.

frosted fudge brownies

yield 2 dozen

1	cup plus 3 tablespoons butter
3/4	cup baking cocoa
4	eggs
2	cups sugar
1-1/2	cups all-purpose flour
1	teaspoon baking powder
1	teaspoon salt
1	teaspoon vanilla extract

FROSTING:

6	tablespoons butter, softened
2-2/3	cups confectioners' sugar
1/2	cup baking cocoa
1	teaspoon vanilla extract
1/4	to 1/3 cup milk

In a saucepan, melt butter. Remove from the heat. Stir in cocoa; cool. In a large bowl, beat eggs and sugar. Combine flour, baking powder and salt; gradually add to egg mixture. Stir in vanilla and the cooled chocolate mixture; mix well.

Spread into a greased 13-in. x 9-in. baking pan. Bake at 350° for 25-28 minutes or until a toothpick inserted near the center comes out clean (do not overbake). Cool in pan on a wire rack.

For frosting, in a large bowl, cream butter, confectioners' sugar, cocoa and vanilla. Add enough milk until the frosting achieves spreading consistency. Spread over brownies. Cut into bars.

Sue Soderlund ✳
Elgin, Illinois

A neighbor brought over a pan of these rich brownies along with the recipe when I came home from the hospital with our baby daughter years ago. I've made them ever since.

✳ Janet Farley, Snellville, Georgia
A mix of tasty, good-for-you ingredients makes these chewy blond brownies impossible to pass up. The granola adds crunch while dried fruit lends pleasing sweetness. I serve them to just about anybody who walks in our front door.

granola blondies

yield 1 dozen

1	egg
1	egg white
1-1/4	cups packed brown sugar
1/4	cup canola oil
1	cup all-purpose flour
1	teaspoon baking powder
1/2	teaspoon salt
2	cups reduced-fat granola with raisins
1	cup dried cranberries *or* cherries

In a large bowl, combine the egg, egg white, brown sugar and oil; mix well. Combine the flour, baking powder and salt; stir into sugar mixture just until blended. Stir in granola and cranberries (batter will be thick).

Spread into a 9-in. square baking pan coated with cooking spray. Bake at 350° for 25-30 minutes or until golden and set. Cool in pan on a wire rack. Cut into bars.

✳ Emily Engel
Quill Lake, Saskatchewan
The brownie base makes this recipe different from other macaroon bars. If time is short, substitute a boxed brownie mix for the base.

chocolate macaroon brownies

yield about 2 dozen

1-1/2	cups sugar
2/3	cup canola oil
4	eggs, beaten
2	teaspoons vanilla extract, *divided*
1-1/3	cups all-purpose flour
2/3	cup baking cocoa
1	teaspoon baking powder
1/2	teaspoon salt
1	can (14 ounces) sweetened condensed milk
3	cups flaked coconut

BUTTER FROSTING:

2	cups confectioners' sugar
1/2	cup baking cocoa
1/2	cup butter, softened
1	teaspoon vanilla extract
1	to 2 tablespoons milk

In a large bowl, combine sugar and oil. Add the eggs and 1 teaspoon vanilla; mix well. Combine dry ingredients; add to bowl and mix until smooth.

Pour into a greased 13-in. x 9-in. x baking pan. In a small bowl, combine condensed milk, coconut and remaining vanilla; spoon over brownie base. Bake at 350° for 30-35 minutes or until a toothpick inserted near the center comes out clean. Cool in pan on a wire rack.

For frosting, in a small bowl, combine the sugar, cocoa, butter, vanilla and enough milk to achieve desired spreading consistency. Spread over filling. Cut into bars.

Brenda Wood, Egbert, Ontario *
This mouthwatering idea is from a family reunion cookbook that I compiled. My niece contributed the recipe.

really rocky road brownies

yield 4 dozen

8	squares (1 ounce *each*) unsweetened chocolate
1-1/2	cups butter
6	eggs
3	cups sugar
1	tablespoon vanilla extract
1-1/2	cups all-purpose flour
1	cup chopped walnuts, optional

TOPPING:

2	cups miniature marshmallows
1	square (1 ounce) unsweetened chocolate, melted

In a microwave, melt chocolate and butter; stir until smooth. Cool slightly. In a large bowl, beat eggs for 2 minutes. Gradually add sugar; beat until thick, about 3 minutes. Stir in chocolate mixture and vanilla. Fold in the flour and nuts if desired.

Pour into two greased and floured 9-in. square baking pans. Bake at 350° for 25-30 minutes or until a toothpick inserted in the center comes out with moist crumbs (do not overbake). Sprinkle each pan with 1 cup of marshmallows. Broil until the marshmallows are golden brown, about 30-60 seconds. Drizzle with the melted chocolate. Cool in pans on wire racks. Cut into bars.

Jennifer Ann Sopko, Battle Creek, Michigan *
I do a lot of cooking for the police officers I work with, and they always line up for these delicious bars. Toffee and chocolate dot the golden-brown batter of these fudge-like brownies.

blond butterscotch brownies

yield 2 dozen

2	cups all-purpose flour
2	cups packed brown sugar
2	teaspoons baking powder
1/4	teaspoon salt
1/2	cup butter, melted and cooled
2	eggs
1	teaspoon vanilla extract
1	cup semisweet chocolate chunks
4	Heath candy bars (1.4 ounces *each*), coarsely chopped

In a large bowl, combine the flour, brown sugar, baking powder and salt. In another bowl, beat the butter, eggs and vanilla until smooth. Stir into dry ingredients just until combined (batter will be thick).

Spread into a 13-in. x 9-in. baking pan coated with cooking spray. Sprinkle with chocolate chunks and chopped candy bars; press gently into batter.

Bake at 350° for 20-25 minutes or until a toothpick inserted near the center comes out clean. Cool on a wire rack. Cut into bars.

* Christine Mol, Grand Rapids, Michigan
This recipe comes from my Grandma Schlientz. Anytime there are ripe bananas around our house, it's Banana Nut Brownie time! People are always surprised to learn there are bananas in these brownies.

banana nut brownies

yield 16 servings

1/2	cup butter, melted and cooled
1	cup sugar
3	tablespoons baking cocoa
2	eggs, lightly beaten
1	tablespoon milk
1	teaspoon vanilla extract
1/2	cup all-purpose flour
1	teaspoon baking powder
1/4	teaspoon salt
1	cup mashed ripe bananas (2-1/2 to 3 medium)
1/2	cup chopped walnuts

Confectioners' sugar, optional

In a bowl, combine the butter, sugar and cocoa. Stir in eggs, milk and vanilla. Blend in the flour, baking powder and salt. Stir in the bananas and walnuts.

Pour into a greased 9-in. square baking pan. Bake at 350° for 40-45 minutes or until the top of brownies spring back when lightly touched. Cool in pan on a wire rack. Just before serving, dust with confectioners' sugar if desired. Cut into bars.

* Linda Hardin-Eldridge, Lake Alfred, Florida
You can't beat the homemade goodness of my from-scratch brownies that are topped with a rich chocolate frosting. With just one taste, your family will think the treats are divinely inspired.

brownies from heaven

yield 2 dozen

1	cup butter, softened
2	cups sugar
2	eggs
1	teaspoon vanilla extract
2	cups all-purpose flour
1/2	cup baking cocoa
1	cup chopped walnuts

FROSTING:

1/2	cup butter, softened
3-1/2	cups confectioners' sugar
1/3	cup baking cocoa
1/4	cup milk
1	teaspoon vanilla extract

In a large bowl, cream butter and sugar until light and fluffy. Add eggs, one at a time, beating well after each addition. Beat in vanilla. Combine flour and cocoa; add to creamed mixture just until combined. Stir in walnuts.

Spread into an ungreased 13-in. x 9-in. baking pan. Bake at 350° for 23-28 minutes or until a toothpick inserted near the center comes out clean. Cool on a wire rack.

For frosting, in a small bowl, beat butter until fluffy. Beat in the confectioners' sugar, cocoa, milk and vanilla until smooth. Spread over brownies. Cut into bars.

Michelle Tiemstra, Lacombe, Alberta ✳

A friend gave me the recipe for these cake-like brownies topped with a creamy, coffee-enhanced filling and a chocolate glaze. I like to garnish each square with a coffee bean.

coffee 'n' cream brownies

yield 16 servings

1/2	**cup butter, cubed**
3	**squares (1 ounce** *each***) unsweetened chocolate, chopped**
2	**eggs**
1	**cup sugar**
1	**teaspoon vanilla extract**
2/3	**cup all-purpose flour**
1/4	**teaspoon baking soda**

FILLING:

1	**tablespoon heavy whipping cream**
1	**teaspoon instant coffee granules**
2	**tablespoons butter, softened**
1	**cup confectioners' sugar**

GLAZE:

1	**cup (6 ounces) semisweet chocolate chips**
1/3	**cup heavy whipping cream**

In a microwave, melt butter and chocolate; stir until smooth. Cool slightly. In a small bowl, beat eggs, sugar and vanilla; stir in the chocolate mixture. Combine flour and baking soda; gradually add to chocolate mixture.

Spread into a greased 8-in. square baking dish. Bake at 350° for 25-30 minutes or until a toothpick inserted near the center comes out clean (do not overbake). Cool on a wire rack.

For filling, combine cream and coffee granules in a small bowl; stir until coffee is dissolved. In a small bowl, cream butter and confectioners' sugar until light and fluffy. Beat in coffee mixture; spread over brownies.

In a small saucepan, combine chips and cream. Cook and stir over low heat until chocolate is melted and mixture is thickened. Cool slightly. Carefully spread over filling. Let stand for 30 minutes or until glaze is set. Cut into squares. Store in the refrigerator.

cinnamon brownies

yield 2 dozen

1-2/3	**cups sugar**
3/4	**cup butter, melted**
2	**tablespoons strong brewed coffee**
2	**eggs**
2	**teaspoons vanilla extract**
1-1/3	**cups all-purpose flour**
3/4	**cup baking cocoa**
1	**tablespoon ground cinnamon**
1/2	**teaspoon baking powder**
1/4	**teaspoon salt**
1	**cup chopped walnuts**

Confectioners' sugar

In a large bowl, beat the sugar, butter and coffee. Add eggs and vanilla. Combine the flour, cocoa, cinnamon, baking powder and salt; gradually add to the sugar mixture and mix well. Stir in walnuts.

Spread into a greased 13-in. x 9-in. baking pan. Bake at 350° for 18-22 minutes or until a toothpick inserted near the center comes out clean. Cool in pan on a wire rack. Dust with confectioners' sugar. Cut into bars.

Christopher Wolf ✳ Belvidere, Illinois
No frosting is needed on top of these chewy, fudge-like brownies. This nice, basic bar packs a delicious burst of cinnamon in every bite.

✳ Connie Poto, Canton, Ohio

These moist, cake-like brownies are so chocolaty-good that they'll go fast at any get-together. Sour cream in the chocolate frosting gives the squares a little tang that makes them special.

frosted chocolate chip brownies

yield 1 dozen

1/2	cup butter, softened
1	cup sugar
4	eggs
1	can (16 ounces) chocolate syrup
2	teaspoons vanilla extract
1	cup all-purpose flour
1	cup (6 ounces) semisweet chocolate chips
1	cup chopped nuts

CHOCOLATE SOUR CREAM FROSTING:

1	cup (6 ounces) semisweet chocolate chips
1/4	cup butter, cubed
1/2	cup sour cream
2-1/4	cups confectioners' sugar

In a large bowl, cream butter and sugar until light and fluffy. Add eggs, one at a time, beating well after each addition. Beat in chocolate syrup and vanilla. Gradually add flour. Stir in chocolate chips and nuts.

Pour into a greased 13-in. x 9-in. baking pan. Bake at 350° for 35-40 minutes or until a toothpick inserted near the center comes out clean. Cool on a wire rack.

For frosting, in a microwave, melt chocolate chips and butter; stir until smooth. Cool for 5 minutes. Whisk in sour cream. Gradually stir in confectioners' sugar until smooth. Frost brownies. Cut into bars. Store in the refrigerator.

✳ Tamara Sellman
Barrington, Illinois

To tell the truth, I'm not a "chocoholic." I enjoy fruit desserts and custards more than anything. So my brownies have neither milk nor dark chocolate—but still satisfy every sweet tooth.

apricot angel brownies

yield about 2 dozen

4	squares (1 ounce *each*) white baking chocolate
1/3	cup butter
1/2	cup packed brown sugar
2	eggs, beaten
1/4	teaspoon vanilla extract
3/4	cup all-purpose flour
1/2	teaspoon baking powder
1/4	teaspoon salt
1	cup finely chopped dried apricots
1/4	cup sliced almonds
1/4	cup flaked coconut

In a saucepan, melt chocolate and butter over low heat, stirring constantly until all of the chocolate is melted. Remove from the heat; stir in brown sugar, eggs and vanilla until blended. Set aside.

In a large bowl, combine flour, baking powder and salt. Stir in chocolate mixture. Combine the apricots, almonds and coconuts; stir half into the batter.

Pour into a greased 9-in. square baking pan. Sprinkle the remaining apricot mixture on top. Bake at 350° for 25-30 minutes or until golden brown. Cool on a wire rack. Cut into bars.

Anna Jean Allen, West Liberty, Kentucky ✳

If you love chocolate and butterscotch, you won't be able to resist these chewy brownies. I often include this recipe inside a baking dish as a wedding present. Everyone, young and old, enjoys these sweet treats.

chippy blond brownies

yield 2 dozen

6	tablespoons butter, softened
1	cup packed brown sugar
2	eggs
1	teaspoon vanilla extract
1-1/4	cups all-purpose flour
1	teaspoon baking powder
1/2	teaspoon salt
1	cup (6 ounces) semisweet chocolate chips
1/2	cup chopped pecans

In a large bowl, cream butter and brown sugar until light and fluffy. Add the eggs, one at a time, beating well after each addition. Beat in vanilla. Combine the flour, baking powder and salt; gradually add to creamed mixture. Stir in the chocolate chips and pecans.

Spread into a greased 11-in. x 7-in. baking pan. Bake at 350° for 25-30 minutes or until a toothpick inserted near the center comes out clean. Cool on a wire rack.

Priscilla Renfrow, Wilson, North Carolina ✳

These brownies are so rich and yummy, you'll never guess they're actually lighter than most. The addition of caramel is a nice surprise most folks enjoy.

caramel fudge brownies

yield 9 servings

4	squares (1 ounce *each*) unsweetened chocolate
3	egg whites, lightly beaten
1	cup sugar
2	jars (2-1/2 ounces *each*) prune baby food
1	teaspoon vanilla extract
1/2	cup all-purpose flour
1/2	teaspoon salt
1/4	cup chopped walnuts
6	tablespoons fat-free caramel ice cream topping
9	tablespoons reduced-fat whipped topping

In a microwave, melt chocolate; stir until smooth. Cool slightly. In a large bowl, beat eggs whites and sugar. Stir in prunes, vanilla and chocolate mixture. Combine flour and salt; gradually add to chocolate mixture just until moistened.

Pour into an 8-in. square baking dish coated with cooking spray. Sprinkle with walnuts. Bake at 350° for 30-32 minutes or until the top springs back when lightly touched.

Cool on a wire rack. Cut into squares; drizzle with the caramel topping and dollop with whipped topping.

* Lynn Snow, Taylors, South Carolina
My mom just had to share this wonderful recipe with me after she baked these fudgy almond delights. They're made in several steps, but the extra effort is well worth it!

almond truffle brownies

yield 1-1/2 dozen

1	**package fudge brownie mix (13-inch x 9-inch pan size)**
1/2	**cup water**
1/2	**cup canola oil**
1	**egg**
3/4	**cup chopped almonds**
1	**teaspoon almond extract**

FILLING:

1	**cup (6 ounces) semisweet chocolate chips**
1	**package (8 ounces) cream cheese, softened**
1/4	**cup confectioners' sugar**
2	**tablespoons milk**
1/2	**teaspoon almond extract**

TOPPING:

1/2	**cup semisweet chocolate chips**
1/4	**cup heavy whipping cream**
1/2	**cup sliced almonds, toasted**

In a large bowl, combine the first six ingredients. Pour into a greased 13-in. x 9-in. baking pan. Bake at 350° for 23-25 minutes or until a toothpick inserted near the center comes out clean (do not overbake). Cool on a wire rack.

In a microwave, melt chocolate chips; stir until smooth. In a large bowl, beat cream cheese and confectioners' sugar until smooth. Beat in the milk, extract and melted chips. Spread over brownies. Refrigerate for 1 hour or until firm.

For topping, in a small saucepan, melt chips and cream over low heat, stirring occasionally. Spread over filling. Sprinkle with almonds. Chill at least 1 hour longer before cutting.

malted milk ball brownies

yield 2 dozen

* Mitzi Sentiff
Annapolis, Maryland
You don't have to be a kid to love these delicious brownies! Malted milk balls in the batter and sprinkled on top make them real tasty. Everyone loves them.

1	**package fudge brownie mix (13-inch x 9-inch pan size)**
1-1/3	**cups chopped malted milk balls, *divided***
1	**cup (6 ounces) semisweet chocolate chips**
2	**tablespoons butter**
2	**tablespoons milk**
1/4	**teaspoon vanilla extract**

Prepare brownie batter according to package directions; stir in 1 cup malted milk balls.

Spread into a greased 13-in. x 9-in. baking pan.

Bake at 350° for 28-30 minutes or until a toothpick inserted 2 in. from an edge comes out with moist crumbs. Cool completely on a wire rack.

In a microwave, melt chocolate chips and butter; stir until smooth. Cool slightly. Stir in milk and vanilla. Spread over brownies. Sprinkle with the remaining malted milk balls. Refrigerate for 10-15 minutes or until set. Cut into bars.

Janet Taylor, Mayville, New York ✳
These brownies travel well, and I often bake them in a disposable foil pan for camping. That way, I don't have to worry about lugging a baking pan back home with me.

fudgy saucepan brownies
yield 1 dozen

1/2	**cup butter**
2	**squares (1 ounce** *each***) unsweetened chocolate, coarsely chopped**
2	**eggs, beaten**
1	**cup sugar**
2/3	**cup all-purpose flour**
1/2	**cup chopped nuts**
1/2	**teaspoon baking powder**
1/2	**teaspoon vanilla extract**

Confectioners' sugar, optional

In a microwave, melt butter and chocolate; stir until smooth. Cool. Transfer to a large bowl. Stir in the eggs, sugar, flour, nuts, baking powder and vanilla.

Pour into a greased 8-in. square baking pan. Bake at 350° for 16-20 minutes or until top is set. Cool on a wire rack. Dust with confectioners' sugar if desired.

cherry-nut brownie bars
yield about 2 dozen

3	**cups all-purpose flour**
2	**cups sugar**
1	**cup baking cocoa**
1/2	**teaspoon baking powder**
1/2	**teaspoon baking soda**
1/2	**teaspoon salt**
2	**eggs**
1	**cup butter, melted**
3	**teaspoons vanilla extract**
1	**can (21 ounces) cherry pie filling**
1	**cup chopped walnuts**
1/2	**cup vanilla** *or* **white chips**
1	**tablespoon milk**

In a large bowl, combine the first six ingredients. In another bowl, whisk the eggs, butter and vanilla; add to dry ingredients. Beat until well blended (mixture will be thick).

Set aside 1 cup dough for topping. Press remaining dough into a greased 13-in. x 9-in. baking dish. Spread evenly with pie filling. Crumble reserved dough over the top; sprinkle with walnuts.

Bake at 350° for 35-40 minutes or until the top is dry and nuts are golden brown. Cool completely on a wire rack.

In a microwave, melt vanilla chips and milk at 70% power; stir until smooth. Microwave at additional 10- to 20-second intervals, stirring until smooth. Drizzle over bars.

Richell Welch ✳
Buffalo, Texas
I created these bars by accident one day, but now I make a point of preparing them often. Cherry pie filling gives them a Black Forest flavor.

✳ Radelle Knappenberger, Oviedo, Florida
A brownie mix base makes this a simple treat that will appeal to adults and children alike. Creamy peanut butter, crunchy peanuts and crisp cereal make the bars an adventure to bite into.

peanut butter brownie bars

yield 3 dozen

1	package fudge brownie mix (13-inch x 9-inch pan size)
12	peanut butter cups, chopped
1/2	cup salted peanuts, chopped
2	cups (12 ounces) semisweet chocolate chips
1-1/4	cups creamy peanut butter
1	tablespoon butter
1/8	teaspoon salt
1-1/2	cups crisp rice cereal
1	teaspoon vanilla extract

Prepare brownie batter according to package directions. Spread into a greased 13-in. x 9-in. baking pan. Bake at 350° for 20-25 minutes or until a toothpick inserted near the center comes out with moist crumbs.

Sprinkle with peanut butter cups and peanuts. Bake 4-6 minutes longer or until chocolate is melted. Cool on a wire rack.

Meanwhile, in a large saucepan, combine the chocolate chips, peanut butter, butter and salt. Cook and stir until chips are melted and mixture is smooth. Remove from the heat; stir in cereal and vanilla. Carefully spread over brownies. Cover and refrigerate for at least 2 hours before cutting.

choco-cloud brownies

yield about 2-1/2 dozen

✳ Linda Roecker
Hazelton, North Dakota
True to its name, this mild chocolate brownie is covered by a cloud of fluffy frosting. The recipe has earned lots of raves at our table.

1	cup butter, softened
2	cups sugar
4	eggs
1	milk chocolate candy bar (7 ounces), melted
3	teaspoons vanilla extract
2	cups all-purpose flour
1/2	teaspoon salt
2	cups chopped pecans

FROSTING:

5	tablespoons all-purpose flour
1	cup milk
1	cup butter, softened
1	cup confectioners' sugar
2	teaspoons vanilla extract

Baking cocoa

In a large bowl, cream butter and sugar. Add the eggs, one at a time, beating well after each. Add chocolate and vanilla; mix well. Gradually add flour and salt. Stir in pecans.

Spread into a greased 13-in. x 9-in. baking pan. Bake at 350° for 35-40 minutes or until center is set and edges pull away from pan. Cool in pan on a wire rack.

For frosting, combine flour and milk in a small saucepan until smooth. Bring to a boil; cook and stir for 2 minutes or until thickened. Remove from the heat; cool completely. In a small bowl, cream butter and confectioners' sugar. Add vanilla; mix well. Gradually add milk mixture; beat for 5 minutes or until fluffy. Frost brownies; dust with cocoa. Cut into bars. Store in the refrigerator.

walnut oat brownies

yield 1 dozen

1/3	cup quick-cooking oats
1/3	cup nonfat dry milk powder
1/4	cup toasted wheat germ
1/4	cup packed brown sugar
2	tablespoons sugar
1/2	teaspoon baking powder
1/4	teaspoon salt
6	squares (1 ounce *each*) semisweet chocolate
1/4	cup butter
1/2	cup egg substitute
1/4	cup chopped walnuts
1	teaspoon vanilla extract

Confectioners' sugar, optional

In a large bowl, combine the first seven ingredients. In a microwave-safe bowl, melt chocolate and butter; cool slightly. Stir in the egg substitute, walnuts and vanilla. Stir into the dry ingredients.

Pour into an 8-in. square baking dish coated with cooking spray. Bake at 350° for 25-30 minutes or until a toothpick inserted near the center comes out clean. Cool on a wire rack. Dust with confectioners' sugar if desired. Cut into bars.

cream cheese brownies

yield 2-1/2 dozen

2	packages (8 ounces *each*) cream cheese, softened
2	cups sugar, *divided*
3	tablespoons milk
1	cup butter, softened
2/3	cup instant hot cocoa mix
4	eggs
2	teaspoons vanilla extract
1-1/2	cups all-purpose flour
1	cup chopped nuts

In a small bowl, beat cream cheese, 1/2 cup sugar and milk until fluffy; set aside. In a large bowl, cream the butter, hot cocoa mix and remaining sugar. Beat in eggs and vanilla. Stir in flour and nuts.

Pour half of the batter into a greased 13-in. x 9-in. baking pan. Spread with the cream cheese mixture. Top with remaining batter. Cut through batter with a knife to swirl the cream cheese.

Bake at 350° for 35-40 minutes or until a toothpick inserted near the center comes out clean. Cool in pan on a wire rack. Cut into bars.

editor's note: This recipe was tested with Swiss Miss instant cocoa.

Carolyn Reed ✳
North Robinson, Ohio
A friend from church shared this recipe with me. Cream cheese lends itself to a moist and chewy bar that's finger-lickin' good!

✳ Carol Gillespie, Chambersburg, Pennsylvania
You'll never want to try another brownie recipe after eating these delicious treats. They have an orange-flavored cream cheese filling and yummy chocolate frosting.

orange cream cheese brownies

yield 16 brownies

1	package fudge brownie mix (13-inch x 9-inch pan size)
1/2	cup vanilla *or* white chips

FILLING:

1	package (3 ounces) cream cheese, softened
2	tablespoons butter, softened
1/4	cup sugar
1	egg
1	tablespoon all-purpose flour
1/2	teaspoon orange extract

FROSTING:

1	ounce unsweetened chocolate
1	ounce semisweet chocolate
2	tablespoons butter
1	cup confectioners' sugar
2	to 3 tablespoons milk

Prepare brownies according to package directions for cake-like brownies; fold in vanilla chips. Spread half of the batter in a greased 13-in. x 9-in. baking pan.

In a small bowl, beat the cream cheese, butter and sugar until smooth. Beat in egg, flour and orange extract.

Carefully spread cream cheese mixture over batter. Drop remaining brownie batter by tablespoonfuls over cream cheese layer. Cut through batter with a knife to swirl.

Bake at 350° for 30-35 minutes or until a toothpick inserted near the center comes out almost clean. Cool on a wire rack.

For frosting, in a microwave-safe bowl, melt chocolate and butter; stir until smooth. Cool slightly; stir in confectioners' sugar and enough milk to achieve spreading consistency. Frost the brownies.

brownies in a cone

✳ Mitzi Sentiff
Annapolis, Maryland
These brownie-filled ice cream cones are a fun addition to any summer get-together. They appeal to the child in everyone.

yield 17 servings

1	package fudge brownie mix (13-inch x 9-inch pan size)
17	ice cream cake cones (about 2-3/4-inches tall)
1	cup (6 ounces) semisweet chocolate chips
1	tablespoon shortening

Colored sprinkles

Prepare brownie batter according to package directions, using 3 eggs. Place the ice cream cones in muffin cups; spoon about 3 tablespoons batter into each cone.

Bake at 350° for 25-30 minutes or until a toothpick comes out clean and top is dry (do not overbake). Cool completely.

In a microwave, melt chocolate chips and shortening; stir until smooth. Dip tops of brownies in melted chocolate; allow excess to drip off. Decorate with sprinkles.

Judy Sims, Weatherford, Texas ✳

A recipe for layered brownies was modified to include the addition of chunky peanut butter. It's a real crowd-pleaser!

chunky peanut butter brownies

yield 4 dozen

1-1/2	cups butter, *divided*
3/4	cup baking cocoa, *divided*
4	eggs
2	cups sugar
1	teaspoon vanilla extract
1-1/2	cups all-purpose flour
1/2	teaspoon salt
1	jar (18 ounces) chunky peanut butter
1/3	cup milk
10	large marshmallows
2	cups confectioners' sugar

In a small saucepan, melt 1 cup butter; stir in 1/2 cup cocoa until smooth. Remove from the heat. In a large bowl, beat the eggs, sugar and vanilla until blended. Combine the flour and salt; gradually add to the egg mixture. Beat in the cocoa mixture.

Transfer to a greased 15-in. x 10-in. x 1-in. baking pan. Bake at 350° for 18-22 minutes or until toothpick inserted near the center comes out clean. Cool for 3-4 minutes on a wire rack.

Microwave peanut butter at 50% power for 2 minutes, stirring once. Stir until the peanut butter is blended. Spread over warm brownies. Chill for 45 minutes or until peanut butter is set.

In a saucepan, combine milk, remaining cocoa, marshmallows and remaining butter. Cook and stir over medium heat until butter and marshmallows are melted and mixture is smooth. Remove from the heat. Gradually stir in confectioners' sugar until smooth. Spread over peanut butter layer. Chill for at least 30 minutes. Cut into squares.

editor's note: This recipe was tested in a 1,100-watt microwave.

fudge-filled brownie bars

yield 4 dozen

1-1/2	cups all-purpose flour
3/4	cup packed brown sugar
3/4	cup butter, softened
1	egg yolk
3/4	teaspoon vanilla extract

FILLING:

1	package fudge brownie mix (13-inch x 9-inch pan size)
1	egg
1/3	cup water
1/3	cup canola oil

TOPPING:

1	package (11-1/2 ounces) milk chocolate chips, melted
3/4	cup chopped walnuts, toasted

In a large bowl, combine the first five ingredients. Press onto the bottom of a greased 15-in. x 10-in. x 1-in. baking pan. Bake at 350° for 15-18 minutes or until golden brown.

In a large bowl, combine the filling ingredients. Spread over hot crust. Bake for 15 minutes or until set. Cool on a wire rack for 30 minutes.

Spread melted chocolate over filling; sprinkle with walnuts. Cool completely. Cut into bars.

Nola Burski ✳
Lakeville, Minnesota
I always have the ingredients to put together these soft chewy bars. They have been a hit at many potlucks, and someone is always asking for the recipe.

✳ Jill Bonanno, Prineville, Oregon

These rich, cake-like brownies are generously topped with a scrumptious mocha frosting. They're an excellent dessert to serve to company or to share when you need a dish to pass. Be sure to hold back a few if you want leftovers.

mocha walnut brownies

yield about 2 dozen

4	squares (1 ounce *each*) unsweetened chocolate
1	cup butter
4	eggs
2	cups sugar
1	teaspoon vanilla extract
1-1/4	cups all-purpose flour
1/2	teaspoon baking powder
1/2	teaspoon salt
1	cup chopped walnuts

MOCHA FROSTING:

4	cups confectioners' sugar
1/2	cup butter, melted
1/3	cup baking cocoa
1/4	cup strong brewed coffee
2	teaspoons vanilla extract

In a microwave, melt the chocolate and butter; stir until smooth. Cool slightly. In a large bowl, beat eggs and sugar. Stir in vanilla and chocolate mixture. Combine flour, baking powder and salt; gradually add to chocolate mixture. Stir in walnuts.

Pour into a greased 13-in. x 9-in. baking pan. Bake at 375° for 30 minutes or until a toothpick inserted near the center comes out clean. Cool on a wire rack.

In a large bowl, beat frosting ingredients until smooth. Spread over brownies.

✳ Annmarie Savage, Skowhegan, Maine

With a creamy frosting and crunchy topping, these three-layer brownie bars are a decadent treat.

triple-tier brownies

yield about 5 dozen

1	package fudge brownie mix (13-inch x 9-inch pan size)
1	package (11-1/2 ounces) milk chocolate chips
1	cup peanut butter
3	cups crisp rice cereal
1	can (16 ounces) cream cheese frosting
1	cup salted peanuts, chopped

Prepare and bake brownie mix according to package directions, using a greased 13-in. x 9-in. baking pan. Cool on a wire rack.

In a large saucepan, combine chocolate chips and peanut butter. Cook over low heat for 4-5 minutes or until blended, stirring occasionally. Stir in cereal; set aside.

Spread frosting over brownies. Sprinkle with peanuts. Spread with peanut butter mixture. Chill for 30 minutes or until set before cutting. Store in the refrigerator.

Susan Myers, Dublin, Ohio ✻

These chewy, from-scratch brownies are topped with mini marshmallows, maraschino cherries and a chocolate drizzle.

chocolate-covered cherry brownies

yield 2 dozen

2	cups sugar
1	cup butter, melted
4	eggs
1	cup all-purpose flour
1	cup baking cocoa
2	teaspoons baking powder
1/2	teaspoon salt
2	cups miniature marshmallows
1	jar (10 ounces) maraschino cherries, chopped and well drained
1/2	cup semisweet chocolate chips
1	to 2 tablespoons heavy whipping cream

In a large bowl, cream sugar and butter until light and fluffy. Beat in eggs. Combine the flour, cocoa, baking powder and salt; gradually add to creamed mixture.

Pour into a greased 13-in. x 9-in. baking pan. Bake at 350° for 28 minutes. Sprinkle with marshmallows. Bake 1-2 minutes longer or until marshmallows are soft but not browned. Sprinkle with cherries. Cool on a wire rack.

In a microwave, melt chocolate chips and cream; stir until smooth. Drizzle over brownies. Let stand until chocolate is set.

orange brownies

yield 16 servings

1/2	cup butter
1/4	cup baking cocoa
2	eggs
1	cup sugar
3/4	cup all-purpose flour
1/2	cup chopped pecans
2	tablespoons orange juice concentrate
1	tablespoon grated orange peel
1/8	teaspoon salt

FROSTING:

1-1/2	cups confectioners' sugar
3	tablespoons butter, softened
2	tablespoons orange juice concentrate
1	tablespoon grated orange peel, optional

In a small saucepan, melt butter. Stir in cocoa until smooth. In a large bowl, beat eggs until frothy. Without stirring, add the sugar, flour, pecans, orange juice concentrate, peel and salt. Pour cocoa mixture over the top; mix well. Transfer to a greased 8-in. square baking pan.

Bake at 350° for 28-32 minutes or until edges begin to pull away from sides of pan. Cool completely on a wire rack.

For frosting, combine confectioners' sugar, butter and orange juice concentrate. Spread over the brownies. Cut into bars; garnish with orange peel if desired.

Rosella Peters ✻
Gull Lake, Saskatchewan
Chocolate and orange go together deliciously in these moist, fudgy brownies. Pecans add crunch while orange peel sprinkled on the frosting lends the finishing touch.

delectable bars

apricot date squares, p. 256

One pan, so many varieties!

Bar cookies, whether they're patted or poured, layered or filled, frosted or sprinkled are satisfying sweets for so many reasons. Many are easy to make, so you'll find plenty for quick weeknight desserts as well as some that impress weekend company.

almond coconut bars, p. 254

raspberry patch crumb bars, p. 259

✳ Janet Coops, Duarte, California

With an oh-so-chocolaty crust, a crunchy crumb topping and soft cream cheese filling, these delectable bars are over-the-top indulgent. But they've been lightened up, so you can enjoy one without feeling guilty.

light cream cheese streusel bars

yield 15 servings

1-1/4	cups confectioners' sugar
1	cup all-purpose flour
1/3	cup baking cocoa
1/4	teaspoon salt
1/2	cup cold butter
1	package (8 ounces) reduced-fat cream cheese
1	can (14 ounces) fat-free sweetened condensed milk
1	egg, lightly beaten
2	teaspoons vanilla extract

In a large bowl, combine confectioners' sugar, flour, cocoa and salt; cut in butter until crumbly. Set aside 1/2 cup for topping; press remaining crumb mixture into an 11-in. x 7-in. baking pan coated with cooking spray. Bake at 325° for 8-12 minutes or until set.

In a small bowl, beat the cream cheese, milk, egg and vanilla until blended. Pour over crust. Bake for 15 minutes. Top with reserved crumb mixture; bake 5-10 minutes longer or until filling is set. Cool on a wire rack. Store in the refrigerator.

Barbara Robbins, Chandler, Arizona ✳

I've made these easy berry squares for many years, and they never fail to bring raves from people of all ages. When things get really busy, I like the convenience of being able to make the fuss-free treats a day ahead of time.

blueberry squares

yield 9 servings

1	cup crushed vanilla wafers (about 30 wafers)
2	tablespoons butter, melted
3/4	cup sugar
1/4	cup cornstarch
1/4	cup cold water
3	cups fresh blueberries, *divided*
3	tablespoons lemon juice
1	teaspoon grated lemon peel
1	cup heavy whipping cream
2	tablespoons confectioners' sugar
1-1/2	cups miniature marshmallows

In a small bowl, combine wafers and butter. Press into a greased 8-in. square baking dish. Bake at 350° for 8-10 minutes or until lightly browned. Cool on a wire rack.

In a small saucepan, combine the sugar and cornstarch. Gradually whisk in water until smooth. Stir in 1-1/2 cups blueberries. Bring to a boil; cook and stir for 1-2 minutes or until thickened. Stir in the lemon juice, peel and remaining blueberries. Cool completely.

In a small bowl, beat cream until it begins to thicken. Add confectioners' sugar; beat until soft peaks form. Fold in marshmallows. Spread over crust. Top with blueberry mixture. Cover and refrigerate until set, about 45 minutes.

frosted creams

yield 3 dozen

1/4	cup shortening
1/4	cup sugar
1/2	cup molasses
1	egg
2	cups all-purpose flour
1	teaspoon baking soda
1	to 2 teaspoons ground ginger
1	teaspoon ground cinnamon
1/2	teaspoon salt
3/4	cup water

GLAZE:

1-1/2	cups confectioners' sugar
2	tablespoons plus 1-1/2 teaspoons milk
1/4	teaspoon vanilla extract

Vivian Clark ✳
Milwaukee, Wisconsin

Molasses, cinnamon and ginger nicely spice these old-fashioned bars that are spread with a sweet and simple glaze.

In a large bowl, cream shortening and sugar until light and fluffy. Beat in molasses and egg. Combine the flour, baking soda, ginger, cinnamon and salt; gradually add to the creamed mixture alternately with water, mixing well after each addition.

Pour into a greased 13-in. x 9-in. baking pan. Bake at 400° for 13-15 minutes or until a toothpick inserted near the center comes out clean. Cool completely on a wire rack.

In a small bowl, combine the glaze ingredients until smooth. Spread over cooled bars.

✳ Beverly Zdurne, East Lansing, Michigan
Folks who have a sweet tooth make a beeline for my dessert tray whenever these rich squares show up. They look attractive on the platter and taste delectable with chocolate, coconut and walnuts.

fudgy macaroon bars
yield 3 dozen

4	squares (1 ounce *each*) unsweetened chocolate
1	cup butter
2	cups sugar
1	cup all-purpose flour
1/4	teaspoon salt
1	teaspoon vanilla extract
3	eggs, lightly beaten

FILLING:

3	cups flaked coconut
1	can (14 ounces) sweetened condensed milk
1	teaspoon vanilla extract
1/2	teaspoon almond extract

TOPPING:

1	cup (6 ounces) semisweet chocolate chips
1/2	cup chopped walnuts

In a microwave, melt chocolate and butter; stir until smooth. Remove from the heat; cool slightly. Stir in the sugar, flour, salt, vanilla and eggs. Spread half of the batter into a greased 13-in. x 9-in. baking pan.

In a large bowl, combine the filling ingredients. Spoon over chocolate layer. Carefully spread remaining chocolate mixture over filling.

Bake at 350° for 35-40 minutes or until the sides pull away from the pan. Immediately sprinkle with chocolate chips. Allow chips to soften for a few minutes, then spread over bars. Sprinkle with walnuts. Cool completely before cutting.

✳ Marilyn Forsell, Hydesville, California
I adapted this easy recipe from a friend who made it with strawberry jam. Instead, I use raspberry jam.

raspberry walnut bars
yield 16 bars

1	cup butter, softened
1	cup sugar
2	egg yolks
2	cups all-purpose flour
1	cup finely chopped walnuts
1/2	cup seedless raspberry jam

In a large bowl, cream butter and sugar until light and fluffy. Beat in egg yolks. Gradually add flour and mix well. Stir in walnuts.

Pat half of the mixture into a greased 8-in. square baking pan. Spread with jam. Crumble remaining crust mixture over jam. Bake at 350° for 35-40 minutes or until lightly browned. Cool on a wire rack.

Susan Huckaby, Smiths, Alabama ✳

My sister gave me this recipe, which is always in demand with family, friends and co-workers. It's amazing how fast these tempting bars vanish when I serve them! The cream cheese frosting is heavenly.

banana nut bars

yield 3 dozen

1	cup butter, cubed
1/2	cup water
2	cups all-purpose flour
1-1/2	cups sugar
1/2	cup packed brown sugar
1	teaspoon baking soda
2	eggs
1	cup mashed ripe bananas (about 2 medium)
1/2	cup buttermilk
1	teaspoon vanilla extract
1/2	cup chopped pecans *or* walnuts

FROSTING:

1	package (8 ounces) cream cheese, softened
1/2	cup butter, softened
1	teaspoon vanilla extract
3-1/2	cups confectioners' sugar

In a saucepan, bring butter and water to a boil. Remove from the heat; set aside. In a mixing bowl, combine the flour, sugars, baking soda, eggs, bananas, buttermilk and vanilla. Beat until blended. Carefully add butter mixture; mix well. Stir in nuts.

Pour into a greased 15-in. x 10-in. x 1-in. baking pan. Bake at 350° for 18-22 minutes or until a toothpick inserted near the center comes out clean. Cool in pan on a wire rack.

For frosting, in a large bowl, beat cream cheese and butter until light and fluffy. Beat in vanilla. Gradually add confectioners' sugar.

lemon-glazed pecan slices

yield 4 dozen

1/2	cup cold butter
1	cup plus 2 tablespoons all-purpose flour, *divided*
2	eggs
1-1/2	cups packed brown sugar
1	teaspoon vanilla extract
1/2	teaspoon baking powder
1/2	teaspoon salt
1	cup chopped pecans
1/2	cup flaked coconut
1-1/2	cups confectioners' sugar
2	tablespoons lemon juice

In a small bowl, cut butter into 1 cup flour until crumbly. Press into a greased 13-in. x 9-in. baking pan. Bake at 350° for 12 minutes.

Meanwhile, in a small bowl, beat the eggs, brown sugar and vanilla until blended. Combine the baking powder, salt and remaining flour; gradually add to egg mixture. Stir in pecans and coconut. Spread over warm crust. Bake for 25 minutes or until set. Cool on a wire rack.

For glaze, combine the confectioners' sugar and lemon juice; spread over bars. Let set before cutting.

Joan Hallford ✳
North Richland Hills, Texas

A tart lemon icing pairs well with these decadent bars that resemble pecan pie. Everyone loves them whenever I take them to work or potlucks.

❋ Paula Eriksen, Palm Harbor, Florida
Baking is my favorite pastime. These moist cranberry bars have a refreshing sweet-tart taste and a crumble topping.

crimson crumble bars

yield 2 dozen

1	**cup sugar**
2	**teaspoons cornstarch**
2	**cups fresh or frozen cranberries**
1	**can (8 ounces) unsweetened crushed pineapple, undrained**
1	**cup all-purpose flour**
2/3	**cup old-fashioned oats**
2/3	**cup packed brown sugar**
1/4	**teaspoon salt**
1/2	**cup cold butter**
1/2	**cup chopped pecans**

In a saucepan, combine the sugar, cornstarch, cranberries and pineapple; bring to a boil, stirring often. Reduce heat; cover and simmer for 10-15 minutes or until the berries pop. Remove from the heat.

In a large bowl, combine the flour, oats, brown sugar and salt. Cut in butter until mixture resembles coarse crumbs. Stir in pecans. Set aside 1-1/2 cups for topping.

Press remaining crumb mixture onto bottom of a 13-in. x 9-in. baking pan coated with cooking spray. Bake at 350° for 8-10 minutes or until firm. Cool for 10 minutes.

Pour fruit filling over crust. Sprinkle with reserved crumb mixture. Bake 25-30 minutes longer or until golden brown. Cool in pan on a wire rack. Cut into bars.

❋ Loretta Coverdell
Amanda, Ohio
This good-looking, great-tasting bar cookie classic has a hint of almond flavoring.

dreamy fudge bar cookies

yield about 3 dozen

1	**cup shortening**
2	**cups packed brown sugar**
2	**eggs**
2-1/2	**cups all-purpose flour**
1	**teaspoon baking soda**
Dash salt	
3	**cups rolled oats**

CHOCOLATE FILLING:

2	**cups (12 ounces) semisweet chocolate chips**
1	**can (14 ounces) sweetened condensed milk**
1	**tablespoon butter**
1	**cup chopped walnuts**
1/4	**to 1/2 teaspoon almond extract**

In a large bowl, cream shortening and sugar until light and fluffy. Add eggs, one at a time, beating well after each addition. Combine flour, baking soda, salt and oats; stir into creamed mixture; set aside.

For filling, combine the chips, milk and butter in a saucepan. Heat over low heat until chips are melted, stirring until smooth. Cool slightly. Stir in the walnuts and extract. Press two-thirds of the oat mixture into bottom of a greased 15-in. x 10-in. x 1-in. baking pan. Cover with the filling and sprinkle remaining oat mixture on top. Flatten slightly.

Bake at 350° for 20 minutes or until set. Cool in pan on a wire rack. Cut into bars.

Nola Burski, Lakeville, Minnesota ✳

You'll need only a handful of ingredients to fix these no-bake bars that are packed with peanut flavor. The recipe makes a small pan, so you won't be tempted with lots of leftovers!

crunchy peanut bars

yield 8 bars

1/4	cup light corn syrup
2	tablespoons brown sugar
1	tablespoon sugar
1/4	cup creamy peanut butter
1-1/2	cups cornflakes
1/4	cup Spanish peanuts
1/2	cup milk chocolate chips, melted

In a large saucepan over medium heat, bring corn syrup and sugars to a boil. Remove from the heat; stir in the peanut butter. Fold in the cornflakes and peanuts.

Gently press into a 9-in. x 5-in. loaf pan coated with cooking spray. Spread melted chocolate evenly over top. Cover and refrigerate for 1 hour or until firm. Cut into bars.

Katie Rose, Pewaukee, Wisconsin ✳

This sweet-tart dessert gets its tropical taste from lime, coconut and macadamia nuts. With its shortbread-nut crust and tangy filling, this small batch of bars makes a satisfying ending to a meal.

macadamia-coconut lime bars

yield 6 servings

1/2	cup all-purpose flour
3	tablespoons confectioners' sugar
2	tablespoons macadamia nuts, toasted
1/4	teaspoon grated lime peel
3	tablespoons cold butter, cubed

FILLING:

1	egg
1/2	cup sugar
3	tablespoons flaked coconut, chopped
2	tablespoons lime juice
1	tablespoon all-purpose flour
1/4	teaspoon grated lime peel
1/8	teaspoon baking powder

Confectioners' sugar

In a food processor, combine the flour, confectioners' sugar, nuts and lime peel; cover and process until nuts are finely chopped. Add the butter; pulse just until mixture is crumbly.

Press into an 8-in. x 4-in. loaf pan coated with cooking spray. Bake at 350° for 20-22 minutes or until golden brown.

In a small bowl, whisk the egg, sugar, coconut, lime juice, flour, lime peel and baking powder until blended. Pour over hot crust. Bake 20-22 minutes longer or until light golden brown. Cool on a wire rack. Dust with confectioners' sugar. Cut into bars.

✳ Debbie Knight, Marion, Iowa

These bars are always a hit at potlucks in the small farming community where my husband and I live. I also provide them for coffee hour after church. They don't last long.

frosted banana bars

yield 3-4 dozen

1/2	cup butter, softened
1-1/2	cups sugar
2	eggs
1	cup (8 ounces) sour cream
1	teaspoon vanilla extract
2	cups all-purpose flour
1	teaspoon baking soda
1/4	teaspoon salt
2	medium ripe bananas, mashed (about 1 cup)

FROSTING:

1	package (8 ounces) cream cheese, softened
1/2	cup butter, softened
2	teaspoons vanilla extract
3-3/4	to 4 cups confectioners' sugar

In a large bowl, cream butter and sugar. Add the eggs, sour cream and vanilla. Combine the flour, baking soda and salt; gradually add to the creamed mixture. Stir in bananas.

Spread into a greased 15-in. x 10-in. x 1-in. baking pan. Bake at 350° for 20-25 minutes or until a toothpick inserted near the center comes out clean. Cool.

For frosting, in a large bowl, beat the cream cheese, butter and vanilla. Gradually beat in enough confectioners' sugar to achieve desired consistency. Frost the bars. Store, covered, in the refrigerator.

spicy butter thins

yield about 3 dozen

✳ Elsie Vince
Peoria, Arizona

I spotted this recipe in a newspaper when teaching in California more than 20 years ago. Even today, my son says these are his favorite treat.

3/4	cup all-purpose flour
1/4	cup sugar
1	teaspoon ground cinnamon
1	teaspoon instant coffee granules
1/2	teaspoon ground ginger
1/2	cup butter
1	cup butterscotch chips, *divided*
1	egg
1/2	cup chopped salted peanuts

In a bowl, combine the first five ingredients; set aside. In a heavy saucepan over low heat, melt the butter and 2/3 cup butterscotch chips. Remove from the heat. Stir in the flour mixture and egg; mix well.

Spread into an ungreased 15-in. x 10-in. x 1-in. baking pan. Sprinkle with the peanuts and remaining chips. Bake at 300° for 25-30 minutes or until lightly browned. Immediately cut into bars and remove from pan. Cool on wire racks. Store in an airtight container.

Marie Martin, Lititz, Pennsylvania ✳
I received this recipe from a friend at our local fire hall's annual quilting bee, where ladies bring in treats to serve at break time. It was a big hit with our family.

chocolate peanut squares

yield 2 dozen

1	cup butter, *divided*
6	squares (1 ounce *each*) semisweet chocolate, *divided*
1-1/2	cups graham cracker crumbs
1/2	cup unsalted dry roasted peanuts, chopped
2	packages (8 ounces *each*) cream cheese, softened
1	cup sugar
1	teaspoon vanilla extract

In a small microwave-safe bowl, melt 3/4 cup butter and two squares of chocolate; stir until smooth. Stir in cracker crumbs and peanuts.

Press into a greased 13-in. x 9-in. pan. Cover and refrigerate for 30 minutes or until set.

In a small bowl, beat the cream cheese, sugar and vanilla until fluffy. Spread over chocolate layer. Melt the remaining butter and chocolate; stir until smooth. Carefully spread over cream cheese layer. Cover and refrigerate until set. Cut into squares.

almond toffee shortbread

yield about 8 dozen

1	cup whole blanched almonds, toasted
3/4	cup confectioners' sugar, *divided*
1	cup butter, softened
1/4	teaspoon almond extract
1-3/4	cups all-purpose flour
1/4	teaspoon salt
1	package English toffee bits (10 ounces) *or* almond brickle chips (7-1/2 ounces)
3/4	cup light corn syrup
3/4	cup sliced almonds, *divided*
3/4	cup flaked coconut, *divided*

In a food processor or blender, place the whole almonds and 1/4 cup confectioners' sugar. Cover and process until the nuts are finely ground; set aside.

In a large bowl, cream butter and remaining sugar until light and fluffy. Beat in extract. Combine the flour, salt and ground almond mixture; gradually add to creamed mixture. Press into a greased 15-in. x 10-in. x 1-in. baking pan. Bake at 350° for 20 minutes.

Meanwhile, combine toffee bits and corn syrup in a heavy saucepan. Cook and stir over medium heat until the toffee is melted. Remove from the heat; stir in 1/2 cup sliced almonds and 1/2 cup coconut. Carefully spread over the hot crust. Sprinkle with remaining almonds and coconut.

Bake for 15 minutes or until golden brown and bubbly. Cool on a wire rack. Cut into squares.

Darlene Brenden ✳
Salem, Oregon
The topping for these yummy shortbread squares tastes like a chewy toffee bar. If you can't find the toffee bits, buy Heath candy bars and chop them up.

Pat Habiger, Spearville, Kansas
A sweet raspberry filling is sandwiched between a crispy crust and a crunchy brown sugar topping in these satisfying snack bars.

raspberry walnut shortbread
yield 16 servings

1-1/4	cups plus 2 tablespoons all-purpose flour, *divided*
1/2	cup sugar
1/2	cup cold butter
1/2	cup raspberry jam
2	eggs
1/2	cup packed brown sugar
1	teaspoon vanilla extract
1/8	teaspoon baking soda
1	cup finely chopped walnuts

In a small bowl, combine 1-1/4 cups flour and sugar; cut in the butter until crumbly. Press into a greased 9-in. square baking pan. Bake at 350° for 20-25 minutes or until edges are lightly browned. Place on a wire rack. Spread jam over hot crust.

In a small bowl, beat eggs, brown sugar and vanilla. Combine baking soda and remaining flour; stir into the egg mixture just until combined. Fold in walnuts. Spoon over jam; spread evenly.

Bake 17-20 minutes longer or until golden brown and set. Cool in pan on a wire rack. Cut into bars.

Jill Moritz, Irvine, California
This recipe is elegant enough to serve for dessert yet casual enough to take to a picnic. For a change of flavor, substitute hazelnuts for the walnuts.

apricot bars
yield 3 dozen

3/4	cup butter, softened
1	cup sugar
1	egg
1/2	teaspoon vanilla extract
2	cups all-purpose flour
1/4	teaspoon baking powder
1-1/3	cups flaked coconut
1/2	cup chopped walnuts
1	jar (12 ounces) apricot preserves

In a large bowl, cream the butter and sugar until light and fluffy. Beat in the egg and vanilla. Combine the flour and baking powder. Gradually add to creamed mixture. Add the coconut and walnuts; mix thoroughly.

Press two-thirds of the dough into a greased 13-in. x 9-in. baking pan. Spread with the preserves; crumble remaining dough over preserves. Bake at 350° for 30-35 minutes or until golden brown. Cool in pan on wire rack. Cut into bars.

A lip-smacking layer of tinted frosting is the crowning touch to these butterscotch bars ladened with crunchy pecans.

blarney stone bars

yield about 3-1/2 dozen

1/2	cup butter, softened
3/4	cup packed brown sugar
2	eggs
1	tablespoon milk
1	teaspoon vanilla extract
3/4	cup all-purpose flour
3/4	cup quick-cooking oats
1/2	teaspoon baking powder
1/4	teaspoon salt
3/4	cup English toffee bits *or* almond brickle chips
1/3	cup chopped pecans
4	drops green food coloring
3/4	cup vanilla frosting

In a large bowl, cream butter and sugar until light and fluffy. Beat in eggs, milk and vanilla. Combine flour, oats, baking powder and salt; add to the creamed mixture. Fold in the toffee bits and pecans.

Spread into a greased 9-in. square baking pan. Bake at 350° for 20-24 minutes or until a toothpick inserted near the center comes out clean. Cool in pan on a wire rack. Add food coloring to frosting; spread over the bars. Cut into diamond shapes.

coconut graham cracker squares

yield 4 dozen

1	cup butter
1	cup sugar
1/2	cup milk
1	egg, beaten
1	cup flaked coconut
1	cup chopped walnuts
1	cup graham cracker crumbs (about 16 squares)
24	whole graham crackers

FROSTING:

1/4	cup butter, softened
2	cups confectioners' sugar
2	tablespoons milk
1	teaspoon vanilla extract
1/8	teaspoon salt

In a heavy saucepan, melt the butter. Stir in the sugar, milk and egg. Bring to a boil; cook and stir for 10 minutes. Remove from the heat. Stir in coconut, nuts and cracker crumbs.

Line a greased 15-in. x 10-in. x 1-in. baking pan with 12 whole crackers. Spread with coconut mixture. Top with remaining crackers; press down gently. Cover with plastic wrap and chill for 30 minutes.

Meanwhile, in a small bowl, combine frosting ingredients; beat until smooth. Break each cracker into four portions; spread with frosting.

Mrs. Victor Wheeler ✳
Girard, Pennsylvania
These bar cookies travel well and feed a lot of people at potlucks and family reunions. Kids, as well as adults, like their rich flavor.

* Marlene Collins, Detroit Lakes, Minnesota

These rich bars are a hit with everyone who tries them. The moist, cake-like crust pairs well with the chewy caramel and salty cashews in the broiled topping.

caramel-cashew cake bars

yield 16 bars

3/4	cup all-purpose flour
1/2	cup sugar
1/2	cup packed brown sugar
1/2	teaspoon baking powder
1/4	teaspoon salt
2	eggs
1/2	cup salted cashews, chopped

CASHEW TOPPING:

1/2	cup salted cashews, chopped
1/4	cup packed brown sugar
2	tablespoons butter, melted
4-1/2	teaspoons heavy whipping cream

In a large bowl, combine the flour, sugars, baking powder and salt. Beat in the eggs just until combined. Fold in the cashews. Spread into a greased 8-in. square baking dish.

Bake at 350° for 20-25 minutes or until top springs back when lightly touched.

In a small bowl, combine the topping ingredients. Spread over cake. Broil for 1-2 minutes or until bubbly and lightly browned. Cut into bars while warm. Cool on a wire rack.

* Rita Christianson, Glenburn, North Dakota

These tender bars have a sweet raisin filling tucked between a golden oat crust and topping. The old-fashioned treats are perfect for potlucks.

oatmeal raisin bars

yield about 3 dozen

1	cup sugar
2	tablespoons plus 1-1/2 teaspoons cornstarch
1	teaspoon ground cinnamon
1-1/2	cups (12 ounces) sour cream
3	eggs, lightly beaten
2	cups raisins

CRUMB MIXTURE:

1-3/4	cups all-purpose flour
1-3/4	cups quick-cooking oats
1	cup packed brown sugar
1	teaspoon baking soda
1/2	teaspoon salt
1	cup cold butter, cubed

In a large saucepan, combine the sugar, cornstarch and cinnamon. Stir in sour cream until smooth. Cook and stir over medium-high heat until thickened and bubbly. Reduce heat; cook and stir 2 minutes longer. Remove from the heat. Stir a small amount of hot filling into eggs; return all to pan, stirring constantly. Bring to a gentle boil; cook and stir 2 minutes longer. Remove from the heat. Gently stir in raisins. Cool to room temperature without stirring.

Meanwhile, in a large bowl, combine the flour, oats, brown sugar, baking soda and salt. Cut in butter until crumbly.

Firmly press 3-1/2 cups of the crumb mixture into a greased 13-in. x 9-in. baking pan. Spread with the raisin filling. Sprinkle with the remaining crumb mixture.

Bake at 350° for 25-30 minutes or until golden brown. Cool on a wire rack. Cut into bars. Refrigerate leftovers.

Our home economists combined cranberries, coconut and white chocolate to create these pretty bars. Colorful and tasty, one of these snacks and a glass of milk make the perfect treat on a cool autumn afternoon.

cranberry shortbread bars

yield 2 dozen

1	cup butter, softened
1/2	cup confectioners' sugar
1	egg
1-1/2	cups all-purpose flour
1/2	cup flaked coconut
1/8	teaspoon salt
1/2	cup sugar
1/2	cup packed brown sugar
3	tablespoons cornstarch
1	package (12 ounces) fresh *or* frozen cranberries
1	cup unsweetened apple juice
1	cup chopped walnuts
2	squares (1 ounce *each*) white baking chocolate, melted

In a large bowl, cream the butter and confectioners' sugar until light and fluffy. Beat in egg. Combine the flour, coconut and salt; gradually add to creamed mixture and mix well. Set aside 1 cup for topping. Spread the remaining mixture into a greased 13-in. x 9-in. baking dish. Bake at 425° for 10 minutes.

Meanwhile, in a small saucepan, combine the sugars and cornstarch. Stir in cranberries and apple juice. Bring to a boil. Reduce heat; cook and stir for 5 minutes or until thickened. Remove from the heat; stir in walnuts.

Spread over crust. Sprinkle with reserved crumb mixture. Bake for 20-25 minutes or until golden brown and bubbly. Cool on a wire rack. Drizzle with white chocolate. Cut into bars.

Rene Wright, Ferryville, Wisconsin ✳

These bars stay very moist, and their rich banana and chocolate flavors are even better the second day. My mother-in-law gave me this recipe, and it's a big favorite with both my husband and sons.

black-bottom banana bars

yield 2-1/2 to 3 dozen

1/2	cup butter, softened
1	cup sugar
1	egg
1	teaspoon vanilla extract
1-1/2	cups mashed ripe bananas (about 3 medium)
1-1/2	cups all-purpose flour
1	teaspoon baking powder
1	teaspoon baking soda
1/2	teaspoon salt
1/4	cup baking cocoa

In a large bowl, cream butter and sugar. Add the egg and vanilla; beat until thoroughly combined. Blend in the bananas. Combine the flour, baking powder, baking soda and salt; add to creamed mixture and mix well.

Divide batter in half. Add cocoa to half; spread into a greased 13-in. x 9-in. baking pan. Spoon remaining batter on top and swirl with a knife. Bake at 350° for 25 minutes or until a toothpick inserted near the center comes out clean. Cool in pan on a wire rack. Cut into bars.

Penny Reifenrath, Wynot, Nebraska
Peanut butter, Cherrios and candies put a tooth-tingling spin on marshmallow-cereal bars. Whether I take them to picnics or bake sales, I'm always asked for the recipe.

oaty cereal treats

yield 15 servings

3	**tablespoons butter**
1	**package (10-1/2 ounces) miniature marshmallows**
1/2	**cup peanut butter**
5	**cups Cheerios**
1	**cup milk chocolate M&M's**

Place the butter and marshmallows in a large microwave-safe bowl. Microwave, uncovered, on high for 1-2 minutes or until puffed. Stir in the peanut butter until blended. Add the cereal and M&M's; mix well.

Spoon into a greased 13-in. x 9-in. pan; press down gently. Cool slightly before cutting.

editor's note: Reduced-fat or generic brands of peanut butter are not recommended for this recipe. This recipe was test in a 1,100-watt microwave.

Bettie Martin, Oneida, Wisconsin
Whenever there is a potluck at work or a family gathering, I'm asked to bring these delectable bars. I found the recipe years ago and have made it countless times since.

cherry cocoa shortbread squares

yield 3 dozen

1/2	**cup plus 2 tablespoons butter, softened,** *divided*
1/4	**cup sugar**
1	**cup all-purpose flour**
2	**tablespoons baking cocoa**
2	**cups confectioners' sugar**
2	**tablespoons milk**
1/2	**teaspoon vanilla extract**
18	**maraschino cherries, halved**
GLAZE:	
1	**square (1 ounce) unsweetened chocolate**
1-1/2	**teaspoons butter**

In a large bowl, cream 1/2 cup butter and sugar until light and fluffy. Beat in flour and cocoa (mixture will be crumbly). Spread into a greased 9-in. square baking pan. Bake at 350° for 15 minutes or until surface is set. Cool in pan on a wire rack for 15 minutes.

Meanwhile, in a large bowl, combine confectioners' sugar and the remaining butter; beat in the milk and vanilla until smooth. Spread over the crust. Pat the cherries dry with a paper towel; arrange over the frosting and press down gently.

In a microwave-safe bowl, melt the chocolate and butter; stir until smooth. Drizzle over the cherries. Refrigerate until the glaze has set. Cut into squares.

Brooke Pike, Pierre, South Dakota ✳

These bars smell so good while they are baking—the spicy aroma brings everyone to the kitchen in a hurry!

spice bars

yield 1 dozen

6	tablespoons buttermilk
1/3	cup packed brown sugar
1/4	cup molasses
3	tablespoons butter, melted
1	egg
1	teaspoon vanilla extract
1-1/4	cups all-purpose flour
3/4	teaspoon ground cinnamon, *divided*
1-1/4	teaspoons Chinese five-spice powder
1/2	teaspoon baking powder
1/4	teaspoon baking soda
1/4	teaspoon salt
1/3	cup raisins
1	tablespoon confectioners' sugar

In a small bowl, combine the buttermilk, brown sugar, molasses, butter, egg and vanilla; mix well. Combine flour, 1/2 teaspoon cinnamon, five-spice powder, baking powder, baking soda and salt; add to the buttermilk mixture and beat until smooth. Stir in raisins.

Pour into a 9-in. square baking pan coated with cooking spray. Bake at 350° for 18-20 minutes or until a toothpick inserted near the center comes out clean. Cool in pan on a wire rack. Combine confectioners' sugar and remaining cinnamon; sprinkle over bars. Cut into bars.

Carol Horne, Perth, Ontario ✳

Only four ingredients make up these toffee bars loaded with crunchy almonds. My sister gave me the recipe years ago, and it's still a family favorite to this day.

toffee crunch grahams

yield 4 dozen

12	whole graham crackers (about 5 inches x 2-1/2 inches)
1-1/2	cups butter
1	cup packed brown sugar
2	cups sliced almonds

Line a 15-in. x 10-in. x 1-in. baking pan with heavy-duty foil. Place graham crackers in pan. In a saucepan, combine butter and brown sugar; bring to a boil, stirring constantly. Carefully pour over graham crackers. Sprinkle with almonds.

Bake at 400° for 6-8 minutes or until bubbly. Cool in pan for 4 minutes. Cut each cracker into four sections; transfer to wire racks to cool.

＊ Anna Miller, Quaker City, Ohio
I'm always looking for a great new cookie or bar to try, but I often return to this tried-and-true recipe that calls for lemon cake mix and saltines. My husband loves the combination of sweet and salty.

lemon crumb bars

yield 2 dozen

1	package (18-1/4 ounces) lemon cake mix
1/2	cup cold butter
1	egg
2	cups crushed saltines (about 60 crackers)
3	egg yolks
1	can (14 ounces) sweetened condensed milk
1/2	cup lemon juice

In a large bowl, beat the cake mix, butter and egg until crumbly. Stir in cracker crumbs; set aside 2 cups for topping.

Press remaining crumb mixture into a 13-in. x 9-in. baking dish coated with cooking spray. Bake at 350° for 18-20 minutes or until edges are lightly browned.

In a small bowl, beat the egg yolks, milk and lemon juice. Pour over crust; sprinkle with reserved crumb mixture. Bake 20-25 minutes longer or until edges are lightly browned. Cool on a wire rack. Cut into bars. Store in the refrigerator.

＊ Susan Hamilton
Fulton, Missouri
With their a butterscotch flavor, these tasty bars have always been welcomed with open arms by my family. Since they're simple to make, kids can have fun pitching in, too.

coconut pecan bars

yield 4 dozen

1	cup butter, softened
2	cups packed brown sugar
2	eggs
2	teaspoons vanilla extract
2	cups all-purpose flour
1	teaspoon salt
1	teaspoon baking powder
1-1/2	cups flaked coconut
1	cup chopped pecans
Confectioners' sugar	

In a large bowl, cream the butter and brown sugar until light and fluffy. Add eggs, one at a time, beating well after each addition. Beat in vanilla. Combine flour, salt and baking powder; gradually add to the creamed mixture. Stir in coconut and pecans (batter will be thick).

Spread into a greased 15-in. x 10-in. x 1-in. baking pan. Bake at 350° for 20-25 minutes or until a toothpick inserted near the center comes out clean. Cool in pan on a wire rack. Dust with confectioners' sugar, then cut into bars.

Lynn Hamilton, Naperville, Illinois ✻

No one ever guesses these sweet "apple" slices are made with zucchini. In fact, there isn't a bit of apple in them. What I like about this yummy recipe is that it makes a lot using economical ingredients.

mock apple pie squares

yield about 2-1/2 dozen

4	cups all-purpose flour
2	cups sugar
1/2	teaspoon salt
1-1/2	cups cold butter

FILLING:

8	cups sliced peeled zucchini
2/3	cup lemon juice
1	cup sugar
1	teaspoon ground cinnamon
1/4	teaspoon ground nutmeg
1/2	cup chopped walnuts
1/2	cup golden raisins

In a large bowl, combine the flour, sugar and salt. Cut in the butter until mixture resembles coarse crumbs. Press half of the crumb mixture into a greased 15-in. x 10-in. x 1-in. baking pan. Bake at 375° for 10-12 minutes or until lightly browned. Set remaining crumb mixture aside.

Meanwhile, in a large saucepan, bring zucchini and lemon juice to a boil. Reduce heat; cover and simmer for 5-6 minutes or until tender. Drain. Stir in the sugar, cinnamon, nutmeg and 1/2 cup reserved crumb mixture. Cook and stir for 2-3 minutes. Stir in walnuts and raisins.

Spread filling evenly over crust. Sprinkle with the remaining crumb mixture. Bake for 25-30 minutes or until golden brown. Cool on a wire rack. Cut into squares. Store in the refrigerator.

Laurie Lingenfelter, Nevada, Iowa ✻

I've gotten a lot of compliments on these bars. Even my husband's friends at work request the sweet, crispy treats.

caramel cereal treats

yield 3-1/2 dozen

8	cups Sugar Smacks cereal
1-3/4	cups dry roasted peanuts
1	package (14 ounces) caramels
1/2	cup sweetened condensed milk
1	tablespoon butter
1/2	cup milk chocolate chips, melted and cooled

In a large bowl, combine cereal and peanuts; set aside. In a large microwave-safe bowl, combine the caramels, milk and butter. Microwave, uncovered, on high for 1-2 minutes or until caramels are melted, stirring every 30 seconds.

Pour over cereal mixture; stir to coat. With greased hands, pat mixture into a greased 15-in. x 10-in. x 1-in. pan. Drizzle with chocolate. Let stand until set. Cut into bars.

editor's note: This recipe was tested in a 1,100-watt microwave.

 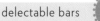

✳ Sharon Skildum, Maple Grove, Minnesota
A middle layer of coconut makes these sweet chocolaty treats taste similar to a Mounds candy bar!

chocolate coconut bars

yield about 3 dozen

2	cups graham cracker crumbs
1/2	cup butter, melted
1/4	cup sugar
2	cups flaked coconut
1	can (14 ounces) sweetened condensed milk
1/2	cup chopped pecans
1	plain chocolate candy bar (7 ounces)
2	tablespoons creamy peanut butter

Combine the crumbs, butter and sugar. Press into a greased 13-in. x 9-in. x baking pan. Bake at 350° for 10 minutes.

Meanwhile, in a bowl, combine the coconut, milk and pecans; spread over the crust. Bake at 350° for 15 minutes. Cool in pan on a wire rack.

In a small saucepan, melt candy bar and peanut butter over low heat; spread over cooled bars. Let stand until frosting is set. Cut into bars.

editor's note: Reduced-fat or generic brands of peanut butter are not recommended for this recipe.

✳ Krissy Fossmeyer
Huntley, Illinois
I'm expected to bring these wonderful treats to our family picnic each year. Their sweet apricot filling and delicate meringue topping make them everyone's favorite. I wouldn't dream of hosting a get-together without serving these bars.

apricot meringue bars

yield 32 bars

3	cups all-purpose flour
1	cup sugar, *divided*
1	cup cold butter
4	eggs, *separated*
1	teaspoon vanilla extract
2	cans (12 ounces *each*) apricot filling
1/2	cup chopped pecans

In a large bowl, combine flour and 1/2 cup sugar; cut in butter until crumbly. Add egg yolks and vanilla; mix well. Press into a greased 15-in. x 10-in. x 1-in. baking pan. Bake at 350° for 12-15 minutes or until lightly browned. Spread apricot filling over crust.

In a large bowl, beat egg whites until soft peaks form. Gradually add the remaining sugar, 1 tablespoon at a time, beating until stiff peaks form. Spread over apricot layer; sprinkle with the pecans.

Bake for 25-30 minutes or until lightly browned. Cool in pan on a wire rack. Cut into bars. Store in the refrigerator.

Esther Horst, Augusta, Wisconsin

While visiting a friend, I tried one of these tempting treats that her daughter made. After one bite, I knew I had to have the recipe. The cake-like bars have a fruity filling and creamy frosting.

frosted raspberry bars

yield about 2 dozen

1	cup butter, softened
1/4	cup sugar
3	cups all-purpose flour
3	teaspoons baking powder
1	teaspoon salt
2	eggs
1/2	cup milk
1	teaspoon vanilla extract
1	can (21 ounces) raspberry pie filling

FROSTING:

1	tablespoon butter, softened
1	tablespoon shortening
1	ounce cream cheese, softened
2	tablespoons marshmallow creme
1/2	cup plus 1 tablespoon confectioners' sugar
1	tablespoon milk

In a large bowl, cream butter and sugar until light and fluffy. Combine the flour, baking powder and salt. Combine eggs, milk and vanilla. Add flour mixture to the creamed mixture alternately with egg mixture; mix well. Divide dough in half; cover and refrigerate for 2 hours or until firm.

Roll out one portion of dough into a 15-in. x 10-in. rectangle; carefully transfer to a greased 15-in. x 10-in. x 1-in. baking pan. Spread with the raspberry filling. Roll out remaining dough to 1/4-in. thickness. Cut into 1/2-in.-wide strips; make a lattice crust over filling. Bake at 350° for 30 minutes or until golden brown. Cool in pan on a wire rack.

In a small bowl, beat the butter, shortening, cream cheese and marshmallow cream until smooth. Add the confectioners' sugar and milk; mix well. Drizzle over bars. Refrigerate until set before cutting into bars. Store in the refrigerator.

✳ Rhonda McKee, Greensburg, Kansas

These chewy bars have a tasty oatmeal crust that's covered with gooey caramel topping, chocolate chips and nuts. To cut down on last-minute prep, you can bake them ahead of time, seal them in a container and keep them in the fridge.

caramelitas

yield 3 dozen

1	cup plus 1 tablespoon all-purpose flour, *divided*
1	cup quick-cooking oats
3/4	cup packed brown sugar
1/2	teaspoon baking soda
1/4	teaspoon salt
3/4	cup butter, melted
1	cup (6 ounces) semisweet chocolate chips
1	jar (12-1/4 ounces) caramel ice cream topping
1/2	cup chopped walnuts

In a large bowl, combine 1 cup flour, oats, brown sugar, baking soda and salt. Stir in butter; mix well.

Press into a greased 13-in. x 9-in. baking pan. Bake at 350° for 10 minutes or until set. Sprinkle with chocolate chips.

Combine caramel topping and remaining flour until blended; drizzle over chips. Sprinkle with nuts. Bake 20-22 minutes longer or until bubbly. Cool completely; cut into bars.

✳ Dolores Skrout, Summerhill, Pennsylvania

I think my sweet bars taste like Almond Joy candy bars—with a bit of a twist from peanut butter.

almond coconut bars

yield 2 dozen

1-1/2	cups graham cracker crumbs
1/2	cup butter, melted
1	can (14 ounces) sweetened condensed milk
1	package (7 ounces) flaked coconut
2	cups (12 ounces) semisweet chocolate chips
1/2	cup peanut butter
24	blanched almonds

In a small bowl, combine the graham cracker crumbs and butter. Press into an ungreased 13-in. x 9-in. baking pan. Combine the milk and coconut; carefully spread over crust. Bake at 350° for 18-20 minutes or until lightly browned.

In a microwave-safe bowl, combine chocolate chips and peanut butter. Microwave on high for 1 minute; stir. Microwave 30-60 seconds longer or until chips are melted; stir until smooth.

Spread over warm bars. Garnish with almonds. Refrigerate for 1 hour before cutting.

Our staff created these delicious bars sure to satisfy any health-conscious cook. Applesauce moistens the batter while colorful dried cranberries, vanilla chips and heart-healthy pecans flavor each bite.

vanilla chip cranberry blondies

yield 20 bars

2	**eggs**
1/4	**cup canola oil**
1/4	**cup unsweetened applesauce**
1-1/2	**teaspoons vanilla extract**
1-1/3	**cups all-purpose flour**
2/3	**cup packed brown sugar**
1	**teaspoon baking powder**
1/2	**teaspoon salt**
1	**cup dried cranberries,** *divided*
1/2	**cup vanilla** *or* **white chips**
1/2	**cup chopped pecans**

In a large bowl, beat the eggs, oil, applesauce and vanilla. Combine the flour, brown sugar, baking powder and salt; stir into egg mixture until blended. Stir in 1/2 cup cranberries (batter will be thick).

Spread into a 13-in. x 9-in. baking pan coated with cooking spray. Top with the chips, pecans and remaining cranberries; gently press the topping down.

Bake at 350° for 15-20 minutes or until a toothpick inserted near the center comes out clean. Cool on a wire rack. Cut into bars.

ginger-cream bars

yield 5-6 dozen

1	**cup butter, softened**
1	**cup sugar**
2	**cups all-purpose flour**
1	**teaspoon salt**
2	**teaspoons baking soda**
1	**tablespoon ground cinnamon**
1	**tablespoon ground cloves**
1	**tablespoon ground ginger**
2	**eggs**
1/2	**cup molasses**
1	**cup hot coffee**

FROSTING:

1/2	**cup butter, softened**
1	**package (3 ounces) cream cheese, softened**
2	**cups confectioners' sugar**
2	**teaspoons vanilla extract**

Chopped nuts, optional

In a large bowl, cream butter and sugar until light and fluffy. Sift together flour, salt, baking soda and spices; add to creamed mixture. Add eggs, one at a time, beating well after each addition. Beat in molasses. Blend in coffee.

Spread in a 15-in. x 10-in. x 1-in. baking pan. Bake at 350° for 20-25 minutes. Cool in pan on a wire rack.

For frosting, in a small bowl, cream butter and cream cheese. Add sugar and vanilla. Spread over bars. Top with nuts if desired. Cut into bars. Store in the refrigerator.

Carol Nagelkirk ✳
Holland, Michigan
I rediscovered this old-time recipe recently and found it's everyone's favorite. Even four-year-olds have asked for these bars as nursery school treats.

* Shannon Koene, Blacksburg, Virginia
Memories of my mom's fruity date bars inspired me to create this wonderful recipe. I've had great results replacing the apricot jam with orange marmalade.

apricot date squares

yield: 3 dozen

1	cup water
1	cup sugar
1	cup chopped dates
1/2	cup 100% apricot spreadable fruit *or* jam
1-3/4	cups old-fashioned oats
1-1/2	cups all-purpose flour
1	cup flaked coconut
1	cup packed brown sugar
1	teaspoon ground cinnamon
1/4	teaspoon salt
3/4	cup cold butter, cubed

In a small saucepan, combine the water, sugar and dates. Bring to a boil. Reduce heat; simmer, uncovered, for 30-35 minutes or until mixture is reduced to 1-1/3 cups and is slightly thickened, stirring occasionally.

Remove from the heat. Stir in the spreadable fruit until blended; set aside. In a food processor, combine the oats, flour, coconut, brown sugar, cinnamon and salt. Add the butter; cover and process until the mixture resembles coarse crumbs.

Press 3 cups crumb mixture into a 13-in. x 9-in. baking dish coated with cooking spray. Spread date mixture to within 1/2 in. of edges. Sprinkle with the remaining crumb mixture; press down gently on crumbs.

Bake at 350° for 20-25 minutes or until edges are lightly browned. Cool on a wire rack. Cut into squares.

* Pat Habiger
Spearville, Kansas
I love almonds, and they really shine in these chewy bars that have a rich golden crust and sweet almond filling.

almond pie bars

yield 6-1/2 dozen

2	cups all-purpose flour
1/2	cup confectioners' sugar
1	cup cold butter, cubed
FILLING:	
2	cups sugar
1	cup chopped almonds
2	tablespoons all-purpose flour
4	eggs, lightly beaten
1/2	cup butter, melted
1/3	cup light corn syrup
1/2	teaspoon almond extract

For the crust, combine flour and confectioners' sugar. Cut in butter until mixture resembles coarse crumbs. Press into a greased 13-in. x 9-in. baking pan.

Bake at 350° for 10-15 minutes or until lightly browned. Meanwhile, in a large bowl, combine sugar, almonds and flour; stir in remaining filling ingredients.

Pour over crust. Bake at 350° for 25-30 minutes or until center is almost set. Cool on a wire rack. Cut into bars. Store in the refrigerator.

Chante Jones, Antioch, California ✳

Walnuts grow everywhere in California. I grew up on a "walnut acre" and love them. When I use walnuts, I always think back to my family and harvesttime. I hope you enjoy these bars as much as we do.

walnut bars

yield 2-1/2 dozen

- 1/2 **cup butter, softened**
- 1/4 **cup sugar**
- 1 **egg**
- 1/2 **teaspoon vanilla extract**
- 1-1/4 **cups all-purpose flour**
- 1/2 **teaspoon salt**

FILLING:

- 2 **eggs**
- 1-1/2 **cups packed brown sugar**
- 2 **tablespoons all-purpose flour**
- 1 **teaspoon vanilla extract**
- 1/2 **teaspoon salt**
- 1/2 **teaspoon baking powder**
- 1-1/2 **cups chopped walnuts**

LEMON GLAZE:

- 1-1/2 **cups confectioners' sugar**
- 2 **to 3 tablespoons lemon juice**

In a small bowl, cream butter and sugar until light and fluffy. Beat in egg and vanilla. Combine flour and salt; gradually add to creamed mixture and mix well.

Press onto the bottom of a greased 13-in. x 9-in. baking pan. Bake at 350° for 20 minutes or until edges are lightly browned.

For filling, in a bowl, combine the eggs, brown sugar, flour, vanilla, salt and baking powder. Stir in walnuts. Spread over crust. Bake for 25 minutes or until filling is golden brown. Cool on a wire rack.

Combine glaze ingredients; spread over filling. Let stand until set before cutting.

Brenda Lewing, Many, Louisiana ✳

These sweet peanut butter treats get plenty of crunch from a generous supply of sunflower kernels plus crisp rice cereal.

no-bake sunflower bars

yield 3 dozen

- 3 **cups sunflower kernels**
- 2 **cups flaked coconut**
- 1 **cup crisp rice cereal**
- 1 **cup packed brown sugar**
- 1 **cup light corn syrup**
- 1 **cup peanut butter**

In a large bowl, combine the sunflower kernels, coconut and rice cereal. In a saucepan, combine brown sugar and syrup. Bring to a boil; boil and stir for 2 minutes.

Remove from the heat; stir in peanut butter until well blended. Pour over sunflower mixture; stir until coated. Press into a greased 13-in. x 9-in. pan. Cool; cut into bars.

✳ Renette Cressey, Fort Mill, South Carolina
These soft bars provide just the right amount of tartness and sweetness. They are simply unbeatable!

rhubarb oat bars

yield 16 bars

1-1/2	cups chopped fresh *or* frozen rhubarb
1	cup packed brown sugar, *divided*
4	tablespoons water, *divided*
1	teaspoon lemon juice
4	teaspoons cornstarch
1	cup old-fashioned oats
3/4	cup all-purpose flour
1/2	cup flaked coconut
1/2	teaspoon salt
1/3	cup butter, melted

In a large saucepan, combine the rhubarb, 1/2 cup brown sugar, 3 tablespoons water and lemon juice. Bring to a boil. Reduce heat to medium; cook and stir for 4-5 minutes or until rhubarb is tender.

Combine the cornstarch and remaining water until smooth; gradually stir into rhubarb mixture. Bring to a boil; cook and stir for 2 minutes or until thickened. Remove from the heat; set aside.

In a large bowl, combine the oats, flour, coconut, salt and remaining brown sugar. Stir in butter until mixture is crumbly. Press half of the mixture into a greased 8-in. square baking dish. Spread with rhubarb mixture. Sprinkle with remaining oat mixture and press down lightly.

Bake at 350° for 25-30 minutes or until golden brown. Cool on a wire rack. Cut into squares.

springtime strawberry bars

yield about 3 dozen

✳ Marna Heitz
Farley, Iowa

Warmer weather calls for a dessert like these berry bars. The recipe makes a big batch, so it's perfect for company.

1	cup butter, softened
1-1/2	cups sugar
2	eggs
1	teaspoon grated lemon peel
3-1/4	cups all-purpose flour, *divided*
3/4	cup slivered almonds, chopped
1	teaspoon baking powder
1/2	teaspoon salt
1	jar (12 ounces) strawberry preserves

In a large bowl, cream the butter and sugar until light and fluffy. Add eggs, one at a time, beating well after each addition. Beat in lemon peel. Combine 3 cups flour, almonds, baking powder and salt; gradually add to creamed mixture until mixture resembles coarse crumbs (do not over mix).

Set aside 1 cup of dough. Press remaining dough into a greased 15-in. x 10-in. x 1-in. baking pan. Spread preserves to within 1/4 in. of edges. Combine the reserved dough with the remaining flour; sprinkle over preserves. Bake at 350° for 25-30 minutes or until lightly browned. Cool in pan on wire rack. Cut into bars.

Leanna Thorne, Lakewood, Colorado ✳
To give these fresh, fruity bars even more crunch, add a sprinkling of nuts to the yummy crumb topping.

raspberry patch crumb bars

yield 3 dozen

3	cups all-purpose flour
1-1/2	cups sugar, *divided*
1	teaspoon baking powder
1/4	teaspoon salt
1/4	teaspoon ground cinnamon
1	cup shortening
2	eggs, lightly beaten
1	teaspoon almond extract
1	tablespoon cornstarch
4	cups fresh *or* frozen raspberries

In a large bowl, combine the flour, 1 cup sugar, baking powder, salt and cinnamon. Cut in shortening until mixture resembles coarse crumbs. Stir in eggs and extract. Press two-thirds of the mixture into a greased 13-in. x 9-in. baking dish.

In a large bowl, combine cornstarch and remaining sugar; add berries and gently toss. Spoon over crust. Sprinkle with remaining crumb mixture.

Bake at 375° for 35-45 minutes or until bubbly and golden brown. Cool on a wire rack. Cut into bars. Store in the refrigerator.

editor's note: If using frozen raspberries, do not thaw before tossing with cornstarch mixture.

spiced pumpkin bars

yield 2-1/2 dozen

2	cups all-purpose flour
1-1/2	cups sugar
1	tablespoon baking powder
2	teaspoons ground cinnamon
1	teaspoon baking soda
1/2	teaspoon salt
1/2	teaspoon ground ginger
1/4	teaspoon ground nutmeg
1/4	teaspoon ground cloves
4	eggs
1-3/4	cups canned pumpkin
1	cup unsweetened applesauce

Confectioners' sugar, optional

In a bowl, combine the dry ingredients. In another bowl, combine the eggs, pumpkin and applesauce; mix well. Stir into dry ingredients.

Spread into a greased 15-in. x 10-in. x 1-in. baking pan. Bake at 350° for 20-25 minutes or until lightly browned. Do not overbake. Cool in pan on a wire rack. Cut into bars. Dust with confectioners' sugar if desired.

Richard Case ✳
Johnstown, Pennsylvania
My bars are moist, with bold pumpkin and spice flavors. When I want to lower the cholesterol, I use egg whites in place of the eggs.

※ Lynn Newman, Gainesville, Florida

These beautiful bars with a meringue and almond topping were among the winners of a cranberry festival baking contest. They're tangy, crunchy and subtly sweet.

ginger cranberry bars

yield 2 dozen

1	cup butter, softened
1/2	cup sugar
2	teaspoons almond extract, *divided*
2	cups all-purpose flour
2	cans (16 ounces *each*) whole-berry cranberry sauce
2	tablespoons candied *or* crystallized ginger, chopped
3	egg whites
1/2	cup confectioners' sugar
1/2	cup sliced almonds

In a large bowl, cream butter and sugar until light and fluffy. Stir in 1-1/2 teaspoons almond extract. Beat in flour until crumbly.

Press into a greased 13-in. x 9-in. baking dish. Bake at 350° for 25-28 minutes or until golden brown.

Meanwhile, in a small saucepan, heat cranberry sauce and ginger. In a small bowl, beat egg whites on medium speed until soft peaks form. Gradually beat in confectioners' sugar, 1 tablespoon at a time, and remaining extract on high until stiff glossy peaks form. Spread cranberry mixture over crust. Spread meringue over cranberry layer; sprinkle with almonds.

Increase heat to 400°. Bake for 14-15 minutes or until lightly browned. Cool completely before cutting. Refrigerate leftovers.

※ Valarie Wheeler, DeWitt, Michigan

This combination of buttery shortbread and sweet chocolate is wonderful. Whenever I make it, there is nothing but crumbs left. Be sure to cut these into small squares because they are very rich.

fudge-topped shortbread

yield 4 dozen

1	cup butter, softened
1/2	cup confectioners' sugar
1/4	teaspoon salt
1-1/4	cups all-purpose flour
1	can (14 ounces) sweetened condensed milk
2	cups (12 ounces) semisweet chocolate chips
1/2	teaspoon almond extract
1/3	cup sliced almonds, toasted

In a large bowl, cream the butter, sugar and salt until fluffy. Gradually beat in flour. Spread into a greased 13-in. x 9-in. baking pan. Bake at 350° for 16-20 minutes or until lightly browned.

In a microwave-safe bowl, combine condensed milk and chocolate chips. Microwave, uncovered, on high for 1-2 minutes or until chips are melted; stir until smooth. Stir in extract. Spread over the shortbread. Sprinkle with almonds and press down. Chill until set. Cut into squares.

Clara Honeyager, North Prairie, Wisconsin ✳
I love to cook large quantities and do most of the cooking for our church functions. People seem to enjoy these scrumptious bars even more than pecan pie.

pecan pie bars
yield 6-8 dozen

6	**cups all-purpose flour**
1-1/2	**cups sugar**
1	**teaspoon salt**
2	**cups cold butter, cubed**

FILLING:

8	**eggs**
3	**cups sugar**
3	**cups corn syrup**
1/2	**cup butter, melted**
3	**teaspoons vanilla extract**
5	**cups chopped pecans**

In a large bowl, combine the flour, sugar and salt. Cut in butter until crumbly. Press onto the bottom and up the sides of two greased 15-in. x 10-in. x 1-in. baking pans. Bake at 350° for 18-22 minutes or until crust edges are beginning to brown and bottom is set.

For filling, combine the eggs, sugar, corn syrup, butter and vanilla in a large bowl. Stir in pecans. Pour over crust.

Bake 25-30 minutes longer or until edges are firm and center is almost set. Cool on wire racks. Cut into bars. Refrigerate until serving.

cheesecake diamonds
yield 16 servings

5	**tablespoons butter, softened**
1/3	**cup packed brown sugar**
1	**cup all-purpose flour**
1/4	**cup chopped pecans**

FILLING:

1	**package (8 ounces) cream cheese, softened**
1/2	**cup sugar**
1	**egg**
2	**tablespoons heavy whipping cream**
1	**tablespoon lemon juice**
2	**teaspoons lemon peel**
1/2	**teaspoon vanilla extract**

In a small bowl, cream butter and brown sugar until light and fluffy. Gradually add flour to creamed mixture and mix well. Stir in pecans.

Set aside 1 cup for topping. Press the remaining mixture into a greased 8-in. square baking pan. Bake at 350° for 10-12 minutes or until set. Cool on a wire rack.

In another small bowl, beat cream cheese and sugar until smooth. Add egg, beating just until combined. Beat in the cream, lemon juice, peel and vanilla. Spread over crust. Sprinkle with reserved topping.

Bake at 350° for 20-22 minutes or until center is almost set. Cool on a wire rack for 1 hour. Refrigerate overnight. Cut into diamonds. Refrigerate leftovers.

Gloria Williams ✳
Chesapeake, Virginia
I found this simple recipe in an old cookbook. It's good to make when you know guests are coming the next day. The cheesecake bars have a pretty diamond shape and pleasant lemon flavor.

✱ Ron Roth, Three Rivers, Michigan
This Hungarian pastry has always been a family favorite. The dough is rich and soft, and the layers of nuts and jam make a delicious filling. Try using a floured pastry cloth when rolling out the dough. It makes placing the dough into the pan easier.

hungarian strawberry pastry bars
yield 2 dozen

5	cups all-purpose flour
1	cup plus 3 tablespoons sugar, *divided*
4	teaspoons baking powder
2	teaspoons baking soda
1/8	teaspoon salt
1-1/4	cups shortening
4	egg yolks
1/2	cup sour cream
1/4	cup water
1	teaspoon vanilla extract
2-1/2	cups chopped walnuts, *divided*
1	jar (18 ounces) seedless strawberry jam

In a large bowl, combine the flour, 1 cup sugar, baking powder, baking soda and salt. Cut in shortening until mixture resembles coarse crumbs. In a bowl, whisk the egg yolks, sour cream, water and vanilla; gradually add to crumb mixture, tossing with a fork until dough forms a ball. Divide into thirds. Chill for 30 minutes.

Between two large sheets of waxed paper, roll out one portion of dough into a 15-in. x 10-in. rectangle. Transfer to an ungreased 15-in. x 10-in. x 1-in. baking pan. Sprinkle with 1-1/4 cups walnuts and 2 tablespoons sugar. Roll out another portion of dough into a 15-in. x 10-in. rectangle; place over walnuts. Spread with jam; sprinkle with remaining walnuts and sugar.

Roll out the remaining pastry; cut into strips. Arrange in a crisscross pattern over filling. Trim and seal edges. Bake at 350° for 25-30 minutes or until golden brown. Cool on a wire rack. Cut into bars.

✱ Jeanne Gerlach
Frisco, Colorado
A friend from Texas gave me this recipe years ago. Because it's so easy to make, I've relied on it quite often.

chewy pecan bars
yield 3 dozen

1/4	cup butter, melted
4	eggs
2	cups packed brown sugar
2	teaspoons vanilla extract
2/3	cup all-purpose flour
1/4	teaspoon baking soda
1/4	teaspoon salt
2	cups chopped pecans

Confectioners' sugar

Spread butter evenly in an ungreased 13-in. x 9-in. baking pan. In a small bowl, beat eggs, brown sugar and vanilla. Combine flour, baking soda and salt; gradually add to egg mixture. Stir in pecans.

Spread into prepared pan. Bake at 350° for 30-35 minutes or until browned. Dust with confectioners' sugar. Cool on a wire rack. Cut into bars.

Wanda Borgen, Minot, North Dakota ✳
If your family likes corn chips, they'll love the sweet and salty blend in these stovetop bars. They also make great take-along treats for picnics or tailgate parties and are so easy, the kids may want to make their own batch.

salty peanut squares
yield 2 dozen

1	package (10 ounces) corn chips, lightly crushed, *divided*
1	cup unsalted peanuts, *divided*
1	cup light corn syrup
1	cup sugar
1	cup peanut butter
1/2	cup milk chocolate chips, melted

Place half of the corn chips and peanuts in a greased 13-in. x 9-in. pan; set aside. In a large saucepan, bring the corn syrup and sugar to a boil. Stir in peanut butter until blended. Drizzle half over corn chip mixture in pan.

Add remaining corn chips and peanuts to remaining syrup; stir until combined. Spoon over mixture in pan; press down lightly. Drizzle with melted chocolate. Cool before cutting.

simple raspberry almond bars
yield about 3 dozen

2	cups butter, softened
2	cups sugar
2	eggs
1	teaspoon almond extract
5	cups all-purpose flour
1	teaspoon baking powder
1	jar (12 ounces) raspberry jam

In a large bowl, cream the butter and sugar. Add eggs, one at a time, beating well after each addition. Beat in extract. Combine flour and baking powder; gradually add to the creamed mixture.

Press into a greased 13-in. x 9-in. x baking pan. With a moistened finger, make diagonal indentations every 2 in. in both directions, about 1/3 in. deep. Fill indentations with jam. Bake at 350° for 40 minutes or until lightly browned. Cool in pan on a wire rack. Cut into bars.

Ann Midkiff ✳
Jackson, Michigan
A pan of these thick bars makes a pretty presentation at any gathering. The buttery crust has a light almond flavor.

BAKING
tip

cut like a pro — For a bake shop appearance, remove bars without soft fillings and toppings from pan before cutting. Trim sides and then cut into rectangles, squares or diamonds. The trimmings can be crumbled and used as a topping for ice cream or pudding.

＊ Jennifer Dzubinski, San Antonio, Texas
If you need a homespun snack or bake sale treat that can be assembled in a hurry, try these moist, nutty bars. The squares are sweet, flavorful and loaded with chopped apple and nuts.

apple walnut squares

yield 16 servings

1/2	cup butter, softened
1	cup sugar
1	egg
1	cup all-purpose flour
1/2	teaspoon baking powder
1/2	teaspoon baking soda
1/2	teaspoon ground cinnamon
1	medium tart apple, peeled and chopped
3/4	cup chopped walnuts

In a large bowl, cream butter and sugar. Add the egg. Combine the flour, baking powder, baking soda and cinnamon; gradually add to the creamed mixture, beating just until combined. Stir in apple and walnuts.

Pour into a greased 8-in. square baking dish. Bake at 350° for 35-40 minutes or until a toothpick inserted near the center comes out clean. Cool on a wire rack.

＊ Marguerite Emery, Orland, California
I came across these bars while stationed at a Michigan Air Force base in 1964, and have been making them ever since. My children don't think an event is special unless these bars are part of it.

cherry coconut bars

yield 3 dozen

1	cup all-purpose flour
3	tablespoons confectioners' sugar
1/2	cup cold butter

FILLING:

2	eggs
1	cup sugar
1	teaspoon vanilla extract
1/4	cup all-purpose flour
1/2	teaspoon baking powder
1/4	teaspoon salt
3/4	cup chopped walnuts
1/2	cup quartered maraschino cherries
1/2	cup flaked coconut

In a bowl, combine flour and confectioners' sugar; cut in butter until crumbly. Press into a lightly greased 13-in. x 9-in. baking pan. Bake at 350° for 10-12 minutes or until lightly browned. Cool in pan on wire rack.

For filling, combine the eggs, sugar and vanilla in a bowl. Combine flour, baking powder and salt; add to the egg mixture. Stir in walnuts, cherries and coconut. Spread over crust. Bake at 350° 20-25 minutes longer or until firm. Cool in pan on a wire rack. Cut into bars.

Shari Roach, South Milwaukee, Wisconsin ✳

Once I tried these rich, gooey bars, I just had to have the recipe so I could make them for my family and friends. The shortbread-like crust and rhubarb and custard layers inspire people to find rhubarb they can use to fix a batch for themselves.

rhubarb custard bars

yield 3 dozen

- 2   cups all-purpose flour
- 1/4   cup sugar
- 1   cup cold butter

FILLING:

- 2   cups sugar
- 7   tablespoons all-purpose flour
- 1   cup heavy whipping cream
- 3   eggs, beaten
- 5   cups finely chopped fresh *or* frozen rhubarb, thawed

TOPPING:

- 2   packages (3 ounces *each*) cream cheese, softened
- 1/2   cup sugar
- 1/2   teaspoon vanilla extract
- 1   cup heavy whipping cream, whipped

In a bowl, combine the flour and sugar; cut in butter until the mixture resembles coarse crumbs. Press into a greased 13-in. x 9-in. baking pan. Bake at 350° for 10 minutes.

Meanwhile, for filling, combine sugar and flour in a bowl. Whisk in cream and eggs. Stir in the rhubarb. Pour over crust. Bake at 350° for 40-45 minutes or until custard is set. Cool in pan on a wire rack.

For topping, beat cream cheese, sugar and vanilla until smooth; fold in whipped cream. Spread over top. Cover and refrigerate. Cut into bars. Store in the refrigerator.

editor's note: If using frozen rhubarb, measure rhubarb while still frozen, then thaw completely. Drain in a colander, but do not press liquid out.

cranberry nut bars

yield 3 dozen

- 1/2   cup butter, softened
- 3/4   cup sugar
- 3/4   cup packed brown sugar
- 2   eggs
- 1   teaspoon vanilla extract
- 1-1/2   cups all-purpose flour
- 1   teaspoon baking powder
- 1/2   teaspoon salt
- 1   cup chopped fresh *or* frozen cranberries
- 1/2   cup chopped walnuts

In a large bowl, cream butter and sugars. Add the eggs, one at a time, beating well after each addition. Beat in the vanilla. Combine the flour, baking powder and salt; gradually add to creamed mixture. Stir in cranberries and nuts.

Spread into a greased 13-in. x 9-in. baking pan. Bake at 350° for 20-25 minutes or until golden brown. Cool on a wire rack. Cut into bars.

Karen Jarocki ✳
Monte Vista, Colorado

My husband's aunt sent us these bars one Christmas. The fresh cranberry flavor was such a nice change from the usual cookies. I had to have the recipe, and she was gracious enough to provide it.

✳ Janis Luedtke, Thornton, Colorado

Memories of lunchtime at school and my Aunt Shelly's kitchen come to mind when I bite into these sweet, chewy bars. My husband is the biggest fan of these peanut butter and chocolate treats.

glazed peanut butter bars
yield 4 dozen

3/4	cup butter, softened
3/4	cup creamy peanut butter
3/4	cup sugar
3/4	cup packed brown sugar
2	teaspoons water
2	eggs
1-1/2	teaspoons vanilla extract
1-1/2	cups all-purpose flour
1-1/2	cups quick-cooking oats
3/4	teaspoon baking soda
1/2	teaspoon salt

GLAZE:

1-1/4	cups milk chocolate chips
1/2	cup butterscotch chips
1/2	cup creamy peanut butter

In a large bowl, cream the butter, peanut butter, sugars and water. Beat in eggs and vanilla. Combine the flour, oats, baking soda and salt; gradually add to creamed mixture.

Spread into a greased 15-in. x 10-in. x 1-in. baking pan. Bake at 325° for 18-22 minutes or until lightly browned.

For glaze, in a microwave-safe bowl, melt chips and peanut butter; pour over warm bars and spread evenly. Cool completely on a wire rack before cutting.

Cora Dunlop, Boston Bar, British Columbia ✳

Ginger complements the flavor of fresh pears and chewy coconut in these delicious, fast-to-fix fruit bars.

pear bar cookies
yield 16 bars

1-1/4	cups all-purpose flour
1/2	cup sugar
1/2	cup cold butter

FILLING:

2	eggs
1/2	cup packed brown sugar
1/2	teaspoon vanilla extract
1/3	cup all-purpose flour
1/4	teaspoon baking powder
1/4	teaspoon salt
1/4	teaspoon ground ginger
2	medium pears, peeled and diced
1/2	cup flaked coconut

In a small bowl, combine the flour and sugar. Cut in butter until mixture resembles coarse crumbs. Press into a greased 9-in. square baking pan. Bake at 350° for 25-28 minutes or until golden brown.

In a small bowl, beat the eggs, brown sugar and vanilla. Combine the flour, baking powder, salt and ginger; stir into egg mixture just until moistened. Gently stir in pears and coconut.

Spread over warm crust. Bake 20-23 minutes longer or until golden brown. Cool on a wire rack. Cut into bars.

grandma's chocolate chip bars
yield 2 dozen

1	cup shortening
1/2	cup sugar
1/2	cup packed brown sugar
3	egg yolks
1	tablespoon water
1	teaspoon vanilla extract
2	cups all-purpose flour
1	teaspoon baking powder
1/2	teaspoon salt
1/4	teaspoon baking soda
1	cup semisweet chocolate chips

TOPPING:

3	egg whites
1	teaspoon vanilla extract
1/8	teaspoon salt
1	cup packed brown sugar
1/4	cup chopped walnuts

In a large bowl, cream shortening and sugars until light and fluffy. Beat in the egg yolks, water and vanilla. Combine the flour, baking powder, salt and baking soda; gradually add to the creamed mixture and mix well. Stir in the chocolate chips.

Spread into a greased 13-in. x 9-in. baking pan. Bake at 350° for 15 minutes or until top is dry.

Meanwhile, in a large bowl, beat egg whites, vanilla and salt on medium speed until soft peaks form. Gradually beat in sugar, 1 tablespoon at a time on high until stiff peaks form.

Spread over warm crust to within 1 in. of edges. Sprinkle with walnuts. Bake for 25 minutes or until a toothpick comes out clean. Cool on a wire rack. Cut into bars.

Sandy Hartig ✳
New Berlin, Wisconsin
My grandmother made these delicious bar cookies with a unique meringue topping for every holiday and birthday gathering. She's now gone, but her wonderful recipe lives on.

※ Mimi Priesman, Pace, Florida

A co-worker's mother gave me this gem of a recipe a few years back. I can never decide what's more appealing—the attractive look of the bars or their incredible aroma while baking! Everyone who tries them asks for the recipe.

raspberry almond bars

yield 2 dozen

1/2	cup butter, cubed
1	package (10 to 12 ounces) vanilla *or* white chips, *divided*
2	eggs
1/2	cup sugar
1	teaspoon almond extract
1	cup all-purpose flour
1/2	teaspoon salt
1/2	cup seedless raspberry jam
1/4	cup sliced almonds

In a small saucepan, melt butter. Remove from the heat; add 1 cup chips (do not stir). In a small bowl, beat eggs until foamy; gradually add sugar. Stir in chip mixture and almond extract. Combine flour and salt; gradually add to egg mixture just until combined.

Spread half of the batter into a greased 9-in. square baking pan. Bake at 325° for 15-20 minutes or until golden brown.

In a small saucepan, melt jam over low heat; spread over warm crust. Stir remaining chips into the remaining batter; drop by teaspoonfuls over the jam layer. Sprinkle with almonds.

Bake 30-35 minutes longer or until a toothpick inserted near the center comes out clean. Cool on a wire rack. Cut into bars.

※ Weda Mosellie, Phillipsburg, New Jersey

My mom tops a pistachio crust with apricot preserves and more chopped nuts to make these moist and buttery shortbread-like bars. They're the perfect dessert for a Syrian menu...or most any meal.

pistachio apricot bars

yield 2-1/2 dozen

1	cup butter, softened
1	cup sugar
1	egg
1	teaspoon vanilla extract
2-1/2	cups all-purpose flour
1/2	cup chopped pistachios
1	jar (18 ounces) apricot preserves
	Additional chopped pistachios, optional

In a small bowl, cream butter and sugar until light and fluffy. Beat in the egg and vanilla. Gradually add flour to the creamed mixture and mix well. Stir in the pistachios. Press into a greased 13-in. x 9-in. baking dish. Spread with the preserves.

Bake at 350° for 25-30 minutes or until edges begin to brown. Cool on a wire rack. Cut into bars. Garnish with pistachios if desired.

Margery Richmond, Fort Collins, Colorado ✳

With lots of peanuts and butterscotch flavor plus a rich, buttery crust, these easy-to-make bars are so good.

butterscotch peanut bars

yield 4 dozen

- 1/2 **cup butter, softened**
- 3/4 **cup packed brown sugar**
- 1-1/2 **cups all-purpose flour**
- 1/2 **teaspoon salt**
- 3 **cups salted peanuts**

TOPPING:

- 1 **package (10 to 11 ounces) butterscotch chips**
- 1/2 **cup light corn syrup**
- 2 **tablespoons butter**
- 1 **tablespoon water**

Line a 15-in. x 10-in. x 1-in. baking pan with aluminum foil. Coat the foil with cooking spray; set aside.

In a small bowl, cream butter and brown sugar until light and fluffy. Combine flour and salt; gradually add to creamed mixture and mix well. Press into prepared pan. Bake at 350° for 6 minutes. Sprinkle with peanuts.

In a large saucepan, combine topping ingredients. Cook and stir over medium heat until chips and butter are melted. Spread over hot crust. Bake for 12-15 minutes longer or until topping is bubbly. Cool on a wire rack. Cut into bars.

fruit 'n' nut bars

yield 1-1/2 dozen

- 1-1/4 **cups chopped almonds**
- 1 **jar (2 ounces) sesame seeds**
- 4 **cups quick-cooking oats**
- 1 **cup dark seedless raisins**
- 1 **cup light corn syrup**
- 2/3 **cup canola oil**
- 1/2 **cup hulled sunflower seeds**
- 1/2 **cup toasted wheat germ**
- 1/2 **cup nonfat dry milk powder**
- 2 **teaspoons ground cinnamon**
- 1 **teaspoon vanilla extract**
- 1/2 **teaspoon salt**

In a large bowl, combine all ingredients; mix well. Press mixture firmly and evenly into a greased 15-in. x 10-in. x 1-in. baking pan.

Bake at 350° for 25 minutes or until golden brown. Cool in pan on wire rack for at least 2 hours. Cut into bars. Store in refrigerator.

Mrs. John Nagel ✳
Deerbrook, Wisconsin

Here's a healthy treat that grandchildren are sure to enjoy. These granola-like bars are filled with flavor and good-for-you ingredients. For convenient snacking, wrap the bars individually in plastic wrap.

✳ Janis Loomis, Madison, Virginia

I created these chewy granola bars while searching for a healthy snack for my family. Now, wherever we go, folks request these bars—and the recipe.

white chocolate cranberry granola bars

yield 2 dozen

1/4	cup sugar
1/4	cup honey
1/4	cup maple syrup
2	tablespoons reduced-fat peanut butter
1	egg white
1	tablespoon fat-free evaporated milk
1	teaspoon vanilla extract
1	cup whole wheat flour
1/2	teaspoon baking soda
1/2	teaspoon ground cinnamon
1/4	teaspoon ground allspice
2	cups old-fashioned oats
1-1/2	cups crisp rice cereal
1/3	cup vanilla *or* white chips
1/4	cup dried cranberries
1/4	cup chopped walnuts

In a large bowl, combine the first seven ingredients. Combine the flour, baking soda, cinnamon and allspice; stir into sugar mixture. Stir in oats, cereal, chips, cranberries and walnuts.

Press into a 13-in. x 9-in. baking pan coated with cooking spray. Bake at 350° for 18-20 minutes or until golden brown. Cool in pan on a wire rack. Cut into bars. Store in the refrigerator.

✳ Connie Craig
Lakewood, Washington

These chewy crowd-pleasers feature all sorts of goodies, including chocolate chips, raisins, coconut and candy-coated baking bits. For a more colorful look, press the baking bits on top of the bars instead of stirring them into the mixture.

cereal cookie bars

yield 6 dozen

9	cups crisp rice cereal
6-1/2	cups quick-cooking oats
1	cup cornflakes
1	cup flaked coconut
2	packages (one 16 ounces, one 10-1/2 ounces) miniature marshmallows
1	cup butter, cubed
1/2	cup honey
1/2	cup chocolate chips
1/2	cup raisins
1/2	cup M&M miniature baking bits

In a large bowl, combine the cereal, oats, cornflakes and coconut; set aside. In a large saucepan, cook and stir the marshmallows and butter over low heat until melted and smooth. Stir in honey. Pour over cereal mixture; stir until coated. Cool for 5 minutes.

Stir in chocolate chips, raisins and baking bits. Press into two greased 15-in. x 10-in. x 1-in. pans. Cool for 30 minutes before cutting.

Oats and almonds are a crunchy complement to the sweet pineapple filling in these delectable bars.

pineapple almond bars

yield 1 dozen

3/4	cup all-purpose flour
3/4	cup quick-cooking oats
1/3	cup packed brown sugar
5	tablespoons cold butter
1/2	teaspoon almond extract
3	tablespoons sliced almonds
1	cup pineapple preserves

In a food processor, combine the flour, oats and brown sugar; cover and process until blended. Add butter and extract; cover and pulse until crumbly. Remove 1/2 cup crumb mixture to a bowl; stir in sliced almonds.

Press remaining crumb mixture into a 9-in. square baking pan coated with cooking spray. Spread preserves over crust. Sprinkle with reserved crumb mixture. Bake at 350° for 25-30 minutes or until golden. Cool in pan on a wire rack. Cut into bars.

chocolaty raisin oat bars

yield 4 dozen

1	can (14 ounces) sweetened condensed milk
2	squares (1 ounce *each*) unsweetened chocolate
2	cups raisins
1	cup butter, softened
1-1/3	cups packed brown sugar
1-1/2	teaspoons vanilla extract
2-1/2	cups quick-cooking oats
2	cups all-purpose flour
3/4	teaspoon salt
1/2	teaspoon baking soda

In a microwave-safe bowl, combine milk and chocolate. Microwave on high for 2 minutes or until chocolate is melted; stir until smooth. Stir in raisins; set aside to cool slightly.

In a large bowl, cream butter and brown sugar. Beat in vanilla. Combine the remaining ingredients; gradually add to creamed mixture (dough will be crumbly). Set aside half for topping.

Press remaining crumb mixture into an ungreased 13-in. x 9-in. baking pan. Spread with the chocolate raisin mixture. Sprinkle with reserved crumb mixture; press down lightly. Bake at 375° for 25-30 minutes or until golden brown. Cool in pan on a wire rack. Cut into bars.

Linda Ploeg ✳
Rockford, Michigan
These attractive layered bars have a similar taste to chocolate-covered raisins. "Yum!" is usually how folks describe every bite.

BAKING tip

perfectly sized bars — For uniform bars or squares, use a ruler and make cut marks with the point of a sharp knife. Lay the ruler on top of the bars between the guide marks and use the edge as a cutting guide. If you're cutting the bars in the pan, remove a corner piece first, then the rest will be easier to remove.

✳ Karla Johnson, East Helena, Montana
My family loves the warm pumpkin fragrance that wafts through our kitchen on cool, fall afternoons when I make these bars. Jack-o'-lantern faces only add to the festive autumn flavor.

halloween pumpkin bars

yield 35 bars

1-1/2	cups pumpkin pie filling
2	cups sugar
1	cup canola oil
4	eggs
1	teaspoon vanilla extract
2	cups all-purpose flour
2	teaspoons baking powder
1	teaspoon baking soda
1/2	teaspoon salt
1	cup chopped pecans
1	can (16 ounces) cream cheese frosting

Yellow and red food coloring

70	pieces candy corn
1/2	cup milk chocolate chips

In a large bowl, beat the pumpkin, sugar, oil, eggs and vanilla. Combine the flour, baking powder, baking soda and salt; gradually add to pumpkin mixture and mix well. Stir in pecans.

Pour into a greased 15-in. x 10-in. x 1-in. baking pan. Bake at 350° for 20-25 minutes or until a toothpick inserted near the center comes out clean. Cool on a wire rack.

Tint the frosting orange with yellow and red food coloring. Frost bars; cut into 35 squares. For eyes, place two pieces of the candy corn on each bar.

In a microwave, melt chocolate chips; stir until smooth. Transfer to a heavy-duty resealable plastic bag; cut a small hole in a corner of the bag. Pipe dots on candy corn for pupils; decorate faces as desired.

✳ Renee Schwebach
Dumont, Minnesota
To satisfy a sweet tooth, try these deliciously different bars. A tasty variety of flavors and textures guarantees that the treats never last long.

graham coconut treats

yield 3 dozen

3	eggs, lightly beaten
1-1/2	cups sugar
1	cup butter
4	cups miniature marshmallows
3	cups graham cracker crumbs (about 48 squares)
3/4	cup flaked coconut
3/4	cup chopped pecans
1-1/2	teaspoons vanilla extract

In a heavy saucepan over low heat or double boiler over simmering water, combine the eggs, sugar and butter. Cook and stir until mixture thickness and reaches 160°. Remove from the heat; cool.

Add remaining ingredients; mix well. Spoon into a greased 13-in. x 9-in. baking pan. Chill for at least 2 hours. Cut into squares.

Taste of Home Test Kitchen ✳

Honey and spices give great flavor to these cake-like bars topped with a thin sugar glaze.

glazed lebkuchen

yield about 2 dozen

3/4	cup honey
1/2	cup sugar
1/4	cup packed brown sugar
2	eggs
2-1/2	cups all-purpose flour
1-1/4	teaspoons ground cinnamon
1	teaspoon baking soda
1/4	teaspoon ground cloves
1/8	teaspoon ground allspice
3/4	cup chopped slivered almonds
1/2	cup finely chopped citron
1/2	cup finely chopped candied lemon peel

FROSTING:

1	cup confectioners' sugar
3	tablespoons hot milk *or* water
1/4	teaspoon vanilla extract

Candied cherries and additional citron

In a saucepan, bring honey to a boil. Remove from the heat; cool to room temperature. In a large bowl, combine honey and sugars; mix well. Add eggs, one at a time, beating well after each addition. Combine the flour, cinnamon, baking soda, cloves and allspice; gradually add to honey mixture. Stir in nuts, citron and lemon peel (mixture will be thick).

Press into a greased 15-in. x 10-in. x 1-in. baking pan. Bake at 350° for 20-28 minutes or until top springs back with lightly touched.

Meanwhile, combine the confectioners' sugar, milk and vanilla; mix well. Spread over bars while warm. Immediately cut into bars. Decorate with cherries and citron. Cool in pan on a wire rack.

shortcut creations

peach almond bars, p. 287

Make fabulous cookies without

all the mixing and measuring. These cookies all start with a convenience product such as cake mixes, refrigerated cookie dough or store-bought cookies. Just add a few items to quickly create rave-winning homemade delights.

peanut butter cookie cups, p. 294

mexican cookies, p. 280

※ Barb Wyman, Hankinson, North Dakota

Because I love candy bars and marshmallows, this recipe was a cinch to invent—and I've yet to find anyone who doesn't enjoy it! The quick bars make great individually wrapped treats for picnics, lunch boxes or out-the-door snacking. And with all the different layers and flavors, they're sure to please just about everyone.

almost a candy bar

yield 3 dozen

1	tube (16-1/2 ounces) refrigerated chocolate chip cookie dough
4	nutty s'mores trail mix bars (1.23 ounces *each*), chopped
1	package (11 ounces) butterscotch chips
2-1/2	cups miniature marshmallows
1	cup chopped walnuts
1-1/2	cups miniature pretzels
1	package (10 ounces) peanut butter chips
3/4	cup light corn syrup
1/4	cup butter, cubed
1	package (11-1/2 ounces) milk chocolate chips

Let dough stand at room temperature for 5-10 minutes to soften. In a large bowl, combine dough and trail mix bars. Press into an ungreased 13-in. x 9-in. baking pan. Bake, uncovered, at 350° for 10-12 minutes or until golden brown.

Sprinkle with butterscotch chips and marshmallows. Bake 3-4 minutes longer or until marshmallows begin to brown. Sprinkle with walnuts; arrange pretzels over the top. In a small saucepan, melt peanut butter chips, corn syrup and butter; spoon over bars.

In a microwave, melt chocolate chips; stir until smooth. Transfer to a small plastic bag; cut a small hole in a corner of the bag. Drizzle chocolate over bars. Refrigerate for 1 hour or until firm before cutting.

Shirley Dehler, Columbus, Wisconsin ✳
Looking for a speedy way to transform plain old refrigerated cookie dough into something special enough for unexpected guests? Try this treat! I dress up the bars with chocolate chips, coconut and whatever nuts I have on hand.

fancy sugar cookie bars

yield 2 dozen

1 tube (16-1/2 ounces) refrigerated sugar cookie dough
1 cup semisweet chocolate chips
1/2 cup flaked coconut
1/4 cup chopped pecans

Let dough stand at room temperature for 5-10 minutes to soften. Press into an ungreased 13-in. x 9-in. baking pan. Bake at 350° for 10-12 minutes or until golden brown.

Sprinkle with chocolate chips, coconut and pecans. Bake 10-12 minutes longer or until golden brown. Cool on a wire rack.

pecan-topped sugar cookies

yield about 3-1/2 dozen

Betty Lech ✳
St. Charles, Illinois
This recipe jazzes up refrigerated cookie dough with cream cheese and coconut. Folks love the almond flavor.

1 can (8 ounces) almond paste
1 package (3 ounces) cream cheese, softened
1/4 cup flaked coconut
1 tube (18 ounces) refrigerated sugar cookie dough
1 cup pecan halves

In a large bowl, beat almond paste and cream cheese. Add coconut; mix well. Cut cookie dough into 1/2-in. slices; divide each slice into four portions.

Roll into balls. Place 2 in. apart on greased baking sheets. Shape 1/2 teaspoonfuls of almond mixture into balls; place one on each ball of dough. Lightly press pecans into tops.

Bake at 350° for 10-12 minutes or until lightly browned. Remove to wire racks to cool.

BAKING
tip

baking cookies — Always preheat the oven before baking cookies. If you find your baking time is significantly different from the time stated in the recipe, check the oven temperature with an oven thermometer. If it is off from the set temperature, adjust the set temperature to compensate for the difference.

Julie Plummer, Sykesville, Maryland
Make any day special with these crispy coffee-dunkers. They're great for bake sales, too. Simply bake up a batch, wrap several slices in bright cellophane and decorate with fun stickers and curly ribbon. They are sure to go fast.

toffee-almond cookie slices

yield 2-1/2 dozen

1	**package (17-1/2 ounces) sugar cookie mix**
1/2	**cup all-purpose flour**
1/2	**cup butter, softened**
1	**egg**
1/3	**cup slivered almonds, toasted**
1/3	**cup miniature semisweet chocolate chips**
1/3	**cup English toffee bits *or* almond brickle chips**

In a large bowl, combine the sugar cookie mix, flour, butter and egg. Stir in the almonds, chocolate chips and toffee bits.

Divide dough in half. On an ungreased baking sheet, shape each portion into a 10-in. x 2-1/2-in. rectangle. Bake at 350° for 25-30 minutes or until lightly browned.

Carefully remove to wire racks; cool for 10 minutes. Transfer to a cutting board; with a serrated knife, cut each rectangle diagonally into 15 slices.

Place cut side down on ungreased baking sheets. Bake for 15-20 minutes or until golden brown. Remove to wire racks to cool. Store in an airtight container.

Ellen Govertsen, Wheaton, Illinois
Chocolate chips and a fudge brownie mix create the rich flavor in these sweet cookies. Rolling the dough in powdered sugar gives them their inviting crackled appearance.

brownie crackles

yield 4-1/2 dozen

1	**package fudge brownie mix (13-inch x 9-inch pan size)**
1	**cup all-purpose flour**
1	**egg**
1/2	**cup water**
1/4	**cup canola oil**
1	**cup (6 ounces) semisweet chocolate chips**

Confectioners' sugar

In a large bowl, combine brownie mix, flour, egg, water and oil; mix well. Stir in chocolate chips. Place confectioners' sugar in a shallow dish. Drop dough by tablespoonfuls into sugar; roll to coat.

Place 2 in. apart on greased baking sheets. Bake at 350° for 8-10 minutes or until set. Remove to wire racks to cool.

Carolyn Mulloy, Davison, Michigan ✳

My two sons are crazy about these simple, fast-fixing cookie bars. And as a busy mom, I can rely on this dessert's easy preparation—even at the last minute. You can vary the jam or jelly to suit your family's tastes.

peanut butter 'n' jelly bars

yield 2 dozen

1 tube (16-1/2 ounces) refrigerated peanut butter cookie dough
1/2 cup peanut butter chips
1 can (16 ounces) buttercream frosting
1/4 cup creamy peanut butter
1/4 cup seedless raspberry jam *or* grape jelly

Let dough stand at room temperature for 5-10 minutes to soften. Press into an ungreased 13-in. x 9-in. baking dish; sprinkle with peanut butter chips.

Bake at 375° for 15-18 minutes or until lightly browned and edges are firm to the touch. Cool on a wire rack.

In a small bowl, beat frosting and peanut butter until smooth. Spread over bars. Drop jam by teaspoonfuls over frosting; cut through frosting with a knife to swirl the jam.

Kathy Ybarra, Rock Springs, Wyoming
Add a sweet treat to a meal of tacos, enchiladas or fajitas with this easy no-fuss dessert.

mexican cookies

yield 32 cookies

4	flour tortillas (6 inches)
1/2	cup semisweet chocolate chips
3/4	teaspoon shortening
1/4	cup confectioners' sugar
1/4	teaspoon ground cinnamon

Cut each tortilla into eight wedges; place on ungreased baking sheets. Bake at 400° for 10-12 minutes or until lightly browned.

Meanwhile, in a microwave or heavy saucepan, melt chocolate chips and shortening. Stir until smooth; keep warm. In a large resealable plastic bag, combine confectioners' sugar and cinnamon. Add tortilla wedges a few at a time; shake to coat. Place on waxed paper-lined baking sheets. Drizzle with melted chocolate. Refrigerate until serving.

Betty Janway
Ruston, Louisiana
No one will guess these buttery treats start with a simple cake mix and a package of instant pudding!

butterscotch pecan cookies

yield 4 dozen

1	package (18-1/4 ounces) butter recipe cake mix
1	package (3.4 ounces) instant butterscotch pudding mix
1/4	cup all-purpose flour
3/4	cup canola oil
1	egg
1	cup chopped pecans

In large bowl, combine the first five ingredients; mix well. Stir in the pecans (the dough will be crumbly).

Roll tablespoonfuls into balls; place 2 in. apart on greased baking sheets. Bake at 350° for 10-12 minutes or until golden brown. Cool for 2 minutes before removing to wire racks.

editor's note: This recipe was tested with Pillsbury brand butter recipe cake mix.

Clara Hielkema
Wyoming, Michigan
You'll be amazed and delighted with how quickly you can whip up a batch of these cookies.

cookies in a jiffy

yield 2 dozen

1	package (9 ounces) yellow cake mix
2/3	cup quick-cooking oats
1/2	cup butter, melted
1	egg
1/2	cup red and green Holiday M&M's *or* butterscotch chips

In a large bowl, beat the first four ingredients. Stir in the M&M's or chips.

Drop by tablespoonfuls 2 in. apart onto ungreased baking sheets. Bake at 375° for 10-12 minutes or until lightly browned. Immediately remove to wire racks to cool.

Kimberly Biel, Java, South Dakota ✳

I bring these quick-and-easy treats to church meetings, potlucks and housewarming parties. I often make a double batch so we can enjoy some at home.

can't leave alone bars

yield 3 dozen

1	package (18-1/4 ounces) white cake mix
2	eggs
1/3	cup canola oil
1	can (14 ounces) sweetened condensed milk
1	cup (6 ounces) semisweet chocolate chips
1/4	cup butter, cubed

In a large bowl, combine the dry cake mix, eggs and oil. Press two-thirds of the mixture into a greased 13-in. x 9-in. baking pan. Set remaining cake mixture aside.

In a microwave-safe bowl, combine the milk, chocolate chips and butter. Microwave, uncovered, until chips and butter are melted; stir until smooth. Pour over crust.

Drop teaspoonfuls of remaining cake mixture over top. Bake at 350° for 20-25 minutes or until lightly browned. Cool before cutting.

editor's note: This recipe was tested in a 1,100-watt microwave.

Melanie Steele, Plano, Texas ✳

I rely on a cake mix and chocolate-covered caramels to fix these popular cookies. They are very fast to prepare, yet they taste so good when served fresh from the oven. People are surprised to find a gooey caramel center.

easy chocolate caramel cookies

yield 3 dozen

1	package (18-1/4 ounces) devil's food cake mix
1	egg
1/4	cup water
3	tablespoons canola oil
38	Rolo candies

Chopped hazelnuts

In a large bowl, combine the dry cake mix, egg, water and oil; mix well. Roll rounded teaspoonfuls of dough into balls. Press a candy into each; reshape balls. Dip tops in hazelnuts.

Place on ungreased baking sheets. Bake at 350° for 8-10 minutes or until tops are cracked. Cool for 2 minutes before removing to wire racks.

editor's note: If the dough is sticky, spray hands lightly with cooking spray before rolling into balls.

*✳ Mary White, Pawnee City, Nebraska
Prepared cookie dough and instant pudding mix hurry along the preparation of this lovely layered dessert.*

chocolate chip cookie pizza

yield 14-16 slices

1	**tube (18 ounces) chocolate chip cookie dough**
1	**package (8 ounces) cream cheese, softened**
1/3	**cup sugar**
2	**cups cold half-and-half cream**
1	**package (3.9 ounces) instant chocolate pudding mix**
1/4	**cup chopped pecans *or* walnuts**

Press cookie dough onto an ungreased 12-in. pizza pan. Bake at 350° for 13-16 minutes or until center is set and cookie is lightly browned. Cool in pan for 5 minutes; gently run a flexible metal spatula under the crust to loosen. Cool completely.

In a small bowl, beat cream cheese and sugar until blended. Spread over crust. In a large bowl, whisk cream and pudding mix for 2 minutes. Let stand for 2 minutes or until soft-set. Spread over cream cheese mixture; sprinkle with nuts. Refrigerate until serving.

*✳ Geraldine Sliva, Elgin, Illinois
Because so many people seem to love the combination of chocolate and peanut butter, I came up with this no-bake cookie recipe.*

chocolate peanut butter grahams

yield 5 dozen

1	**jar (18 ounces) peanut butter**
1	**package (16 ounces) graham crackers, broken into rectangles**
1-1/2	**pounds milk chocolate candy coating**

Spread a rounded teaspoonful of peanut butter on one side of half of the graham crackers. Top with remaining crackers.

In a heavy saucepan over low heat, melt candy coating; stir until smooth. Dip cookies in coating to completely cover; allow excess to drip off. Place on waxed paper-lined baking sheets; let stand until set. Store in an airtight container in a cool, dry place.

Susan Laubach, Vida, Montana ✳
To keep my holiday baking quick and easy, I've come to rely on fast recipes like this one. The crunchy-chewy tidbits are our youngsters' favorite treat.

chocolate caramel wafers

yield about 7 dozen

1	**package (14 ounces) caramels**
1/4	**cup evaporated milk**
1	**package (12 ounces) vanilla wafers**
8	**plain milk chocolate candy bars (1.55 ounces *each*), broken into squares**

Chopped pecans, optional

Place caramels and milk in a microwave-safe bowl; microwave, uncovered, on high for 2 minutes or until melted. Stir until smooth. Spread over vanilla wafers; place on ungreased baking sheets.

Top each with a chocolate square. Place in a 225° oven for 1-2 minutes or until chocolate is melted. Spread with an icing knife. Sprinkle with pecans if desired.

editor's note: This recipe was tested in a 1,100-watt microwave.

lemon-lime crackle cookies

yield about 3 dozen

1/2	**cup flaked coconut**
2	**teaspoons grated lemon peel**
2	**teaspoons grated lime peel**
2	**cups whipped topping**
2	**eggs**
2	**tablespoons whipped topping mix**
1	**teaspoon lemon juice**
1	**package (18-1/4 ounces) lemon cake mix**

Confectioners' sugar

In a blender or food processor, combine the coconut, lemon peel and lime peel. Cover and process until finely chopped, about 30 seconds; set aside. In a large bowl, combine whipped topping, eggs, dry whipped topping mix and lemon juice. Add the dry cake mix and coconut mixture; mix well.

Drop by tablespoonfuls into a bowl of confectioner's sugar. Shape into balls. Place 2 in. apart on greased baking sheets. Bake at 350° for 10-12 minutes or until the edges are golden brown. Remove to wire racks to cool.

editor's note: This recipe was tested with Dream Whip topping.

Ada Merwin ✳
Waterford, Michigan
You can taste the spirit of Christmases past in these chewy old-time cookies with their crackle tops and lemony flavor. They're a luscious addition to cookie exchanges.

✳ Taste of Home Test Kitchen
Refrigerated cookie dough gives you a head start on making this easy biscotti. For true chocolate lovers, substitute chocolate chips for the vanilla.

double chip biscotti

yield about 2 dozen

1	tube (18 ounces) refrigerated chocolate chip cookie dough
1/2	cup vanilla *or* white chips
1/2	cup coarsely chopped macadamia nuts

In a large bowl, combine dough, chips and nuts; knead until well combined. Divide dough in half. On greased baking sheets, shape each piece into a 13-in. x 2-1/2-in. log. Bake at 375° for 12-14 minutes or until golden brown.

Remove from oven; cut diagonally with a serrated knife into 1-in. slices, separating each piece about 1/4 in. after cutting. Bake 5-6 minutes longer or until firm. Cool for 2 minutes before removing to wire racks.

✳ Mary Pulyer, Port St. Lucie, Florida
It's a snap to make a batch of tasty cookies using this recipe, which starts with a basic boxed cake mix. My husband and son gobble them up.

chocolate peanut butter cookies

yield 4 dozen

1	package (18-3/4 ounces) devil's food cake mix
2	eggs
1/3	cup canola oil
1	package (10 ounces) peanut butter chips

In a large bowl, beat the dry cake mix, eggs and oil (batter will be very stiff). Stir in chips.

Roll into 1-in. balls. Place on lightly greased baking sheets; flatten slightly. Bake at 350° for 10 minutes or until a slight indentation remains when lightly touched. Cool for 2 minutes before removing to wire racks.

editor's note: Reduced-fat or generic brands of peanut butter are not recommended for this recipe.

Beverly Wilkerson, Crocker, Missouri ✳
We call these "magic bars" because they're fast and easy to make, and they disappear quickly when finished—just like magic!

chocolate chip brownies

yield 2 dozen

2	**tubes (18 ounces *each*) refrigerated chocolate chip cookie dough**
3/4	**cup flaked coconut, *divided***
1	**package fudge brownie mix (8-inch square pan size)**
1/2	**cup semisweet chocolate chips**
1/2	**cup chopped pecans**

Press cookie dough into a greased 13-in. x 9-in. baking pan. Sprinkle with 1/2 cup coconut and press firmly into dough.

Prepare brownie batter according to package directions; carefully spread over coconut. Sprinkle with remaining coconut; top with chocolate chips and pecans.

Bake at 350° for 45-50 minutes or until a toothpick inserted near the center comes out clean (do not overbake). Cool on a wire rack.

graham cracker cookies

yield 2-1/2 dozen

1-1/2	**cups sugar**
6	**tablespoons butter, cubed**
1/3	**cup evaporated milk**
1	**cup marshmallow creme**
3/4	**cup peanut butter**
1/3	**cup chopped salted peanuts, optional**
1/2	**teaspoon vanilla extract**
1	**package (14.4 ounces) graham crackers**

In a large saucepan, combine the sugar, butter and milk. Cook and stir over medium heat until mixture comes to a boil. Cook 4-5 minutes longer or until thickened and bubbly. Remove from heat; stir in marshmallow creme, peanut butter, and peanuts if desired and vanilla.

Break graham crackers in half. Spread about 2 tablespoons filling on the bottoms of half of the crackers; top with remaining crackers.

Lois McKnight ✳
Freeport, Illinois
My brother and I enjoyed these yummy peanut butter sandwich cookies when we were young. I often made the graham cracker treats for my children, and now I make them for my grandchildren.

BAKING tip

about biscotti — Biscotti (bee-skawt-tee) is an Italian cookie that is baked twice. First it's baked as a loaf and cut into individual cookies. Then the cookies are baked again to produce a dry, crunchy cookie that goes great with coffee.

Michelle Kester, Cleveland, Ohio

I created these melt-in-your-mouth thin mints for a cookie exchange, and everyone raved about them. They're often requested by my family and have become one of my daughter's favorites. To switch up the flavor, try using different extracts, such as raspberry, orange, almond or vanilla, instead of peppermint.

chocolate mint wafers

yield about 1-1/2 dozen

4	ounces dark chocolate candy coating
1/8	to 1/4 teaspoon peppermint extract
18	to 24 vanilla wafers

Place the candy coating and extract in a microwave-safe bowl. Microwave, uncovered, on high for 30-60 seconds or until smooth, stirring every 15 seconds.

Dip vanilla wafers in coating; allow excess to drip off. Place on waxed paper; let stand until set. Store in an airtight container.

editor's note: This recipe was tested in a 1,100-watt microwave.

Melanie Van Den Brink, Rock Rapids, Iowa

Most people don't realize that these cookies are low in fat. You get more than 2 dozen of the treats from a cake mix and just four other common ingredients.

devil's food cookies

yield about 2 dozen

1	package (18-1/4 ounces) devil's food cake mix
2	eggs
2	tablespoons butter, softened
3	tablespoons water
1/2	cup miniature semisweet chocolate chips

In a large bowl, combine the dry cake mix, eggs, butter and water (batter will be thick). Fold in chocolate chips.

Drop by tablespoonfuls 2 in. apart onto baking sheets coated with cooking spray. Bake at 350° for 10-13 minutes or until set and edges are lightly browned. Cool for 2 minutes before removing to wire racks.

Justine Furman-Olshan, Willow Street, Pennsylvania ✳

These delicious, crisp and nutty treats have been a favorite with our family for years—and they're so pretty! When my dad retired, he took over all the baking in our home. He'd make these and say, "Put on a pot of coffee; let's invite company!" What an effortless way to recall what's most important in life: family and friends.

peach almond bars

yield 2 dozen

1	**tube (16-1/2 ounces) refrigerated sugar cookie dough**
1	**jar (18 ounces) peach preserves**
1-1/2	**cups slivered almonds**, *divided*
4	**egg whites**
1/2	**cup sugar**

Let dough stand at room temperature for 5-10 minutes to soften. Press into an ungreased 13-in. x 9-in. baking pan. Bake at 350° for 12-15 minutes or until golden brown.

Spread preserves over crust. Sprinkle with 3/4 cup almonds. In a large bowl, beat egg whites on medium speed until soft peaks form. Gradually beat in sugar, 1 tablespoon at a time, on high until stiff glossy peaks form and sugar is dissolved.

Spread meringue evenly over almonds. Sprinkle with remaining almonds. Bake for 20-25 minutes or until lightly browned. Cool on a wire rack. Store in the refrigerator.

cherry oatmeal wedges

yield 12 servings

1	**tube (16-1/2 ounces) refrigerated chocolate chip cookie dough**
3/4	**cup old-fashioned oats**
1	**can (21 ounces) cherry pie filling**

In a large bowl, combine cookie dough and oats. Press onto an ungreased 12-in. pizza pan.

Bake at 350° for 14-16 minutes or until golden brown. Cool on a wire rack for 5 minutes. Cut into wedges; top with pie filling.

Richelle White ✳
Adair, Oklahoma
Oatmeal and cherries add extra flavor and a special touch to this one-of-a-kind chocolate-chip cookie. My kids help me make this, and it's so good!

BAKING tip

easy cleanup — When baking several batches of cookies, try this trick for easier cleanup. Cut several pieces of parchment paper to fit your baking sheet. Lay them on the countertop and drop the cookie dough on them. Slide one cookie-filled piece of parchment on top of the baking sheet and bake. When the cookies are done, slide the parchment paper with the cookies off the baking sheet and onto wire racks to cool.

Here is a fancy meal finale that couldn't be quicker to whip up. Start with purchased Pirouette cookies, dip in a rich chocolate and peanut-butter coating and dust with nuts or sprinkles. Serve alone or with your favorite after-dinner beverage.

nuts-about-you cookie sticks

yield 2 servings

1/4	cup semisweet chocolate chips
3/4	teaspoon shortening
1-1/2	teaspoons creamy peanut butter
4	French vanilla Pirouette cookies
1/2	cup chopped nuts

In a microwave, melt the chocolate chips, shortening and peanut butter; stir until smooth. Dip one end of each cookie into chocolate mixture; allow excess to drip off. Sprinkle with nuts. Place on waxed paper; let stand until set.

✳ Barbara Wentzel
Fort Bragg, California
A boxed cake mix brings these cookies together in a snap. Big on orange flavor but short on kitchen time, this crowd-pleaser is the solution to your bake sale needs.

orange crispy cookies

yield about 4 dozen

1	package (18-1/4 ounces) white cake mix
1/2	cup butter, melted
1	egg, beaten
2	teaspoons grated orange peel
2	teaspoons orange extract
1	cup crisp rice cereal
1	cup chopped walnuts, optional

In a large bowl, combine the first five ingredients; mix well. Stir in the cereal and walnuts if desired.

Roll into 1-in. balls. Place 2 in. apart on ungreased baking sheets. Bake at 350° for 12-14 minutes or until lightly browned. Cool for 1 minute before removing to wire racks.

✳ Robert Moon
Tampa, Florida
The only problem with these cookies is that once you eat one, you want more. This makes a small batch so you won't have too many around to tempt you.

brickle cookies

yield about 1-1/2 dozen

1	package (9 ounces) yellow cake mix
1/4	cup canola oil
1	egg, lightly beaten
1/2	teaspoon vanilla extract
1/2	cup chopped pecans
1/2	cup almond brickle chips *or* English toffee bits

In a small bowl, combine the dry cake mix, oil, egg and vanilla; mix well. Stir in pecans. Chill for 1 hour or until firm enough to handle.

Roll into 1-in. balls; dip top of each ball into toffee bits and set 2 in. apart on greased baking sheets. Bake at 350° for 10-12 minutes or until golden brown. Cool for 3 minutes before removing to wire racks.

Jan Thomas, Richmond, Virginia ✳
These frozen sandwich cookies are a favorite after-school snack for my kids, and even my diabetic husband enjoys one now and then.

chocolate pudding sandwiches

yield 43 sandwiches

- 1-1/2 **cups cold fat-free milk**
- 1 **package (1.4 ounces) sugar-free instant chocolate pudding mix**
- 1 **carton (8 ounces) frozen reduced-fat whipped topping, thawed**
- 1 **cup miniature marshmallows**
- 2 **packages (9 ounces *each*) chocolate wafers**

In a large bowl, whisk milk and pudding mix for 2 minutes; let stand for 2 minutes or until slightly thickened. Fold in whipped topping and marshmallows.

For each sandwich, spread about 2 tablespoons of pudding mixture on the bottom of a chocolate wafer; top with another wafer. Stack sandwiches in an airtight container.

Freeze until firm, about 3 hours. Remove from the freezer 5 minutes before serving.

Convenient refrigerated sugar cookie dough and a few spices from your cupboard are all you need to bake a batch of these yummy cookie strips. Your family will want to gobble them up right out of the oven. They're that good!

spiced cookie strips

yield 2 dozen

1	tube (18 ounces) refrigerated sugar cookie dough
2	tablespoons all-purpose flour
2	tablespoons butter, melted
1/2	teaspoon ground nutmeg
1/4	teaspoon ground cinnamon
1/4	teaspoon ground cloves

Remove cookie dough from package and coat with flour. Shake excess flour onto work surface. Roll out dough on floured surface into a 12-in. x 8-in. rectangle. Using a pizza cutter or sharp knife, cut rectangle in half lengthwise. Cut widthwise into 1-in. strips. Carefully transfer strips to two ungreased baking sheets.

Combine butter and spices; brush over strips. Bake at 425° for 10-12 minutes or until edges are golden brown. Cool for 2 minutes before removing to wire racks.

easy macaroons

yield about 10-1/2 dozen

✳ Judy Farlow
Boise, Idaho
My family likes macaroons, so when they raved about this easy-to-make pastel version, I knew I had a keeper.

1	pint lemon *or* orange sherbet
2	tablespoons almond extract
1	package (18-1/4 ounces) white cake mix
6	cups flaked coconut

In a large bowl, beat sherbet and almond extract until sherbet is slightly softened. Gradually add dry cake mix. Stir in coconut.

Drop by rounded teaspoonfuls 2 in. apart onto greased baking sheets. Bake at 350° for 12-15 minutes or until edges are lightly browned. Remove to wire racks to cool.

strawberry cookies

yield about 5 dozen

✳ Nancy Shelton
Boaz, Kentucky
My family finds these fruity cookies to be a light treat in summer. I sometimes use lemon cake mix in place of the strawberry.

1	package (18-1/4 ounces) strawberry cake mix
1	egg, lightly beaten
1	carton (8 ounces) frozen whipped topping, thawed
2	cups confectioners' sugar

In a large bowl, combine the dry cake mix, egg and whipped topping until well combined. Place confectioners' sugar in a shallow dish.

Drop dough by tablespoonfuls into sugar; turn to coat. Place 2 in. apart on greased baking sheets. Bake at 350° for 10-12 minutes or until lightly browned around the edges. Remove to wire racks to cool.

Carolyn Kyzer, Alexander, Arkansas ✳
Guests will never recognize the refrigerated crescent roll dough that goes into these almond-flavored bars. You can assemble these chewy coconut treats in no time at all.

macaroon bars

yield 3 dozen

3-1/4 **cups flaked coconut, _divided_**
1 **can (14 ounces)**
   sweetened condensed milk
1 **teaspoon almond extract**
1 **tube (8 ounces)**
   refrigerated crescent rolls

Sprinkle 1-1/2 cups coconut into a well-greased 13-in. x 9-in. baking pan. Combine milk and extract; drizzle half over the coconut. Unroll crescent dough; arrange in a single layer over coconut. Drizzle with remaining coconut.

Bake at 350° for 30-35 minutes or until golden brown. Cool completely on a wire rack before cutting. Store in the refrigerator.

Linda Hutmacher, Teutopolis, Illinois ✳
You'll need just six ingredients, including a convenient boxed cake mix, to bake up these chewy bars. They are my husband's favorite snack, and he loves to take them to work. I often whip up a batch for bake sales or to share with my co-workers at our local car dealership.

chewy date nut bars

yield 3 dozen

1 **package (18-1/4 ounces) yellow**
   cake mix
3/4 **cup packed brown sugar**
3/4 **cup butter, melted**
2 **eggs**
2 **cups chopped dates**
2 **cups chopped walnuts**

In a large bowl, combine dry cake mix and brown sugar. Add butter and eggs; beat on medium speed for 2 minutes. Combine the dates and walnuts; stir into batter (the batter will be stiff).

Spread into a greased 13-in. x 9-in. baking pan. Bake at 350° for 35-45 minutes or until edges are golden brown. Cool on a wire rack for 10 minutes. Run a knife around sides of pan to loosen; cool completely before cutting.

Jackie Howell, Gordo, Alabama

This is a tempting treat you'll love to give. The recipe is almost too simple to believe!

dipped peanut butter sandwich cookies

yield 9 cookies

1/2	**cup creamy peanut butter**
1	**sleeve (4 ounces) round butter-flavored crackers**
1	**cup white, semisweet *or* milk chocolate chips**
1	**tablespoon shortening**

Spread peanut butter on half of the crackers; top with the remaining crackers to make sandwiches. Refrigerate.

In microwave, melt chocolate chips and shortening, stirring until smooth. Dip sandwiches and place on waxed paper until chocolate sets.

Flora Alers, Clinton, Maryland

A package of cake mix is transformed into a big batch of tasty cookies that are filled with coconut, nuts and chocolate chips. With just six ingredients, this recipe can be whipped up in a jiffy.

coconut chip cookies

yield 3-1/2 dozen

1	**package (18-1/4 ounces) white cake mix**
2	**eggs**
1/3	**cup canola oil**
1	**cup flaked coconut**
1/2	**cup semisweet chocolate chips**
1/4	**cup chopped macadamia nuts *or* almonds**

In a large bowl, beat dry cake mix, eggs and oil (batter will be very stiff). Stir in coconut, chips and nuts.

Roll into 1-in. balls. Place on lightly greased baking sheets. Bake at 350° for 10 minutes or until a slight indentation remains when lightly touched. Cool for 2 minutes before removing to wire racks.

Christina Hitchcock, Blakely, Pennsylvania ✳

Because you start with a store-bought cookie mix, it takes no time at all to make these minty treats. I usually drizzle melted chocolate chips over the cookie tops, but pink candy coating looks lovely for Valentine's Day.

mint candy cookies

yield about 3-1/2 dozen

- **1 package (17-1/2 ounces) sugar cookie mix**
- **40 to 45 mint Andes Candies**
- **6 ounces pink candy coating disks**
- **Heart-shaped decorating sprinkles, optional**

Prepare the cookie dough according to package directions. Cover and chill for 15-20 minutes or until easy to handle.

Pat a scant tablespoonful of dough in a thin layer around each mint candy. Place 2 in. apart on ungreased baking sheets. Bake at 375° for 7-9 minutes or until set. Cool for 1 minute before removing from pans to wire racks to cool completely.

In a microwave-safe bowl, melt candy coating; stir until smooth. Drizzle over cookies. Top with decorating sprinkles if desired.

editor's note: White candy coating tinted with red food coloring may be substituted for the pink candy coating.

※ Ruth Cassis, University Place, Washington

If you like sweet-and-salty snacks, you're sure to enjoy these chocolate-covered crackers with a rich, sweet peanut-butter filling. They're great any time of year—just choose shaped sprinkles that coordinate with the season.

colorful peanut butter crackers

yield 2 dozen

4	ounces cream cheese, cubed
1/2	cup creamy peanut butter
1/4	cup honey
48	butter-flavored crackers
2	cups (12 ounces) semisweet chocolate chips
4	teaspoons shortening
1/4	cup milk

Cake decorator holiday shapes

In a microwave-safe bowl, heat cream cheese on high for 15 seconds or until very soft. Add peanut butter and honey; stir until smooth.

Spread over half of the crackers; top with remaining crackers.

In a microwave, melt chocolate chips and shortening; stir until smooth. Heat milk; stir into chocolate mixture.

Dip each cracker sandwich in chocolate mixture, allowing excess to drip off. Place on waxed paper-lined baking sheets; decorate as desired. Refrigerate for 45 minutes or until set.

editor's note: This recipe was tested in a 1,100-watt microwave.

※ Kristi Tackett, Banner, Kentucky

I'm a busy schoolteacher and pastor's wife who always looks for shortcuts. I wouldn't dare show my face at a church dinner or bake sale without these tempting peanut butter treats. They're quick and easy to make and always a hit.

peanut butter cookie cups

yield 3 dozen

1	package (17-1/2 ounces) peanut butter cookie mix
36	miniature peanut butter cups, unwrapped

Prepare cookie mix according to package directions. Roll the dough into 1-in. balls. Place in greased miniature muffin cups. Press dough evenly onto bottom and up sides of each cup. Bake at 350° for 11-13 minutes or until set.

Immediately place a peanut butter cup in each cup; press down gently. Cool for 10 minutes; carefully remove from pans.

editor's note: 2-1/4 cups peanut butter cookie dough of your choice can be used for the mix.

quick ghost cookies

yield about 3 dozen

- 1 **pound white candy coating, cut into chunks**
- 1 **package (1 pound) Nutter Butter peanut butter cookies**

Mini semisweet chocolate chips

In a small, heavy saucepan or microwave, melt the candy coating, stirring occasionally. Dip cookies into coating, covering completely. Place on waxed paper.

Brush ends with a pastry brush dipped in coating where fingers touched cookies. While coating is still warm, place two chips on each cookie for eyes. Let stand until set. Store in an airtight container.

lemon basil cookies

yield 3-1/2 dozen

- 1 **package (8 ounces) cream cheese, softened**
- 1/4 **cup butter, softened**
- 1 **egg yolk**
- 1 **teaspoon lemon juice**
- 1 **package (18-1/4 ounces) lemon cake mix**
- 1/4 **cup flaked coconut**
- 1/4 **cup chopped pecans**
- 1 **tablespoon dried basil**
- 1/2 **teaspoon grated lemon peel**

In a large bowl, beat cream cheese and butter until fluffy. Beat in egg yolk and lemon juice. Gradually add dry cake mix and mix well. Stir in the coconut, pecans, basil and lemon peel.

Drop by teaspoonfuls 2 in. apart onto greased baking sheets. Bake at 350° for 10-14 minutes or until golden brown. Cool for 2 minutes before removing to wire racks.

Pam Frankenfield ✳
Halethorpe, Maryland
These light, lemony cookies
are a breeze to make because
they start with a packaged
cake mix. With flaked coconut,
chopped pecans and flecks of
basil, the golden treats are
sure to be a hit at any
summer gathering.

BAKING
tip

dipping cookies in chocolate — When coating cookies in chocolate or candy coating, such as Quick Ghost Cookies above, use a shallow dish with a wide mouth for the melted chocolate. For the last few cookies, spoon the melted chocolate over the cookies to ensure complete coverage. If the melted chocolate starts to set before you are finished, rewarm at a low power level in the microwave.

✳ Patricia Kaseta, Brockton, Massachusetts
I jazz up a packaged cookie mix, then let Junior Mints melt on top of the warm treats to create an easy frosting. These delicious cookies are requested at every gathering.

chocolate chip mint cookies

yield 4 dozen

1	package (17-1/2 ounces) chocolate chip cookie mix
3	tablespoons water
1	egg
1/4	cup canola oil
1/2	cup semisweet chocolate chips
1/2	cup vanilla *or* white chips
1/2	cup chopped walnuts
1	package (5-1/2 ounces) Junior Mints

In a large bowl, combine cookie mix, water, egg and oil; mix well. Stir in the chips and nuts.

Drop by tablespoonfuls 2 in. apart onto ungreased baking sheets. Bake at 350° for 7-9 minutes or until edges are golden brown.

Remove from the oven; place one candy on each cookie. Remove to wire racks. When candy is melted, spread over cookie. Cool.

✳ Brenda Jackson,
Garden City, Kansas
Whenever I take these cookies, I'm always asked for the recipe. To dress them up, I reserve some chocolate and nuts to press into each cookie before baking.

peanutty chocolate cookies

yield about 3-1/2 dozen

1	cup chunky peanut butter
2	tablespoons canola oil
2	eggs
1	package fudge brownie mix (13-inch x 9-inch pan size)
1/2	cup water
12	ounces milk chocolate candy bars, coarsely chopped
1/2	cup unsalted peanuts

In a large bowl, cream peanut butter and oil. Beat in eggs just until combined. Stir in brownie mix and water. Fold in the chopped candy bars and peanuts.

Drop by heaping tablespoonfuls 2 in. apart onto greased baking sheets. Bake at 350° for 12-14 minutes or until lightly browned. Remove to wire racks to cool.

editor's note: Reduced-fat or generic brands of peanut butter are not recommended for this recipe.

Dress up convenient refrigerated cookie dough to create these sweet summery treats. The orange and lemon cookies taste like the sunny citrus slices they resemble.

citrus cookies

yield about 2 dozen

1	tube (18 ounces) refrigerated sugar cookie dough
2	teaspoons grated orange peel
2	teaspoons orange extract

Orange and yellow paste food coloring

2	teaspoons grated lemon peel
2	teaspoons lemon extract

Granulated sugar

1/2	cup vanilla frosting

Orange and yellow colored sugar

Divide cookie dough in half. Place one half in a bowl. Add the orange peel, orange extract and orange food coloring; mix well. Add lemon peel, lemon extract and yellow food coloring to the remaining dough; mix well. Cover and refrigerate for 2 hours or until firm.

Roll dough into 1-in. balls. Place 2 in. apart on ungreased baking sheets. Coat the bottom of a glass with cooking spray, then dip in granulated sugar. Flatten dough balls, redipping glass in sugar as needed. Bake at 375° for 8-10 minutes or until edges are golden brown. Remove to wire racks to cool completely.

Cut a small hole in the corner of a small plastic bag; add frosting. Pipe circle of frosting on cookie tops; dip in colored sugar. Pipe lines of frosting for citrus sections.

Rhonda Walsh, Cleveland, Tennessee ✳

Along with eight other day school teachers, we created this snack for a fire safety program at the school.

fire truck cookies

yield 16 cookies

16	whole graham crackers (4-3/4 inches x 2-1/2 inches)
1	cup vanilla frosting

Red paste *or* liquid food coloring

32	chocolate cream-filled sandwich cookies

Black shoestring licorice

16	red gumdrops

With a serrated knife, cut the top left- or right-hand corner off of each graham cracker at a 45° angle. Tint frosting red; frost crackers. Place two sandwich cookies on each for wheels.

For each truck, cut licorice into two 2-1/2-in. pieces, five 1/2-in. pieces and two 1-1/2-in. pieces. Place the large pieces parallel to each other above wheels, with the small pieces between to form a ladder. Place the medium pieces at cut edge, forming a windshield. Add a gumdrop for light.

✳ Kelly Loudon, Olathe, Kansas

Here's a fun way to add a musical note to a celebration. You get a jump on the preparation by using packaged gingerbread mix.

gingerbread cookie wreath

yield 1 wreath

1	package (14-1/2 ounces) gingerbread cake/cookie mix *or* 2 cups gingerbread cookie dough of your choice
1/2	pound white candy coating, melted
1/4	cup green colored sugar
15	red-hot candies

Prepare mix according to package directions for cookies. Set aside 1/4 cup dough. On a greased baking sheet, roll out remaining dough into a 9-1/2-in. circle. With a sharp knife, cut a 4-in. circle from the center of the 9-1/2-in. circle. Remove 4-in. circle; add to reserved dough. Bake 9-1/2-in. ring at 375° for 12-15 minutes or until edges are firm (do not overbake). Cool for 1 minute before removing to a wire rack.

Roll out reserved dough to 1/2-in. thickness. Cut out 5 musical notes with a floured 4-in. musical note cutter and 10 holly leaves with a floured 1-1/2-in. leaf cutter. Place 2 in. apart on a greased baking sheet. Bake at 375° for 10-12 minutes or until edges are firm. Remove to a wire rack to cool.

Dip holly leaves halfway in candy coating; sprinkle with green sugar. Place on a ring as shown in photo. Cut a small hole in the corner of pastry or plastic bag; insert round tip #3. Fill with remaining candy coating. Squeeze a small amount on the back of cookies; attach to wreath. Pipe around edges of notes. Pipe small dots of coating above holly leaves to attach candies. Allow coating to set completely, about 30 minutes.

Sandy Pyeatt, Rockaway Beach, Oregon
I heard this cookie recipe over the radio sometime around 1950—shortly after my husband and I married. The goodies remain my favorite to this day.

giant spice cookies

yield 10 cookies

1	package (18-1/4 ounces) spice cake mix
1/2	teaspoon ground ginger
1/4	teaspoon baking soda
1/4	cup water
1/4	cup molasses
6	teaspoons vanilla extract

In a large bowl, combine the dry cake mix, ginger and baking soda. Stir in water, molasses and vanilla and mix well. Roll into 10 balls.

Place 3 in. apart on greased baking sheets. Flatten slightly with a glass coated with cooking spray.

Bake at 375° for 13-15 minutes or until surface cracks and cookies are firm. Remove to wire racks to cool.

mint sandwich cookies

yield 3 dozen

1	can (16 ounces) vanilla frosting
1/2	teaspoon peppermint extract
3	to 5 drops green food coloring, optional
72	butter-flavored crackers
1	pound dark chocolate candy coating, coarsely chopped

In a bowl, combine the frosting, extract and food coloring if desired. Spread over half of the crackers; top with remaining crackers.

Melt candy coating in a microwave; stir until smooth. Dip the cookies in coating. Place on waxed paper; let stand until set. Store in an airtight container at room temperature.

Melissa Thompson
Anderson, Ohio

Canned frosting, peppermint extract and chocolate candy coating quickly turn crackers into these wonderful little no-bake cookies.

soft raisin cookies

yield 2 dozen

1	package (9 ounces) yellow cake mix
1	cup quick-cooking oats
6	tablespoons unsweetened applesauce
1/4	cup egg substitute
2	tablespoons butter, melted
1/2	teaspoon apple pie spice
1/2	cup raisins

In a large bowl, combine the dry cake mix, oats, applesauce, egg substitute, butter and apple pie spice; beat until blended. Stir in raisins.

Drop by tablespoonfuls 2 in. apart onto baking sheets coated with cooking spray. Bake at 375° for 10-12 minutes or until the edges are lightly browned. Cool for 5 minutes before removing to wire racks.

Ray Amet
Kansas City, Missouri

I modified a recipe for cake mix cookies to make it healthier. My family likes my version, with its mild spice flavor and touch of sweetness from raisins, even better than the original.

✳ Marcella Cremer, Decatur, Illinois
I came up with these fudgy peanut butter brownies when I ran out of ingredients I needed for my usual recipe. They take less than 10 minutes to mix up.

very chocolaty pb brownies

yield 2 dozen

1	package (17-1/2 ounces) peanut butter cookie mix
1/2	cup baking cocoa
2/3	cup chocolate syrup
1/4	cup butter, melted
1	egg
1/2	cup chopped walnuts *or* peanuts

FROSTING:

2	cups plus 2 tablespoons confectioners' sugar
1/2	cup chocolate syrup
1/4	cup baking cocoa
1/4	cup butter, melted
1/2	teaspoon vanilla extract

In a large bowl, combine cookie mix and cocoa. Add chocolate syrup, butter and egg; beat until combined. Stir in nuts.

Spread into a greased 13-in. x 9-in. baking pan. Bake at 350° for 28-32 minutes or until a toothpick inserted near the center comes out clean. Cool on a wire rack.

Meanwhile, combine the frosting ingredients in a bowl; stir until smooth. Spread over brownies. Cut into squares.

editor's note: This recipe was tested with Betty Crocker peanut butter cookie mix.

✳ Taste of Home Test Kitchen
These cute cat cookies are so simple to make that even young kids can help. They are great for an after-school treat, fall bake sale or as a contribution to a classroom celebration.

halloween cat cookies

yield 1-1/2 dozen

1	tube (18 ounces) refrigerated chocolate chip cookie dough
54	pieces candy corn
1	can (16 ounces) chocolate frosting

Red shoestring licorice, cut into 1-3/8-inch pieces

9	thin chocolate wafers (2-1/4 inch diameter), quartered

Bake cookies according to package directions. Cool on a wire rack.

Cut off yellow tips from 18 pieces of candy corn (discard orange and white portion or save for another use). Frost cookies with chocolate frosting.

Immediately decorate with two whole candy corns for eyes, a yellow candy corn tip for nose, six licorice pieces for whiskers and two wafer quarters for ears.

Sandy McKenzie, Braham, Minnesota ✳

I rely on this tried-and-true recipe during the holidays. The cream cheese frosting complements the cookies' gingery flavor and sets up nicely for easy packaging and stacking.

easy gingerbread cutouts

yield 2-1/2 dozen

1	package (18-1/4 ounces) spice cake mix
3/4	cup all-purpose flour
2	eggs
1/3	cup canola oil
1/3	cup molasses
2	teaspoons ground ginger
3/4	cup canned cream cheese frosting, warmed slightly

Red-hot candies

In a large bowl, combine dry cake mix, flour, eggs, oil, molasses and ginger; mix well. Chill for 30 minutes or until easy to handle.

On a floured surface, roll out the dough to 1/8-in. thickness. Cut with floured 5-in. cookie cutters.

Place 3 in. apart on ungreased baking sheets. Bake at 375° for 7-10 minutes or until edges are firm and bottom is lightly browned. Remove to wire racks to cool.

Decorate with cream cheese frosting as desired. Use red-hots for eyes, nose and buttons. Store in the refrigerator.

cranberry crispies

yield 2-1/2 dozen

1	package (15.6 ounces) cranberry quick bread mix
1/2	cup butter, melted
1/2	cup finely chopped walnuts
1	egg
1/2	cup dried cranberries

In a bowl, combine the bread mix, butter, walnuts and egg; mix well. Stir in cranberries.

Roll into 1-1/4-in. balls. Place 3 in. apart on ungreased baking sheets. Flatten to 1/8-in. thickness with a glass dipped in sugar. Bake at 350° for 10-12 minutes or until light golden brown. Remove to wire racks to cool.

LaVern Kraft ✳
Lytton, Iowa

At holiday rush time, you can't go wrong with these simple cookies. They're a snap to stir up with a boxed quick bread.

※ Taste of Home Test Kitchen

These big, soft spice cookies have a sweet frosting that makes them an extra-special treat. Enjoy!

easy pumpkin spice cookies

yield about 2-1/2 dozen

1	**package (18-1/4 ounces) yellow cake mix**
1/2	**cup quick-cooking oats**
2	**to 2-1/2 teaspoons pumpkin pie spice**
1	**egg**
1	**can (15 ounces) solid-pack pumpkin**
2	**tablespoons canola oil**
3	**cups confectioners' sugar**
1	**teaspoon grated orange peel**
3	**to 4 tablespoons orange juice**

In a large bowl, combine the dry cake mix, oats and pumpkin pie spice. In another bowl, beat the egg, pumpkin and oil; stir into dry ingredients just until moistened.

Drop by 2 tablespoonfuls onto baking sheets coated with cooking spray; flatten with the back of a spoon. Bake at 350° for 18-20 minutes or until edges are golden brown. Remove to wire racks to cool.

In a large bowl, combine the confectioners' sugar, orange peel and enough orange juice to achieve spreading consistency. Frost the cooled cookies.

Zoraya Jennings, Fredericksburg, Virginia ✳

Making a gaggle of these gobblers is a fun project to do with kids. The cute, easy turkey cookies make great school treats or sweet favors for a Thanksgiving gathering.

a flock of turkeys

yield 2 dozen

48	sugar cookies (3 inches)
1	package (12 ounces) chocolate and marshmallow cookies
1	can (16 ounces) chocolate frosting
1	cup vanilla frosting

Yellow and red paste food coloring

Using a serrated knife, cut 1/2 in. from one side of 24 sugar cookies. Using a sharp knife, cut each marshmallow cookie in half vertically. Spread the chocolate frosting over the bottom of each marshmallow cookie half; align cut edges of a marshmallow cookie and a sugar cookie, and press together to form each turkey body and feathers.

Spread chocolate frosting over the cut edges of each turkey; position and attach near the back edge of a whole sugar cookie.

Cut a small hole in the corner of a pastry or plastic bag. Insert a #12 round pastry tip; fill bag with 3/4 cup chocolate frosting. Pipe a neck and head on each turkey.

Tint 1/2 cup vanilla frosting yellow and 1/2 cup red. With a #3 round pastry tip and yellow frosting, add eyes, beaks and legs. With #3 round tip and red frosting, pipe snood and tail feathers. Store in the refrigerator.

editor's note: This recipe was tested with Nabisco Pinwheels.

Karen Mead, Pittsburgh, Pennsylvania ✳

I bake for a group of seniors every week, and this is one of the goodies they request most. I always keep the ingredients on hand for last-minute baking emergencies. Give these bars your own twist by using the fruit jam of your choice.

no-fuss strawberry bars

yield 2 dozen

1/2	cup butter, softened
1/2	cup packed brown sugar
1	egg
1	package (18-1/4 ounces) white cake mix
1	cup finely crushed cornflakes
1	cup strawberry jam *or* preserves

In a large bowl, cream butter and sugar until smooth. Add egg; mix well. Gradually add dry cake mix and cornflakes. Set aside 1-1/2 cups for topping. Press remaining dough into a greased 13-in. x 9-in. baking pan.

Carefully spread jam over crust. Sprinkle with reserved dough; gently press down. Bake at 350° for 30 minutes or until golden brown. Cool completely on a wire rack. Cut into bars.

✳ Mary Kaufenberg, Shakopee, Minnesota
You'll need just six ingredients to create these cute Kris Kringle confections. Store-bought peanut butter sandwich cookies are dressed up with white chocolate, colored sugar, mini chips and red cinnamon candies for kid-pleasing results.

santa claus cookies

yield 32 cookies

2   **packages (6 ounces *each*) white baking chocolate, chopped**
1   **package (1 pound) Nutter Butter sandwich cookies**
Red colored sugar
32   **vanilla *or* white chips**
64   **miniature semisweet chocolate chips**
32   **red-hot candies**

In a microwave, melt white chocolate at 70% power for 1 minute; stir. Microwave at additional 10- to 20-second intervals, stirring until smooth.

Dip one end of each cookie into melted chocolate, allowing excess to drip off. Place on wire racks. For Santa's hat, sprinkle red sugar on top part of chocolate. Press one vanilla chip off-center on hat for pom-pom; let stand until chocolate is set.

Dip other end of each cookie into melted chocolate for beard, leaving center of cookie uncovered. Place on wire racks. With a dab of melted chocolate, attach semisweet chips for eyes and a red-hot for nose. Place on waxed paper until set.

✳ Taste of Home Test Kitchen
No one will guess these sweet treats with the candy bar center start with store-bought dough. Roll them in colored sugar...or just dip the tops for even faster assembly. Instead of using miniature candy bars, slice regular size Snickers candy bars into 1-inch pieces for the centers.

colorful candy bar cookies

yield 2 dozen

1/2   **tube refrigerated sugar cookie dough, softened**
1/4   **cup all-purpose flour**
24   **miniature Snickers candy bars**
Red and green colored sugar

In a small bowl, beat the cookie dough and flour until combined. Shape 1-1/2 teaspoonfuls of cookie dough around each candy bar. Roll in the colored sugar.

Place 2 in. apart on parchment paper-lined baking sheets. Bake at 350° for 10-12 minutes or until edges are golden brown. Remove to wire racks.

Teri Lindquist, Gurnee, Illinois ✳

This is my most requested dessert recipe. Everyone loves these yummy bars with their soft, delicious cream cheese filling. And what's even better is that they couldn't be easier to make!

chocolate chip cheese bars

yield 12-16 servings

1	tube (18 ounces) refrigerated chocolate chip cookie dough
1	package (8 ounces) cream cheese, softened
1/2	cup sugar
1	egg

Cut cookie dough in half. For crust, press half of the dough onto the bottom of a greased 8-in. square baking dish.

In a small bowl, beat cream cheese, sugar and egg until smooth. Spread over crust. Crumble remaining dough over top. Bake at 350° for 35-40 minutes or until a toothpick inserted near the center comes out clean. Cool on a wire rack. Refrigerate leftovers.

editor's note: 2 cups of your favorite chocolate chip cookie dough can be substituted for the refrigerated dough.

strawberry banana squares

yield 2 dozen

1	package (14 ounces) banana quick bread and muffin mix
1/2	cup chopped walnuts
1/3	cup butter, softened
1	egg
1	can (14 ounces) sweetened condensed milk
1	can (20 ounces) strawberry pie filling
1/2	cup flaked coconut

In a small bowl, combine the bread mix, walnuts, butter and egg until crumbly. Press onto the bottom of a 13-in. x 9-in. baking dish coated with cooking spray. Bake at 350° for 8-10 minutes or until lightly browned.

Spread milk over crust; spoon pie filling over milk. Sprinkle with coconut. Bake 30-40 minutes longer or until golden brown. Cool on a wire rack. Cut into squares.

Lucille Mead ✳
Ilion, New York

It's a snap to make this delicious dessert because it calls for a handful of convenience items. With a combination of strawberry, banana and coconut flavors, these squares really do have it all, and your kids will notice!

christmas classics

lemon ginger cutouts, p. 318

Cookies at Christmas are a

holiday tradition—for gift giving, cookie exchanges and as special treats for family and guests. The variety of festive cookies featured here are sure to create a dazzling assortment on your cookie trays.

cranberry swirl biscotti, p. 312

chocolate mint creams, p. 321

✳ Cindi Bauer, Marshfield, Wisconsin

Here's a nice change of pace from the more traditional sugar cutouts. And children will find that these peanut butter versions are just as much fun to decorate with frosting and a dash of Yuletide imagination.

peanut butter cutout cookies

yield about 4-1/2 dozen

1	cup creamy peanut butter
3/4	cup sugar
3/4	cup packed brown sugar
2	eggs
1/3	cup milk
1	teaspoon vanilla extract
2-1/2	cups all-purpose flour
1/2	teaspoon baking powder
1/2	teaspoon baking soda

Vanilla frosting
Red, green, yellow and blue gel food coloring
Assorted colored sprinkles

In a large bowl, cream peanut butter and sugars. Beat in the eggs, milk and vanilla. Combine the flour, baking powder and baking soda; add to creamed mixture and mix well. Cover and refrigerate for 2 hours or until easy to handle.

On a lightly floured surface, roll out dough to 1/4-in. thickness. Cut with floured 2-in. to 4-in. cookie cutters.

Place 2 in. apart in ungreased baking sheets. Bake at 375° for 7-9 minutes or until edges are browned. Cool for 1 minute before removing to wire racks. Frost and decorate as desired.

editor's note: Reduced-fat or generic brands of peanut butter are not recommended for this recipe.

Janice Poechman, Walkerton, Ontario

These melt-in-your-mouth sandwich cookies have a scrumptious filling. I helped my sister make these in high school when she needed a project in her home economics class. "She got an A!"

christmas sandwich cremes

yield 4 dozen

1	**cup butter, softened**
1/3	**cup heavy whipping cream**
2	**cups all-purpose flour**

Sugar

FILLING:

1/2	**cup butter, softened**
1-1/2	**cups confectioners' sugar**
2	**teaspoons vanilla extract**

Food coloring

In a large mixing bowl, combine the butter, cream and flour. Cover and refrigerate for 2 hours or until dough is easy to handle.

Divide into thirds; let one portion stand at room temperature for 15 minutes (keep remaining dough refrigerated until ready to roll out). On a floured surface, roll out dough to 1/8-in. thickness. Cut with a floured 1-1/2-in.-round cookie cutter. Place cutouts in a shallow dish filled with sugar; turn to coat.

Place 2 in. apart on ungreased baking sheets. Prick with a fork several times. Bake at 375° for 7-9 minutes or until set. Remove to wire racks to cool completely.

For filling, in a small bowl, cream butter and sugar. Add vanilla. Tint with food coloring. Spread about 1 teaspoon of filling over half of the cookies; top with remaining cookies.

jam-filled wreaths

yield 2-1/2 dozen

3/4	**cup butter, softened**
1	**cup sugar**
2	**eggs**
1-1/2	**cups all-purpose flour**
1	**teaspoon baking powder**
1	**teaspoon ground cinnamon**
1/2	**teaspoon ground allspice**
1	**cup quick-cooking oats**
3/4	**cup finely chopped nuts**
1	**jar (18 ounces) seedless raspberry jam**

Confectioners' sugar

In a large bowl, cream butter and sugar. Add the eggs, one at a time, beating well after each addition. Combine the flour, baking powder, cinnamon and allspice; add to the creamed mixture. Stir in the oats and nuts; mix well. Chill for 3 hours or until dough is easy to handle.

On a floured surface, roll out half of the dough to 1/8-in. thickness. Cut with a floured 2-1/2-in. round cookie cutter. Repeat with remaining dough, using a 2-1/2-in. doughnut cutter, so the center is cut out of each cookie.

Place 2 in. apart on lightly greased baking sheets. Bake at 400° for 6-8 minutes or until lightly browned. Cool on wire racks.

Spread 1 teaspoon jam over solid cookies. Place cookies with centers cut out over jam, forming a sandwich. Dust with confectioners' sugar. Fill centers with additional jam if desired.

Monica Wilson ✳
Pomona, New York
I make these beautiful wreath-shaped cookies with jewel-red centers every Christmas. The dusting of powdered sugar gives them a snowy look. My mother cut the recipe out of a newspaper some 30 years ago.

* Taste of Home Test Kitchen
With sweet candy halos and crunchy mini pretzel wings, these easy-to-assemble angels are sure to be popular with kids.

cookie angels

yield 1-1/2 dozen

2/3	cup butter-flavored shortening
1/4	cup sugar
1	egg
1-1/2	cups all-purpose flour
1/2	teaspoon baking powder
1/2	teaspoon salt
36	miniature pretzels
1	can (16 ounces) vanilla frosting, *divided*
1/4	cup confectioners' sugar

Brown paste food coloring

18	yellow Life Savers
10	green Life Savers, crushed

Decorating gels

In a small bowl, cream shortening and sugar until light and fluffy. Beat in egg. Combine the flour, baking powder and salt; gradually add to creamed mixture and mix well. Set aside 1/2 cup of dough; divide remaining dough into three portions.

On a lightly floured surface, roll out each portion into a 6-in. circle; cut each into six wedges. Transfer to ungreased baking sheets.

For angel heads, roll teaspoonfuls of reserved dough into 18 balls; lightly press onto pointed end of each wedge. Press a pretzel into each side for wings.

Bake at 350° for 10-12 minutes or until lightly browned. Remove from pan to wire racks to cool completely.

For hair, in a small bowl, beat 1/4 cup vanilla frosting and confectioners' sugar until smooth; tint with food coloring. Press dough through a garlic press. Trim strands to desired length; place on heads. For halos, attach yellow Life Savers.

Frost gowns with remaining frosting; sprinkle with crushed Life Savers. Use decorating gels to add faces.

* Katherine Both
Rocky Mountain House
Alberta

This chocolate-flavored shortbread requires only a few ingredients, which are always in my pantry.

chocolate shortbread

yield about 4 dozen

1	cup butter, softened
1/3	cup unsweetened cocoa
2/3	cup confectioners' sugar

Dash salt

1-1/2	cups all-purpose flour

In a large bowl, cream butter until light and fluffy. Blend in remaining ingredients. Cover and refrigerate for 1 hour.

Drop by rounded teaspoonfuls 2 in. apart on greased baking sheets. Bake at 300° for about 20 minutes or until the cookies are set. Remove to wire racks to cool.

Marie Capobianco, Portsmouth, Rhode Island ✳

I dreamed up this recipe using two of my favorite flavors, pistachio and raspberry. These pink and green cookies are tasty and eye-catching, too. They're perfect for formal or informal gatherings, and everybody likes them.

two-tone christmas cookies

yield 6-1/2 dozen

1	cup butter, softened
1-1/2	cups sugar
2	egg yolks
2	teaspoons vanilla extract
1	teaspoon almond extract
3-1/2	cups all-purpose flour
1	teaspoon salt
1	teaspoon baking powder
1/2	teaspoon baking soda
9	drops green food coloring
1	tablespoon milk
1/3	cup chopped pistachios
9	drops red food coloring
3	tablespoons seedless raspberry preserves
2	cups (12 ounces) semisweet chocolate chips, melted

Additional chopped pistachios

In a large bowl, cream butter and sugar. Beat in egg yolks and extracts. Combine flour, salt, baking powder and baking soda; gradually add to creamed mixture. Divide dough in half. Stir green food coloring, milk and nuts into one portion; mix well. Add red food coloring and jam to the other half.

Shape each portion between two pieces of waxed paper into an 8-in. x 6-in. rectangle. Cut in half lengthwise. Place one green rectangle on a piece of plastic wrap. Top with pink rectangle; press together lightly. Repeat. Wrap each in plastic wrap and refrigerate overnight.

Unwrap the dough and cut in half lengthwise. Return one rectangle to the refrigerator. Cut the remaining rectangle into 1/8-in. slices. Place 1 in. apart on ungreased baking sheets. Bake at 375° for 7-9 minutes or until set. Remove to wire racks to cool. Repeat with the remaining dough. Drizzle the cooled cookies with melted chocolate. Sprinkle with additional pistachios.

surprise package cookies

yield 3-1/2 dozen

1	cup butter, softened
1	cup sugar
1/2	cup packed brown sugar
2	eggs
1	teaspoon vanilla extract
3	cups all-purpose flour
1	teaspoon baking powder
1/2	teaspoon salt
65	mint Andes candies

In a large bowl, cream the butter and sugars. Add the eggs, one at a time, beating well after each addition. Beat in vanilla. Combine the flour, baking powder and salt; gradually add to creamed mixture. Cover and refrigerate for 2 hours or until easy to handle.

With floured hands, shape a tablespoonful of dough around 42 candies, forming rectangular cookies. Place 2 in. apart on greased baking sheets. Bake at 375° for 10-12 minutes or until edges are golden brown. Remove to wire racks to cool.

In a microwave or heavy saucepan, melt the remaining candies; drizzle over cookies.

Lorraine Meyer ✳
Bend, Oregon
Each of these buttery cookies has a chocolate-mint candy inside. They're my very favorite cookie and are always part of our Christmas cookie selection.

✳ Lisa Kilcup, Gig Harbor, Washington
A friend of mine, who is known for her excellent cookies, shared this recipe with me. The mix of cranberries and cherry preserves is so refreshing.

cranberry swirl biscotti

yield about 2-1/2 dozen

2/3	cup dried cranberries
1/2	cup cherry preserves
1/2	teaspoon ground cinnamon
1/2	cup butter, softened
2/3	cup sugar
2	eggs
1	teaspoon vanilla extract
2-1/4	cups all-purpose flour
3/4	teaspoon baking powder
1/4	teaspoon salt

GLAZE:

3/4	cup confectioners' sugar
1	tablespoon milk
2	teaspoons butter, melted
1	teaspoon almond extract

In a food processor, combine the cranberries, preserves and cinnamon. Cover and process until smooth; set aside.

In a large bowl, cream butter and sugar until light and fluffy. Beat in eggs and vanilla. Combine the flour, baking powder and salt; gradually add to creamed mixture and mix well.

Divide dough in half. On a lightly floured surface, roll each portion into a 12-in. x 8-in. rectangle. Spread each with cranberry filling; roll up jelly-roll style, starting with a short side.

Place seam side down 4 in. apart on a lightly greased baking sheet. Bake at 325° for 25-30 minutes or until lightly browned.

Carefully transfer logs to a cutting board; cool for 5 minutes. With a serrated knife, cut into 1/2-in. slices. Place 2 in. apart on lightly greased baking sheets. Bake 15 minutes longer or until centers are firm and dry. Remove to wire racks.

In a small bowl, combine glaze ingredients; drizzle over warm biscotti. Cool completely. Store in an airtight container.

✳ Agnes Golian
Garfield Heights, Ohio
These cute cherry-topped cookies are as light as air and so easy to make. They're perfect for holiday entertaining or most any time of year.

cream cheese delights

yield 2 dozen

1/2	cup butter-flavored shortening
1	package (3 ounces) cream cheese, softened
1/2	cup sugar
1	egg yolk
1	teaspoon vanilla extract
1	cup all-purpose flour
1	teaspoon salt

Halved maraschino cherries *or* candied cherries

In a small bowl, cream the shortening, cream cheese and sugar until light and fluffy. Beat in the egg yolk and vanilla. Combine the flour and salt; gradually add to the creamed mixture and mix well.

Drop by teaspoonfuls 2 in. apart onto greased baking sheets. Top each with a cherry half. Bake at 350° for 12-15 minutes or until lightly browned. Cool for 1 minute before removing to wire racks.

Susan Beck, Napa, California ✳

These tender, buttery tea cookies have a lovely fennel flavor and add a touch of elegance to any holiday cookie tray.

fennel tea cookies

yield 3 dozen

1	**tablespoon fennel seed, crushed**
2	**tablespoons boiling water**
3/4	**cup butter, softened**
2/3	**cup packed brown sugar**
1	**egg**
2	**cups all-purpose flour**
1/2	**teaspoon baking soda**

Confectioners' sugar

In a small bowl, soak fennel seed in boiling water; set aside. In a large bowl, cream butter and brown sugar. Beat in egg. Drain fennel seed. Combine the flour, baking soda and fennel seed; gradually add to creamed mixture.

Roll into 1-in. balls; place 2 in. apart on ungreased baking sheets. Bake at 350° for 10-12 minutes or until lightly browned. Roll warm cookies in confectioners' sugar. Cool on wire racks.

Lois Hill, Thomasville, North Carolina ✳

These rich and buttery cookies are actually light and with their colorful swirls, each one of these minty sugary bites is unique.

swirled mint cookies

yield 4 dozen

1/2	**cup butter, softened**
1/2	**cup reduced-fat butter, softened**
3/4	**cup plus 1 tablespoon sugar,** *divided*
1	**egg**
1	**teaspoon vanilla extract**
1/2	**teaspoon peppermint extract**
2	**cups all-purpose flour**
1/2	**teaspoon baking powder**
1/4	**teaspoon salt**
10	**to 20 drops red food coloring**
10	**to 20 drops green food coloring**

In a large bowl, cream butters and 3/4 cup sugar until light and fluffy. Beat in egg and extracts. Combine the flour, baking powder and salt; gradually add to creamed mixture and mix well.

Divide dough into thirds. Stir red food coloring into one portion of dough; stir green food coloring into another portion. Leave remaining dough plain. Cover and chill for at least 1 hour.

Divide each portion of dough into four equal pieces. Roll each piece into a 12-in. rope. Place a red, a green and a plain rope next to each other. Cut through all three ropes at 1-in. intervals, forming sets of three differently colored doughs. Repeat.

Roll each set of doughs into a ball; place balls 3 in. apart on ungreased baking sheets. Flatten to 1/8-in. thickness with a glass dipped in remaining sugar. Bake at 375° for 8-10 minutes or until bottoms are lightly browned. Remove to wire racks to cool.

editor's note: This recipe was tested with Land O'Lakes light stick butter.

✳ Carolyn Stromberg, Wever, Iowa
These fun cookies are filled with chewy gumdrops. I use red and green ones at Christmas, black and orange for Halloween and pastel shades for Easter.

gumdrop cookies
yield 3-1/2 dozen

3/4	cup shortening
1	cup sugar, *divided*
1/2	teaspoon almond extract
1-3/4	cups all-purpose flour
1/2	teaspoon baking soda
1/4	teaspoon salt
1	cup chopped fruit-flavored *or* spiced gumdrops
2	egg whites

In a large bowl, cream shortening and 3/4 cup sugar until light and fluffy. Beat in extract. Combine the flour, baking soda and salt; gradually add to creamed mixture and mix well. Stir in gumdrops.

In a small bowl, beat egg whites until soft peaks form. Gradually add remaining sugar, beating until stiff peaks form. Fold into dough.

Drop by heaping teaspoonfuls 2 in. apart onto ungreased baking sheets. Bake at 350° for 12-15 minutes or until golden brown. Cool for 1 minute before removing from pans to wire racks to cool completely.

✳ Elizabeth Flatt
Kelso, Washington
These old-time cookies are always on the goody trays I give to friends and neighbors every holiday. They're great for dunking in milk, and they bring back a spicy flavor of Christmases past.

gingersnaps
yield 2 dozen

1/3	cup shortening
1/2	cup sugar
1	egg
2	tablespoons molasses
1	cup all-purpose flour
1	teaspoon baking soda
1/2	teaspoon *each* ground cinnamon, cloves and ginger
1/8	teaspoon salt

Additional sugar

In a large bowl, cream the shortening and sugar until light and fluffy. Beat in egg and molasses. Combine the flour, baking soda, cinnamon, cloves, ginger and salt; gradually add to creamed mixture and mix well. Cover and refrigerate for at least 4 hours.

Shape tablespoonfuls of the dough into balls. Roll in additional sugar. Place 2 in. apart on lightly greased baking sheets. Flatten slightly with a greased glass.

Bake at 350° for 8-10 minutes or until edges are lightly browned and tops are set and starting to crack. Cool for 2 minutes before removing to wire racks.

editor's note: Cookie dough may be frozen. Freeze balls of dough on waxed paper-lined baking sheets until firm. Remove from the pan and place in resealable freezer bags for up to 3 months. To bake, place frozen balls of dough 2 in. apart on lightly greased baking or until edges are lightly browned and tops are set and starting to crack.

Marlene Robinson, Sexsmith, Alberta

A cross between classic fruitcake and buttery cookies, these treats are perfect for Christmas. Each one is chock-full of raisins and candied cherries.

slice 'n' bake fruitcake cookies

yield 5 dozen

1	cup butter, softened
1	cup confectioners' sugar
1/2	cup sugar
1	egg
2	teaspoons vanilla extract
2-1/4	cups all-purpose flour
1/2	teaspoon baking soda
1/2	cup raisins
1/2	cup *each* red and green candied cherries, chopped

In a large bowl, cream butter and sugars until light and fluffy. Beat in egg and vanilla. Combine flour and baking soda; gradually add to creamed mixture and mix well. Fold in raisins and cherries.

Shape dough into two 2-in.-thick logs; wrap each in plastic wrap. Refrigerate for 2 hours or until firm.

Cut logs into 1/4-in. slices. Place 2 in. apart on ungreased baking sheets. Bake at 350° for 12-15 minutes or until lightly browned. Remove to wire racks to cool.

pfeffernuesse

yield 8 dozen

1	cup butter, softened
1	cup sugar
2	eggs
1/2	cup light corn syrup
1/2	cup molasses
1/3	cup water
6-2/3	cups all-purpose flour
1/4	cup crushed aniseed
1	teaspoon baking soda
1	teaspoon ground cinnamon
1/2	teaspoon ground nutmeg
1/4	teaspoon ground cloves
1/4	teaspoon ground allspice

Confectioners' sugar

In a large bowl, cream the butter and sugar until light and fluffy. Add the eggs, one at a time, beating well after each addition. In a bowl, combine corn syrup, molasses and water; set aside. Combine the flour, aniseed, baking soda and spices; add to creamed mixture alternately with molasses mixture. Cover and refrigerate overnight.

Roll into 1-in. balls. Place 2 in. apart on greased baking sheets. Bake at 400° for 11-12 minutes or until golden brown. Roll the warm cookies in confectioners' sugar. Cool on wire racks.

Betty Hawkshaw
Alexandria, Virginia
These mild spice cookies, perfect for dunking, come from an old family recipe. This German cookie sometimes has black pepper in the dough for an added zip.

✳ Libia Foglesong, San Bruno, California
A twice-baked Italian cookie, biscotti makes a wonderful "dunker." A pretty way to present a batch is on a Christmasy plate arranged in wagon-wheel fashion.

holiday biscotti

yield 2 dozen

1/2	cup butter, softened
1	cup sugar
3	eggs
2	teaspoons vanilla extract
1	teaspoon orange extract
3	cups all-purpose flour
2	teaspoons baking powder
1/2	teaspoon salt
2/3	cup dried cranberries, coarsely chopped
2/3	cup pistachios, coarsely chopped
2	tablespoons grated orange peel

In a large bowl, cream the butter and sugar. Add the eggs, one at a time, beating well after each addition. Stir in extracts. Combine flour, baking powder and salt; gradually add to creamed mixture and mix well (dough will be sticky). Stir in the cranberries, pistachios and orange peel. Cover and chill for 30 minutes.

Divide dough in half. On a floured surface, shape each half into a loaf 1-1/2 to 2-in. diameter. Place on an ungreased baking sheet. Bake at 350° for 30-35 minutes.

Cool on pan for 5 minutes. Cut diagonally into 3/4-in.-thick slices. Place slices cut side down on an ungreased baking sheet. Bake for 9-10 minutes. Turn slices over. Bake 10 minutes longer or until golden brown. Remove to wire racks to cool. Store in an airtight container.

✳ Tami Henke
Lockport, Illinois

There's a nice surprise of chocolate inside these frothy kisses. They're my husband's top choice each Christmas.

meringue kisses

yield 44 cookies

3	egg whites
1	teaspoon vanilla extract
1/4	teaspoon cream of tartar
Dash salt	
1	cup sugar
Red and green food coloring, optional	
44	chocolate kisses

In a large bowl, beat egg whites, vanilla, cream of tartar and salt; on medium speed until soft peaks form. Gradually add sugar, two tablespoons at a time, beating on high until stiff peaks form, about 5-8 minutes. If desired, divide batter in half and fold in red and green food coloring.

Drop by rounded tablespoonfuls 1-1/2 in. apart onto lightly greased baking sheets. Press a chocolate kiss into the center of each cookie and cover it with meringue using a knife.

Bake at 275° for 30-35 minutes or until firm to the touch. Immediately remove to a wire rack to cool. Store in an airtight container.

Debbie Kersh, Springtown, Texas ✳
My mom created this wonderful dessert after tasting something similar. The sweet bars boast a tangy cranberry flavor.

caramel cranberry bars

yield 2 dozen

1	package (12 ounces) fresh *or* frozen cranberries, thawed
1	package (8 ounces) chopped dates
3/4	cup chopped pecans
2	tablespoons plus 1/2 cup sugar, *divided*
2-1/3	cups all-purpose flour, *divided*
2	cups old-fashioned oats
1/2	cup packed brown sugar
1/2	teaspoon baking soda
1	cup butter, melted
3/4	cup caramel ice cream topping

In a small bowl, combine the cranberries, dates, pecans and 2 tablespoons sugar; set aside.

In a large bowl, combine 2 cups flour, oats, brown sugar, baking soda and remaining sugar. Stir in butter; set aside 1 cup for topping. Press remaining crumb mixture into a greased 13-in. x 9-in. baking dish. Bake at 350° for 15 minutes.

Meanwhile, place the remaining flour in a small bowl. Stir in caramel topping until smooth; set aside. Sprinkle cranberry mixture over crust; drizzle with caramel mixture. Sprinkle with reserved crumb mixture.

Bake for 30-35 minutes or until golden brown and bubbly. Cool on a wire rack. Cut into bars. Store in the refrigerator.

Nicole Moskou, New York, New York ✳
In Greece, these buttery golden twists are a traditional treat for celebrations. One side of my family is Greek, and I enjoy making foods that keep me in touch with my heritage.

greek holiday cookies

yield about 6-1/2 dozen

1-1/2	cups butter, softened
1-1/4	cups sugar
4	eggs
2	tablespoons orange juice
3	teaspoons vanilla extract
5-1/4	cups all-purpose flour
1-1/2	teaspoons baking powder
3/4	teaspoon baking soda

In a large bowl, cream butter and sugar. Add 2 eggs; beat well. Beat in orange juice and vanilla. Combine the flour, baking powder and baking soda; gradually add to creamed mixture. Cover and refrigerate for 1 hour or until easy to handle.

Roll dough into 1-1/4-in. balls. Shape each into a 6-in. rope; fold in half and twist twice. Place 2 in. apart on ungreased baking sheets.

In a small bowl, beat the remaining eggs; brush over the dough. Bake at 350° for 7-12 minutes or until edges are golden brown. Remove to wire racks.

✳ Victoria Sampson, Hendersonville, North Carolina
I bake these cutouts for Thanksgiving and Christmas, then decorate them in the colors of the season. If I run out of time before the holidays, I simply skip the frosting step and sprinkle the colored sugar directly on the cookies before they go in the oven.

lemon ginger cutouts

yield about 8 dozen

1	cup butter, softened
2/3	cup packed brown sugar
2/3	cup light corn syrup
1/3	cup honey
1	teaspoon grated lemon peel
4-1/2	cups all-purpose flour
1	teaspoon salt
1	teaspoon baking soda
1	teaspoon ground cinnamon
3/4	teaspoon ground ginger

FROSTING:

1-1/2	cups confectioners' sugar
1	to 2 tablespoons water

Colored sugar, optional

In a large bowl, cream butter and brown sugar until light and fluffy. Gradually add corn syrup, honey and lemon peel. Combine the flour, salt, baking soda, cinnamon and ginger; gradually add to creamed mixture and mix well. Cover and chill for 2 hours or until easy to handle.

Divide dough into fourths. On a lightly floured surface, roll one portion to 1/8-in. thickness. Cut into desired shapes with floured 2-in. cookie cutters. Place 2 in. apart on greased baking sheets. Bake at 350° for 8-10 minutes or until light golden brown. Remove to wire racks to cool. Repeat with remaining dough.

For frosting, in a small bowl, combine confectioners' sugar and enough water to achieve desired consistency. Spread over cookies. Sprinkle with colored sugar if desired.

fruitcake cookies

yield 5-6 dozen

✳ Dorcas Wright
Guelph, Ontario
My old-fashioned goodies are fun, colorful and chewy without being sticky. They are bite-size fruitcake treats.

1/2	cup butter, softened
1/2	cup shortening
1/2	cup sugar
1/2	cup packed brown sugar
1	egg
1	teaspoon vanilla extract
1	cup all-purpose flour
1/2	teaspoon baking soda
1/2	teaspoon salt
2	cups old-fashioned oats
1	cup flaked coconut
1/2	cup chopped dates
1/2	cup *each* chopped red and green candied cherries
1/2	cup chopped candied pineapple

In a large bowl, cream butter, shortening and sugars. Add the egg and vanilla; mix well. Combine flour, baking soda, salt and oats; add to creamed mixture and mix well. Stir in the coconut, dates, cherries and pineapple.

Shape into 1-in. balls; place 1 in. apart on greased baking sheets. Bake at 325° for 15 minutes or until lightly browned. Remove to wire racks to cool.

Karyn Rogers, Hemet, California

I received the recipe for these soft ginger cookies from a dear friend. A comforting classic like this always satisfies.

frosted gingerbread nut cookies

yield 5 dozen

1/2	cup butter, softened
2/3	cup sugar
1	egg
1/2	cup molasses
2-3/4	cups all-purpose flour
1	teaspoon baking soda
1	teaspoon ground cinnamon
1	teaspoon ground ginger
1/2	teaspoon salt
1/4	teaspoon ground cloves
1/2	cup buttermilk
1/2	cup chopped walnuts

FROSTING:

1-1/2	cups confectioners' sugar
4-1/2	teaspoons butter, softened
1/2	teaspoon vanilla extract
2	to 3 tablespoons half-and-half cream

Walnuts halves, optional

In a large bowl, cream butter and sugar until light and fluffy. Beat in egg and molasses. Combine flour, baking soda, cinnamon, ginger, salt and cloves; add to creamed mixture alternately with buttermilk, beating well after each addition. Stir in chopped walnuts.

Drop by tablespoonfuls 2 in. apart onto greased baking sheets. Bake at 350° for 10-12 minutes or until edges are firm. Remove to wire racks to cool.

For frosting, in a small bowl, combine confectioners' sugar, butter, vanilla and enough cream to achieve the desired consistency. Frost cooled cookies. Top each with a walnut half if desired.

peppermint pinwheels

yield about 4 dozen

3/4	cup butter, softened
3/4	cup sugar
1	egg yolk
1	teaspoon vanilla extract
2	cups all-purpose flour
1/2	teaspoon baking powder
1/2	teaspoon salt
1/2	teaspoon peppermint extract
1/4	teaspoon red liquid food coloring

In a large bowl, cream butter and sugar. Beat in egg yolk and vanilla. Combine the flour, baking powder and salt; gradually add to creamed mixture and mix well. Divide dough in half; add extract and red food coloring to one portion. Roll out each portion of dough between waxed paper into a 16-in. x 10-in. rectangle. Remove waxed paper.

Place red rectangle over plain rectangle. Roll up tightly jelly-roll style, starting with a long side. Wrap in plastic wrap. Refrigerate overnight or until firm.

Unwrap the dough and cut into 1/4-in. slices. Place 2 in. apart on lightly greased baking sheets. Bake at 350° for 12-14 minutes or until set. Cool for 2 minutes before removing to wire racks.

Marcia Hostetter
Canton, New York
Put a spin on your holidays with these bright swirls! This recipe makes rich-tasting cookies with a minty flavor that sometimes surprises people.

❋ Dee Lein, Longmont, Colorado
I've never come across another spritz cookie like this—one calling for cream cheese as an ingredient. That helps to keep these wreaths moist a long time, while also adding a delicious flavor.

holly wreaths

yield about 3 dozen

1	cup butter, softened
1	package (3 ounces) cream cheese, softened
1/2	cup sugar
1	teaspoon vanilla extract
2	cups all-purpose flour

Green cherries, cut into thin slices
Cinnamon red-hot candies
Frosting and decorator gel

In a large bowl, cream butter and cream cheese. Add sugar; blend well. Stir in vanilla. Gradually beat in flour.

Using a cookie press fitted with star tip, form dough into 2-1/2-in. wreaths on ungreased baking sheets. Bake at 375° for 10-12 minutes or until set (do not brown). Remove to wire racks to cool.

Decorate wreaths with green cherry "leaves" and cinnamon candy "berries" attached with a drop of frosting. Add bows with decorator gel.

❋ Elizabeth Manzanares, Gloucester, Virginia
These cookies have been a Christmas tradition in my family since I was a little girl. The big bears are delicate and tasty.

gingerbread teddy bears

yield 8 cookies

1	cup butter, cubed
2/3	cup packed brown sugar
2/3	cup molasses
1	egg, lightly beaten
1-1/2	teaspoons vanilla extract
4	cups all-purpose flour
1-1/2	teaspoons ground cinnamon
1	teaspoon ground ginger
3/4	teaspoon baking soda
1/2	teaspoon ground cloves

Miniature chocolate chips
Red decorating frosting

In a small saucepan, combine the butter, brown sugar and molasses. Cook over medium heat until sugar is dissolved. Pour into a large bowl; let stand for 10 minutes. Stir in egg and vanilla. Combine the flour, cinnamon, ginger, baking soda and cloves; gradually add to butter mixture and mix well. Cover and refrigerate for 2 hours or overnight.

Shape dough into eight balls, 2 in. each; eight balls, 1 in. each; 32 balls, 1/2 in. each; and 16 balls, 3/8 in. each. Place the 2-in. balls on three foil-lined baking sheets for the body of eight bears; flatten to 1/2-in. thickness. Position 1-in. balls for heads; flatten to 1/2-in. thickness. Attach four 1/2-in. balls to each bear for arms and legs. Attach two 3/8-in. balls for ears. Add chocolate chips for eyes, nose and buttons.

Bake at 350° for 10-12 minutes or until set. Cool for 10 minutes before carefully removing to wire racks to cool completely. With frosting, pipe bows on bears.

Beverly Fehner, Gladstone, Missouri ✳
This recipe came from an old family friend and is always high on everyone's cookie request list. I make at least six batches for Noel nibbling and also give some away as gifts.

chocolate mint creams

yield about 6 dozen

1	cup butter, softened
1-1/2	cups confectioners' sugar
2	squares (1 ounce *each*) unsweetened chocolate, melted and cooled
1	egg
1	teaspoon vanilla extract
2-1/2	cups all-purpose flour
1	teaspoon baking soda
1	teaspoon cream of tartar
1/4	teaspoon salt

FROSTING:

1/4	cup butter, softened
2	cups confectioners' sugar
2	tablespoons milk
1/2	teaspoon peppermint extract

Green food coloring, optional

In a large bowl, cream butter and confectioners' sugar. Add the chocolate, egg and vanilla; mix well. Combine dry ingredients; gradually add to the creamed mixture, beating well. Shape the dough into a 2-in. diameter roll; wrap in plastic wrap. Refrigerate for 1 hour or until firm.

Unwrap dough and cut into 1/8-in. slices. Place 2 in. apart on ungreased baking sheets. Bake at 400° for 7-8 minutes or until edges are firm. Remove to wire racks to cool.

In a small bowl, combine frosting ingredients. Frost cookies. Store in airtight containers.

peppermint kisses

yield 3 dozen

2	egg whites
1/8	teaspoon salt
1/8	teaspoon cream of tartar
1/2	cup sugar
2	peppermint candy canes (one green, one red), crushed

In a large bowl, beat the egg whites, salt and cream of tartar; on medium speed until soft peaks form. Add sugar, 1 tablespoon at a time, beating on high until stiff, glossy peaks form.

Spoon meringue into a pastry bag or a resealable plastic bag. If using a plastic bag, cut a 1-in. hole in a corner. On ungreased foil-lined baking sheets, pipe meringue into 1-1/2-in.-high mounds, forming a kiss shape. Sprinkle half with red crushed candy cane and half with green crushed candy cane.

Bake at 225° for 1-1/2 to 2 hours or until dry but not brown. Cool; remove from foil. Store in an airtight container.

Lynn Bernstetter ✳
Lake Elmo, Minnesota
These are fun, refreshing and low in fat! I pipe the airy meringue batter, but if your prefer, you can drop it from a tablespoon.

✳ Bobbie Hanks, Tulsa, Oklahoma
As a city kid, I was always eager to visit my grandparents on their Oklahoma farmstead. There I acquired my taste for country food, like these tender cookies with buttery icing.

sour cream cutouts

yield about 9 dozen

1	cup butter, softened
2	cups sugar
3	eggs
6	cups all-purpose flour
2	teaspoons baking soda
1/2	teaspoon salt
1	cup (8 ounces) sour cream

FROSTING:

1/2	cup butter, softened
4	cups confectioners' sugar
3	tablespoons milk

Food coloring, optional

In a large bowl, cream butter and sugar until light and fluffy. Add eggs, one at a time, beating well after each addition. Combine dry ingredients; add to the creamed mixture alternately with sour cream, beating well after each addition (dough will be sticky). Cover and refrigerate for 2 hours or until easy to handle.

On a floured surface, roll out dough to 1/4-in. thickness. Cut into desired shapes with floured cookie cutters.

Place 1 in. apart on greased baking sheets. Bake at 375° for 8-12 minutes or until lightly browned. Cool for 1-2 minutes before removing to wire racks.

For frosting, in a large bowl, beat the butter, confectioners' sugar and milk until smooth. Add food coloring if desired. Frost cookies.

✳ Doris Marshall
Strasburg, Pennsylvania
A single batch of these mouthwatering cookies is never enough. I usually make one to give away and two more to keep at home.

italian christmas cookies

yield 8-1/2 dozen

1	cup butter, softened
2	cups sugar
3	eggs
1	carton (15 ounces) ricotta cheese
2	teaspoons vanilla extract
4	cups all-purpose flour
1	teaspoon salt
1	teaspoon baking soda

FROSTING:

1/4	cup butter, softened
3	to 4 cups confectioners' sugar
1/2	teaspoon vanilla extract
3	to 4 tablespoons milk

Colored sprinkles

In a large bowl, cream butter and sugar. Add the eggs, one at a time, beating well after each addition. Beat in ricotta and vanilla. Combine flour, salt and baking soda; gradually add to creamed mixture.

Drop by rounded teaspoonfuls 2 in. apart onto greased baking sheets. Bake at 350° for 10-12 minutes or until lightly browned. Remove to wire racks to cool.

In a large bowl, cream butter, sugar and vanilla. Add enough milk until frosting reaches spreading consistency. Frost cooled cookies and immediately decorate with sprinkles. Store in the refrigerator.

Gloria Ward, Mesa, Arizona ✳

I adapted a traditional cherry blossom cookie recipe by leaving out the lemon zest and adding food coloring, sprinkles and almond extract to create a more festive look. When I took a batch to a cookie exchange party, everyone raved about them.

poinsettia cookies
yield about 3 dozen

1/2	**cup butter, softened**
1/2	**cup sugar**
1	**egg**
1	**tablespoon milk**
1/2	**teaspoon almond extract**
1/2	**teaspoon cherry** *or* **vanilla extract**
4	**to 5 drops red food coloring, optional**
1-3/4	**cups all-purpose flour**
1	**teaspoon baking powder**
1/4	**teaspoon salt**
1/2	**cup candied cherry halves**

Pink *or* **red sprinkles, optional**

In a large bowl, cream butter and sugar until light and fluffy. Beat in the egg, milk, extracts and food coloring if desired. Combine the flour, baking powder and salt; gradually add to creamed mixture and mix well. Cover and chill for 30 minutes or until easy to handle.

Roll dough into 1-1/4-in. balls. Place 2 in. apart on parchment paper-lined baking sheets. With kitchen scissors, snip the top of each ball in half, cutting three-fourths of the way through. Cut each half into thirds; carefully spread the wedges apart, forming flower petals.

Place a cherry half in the center of each; top with sprinkles if desired. Bake at 350° for 10-12 minutes or until set. Cool for 1-2 minutes before removing from pans to wire racks.

Karla Retzer, Grantsburg, Wisconsin ✳

It just wouldn't be Christmas at our house without these crunchy, chocolate-mint meringue cookies.

mint meringues
yield 32 cookies

2	**egg whites**
1/8	**teaspoon salt**
1/8	**teaspoon cream of tartar**
1/8	**teaspoon peppermint extract**
6	**to 8 drops green food coloring, optional**
1/2	**cup sugar**
1/3	**cup miniature semisweet chocolate chips**

In a small bowl, beat the egg whites, salt, cream of tartar, extract and food coloring if desired on medium speed until soft peaks form. Gradually add sugar, 1 tablespoon at a time, beating on high until stiff glossy peaks form and sugar is dissolved, about 6 minutes. Gently fold in chocolate chips.

Drop by rounded teaspoonfuls 2 in. apart onto parchment paper-lined baking sheets. Bake at 250° for 40-45 minutes or until firm to the touch. Turn oven off; leave meringues in oven for 1-1/2 hours. Remove to wire racks. Store in an airtight container.

✳ Lisa MacLean, Winslow, Arizona

Sour cream keeps my favorite sugar cookies extra moist. Dress them up with a drizzle of tinted white chocolate or dip them in white chocolate, then sprinkle with crushed candy canes.

christmas sugar cookies

yield about 8 dozen

1	cup butter, softened
2	cups confectioners' sugar
1	egg
1/4	cup sour cream
1/4	cup honey
2	teaspoons vanilla extract
3-1/2	cups all-purpose flour
1	teaspoon baking soda
1	teaspoon cream of tartar
1/2	teaspoon ground mace
1/8	teaspoon salt

White candy coating
Green paste food coloring

In a large bowl, cream butter and sugar until light and fluffy. Beat in the egg. Beat in the sour cream, honey and vanilla. Combine the dry ingredients; gradually add to creamed mixture and mix well. Cover and chill for 2 hours or until easy to handle.

On a lightly floured surface, roll out dough to 1/8-in. thickness. Cut with a floured 3-in. cookie cutters. Place 1 in. apart on ungreased baking sheets.

Bake at 325° for 8-10 minutes or until lightly browned. Remove to wire racks to cool.

In a microwave, melt white coating at 70% power for 1 minute; stir. Microwave at additional 10- to 20-second intervals, stirring until smooth. Stir in food coloring; drizzle over cooled cookies.

cranberry nut swirls

yield about 3-1/2 dozen

✳ Carla Hodenfield
Mandan, North Dakota

When we want to "pull a fast one" on the guys in our family, who claim they don't like cranberries in any shape or form, we make this recipe. Everyone, including the guys, enjoys these cookies.

1/2	cup butter, softened
3/4	cup sugar
1	egg
1	teaspoon vanilla extract
1-1/2	cups all-purpose flour
1/4	teaspoon baking powder
1/4	teaspoon salt
1/2	cup finely ground cranberries
1/2	cup finely chopped walnuts
1	tablespoon grated orange peel
3	tablespoons brown sugar
2	teaspoons milk

In a large bowl, cream butter and sugar. Beat until light and fluffy. Beat in egg and vanilla.

Combine dry ingredients; add to the creamed mixture. Cover and refrigerate at least 1 hour.

In a small bowl, combine the cranberries, walnuts and orange peel; set aside. On a lightly floured surface, roll dough into a 10-in. square. Combine brown sugar and milk; spread over dough. Sprinkle with the cranberry mixture, to within a 1/2 in. of edges; roll up tightly, jelly-roll style. Wrap in plastic wrap. Refrigerate for several hours or overnight.

Unwrap dough. Cut roll into 1/4-in. slices and place on well-greased baking sheets. Bake at 375° for 14-15 minutes or until edges are light brown. Remove to wire racks to cool.

Iola Egle, McCook, Nebraska ✳

Dipping the edges of these traditional favorites in icing defines their lacy pattern. These are best when made shortly before they are served.

rosettes

yield 4-5 dozen

2	**eggs**
2	**teaspoons sugar**
1	**cup milk**
1	**tablespoon vanilla extract**
1	**cup all-purpose flour**
1/4	**teaspoon salt**

Oil for deep-fat frying
ICING:

2	**cups confectioners' sugar**
1	**teaspoon vanilla extract**
1	**to 3 tablespoons water**

In a small bowl, beat eggs and sugar; stir in milk and vanilla. Combine flour and salt; add to batter and beat until smooth.

Heat 2-1/2 in. of oil to 365° in a deep-fat fryer or electric skillet. Place rosette iron in hot oil, then dip in batter, three-fourths up on sides of iron (do not let batter run over top of iron). Immediately place into hot oil; loosen rosette with fork and remove iron. Fry 1-2 minutes per side or until golden. Remove to a wire rack covered with paper towel. Repeat with remaining batter.

For icing, combine the sugar, vanilla and enough water to achieve a dipping consistency. Dip edges of rosettes into icing; dry on wire racks.

✳ Kristi Thorpe, Portland, Oregon
My grandma shared her recipe for these old-fashioned sugar cookies with the unexpected taste of nutmeg. They are light, crunchy and so delicious.

nutmeg sugar crisps

yield about 6 dozen

1	cup butter, softened
3/4	cup sugar
1/2	cup confectioners' sugar
1	egg
1	teaspoon vanilla extract
2-1/2	cups all-purpose flour
1/2	teaspoon baking soda
1/2	teaspoon cream of tartar
1/4	to 1/2 teaspoon ground nutmeg
1/8	teaspoon salt

In a large bowl, cream butter and sugars. Beat in egg and vanilla; mix well. Combine the flour, baking soda, cream of tartar, nutmeg and salt; add to the creamed mixture and mix well. Refrigerate for 1 hour.

Roll into 3/4-in. balls. Place the balls 2 in. apart on greased baking sheets. Flatten with a glass dipped in sugar. Bake at 350° for 10-12 minutes or until lightly browned. Remove to wire racks to cool.

✳ Lisa Rupple, Keenesburg, Colorado
These cute cutout reindeer really fly off the plate when my brother's around. They're his favorite! The subtle chocolate color and taste make them a nice alternative to plain vanilla sugar cookies.

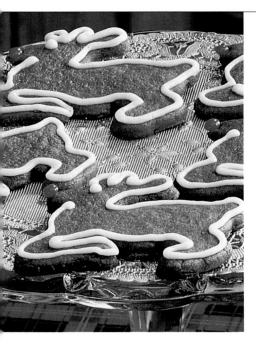

chocolate reindeer

yield about 3-1/2 dozen

1	cup butter, softened
1	cup sugar
1/2	cup packed brown sugar
1	egg
1	teaspoon vanilla extract
2-3/4	cups all-purpose flour
1/2	cup baking cocoa
1	teaspoon baking soda
44	red-hot candies

ICING: (optional)

1-1/2	cups confectioners' sugar
2	to 3 tablespoons milk

In a large bowl, cream butter and sugars until fluffy. Beat in egg and vanilla. Combine flour, cocoa and baking soda; add to creamed mixture and mix well. Cover and refrigerate for at least 2 hours.

On a lightly floured surface, roll dough to 1/8-in. thickness. Cut with a floured reindeer-shaped cookie cutter. Place 2 in. apart on greased baking sheets. Bake at 375° for 8-9 minutes. Immediately press a red-hot onto each nose. Cool for 2-3 minutes before removing to wire racks.

If desired, combine confectioners' sugar and milk until smooth. Cut a small hole in the corner of a heavy-duty resealable plastic bag; fill with icing. Pipe around edges of cookies and add a dot for eye.

Dawn Burns, Troy, Ohio ✳

My mom made these dressy cookies for cookie exchanges when I was little. She'd let me sprinkle on the nuts and coconut.

caramel heavenlies

yield about 6 dozen

12	graham crackers (4-3/4 inches x 2-1/2 inches)
2	cups miniature marshmallows
3/4	cup butter
3/4	cup packed brown sugar
1	teaspoon ground cinnamon
1	teaspoon vanilla extract
1	cup sliced almonds
1	cup flaked coconut

Line a 15-in. x 10-in. x 1-in. baking pan with foil. Place graham crackers in pan; cover with marshmallows. In a saucepan, cook and stir butter, brown sugar and cinnamon over medium heat until the butter is melted and sugar is dissolved. Remove from the heat; stir in the vanilla.

Spoon over the marshmallows. Sprinkle with almonds and coconut. Bake at 350° for 14-16 minutes or until browned. Cool completely. Cut into 2-in. squares, then cut each square in half to form triangles.

frosted ginger creams

yield about 4 dozen

1/4	cup shortening
1/2	cup sugar
1	egg
1/3	cup molasses
2	cups all-purpose flour
1	teaspoon ground ginger
1/2	teaspoon baking soda
1/2	teaspoon salt
1/2	teaspoon ground cinnamon
1/2	teaspoon ground cloves
1/3	cup water

FROSTING:

1-1/2	ounces cream cheese, softened
3	tablespoons butter, softened
1	cup plus 3 tablespoons confectioners' sugar
1/2	teaspoon vanilla extract
1	to 2 teaspoons lemon juice

In a large bowl, cream shortening and sugar until blended. Beat in egg and molasses. Combine the flour, ginger, baking soda, salt, cinnamon and cloves; gradually add to creamed mixture alternately with water (dough will be soft).

Drop by heaping teaspoonfuls 2 in. apart onto greased baking sheets. Bake at 400° for 7-8 minutes or until tops are cracked. Remove to wire racks to cool.

In a small bowl, beat cream cheese, butter and confectioners' sugar until light and fluffy. Beat in vanilla and enough lemon juice to achieve spreading consistency. Frost cookies. Store in the refrigerator.

Shirley Clark ✳
Columbia, Missouri
I have many recipes featuring ginger, but these soft cookies are real gems. The cream cheese frosting is just the perfect topping.

Guests will have a merry time munching these mild mint cookies. The cute, crunchy candy canes are easy to form once you color the dough—just roll into ropes and twist together.

candy cane cookies

yield about 6 dozen

1/2	cup butter, softened
1/2	cup shortening
1	cup sugar
1/4	cup confectioners' sugar
1/2	cup milk
1	egg
1	teaspoon peppermint extract
1	teaspoon vanilla extract
3-1/2	cups all-purpose flour
1/4	teaspoon salt

Green and red food coloring

In a large bowl, cream butter, shortening and sugars. Beat in milk, egg and extracts. Gradually add flour and salt. Set aside half of the dough. Divide remaining dough in half; add the green food coloring to one portion and red food coloring to the other. Wrap each dough separately in plastic wrap. Refrigerate for 1 hour or until easy to handle.

Roll 1/2 teaspoonfuls of each color of dough into 3-in. ropes. Place each green rope next to a white rope; press together gently and twist. Repeat with red ropes and remaining white ropes.

Place 2 in. apart on ungreased baking sheets. Curve one end, forming a cane. Bake at 350° for 11-13 minutes or until set. Cool for 2 minutes; carefully remove to wire racks.

cherry macaroons

yield about 6 dozen

※ Sherma Talbot
Salt Lake City, Utah
I received this recipe along with its ingredients at my bridal shower. Now these are a favorite of our sons.

1-1/3	cups shortening
1-1/2	cups sugar
2	eggs
1	teaspoon almond extract
3-1/2	cups all-purpose flour
2	teaspoons baking powder
2	teaspoons baking soda
1	teaspoon salt
1-1/2	cups flaked coconut
1	cup maraschino cherries, chopped

In a large bowl, cream shortening and sugar. Add eggs and extract; mix well. Combine flour, baking powder, baking soda and salt; gradually add to creamed mixture. Stir in the coconut and cherries (dough will be very stiff).

Drop by rounded teaspoonfuls 2 in. apart onto greased baking sheets. Bake at 375° for 10-12 minutes or until lightly browned. Remove to wire racks to cool.

Sue Bartlett, Berlin, Wisconsin ✳

Making these soft, chewy cookies with a rich flavor has been a family tradition since my children were small.
At Christmastime, I shape the dough into gingerbread men with tasty raisin eyes and buttons.

molasses cutouts

yield about 3 dozen

1	cup butter, softened
1	cup sugar
2	eggs
1	cup molasses
1/2	cup cold water
5-1/2	cups all-purpose flour
4	teaspoons baking soda
1	teaspoon salt
1	teaspoon ground cinnamon
1	teaspoon ground ginger

FROSTING:

4	cups confectioners' sugar
1/4	cup butter, softened
1	teaspoon ground ginger
1/2	teaspoon salt
1/2	teaspoon ground cinnamon
3	to 4 tablespoons boiling water

M&M baking bits, raisins *or* other candies

In a large bowl, cream butter and sugar until light and fluffy. Add eggs, one at a time, beating well after each addition. Beat in molasses and water. Combine the flour, baking soda, salt, cinnamon and ginger; gradually add to creamed mixture and mix well. Cover and refrigerate for 4 hours or until easy to handle.

On a lightly floured surface, roll out dough to 1/8-in. thickness. Cut with a floured 5-in. gingerbread man cutter. Place 1 in. apart on ungreased baking sheets.

Bake at 375° for 6-8 minutes or until edges are golden brown. Remove to wire racks to cool.

For frosting, in a large bowl, combine the confectioners' sugar, butter, ginger, salt, cinnamon and enough water to achieve spreading consistency. Frost and decorate cookies as desired.

mincemeat cookies

yield 4 dozen

1/2	cup butter, softened
1	cup sugar, *divided*
1	egg
1	teaspoon vanilla extract
1-3/4	cups all-purpose flour
1-1/2	teaspoons baking powder
1/4	teaspoon salt
1	package (9 ounces) condensed mincemeat, cut into small pieces
1	egg white, lightly beaten

In a large bowl, cream butter and 3/4 cup sugar until light and fluffy. Beat in egg and vanilla. Combine the flour, baking powder and salt; gradually add to creamed mixture and mix well. Stir in mincemeat. Cover and refrigerate for 2 hours.

Roll dough into 1-in. balls; dip into egg white and remaining sugar. Place sugar side up 2 in. apart on greased baking sheets. Bake at 375° for 10-12 minutes or until set. Remove to wire racks to cool.

Lucie Fitzgerald ✳
Spring Hill, Florida
Shh! Don't reveal the "secret ingredient" in this tender, chewy old-time cookie until after they take a taste. This recipe will win over those who think they don't like mincemeat.

✳ Judy Degenstein, Ottawa, Kansas
These soft sandwich cookies are eye-catching, thanks to the holiday designs you paint on with food coloring.

painted holiday delights

yield about 2 dozen

2	cups all-purpose flour
1/2	cup sugar
1/2	cup confectioners' sugar
2	teaspoons ground cinnamon
3/4	teaspoon baking powder
1/4	teaspoon salt
1/2	cup cold butter
1	egg
1/4	cup orange juice

FILLING:

1	package (8 ounces) cream cheese, softened
3	tablespoons confectioners' sugar
3	tablespoons strawberry preserves

GLAZE:

1	cup confectioners' sugar
1/4	teaspoon vanilla extract
1	to 2 tablespoons milk

Assorted food coloring

In a bowl, combine the first six ingredients. Cut in butter until mixture resembles coarse crumbs. Combine egg and orange juice; stir into crumb mixture just until moistened. Shape into a ball; cover and chill for 1-2 hours or until easy to handle.

On a floured surface, roll out the dough to 1/8-in. thickness. Cut with a floured 2-in. round cookie cutter.

Place 1 in. apart on ungreased baking sheets. Bake at 375° for 8-10 minutes or until lightly browned. Remove to wire racks to cool.

Combine filling ingredients; spread on the bottom of half of cookies. Top with remaining cookies.

For glaze, combine sugar, vanilla and enough milk to achieve desired consistency. Spread over tops of cookies; let stand until set. Using a small new paintbrush and food coloring, paint holiday designs on cookie tops. Store in the refrigerator.

christmas wreaths

yield 8 wreaths

✳ Taste of Home Test Kitchen
Cornflakes take the place of traditional rice cereal in these sweet no-bake treats. Dressed up with green food coloring and red candies, they look nice on cookie platters and dessert buffets.

20	large marshmallows
2	tablespoons butter, cubed

Green food coloring

3	cups cornflakes
72	miniature red M&M baking bits

In a microwave-safe bowl, combine the marshmallows and butter. Microwave, uncovered, on high for 1 minute or until butter is melted and marshmallows are puffed. Add food coloring; mix well. Stir in the cornflakes.

Shape mixture into 3-in. wreaths on a waxed paper-lined baking sheet. Immediately press M&M's in three clusters of three for berries. Let stand until set.

Kim Jordan, Dunsmuir, California ✳

A lady at my church gave me this recipe. I always include these cute little logs in my holiday food gifts.

eggnog logs
yield 4-1/2 dozen

1	**cup butter, softened**
3/4	**cup sugar**
1-1/4	**teaspoons ground nutmeg**
1	**egg**
2	**teaspoons vanilla extract**
1/2	**to 1 teaspoon rum extract**
3	**cups all-purpose flour**

FROSTING:

1/4	**cup butter, softened**
3	**cups confectioners' sugar,** *divided*
1	**teaspoon vanilla extract**
1/2	**to 1 teaspoon rum extract**
2	**tablespoons half-and-half cream**

Ground nutmeg

In a large bowl, cream butter and sugar until light and fluffy. Add the nutmeg, egg and extracts; mix thoroughly. Stir in flour. If necessary, refrigerate dough for easier handling.

On a lightly floured surface, shape dough into 1/2-in.-diameter rolls; cut each into 3-in.-long pieces. Place 2 in. apart on ungreased baking sheets. Bake at 350° for 15 minutes or until lightly browned. Remove to wire racks to cool.

For frosting, cream butter until light and fluffy. Add 2 cups sugar and extracts; mix well. Beat in cream and remaining sugar. Frost cookies. With tines of a small fork, make lines down frosting to simulate bark. Sprinkle with nutmeg.

Patsy Wolfenden, Golden, British Columbia ✳

I make these attractive, buttery cookies to serve at our guest lodge, and all the girls in the kitchen are addicted to them!

raspberry ribbons
yield about 5 dozen

1	**cup butter, softened**
1/2	**cup sugar**
1	**egg**
1	**teaspoon vanilla extract**
2-1/4	**cups all-purpose flour**
1/2	**teaspoon baking powder**
1/4	**teaspoon salt**
1/2	**cup raspberry jam**

GLAZE:

1	**cup confectioners' sugar**
2	**tablespoons evaporated milk**
1/2	**teaspoon vanilla extract**

In a large bowl, cream butter and sugar. Beat in egg and vanilla. Combine the flour, baking powder and salt; gradually add to creamed mixture and mix well.

Divide dough into four portions; shape each into a 10-in. x 2-1/2-in. log. Place 4 in. apart on greased or foil-lined baking sheets. Make a 1/2-in. depression down the center of each log. Bake at 350° for 10 minutes.

Fill depressions with jam. Bake 10-15 minutes longer or until lightly browned. Cool for 2 minutes. Remove to a cutting board; cut into 3/4-in. slices. Place on wire racks.

In a small bowl, combine glaze ingredients until smooth. Drizzle over warm cookies. Cool completely.

* Judith Outlaw, Portland, Oregon
My friend bakes these cookies at Christmas. They're popular at cookie exchanges, but her husband urges her not to trade any of them! I agree with him that they are simply wonderful.

finnish christmas cookies

yield about 6 dozen

2	cups butter, softened
1	cup sugar
4	cups all-purpose flour
1	egg, beaten
2/3	cup finely chopped almonds

Colored sugar, optional

In a large bowl, cream butter and sugar until light and fluffy. Beat in flour. Cover and chill for 1 hour.

On a well-floured surface, roll out dough to 1/4-in. thickness. Brush lightly with egg. Sprinkle with almonds and sugar if desired. Using a fluted pastry cutter or knife, cut into 2-in. x 1-in. strips.

Place 1 in. apart on ungreased baking sheets. Bake at 350° for 10-12 minutes or until lightly browned. Remove to wire racks to cool.

* Pat Habiger
Spearville, Kansas
These delicious mini tarts are lovely for Christmas or to serve at a tea. They're worth the extra time it takes to make them.

pumpkin pecan tassies

yield 2 dozen

1/2	cup butter, softened
1	package (3 ounces) cream cheese, softened
1	cup all-purpose flour

FILLING:

3/4	cup packed brown sugar, *divided*
1/4	cup canned pumpkin
4	teaspoons plus 1 tablespoon butter, melted, *divided*
1	egg yolk
1	tablespoon half-and-half cream
1	teaspoon vanilla extract
1/4	teaspoon rum extract
1/8	teaspoon ground cinnamon
1/8	teaspoon ground nutmeg
1/2	cup chopped pecans

In a small bowl, cream butter and cream cheese. Beat in flour. Shape into 24 balls. With floured fingers, press onto the bottom and up the sides of greased miniature muffin cups. Bake at 325° for 8-10 minutes or until edges are lightly browned.

Meanwhile, in a bowl, combine 1/2 cup brown sugar, pumpkin, 4 teaspoons butter, egg yolk, cream, extracts, cinnamon and nutmeg. Spoon into warm cups. Combine the pecans and remaining brown sugar and butter; sprinkle over filling.

Bake 23-27 minutes longer or until set and edges are golden brown. Cool for 10 minutes before removing to wire racks.

Lorraine Caland, Thunder Bay, Ontario ✳

For as long as I can remember, these fancy little maple logs have been a Christmas tradition at our house. My girls loved working the assembly line and dipping the ends in chocolate.

chocolate-dipped maple logs

yield about 6 dozen

1/2	cup butter, softened
1/2	cup shortening
1/2	cup confectioners' sugar
1	teaspoon vanilla extract
1	teaspoon maple flavoring
1-1/2	cups all-purpose flour
1	cup quick-cooking oats
1/2	teaspoon salt
1	cup (6 ounces) semisweet chocolate chips
3	tablespoons milk
3/4	cup ground walnuts

In a large bowl, cream the butter, shortening and confectioners' sugar until light and fluffy. Beat in vanilla and maple flavoring. Combine the flour, oats and salt; gradually add to creamed mixture and mix well.

On a lightly floured surface, shape dough into 1/2-in.-wide logs. Cut into 2-in. pieces. Place 1 in. apart on ungreased baking sheets. Bake at 325° for 15-18 minutes or until set and very lightly browned. Remove to wire racks to cool.

In a microwave, melt chocolate chips and milk; stir until smooth. Dip one end of each cookie into chocolate; allow excess to drip off. Roll in walnuts. Place on waxed paper until set.

dipped pecan spritz

yield 12-1/2 dozen

1-1/2	cups butter, softened
1	cup sugar
1	egg
1	teaspoon vanilla extract
1/2	teaspoon almond extract
3	cups all-purpose flour
1	cup finely ground pecans
1	teaspoon baking powder
3/4	cup semisweet chocolate chips
1-1/2	teaspoons shortening, *divided*
3/4	cup vanilla *or* white chips

Colored sprinkles

In a large bowl, cream butter and sugar until light and fluffy; beat in egg and extracts. Combine the flour, pecans and baking powder; gradually add to creamed mixture and mix well.

Using a cookie press fitted with disk of your choice, press dough 2 in. apart onto ungreased baking sheets. Bake at 375° for 5-7 minutes or until set (do not brown). Remove to wire racks to cool.

In a microwave, melt chocolate chips and 3/4 teaspoon shortening; stir until smooth. Melt vanilla chips and remaining shortening at 70% power for 1 minute; stir. Microwave at additional 10- to 20-second intervals, stirring until smooth.

Dip half of the cookies halfway in semisweet mixture; allow excess to drip off. Place on waxed paper to set. Dip remaining cookies halfway in vanilla mixture; allow excess to drip off. Place on waxed paper and sprinkle coated area with colored sprinkles. Let stand until set.

Sylvia Neudorf ✳
Abbotsford, British Columbia

With their pretty shapes, these treats look lovely at the center of the cookie plates I arrange for all of our Christmas gatherings, and they are always the first to disappear. This is my husband's favorite Christmas cookie.

※ Glenna Tooman, Boise, Idaho

I created this cookie recipe because my sons liked eggnog so much. After frosting the cookies, you can add to their festive flair by sprinkling them with colored sugar.

eggnog cutout cookies
yield about 4 dozen

1/2	cup butter, softened
1	cup sugar
2	eggs
2	tablespoons plus 1 teaspoon eggnog
2-1/2	cups all-purpose flour
1/2	teaspoon salt
1/4	teaspoon baking soda
1/4	teaspoon ground nutmeg

ICING:

2	cups confectioners' sugar
1/4	teaspoon ground nutmeg, optional
4	to 5 tablespoons eggnog

Liquid *or* paste food coloring, optional

In a large bowl, cream butter and sugar until light and fluffy. Beat in eggs. Stir in eggnog.

Combine the flour, salt, baking soda and nutmeg; gradually add to creamed mixture and mix well. Cover and refrigerate for 1 hour or until easy to handle.

On a lightly floured surface, roll out dough to 1/8-in. thickness. Cut with floured 2-1/2-in. cookie cutters. Place 2 in. apart on greased baking sheets.

Bake at 375° for 8-10 minutes or until edges begin to brown. Remove to wire racks to cool.

In a small bowl, beat the confectioners' sugar, nutmeg if desired and enough eggnog to achieve icing consistency. Add food coloring if desired. Spread over cooled cookies; let stand until set.

editor's note: This recipe was tested with commercially prepared eggnog.

※ Pamela Esposito
Smithville, New Jersey
These rounds filled with fruit preserves were blue-ribbon winners at the county fair two years running. A family favorite, they never last past December 25!

sweetheart cookies
yield about 2 dozen

3/4	cup butter, softened
1/2	cup sugar
1	egg yolk
1-1/2	cups all-purpose flour
2	tablespoons raspberry *or* strawberry preserves

Confectioners' sugar, optional

In a large bowl, cream butter and sugar. Add egg yolk; mix well. Stir in the flour by hand. On a lightly floured surface, gently knead dough for 2-3 minutes or until thoroughly combined.

Roll into 1-in. balls. Place 2 in. apart on greased baking sheets. Using the end of a wooden spoon handle, make an indention in the center of each. Fill each with 1/4 teaspoon preserves. Bake at 350° for 13-15 minutes or until edges are lightly browned. Remove to wire racks. Dust warm cookies with confectioners' sugar if desired. Cool.

Paula Marchesi, Lenhartsville, Pennsylvania ✳
Dipped in melted chocolate and rolled in crushed peppermint candy, this flavorful biscotti is a favorite. It's one of the many sweets I make for Christmas.

peppermint biscotti
yield about 3-1/2 dozen

3/4	cup butter, softened
3/4	cup sugar
3	eggs
2	teaspoons peppermint extract
3-1/4	cups all-purpose flour
1	teaspoon baking powder
1/4	teaspoon salt
1	cup crushed peppermint candy

FROSTING:

2	cups (12 ounces) semisweet chocolate chips
2	tablespoons shortening
1/2	cup crushed peppermint candy

In a large bowl, cream butter and sugar. Add eggs, one at a time, beating well after each addition. Beat in extract. Combine the flour, baking powder and salt; stir in peppermint candy. Gradually add to creamed mixture, beating until blended (dough will be stiff).

Divide dough in half. On an ungreased baking sheet, roll each portion into a 12-in. x 2-1/2-in. rectangle. Bake at 350° for 25-30 minutes or until golden brown. Carefully remove to wire racks; cool for 15 minutes.

Transfer to a cutting board; cut diagonally with a sharp knife into 1/2-in. slices. Place cut side down on ungreased baking sheets. Bake for 12-15 minutes or until firm. Remove to wire racks to cool.

In a microwave-safe bowl, melt chocolate chips and shortening; stir until smooth. Dip one end of each cookie in chocolate; roll in candy. Place on waxed paper until set. Store in an airtight container.

holiday snickerdoodles
yield 6-1/2 dozen

1/2	cup butter, softened
1/2	cup shortening
1-3/4	cups sugar, *divided*
2	eggs
1/4	to 1/2 teaspoon rum extract
2-3/4	cups all-purpose flour
2	teaspoons cream of tartar
1	teaspoon baking soda
1/4	teaspoon salt
2	teaspoons ground nutmeg

In a large bowl, cream butter, shortening and 1-1/2 cups sugar. Beat in eggs and extract. Combine the flour, cream of tartar, baking soda and salt; gradually add to creamed mixture. In a shallow bowl, combine the nutmeg and remaining sugar.

Roll dough into 1-in. balls; roll in sugar mixture. Place 2 in. apart on ungreased baking sheets. Bake at 400° for 10-12 minutes or until lightly browned. Remove to wire racks to cool.

Darlene Brenden ✳
Salem, Oregon
It simply wouldn't be Christmas without these melt-in-your-mouth cookies on my platter! They have a lovely eggnog flavor and look great with their crunchy tops.

❋ Marcy Greenblatt, Redding, California
My grandmother encouraged me to enter these mint brownies in the county fair some years ago—and they earned top honors! They're a great treat to serve during the holidays.

peppermint brownies
yield 2 dozen

3/4	cup canola oil
2	cups sugar
2	teaspoons vanilla extract
4	eggs
1-1/3	cups all-purpose flour
1	cup baking cocoa
1	teaspoon baking powder
1	teaspoon salt
3/4	cup crushed peppermint candy, *divided*

GLAZE:

1	cup (6 ounces) semisweet chocolate chips
1	tablespoon shortening

Line a 13-in. x 9-in. baking pan with foil; grease foil and set aside. In a large bowl, beat oil and sugar until blended. Beat in vanilla. Add eggs, one at a time, beating well after each addition. Combine the flour, cocoa, baking powder and salt; gradually add to oil mixture. Set aside 2 tablespoons peppermint candy for garnish; stir in remaining candy. Spread into prepared pan.

Bake at 350° for 35-40 minutes or until a toothpick inserted near the center comes out clean. Cool on a wire rack.

For glaze, in a microwave, melt chocolate chips and shortening; stir until smooth. Spread over brownies; sprinkle with reserved candy.

candied orange date bars
yield about 3 dozen

❋ Eunice Stoen
   Decorah, Iowa

A good friend of mine gave me the recipe for these yummy, rich date bars. Chopped candied orange slices really make them special. I dip my kitchen shears in hot water to make cutting the orange slices a little easier.

1	package (7 ounces) orange candy slices
1/2	cup sugar
2	tablespoons plus 1-3/4 cups all-purpose flour, *divided*
1/2	cup water
1/2	pound chopped dates
1	cup butter, softened
1	cup packed brown sugar
2	eggs
1	teaspoon baking soda
1/2	teaspoon salt
1/2	cup chopped walnuts

Confectioners' sugar

Cut orange slices horizontally in half, then into 1/4-in. pieces; set aside. In a saucepan, combine the sugar and 2 tablespoons flour. Stir in water until smooth. Add dates. Bring to a boil; cook and stir for 2 minutes or until thickened. Remove from the heat; cool.

In a large bowl, cream butter and brown sugar until light and fluffy. Add eggs, one at a time, beating well after each addition. Combine the baking soda, salt and remaining flour; add to creamed mixture and mix well. Stir in walnuts.

Spread half of the batter into a greased 13-in. x 9-in. baking pan. Spread date mixture over batter; sprinkle with reserved orange pieces. Spread remaining batter over the top.

Bake at 350° for 30-35 minutes or until a toothpick inserted near the center comes out clean. Cool in pan on a wire rack. Dust with the confectioners' sugar.

Start the dough for these crispy cookie-like treats the night before. They're a tasty and delicious with a pot of hot coffee.

danish crispies

yield about 2 dozen

- 1 **package (1/4 ounce) active dry yeast**
- 1/2 **teaspoon plus 3 tablespoons sugar,** *divided*
- 1 **cup warm water (110° to 115°),** *divided*
- 3 **egg yolks**
- 4 **cups all-purpose flour**
- 1/3 **cup nonfat dry milk powder**
- 1 **teaspoon salt**
- 1 **cup cold butter**

FILLING:
- 6 **tablespoons butter, softened**
- 1/2 **cup sugar**
- 1 **teaspoon ground cinnamon**

TOPPING:
- 1-1/2 **cups sugar**
- 1 **teaspoon ground cinnamon**

In a large bowl, dissolve yeast and 1/2 teaspoon sugar in 1/4 cup water; let stand for 5 minutes. Beat in the egg yolks, remaining sugar and water.

Combine the flour, milk powder and salt; cut in butter until mixture resembles coarse crumbs. Gradually add to yeast mixture to make a soft dough. Place in a greased bowl, turning once to grease top; cover and refrigerate overnight.

Turn dough onto a lightly floured surface. Cover with a kitchen towel; let rest for 10 minutes. Roll into an 18-in. x 10-in. rectangle; spread with softened butter. Combine sugar and cinnamon; sprinkle over butter. Roll up jelly-roll style, starting with a long side. Pinch edges to seal. Cut into 3/4-in. slices.

Combine topping ingredients; sprinkle some on waxed paper. Place slices, cut side down, on cinnamon-sugar; roll each into a 5-in. circle, turning to coat both sides and adding cinnamon-sugar as needed. Place 2 in. apart on greased baking sheets. Sprinkle tops with leftover cinnamon-sugar if desired. Bake at 350° for 15-20 minutes or until golden brown. Remove from pans to cool on wire racks.

cranberry macaroons

yield about 4-1/2 dozen

- 4 **egg whites**
- 1/4 **teaspoon cream of tartar**
- 1 **teaspoon almond extract**
- 1-1/3 **cups sugar**
- 2 **drops red food coloring, optional**
- 1 **cup sliced almonds, chopped**
- 3/4 **cup flaked coconut**
- 1/2 **cup finely chopped dried cranberries**
- 3 **cups cornflakes, finely crushed**

In a large bowl, beat the egg whites, cream of tartar and almond extract on medium speed until soft peaks form. Gradually beat in sugar, 2 tablespoons at a time, on high until stiff glossy peaks form. Add food coloring if desired. Fold in almonds, coconut, cranberries and cornflakes.

Drop by rounded teaspoonfuls 2 in. apart onto well-greased baking sheets. Bake at 325° for 20-22 minutes. Remove to wire racks.

Jane Guilbeau ✳
Melbourne, Florida
A doily-lined tray piled high with these cookies never fails to draw exclamations of admiration from all who see them. Crunchy on the outside and chewy on the inside, the cookies have a great texture.

big batch bonanza

white chocolate holiday cookies, p. 358

Need a batch of cookies for

a bake sale, potluck or class trip? Start with any one of these tempting, crowd-pleasing treats. Each one makes at least 7 dozen cookies, and some recipes make over 15 dozen! So, start with your biggest bowl when you mix up one of these recipes.

pumpkin spice cookies, p. 360

jeweled cookies, p. 353

❋ Dolores Deegan, Pottstown, Pennsylvania

Peanut butter sets these scrumptious, delicate cookies apart from other spritz. The chocolate drizzle and chopped peanut topping make them extra-special.

chocolate topped peanut butter spritz

yield 16 dozen

1	**cup butter, softened**
1	**cup peanut butter**
1	**cup granulated sugar**
1	**cup brown sugar**
2	**eggs**
2	**cups all-purpose flour**
1	**teaspoon baking soda**
1/2	**teaspoon salt**

CHOCOLATE TOPPING:

1-1/2	**cups semisweet chocolate chips**
1	**tablespoons shortening**

Chopped peanuts

In a large bowl, cream together butter, peanut butter and sugars. Beat in eggs until fluffy. Combine flour, baking soda and salt; gradually add to creamed mixture; blend well. Cover and refrigerate for 15 minutes.

Using a cookie press fitted with a zigzag disk, press dough into long strips onto ungreased baking sheets. Cut each strip into 2-in. pieces (there is no need to separate the pieces). Bake at 350° for 6-8 minutes or until set (do not brown). Remove to wire racks to cool.

In a microwave or saucepan, melt chocolate and shortening, stirring until smooth. Cut a small hole in the corner of pastry or plastic bag. Fill with chocolate mixture. Pipe a strip of chocolate down center of each cookie. Sprinkle with chopped peanuts.

editor's note: Reduced-fat or generic brands of peanut butter are not recommended for this recipe.

Charleen Block, Hutchinson, Minnesota ✳
Instead of walnuts or pecans, this chocolate chip cookie recipe calls for salted peanuts. Whenever I bake these, friends and family seem to come running! This salty-sweet combination is just delicious.

salted peanut cookies
yield 10 dozen

1-1/2	cups shortening
1	cup sugar
1	cup packed brown sugar
3	eggs
1	teaspoon vanilla extract
3-3/4	cups all-purpose flour
2	teaspoons baking soda
1	teaspoon salt
1-1/2	cups semisweet chocolate chips
1-1/2	cups salted peanuts

In a large bowl, cream shortening and sugars until light and fluffy. Add eggs, one at a time, beating well after each addition. Beat in vanilla. Combine the flour, baking soda and salt; gradually add to creamed mixture and mix well. Stir in chocolate chips and peanuts.

Drop by tablespoonfuls 2 in. apart onto greased baking sheets. Bake at 350° for 10-12 minutes or until lightly browned. Remove to wire racks.

bushel of cookies
yield 24 dozen

2	pounds raisins
1	pound pecans
5	cups butter, softened
11	cups sugar
12	eggs
1	cup maple syrup
1	quart milk
1/4	cup vanilla extract
12	cups quick-cooking oats
21	cups all-purpose flour
2	teaspoons salt
1/4	cup baking powder
1/4	cup baking soda
2	packages (10 to 11 ounces *each*) butterscotch chips

Grind or finely chop raisins and pecans; set aside. In a very large bowl, cream butter and sugar. Add eggs, a few at a time, beating well after each addition. Add syrup, milk and vanilla; mix well. Stir in the oats, raisins and pecans. Combine the flour, salt, baking powder and baking soda; stir into oat mixture. Fold in chips. Cover and chill for 2 hours.

Drop by rounded tablespoonfuls 2 in. apart onto greased baking sheets. Bake at 350° for 13-15 minutes or until set. Remove to wire racks to cool.

Martha Schwartz ✳
Jackson, Ohio
This recipe turns out what seems like a bushelful of cookies—that's probably how it got its name. The flavor of the raisins and pecans comes through in every bite, and the butterscotch chips add a delectable taste.

✳ Britt Strain, Idaho Falls, Idaho
Soft candy orange slices are a refreshing addition to these crispy vanilla chip cookies. To quickly cut the orange candy, use scissors, rinsing the blades with cold water occasionally to reduce sticking.

orange slice cookies

yield about 10 dozen

1	cup candy orange slices
1-1/2	cups sugar, *divided*
1	cup butter, softened
1-1/2	cups packed brown sugar
2	eggs
2	teaspoons vanilla extract
4	cups all-purpose flour
2	teaspoons baking soda
1	teaspoon salt
1	package (10 to 12 ounces) vanilla chips *or* white chips
1	cup chopped pecans

Cut each orange slice into eight pieces. Roll in 1/4 cup sugar; set aside. In a large bowl, cream the butter, shortening, brown sugar and remaining sugar. Add eggs, one at a time, beating well after each addition. Beat in vanilla. Combine the flour, baking soda and salt; gradually add to creamed mixture. Stir in chips, pecans and orange slice pieces.

Roll into 1-in. balls. Place 2 in. apart on ungreased baking sheets. Bake at 375° for 10-12 minutes or until golden brown. Remove to wire racks to cool completely.

✳ Becky Melander
Clinton Township, Michigan
When I was growing up, my mother would make these soft and spicy raisin cookies once a month. Since the recipe makes a huge batch, she would freeze some to snack on later.

jumbo raisin cookies

yield 13 dozen

2	cups water
4	cups raisins
1	cup butter, softened
1	cup shortening
4	cups sugar
6	eggs
2	teaspoons vanilla extract
8	cups all-purpose flour
4	teaspoons baking soda
4	teaspoons baking powder
4	teaspoons salt
1	tablespoon ground cinnamon
1	teaspoon ground nutmeg
1/2	teaspoon ground allspice
2	cups (12 ounces) semisweet chocolate chips

In a saucepan, combine the water and raisins. Bring to a boil. Remove from the heat; cool to room temperature (do not drain).

In a large bowl, cream butter, shortening and sugar until light and fluffy. Add eggs, one at a time, beating well after each addition. Beat in vanilla. Combine the dry ingredients; gradually add to the creamed mixture. Stir in chocolate chips and raisins with any liquid.

Drop by heaping tablespoonfuls 2 in. apart onto greased baking sheets. Bake at 350° for 12-15 minutes or until golden brown. Remove to wire racks to cool completely.

Alice Kahnk, Kennard, Nebraska ✳

Crisp and loaded with goodies, these are my husband's favorite cookies. I used to bake them in large batches when our four sons still lived at home. Now I whip them up for our grandchildren.

whole wheat toffee sandies

yield about 12 dozen

1	**cup butter, softened**
1	**cup sugar**
1	**cup confectioners' sugar**
1	**cup canola oil**
2	**eggs**
1	**teaspoon almond extract**
3-1/2	**cups all-purpose flour**
1	**cup whole wheat flour**
1	**teaspoon baking soda**
1	**teaspoon cream of tartar**
1	**teaspoon salt**
2	**cups chopped almonds**
1	**package (6 ounces) English toffee bits**

Additional sugar

In a large bowl, cream butter and sugars until light and fluffy. Add oil, eggs and extract; mix well. Combine flours, baking soda, cream of tartar and salt; gradually add to creamed mixture. Stir in almonds and toffee bits.

Roll into 1-in. balls; roll in sugar. Place on ungreased baking sheets and flatten with a fork. Bake at 350° for 12-14 minutes or until lightly browned. Remove to wire racks to cool.

Katie Koziolek, Hartland, Minnesota ✳

You'll especially appreciate this recipe around the hurried holidays because the dough can be frozen for up to 2 months. So when planning your holiday cookie baking spree, be sure to include these.

cherry christmas slices

yield about 11 dozen

1	**cup butter, softened**
1	**cup confectioners' sugar**
1	**egg**
1	**teaspoon vanilla extract**
2-1/4	**cups all-purpose flour**
2	**cups red and green candied cherries, halved**
1	**cup pecan halves**

In a large bowl, cream the butter and sugar. Add egg and vanilla; beat until fluffy. Add flour; mix well. Stir in cherries and pecans. Cover and refrigerate for 1 hour. Shape dough into three 10-in. rolls; wrap in plastic wrap and place in a freezer bag. Freeze up to 2 months or until ready to bake.

To bake, unwrap and cut frozen rolls into 1/8-in. slices. Place 1 in. apart on ungreased baking sheets. Bake at 325° for 10-12 minutes or until edges are golden brown. Remove to wire racks to cool.

Susan Bohannon, Kokomo, Indiana
My Great-Aunt Hilda makes this recipe every Christmas, and everybody just raves about it! Kipplens taste a lot like Mexican wedding cakes, but I like them better.

kipplens

yield 12 dozen

2	cups butter, softened
1	cup sugar
2	teaspoons vanilla extract
5	cups all-purpose flour
2	cups chopped pecans
1/4	teaspoon salt

Confectioners' sugar

In a large bowl, cream butter and sugar until light and fluffy. Beat in vanilla. Add the flour, pecans and salt. Mix well.

Roll dough into 1-in. balls and place on ungreased baking sheets. Bake at 325° for 17-20 minutes or until lightly browned. Remove to wire racks. Cool cookies slightly before rolling them in confectioners' sugar.

walnut chip cookies

yield about 12 dozen

Joy Hanje
Gaylord, Michigan
You're sure to enjoy the double-chocolate flavor in these sweet treats. Melted chocolate is added to the batter, then chocolate chips are stirred in before baking. Ground oats add a nice texture.

2	cups butter, softened
2	cups sugar
2	cups packed brown sugar
4	eggs
2	squares (1 ounce *each*) unsweetened chocolate, melted
2	teaspoons vanilla extract
5	cups quick-cooking oats
4	cups all-purpose flour
2	teaspoons baking soda
2	teaspoons baking powder
1	teaspoon salt
4	cups (24 ounces) semisweet chocolate chips
3	cups chopped walnuts

In a large bowl, cream butter and sugars until light and fluffy. Add the eggs, one at a time, beating well after each addition. Beat in melted chocolate and vanilla.

Place half of the oats at a time in a blender or food processor; cover and process until powdery. Combine the oats, flour, baking soda, baking powder and salt; gradually add to creamed mixture and mix well.

Transfer to a large bowl if necessary. Stir in chocolate chips and nuts. Roll the dough into 1-1/4-in. balls.

Place 2 in. apart on lightly greased baking sheets. Bake at 375° for 7-9 minutes or until edges are firm (do not overbake). Remove to wire racks to cool.

This cookie's flavor fits right into the holiday spirit. If you like to have them well into winter, omit the sprinkle of colored sugar and freeze the cookies after baking.

eggnog cookies

yield about 16 dozen

1	cup butter, softened
2	cups sugar
1	cup eggnog
1	teaspoon baking soda
1/2	teaspoon ground nutmeg
5-1/2	cups all-purpose flour
1	egg white, lightly beaten

Colored sugar

In a large bowl, cream the butter and sugar until light and fluffy. Beat in eggnog, baking soda and nutmeg. Gradually add flour and mix well. Cover and chill for 1 hour.

On a lightly floured surface, roll out half of dough to 1/8-in. thickness. Cut into desired shapes; place 2 in. apart on ungreased baking sheets. Repeat with the remaining dough. Brush with the egg white; sprinkle with the colored sugar.

Bake at 350° for 6-8 minutes or until edges are lightly browned. Remove to wire racks to cool.

editor's note: This recipe was tested with commercially prepared eggnog.

soft apple butter delights

yield 10 dozen

1	cup butter, softened
2	cups packed brown sugar
2	eggs
1/2	cup brewed coffee, room temperature
3-1/2	cups all-purpose flour
1	teaspoon baking soda
1	teaspoon salt
1	teaspoon ground nutmeg
2	cups apple butter
1	cup chopped walnuts

In a large bowl, cream the butter and brown sugar until light and fluffy. Add eggs, one at a time, beating well after each addition. Beat in the coffee. Combine flour, baking soda, salt and nutmeg; gradually add to the creamed mixture. Stir in apple butter and walnuts (dough will be soft). Cover and chill for 1 hour.

Drop by teaspoonfuls 2 in. apart onto lightly greased baking sheets. Bake at 400° for 10-12 minutes or until edges are firm. Remove to wire racks to cool.

editor's note: This recipe was tested with commercially prepared apple butter.

Shirley Harter ✳
Greenfield, Indiana
I won first place at a local apple bake-off with this original recipe. I especially like to take these hearty cookies to gatherings in fall.

✳ Kelly McNeal, Derby, Kansas
My husband and two kids are sure to eat the first dozen of these cookies, warm from the oven, before the next tray is even done. A co-worker gave me the recipe for the pumpkin dip, which everyone loves with the cookies.

spice cookies with pumpkin dip

yield about 20 dozen (3 cups dip)

1-1/2	cups butter, softened
2	cups sugar
2	eggs
1/2	cup molasses
4	cups all-purpose flour
4	teaspoons baking soda
2	teaspoons ground cinnamon
1	teaspoon *each* ground ginger and cloves
1	teaspoon salt

PUMPKIN DIP:

1	package (8 ounces) cream cheese, softened
2	cups pumpkin pie filling
2	cups confectioners' sugar
1/2	to 1 teaspoon ground cinnamon
1/4	to 1/2 teaspoon ground ginger

In a very large bowl, cream the butter and sugar until light and fluffy. Add the eggs, one at a time, beating well after each addition. Add the molasses; mix well. Combine flour, baking soda, cinnamon, ginger, cloves and salt; add to creamed mixture and mix well. Cover and refrigerate overnight.

Shape into 1/2-in. balls; roll in sugar. Place 2 in. apart on ungreased baking sheets. Bake at 375° for 6 minutes or until edges begin to brown. Cool for 2 minutes before removing to a wire racks.

For dip, beat cream cheese in a large bowl until smooth. Add pumpkin pie filling; beat well. Add sugar, cinnamon and ginger; beat until smooth. Serve with cookies. Store leftover dip in the refrigerator.

✳ Delia True
Forest Ranch, California
If anything can get you in the Christmas spirit, these minty chocolate chip cookies can. A sprinkle of peppermint candy adds an extra-festive touch. They're excellent for dunking.

chocolate peppermint cookies

yield about 7-1/2 dozen

1	cup butter, softened
3/4	cup sugar
3/4	cup packed brown sugar
2	eggs
2	teaspoons vanilla extract
2-1/2	cups whole wheat flour
1	teaspoon baking soda
1/2	teaspoon salt
1	cup (6 ounces) semisweet chocolate chips
1/2	cup crushed peppermint candy

Additional crushed peppermint candy, optional

In a large bowl, cream butter and sugars until light and fluffy. Beat in eggs and vanilla. Combine the flour, baking soda and salt; gradually add to creamed mixture and mix well. Stir in chocolate chips and crushed candy.

Drop by rounded teaspoonfuls 2 in. apart onto ungreased baking sheets. Sprinkle with the additional candy if desired.

Bake at 350° for 9-10 minutes or until cookies spring back when lightly touched. Remove to wire racks to cool.

Frances Pierce, Waddington, New York ✳

These nutty treats are great for a classroom party or to share with friends. With a glass of cold milk, they're an irresistible snack.

back-to-school cookies

yield 12 dozen

1	cup butter-flavored shortening
1	cup creamy peanut butter
2	cups packed brown sugar
4	egg whites
1	teaspoon vanilla extract
2	cups all-purpose flour
1	teaspoon baking soda
1/2	teaspoon baking powder
2	cups crisp rice cereal
1-1/2	cups chopped nuts
1	cup flaked coconut
1	cup quick-cooking oats

In a large bowl, cream the shortening, peanut butter and brown sugar until light and fluffy. Beat in egg whites and vanilla. Combine the flour, baking soda and baking powder; gradually add to creamed mixture and mix well. Stir in the cereal, nuts, coconut and oats.

Drop by rounded tablespoonfuls 2 in. apart onto ungreased baking sheets. Flatten with a fork, forming a crisscross pattern. Bake at 375° for 7-8 minutes. Remove to wire racks.

editor's note: Reduced-fat or generic brands of peanut butter are not recommended for this recipe.

Mary Dudek, Alliance, Ohio ✳

Crisp outside but chewy inside, these sweet sensations will disappear in a hurry. The kids always have friends over, so I like to keep snacks on hand. They love these cookies.

cocoa chocolate chip cookies

yield about 8-1/2 dozen

2/3	cup butter, softened
1/2	cup canola oil
1	cup sugar
1	cup packed brown sugar
2	eggs
1	package (3.9 ounces) instant chocolate pudding mix
3	tablespoons water
3	cups all-purpose flour
1	teaspoon baking soda
1	teaspoon salt
1	package (12 ounces) miniature semisweet chocolate chips

In a large bowl, beat the butter, oil and sugars until blended. Beat in eggs. Beat in pudding mix and water. Combine the flour, baking soda and salt; gradually add to the chocolate mixture and mix well (dough will be stiff). Stir in the chocolate chips.

Roll into 1-in. balls. Place 2 in. apart on ungreased baking sheets. Bake at 350° for 9-11 minutes or until set and edges are firm. Cool for 2 minutes before removing to wire racks.

✳ Lavon Timken, Cimarron, Kansas
With four daughters, six grandchildren and one great-grandchild, I've baked lots of cookies. These chewy cookies are one of my favorites, and the candy surprise delights the kids.

chewy surprise cookies

yield about 8 dozen

1-1/2	cups butter-flavored shortening
1-1/2	cups peanut butter
2	cups sugar, *divided*
1-1/2	cups packed brown sugar
4	eggs
3-3/4	cups all-purpose flour
2	teaspoons baking soda
1-1/2	teaspoons baking powder
3/4	teaspoon salt
1	package (10 ounces) Milk Duds

In a large bowl, cream the shortening, peanut butter, 1-1/2 cups sugar and brown sugar until light and fluffy. Add eggs, one at a time, beating well after each addition. Combine dry ingredients; gradually add to the creamed mixture and mix well. Chill for at least 1 hour.

Shape 4 teaspoons of dough around each Milk Dud so it is completely covered. Roll balls in remaining sugar.

Place 2 in. apart on ungreased baking sheets. Bake at 350° for 10-12 minutes or until set. Cool for 5 minutes before removing to wire racks to cool completely.

editor's note: Reduced-fat or generic brands of peanut butter are not recommended for this recipe.

lavender cookies

yield about 7 dozen

1/2	cup shortening
1/2	cup butter, softened
1-1/4	cups sugar
2	eggs
1	teaspoon vanilla extract
1/2	teaspoon almond extract
2-1/4	cups all-purpose flour
4	teaspoons dried lavender flowers
1	teaspoon baking powder
1/2	teaspoon salt

In a large bowl, cream the shortening, butter and sugar until light and fluffy. Add eggs, one at a time, beating well after each addition. Beat in extracts. Combine the flour, lavender, baking powder and salt; gradually add to creamed mixture and mix well.

Drop dough by rounded teaspoonfuls 2 in. apart onto baking sheets lightly coated with cooking spray.

Bake at 375° for 8-10 minutes or until golden brown. Cool for 2 minutes before removing to wire racks. Store in an airtight container.

✳ Glenna Tooman
Boise, Idaho
I am a wedding and event planner. One of my brides served these unusual cookies at her reception, and I had to have the recipe. You can guess what her wedding color was!

Paula Pelis, Rocky Point, New York ✳

This recipe makes a lot of terrific cookies! Using a cookie press may be too difficult for children to master. Instead, have them help sprinkle the cookies with colored sugar before baking.

lemon-butter spritz cookies

yield about 12 dozen

2	cups butter, softened
1-1/4	cups sugar
2	eggs
Grated peel of 1 lemon	
2	teaspoons lemon juice
1	teaspoon vanilla extract
5-1/4	cups all-purpose flour
1/4	teaspoon salt
Colored sugar	

In a large mixing bowl, cream butter and sugar. Add the eggs, lemon peel, lemon juice and vanilla; mix well. Stir together flour and salt; gradually add to creamed mixture.

Using a cookie press fitted with the disk of your choice, press dough 2 in. apart onto ungreased baking sheets. Sprinkle with colored sugar. Bake at 400° for 8-10 minutes or until lightly brown around the edges. Remove to wire racks to cool.

peanut oat cookies

yield about 8 dozen

1-1/4	cups butter-flavored shortening
1-1/4	cups chunky peanut butter
1-1/2	cups packed brown sugar
1	cup sugar
3	eggs
4-1/2	cups old-fashioned oats
2	teaspoons baking soda
1	package (11-1/2 ounces) milk chocolate chips
1	cup chopped peanuts

In a large bowl, cream the shortening, peanut butter and sugars until light and fluffy. Add eggs, one at a time, beating well after each addition. Combine oats and baking soda; gradually add to creamed mixture and mix well. Stir in chocolate chips and peanuts.

Drop by tablespoonfuls 2 in. apart onto greased baking sheets. Bake at 350° for 10-12 minutes or until golden brown. Remove to wire racks to cool.

Stacia McLimore ✳
Indianapolis, Indiana
I'm not surprised when people say these are the best cookies they've ever had…I agree! Oats make them hearty and more delicious than traditional peanut butter cookies.

BAKING
tip

selling for a cause — When you bring your items to a bake sale, you should create a sign for each item. The information on the sign should include the name of the item and a list of ingredients. While food allergies to nuts are common, a wide variety of foods can cause an allergic reaction.

※ Judy McCreight, Springfield, Illinois
These tender cutout cookies have a slight lemon flavor that makes them stand out from the rest.
They're very easy to roll out compared to other sugar cookies I've worked with.

lemon butter cookies

yield about 13 dozen

1	**cup butter, softened**
2	**cups sugar**
2	**eggs, beaten**
1/4	**cup milk**
2	**teaspoons lemon extract**
4-1/2	**cups all-purpose flour**
2	**teaspoons baking powder**
1/2	**teaspoon salt**
1/4	**teaspoon baking soda**

Colored sugar, optional

In a large bowl, cream butter and sugar until light and fluffy. Add eggs, milk and extract. Combine dry ingredients; gradually add to creamed mixture. Cover and chill for 2 hours.

Roll out on a lightly floured surface to 1/8-in. thickness. Cut with a floured 2-in. cookie cutter. Place 2 in. apart on ungreased baking sheets. Sprinkle with colored sugar if desired.

Bake at 350° for 8-9 minutes or until the edges just begin to brown. Remove to wire racks to cool.

Marilyn Kutzli, Clinton, Iowa ✳
Before Christmas, my grandmother would bake peppernuts and store them until the "big day." When we'd come home from school, the whole house would smell like anise and we knew the holiday season was about to begin.

itty bitty peppernuts
yield 30 dozen

3	**eggs**
2	**cups sugar**
2-3/4	**cups all-purpose flour**
1	**teaspoon anise extract** *or* **crushed anise seed**

In a large bowl, beat eggs and sugar at medium speed for 15 minutes. Reduce speed and slowly add flour and anise. Mix until well combined. On a lightly floured surface, shape dough into ropes about 1/2 in. in diameter. Cover and refrigerate for 1 hour.

Slice ropes into 1/2-in. lengths. Place on greased baking sheets. Bake at 350° for 6-8 minutes or until set. Cookies will harden upon standing. When cookies are cool, store in airtight containers; they are best if allowed to age before serving.

toffee chip cookies
yield 12 dozen

1	**cup butter, softened**
1/2	**cup canola oil**
1	**cup sugar**
1	**cup packed brown sugar**
1	**teaspoon vanilla extract**
2	**eggs**
3-1/2	**cups all-purpose flour**
1	**teaspoon cream of tartar**
1	**teaspoon baking soda**
1	**teaspoon salt**
3	**cups crisp rice cereal**
1	**cup quick-cooking oats**
1	**cup flaked coconut**
1	**cup chopped pecans**
1	**cup English toffee bits** *or* **almond brickle chips**

In a large bowl, beat butter, oil, sugars and vanilla until blended. Add the eggs, one at a time, beating well after each addition. Combine flour, cream of tartar, baking soda and salt; add to creamed mixture. Stir in remaining ingredients.

Drop by tablespoonfuls 2 in. apart onto ungreased baking sheets. Bake at 350° for 10-12 minutes or until lightly browned. Remove to wire racks to cool.

Kay Frances Ronnenkamp ✳
Albion, Nebraska
These cookies combine several mouthwatering flavors. The generous size of the batch gives me plenty of scrumptious cookies to have on hand and extras to send to our sons at college.

✳ Eleanor Slimak, Chicago, Illinois
These cookies are my grandchildren's favorite. I've even shaped the dough in the form of their initials for special occasions.

valentine butter cookies

yield 18-19 dozen

2	cups butter, softened
2	cups sugar
3	eggs
1	tablespoon vanilla extract
6	cups all-purpose flour
2	teaspoons baking powder

Red decorator's sugar, optional

In a very large bowl, cream butter and sugar. Add eggs and vanilla; mix well. Combine flour and baking powder; gradually add to creamed mixture and mix well.

Using a cookie press fitted with the heart disk, press dough 2 in. apart onto ungreased baking sheets. Decorate with sugar if desired. Bake at 350° for 10-12 minutes or until set (do not brown). Remove to wire racks to cool completely.

✳ Penny Field
Waynesboro, Virginia
"Simply the best" is what most folks say after sampling my rich, flaky cookies. It's a thrill to share them with all of my friends and family.

nut-filled horns

yield 10 dozen

2	cups butter, softened
2	packages (8 ounces *each*) cream cheese, softened
2	egg yolks
4-1/2	cups all-purpose flour
2	teaspoons baking powder

FILLING:

4	cups finely chopped walnuts
1-1/2	to 2 cups sugar
6	tablespoons evaporated milk
1-1/2	teaspoons vanilla extract

In a large bowl, cream the butter and cream cheese until fluffy. Add egg yolks. Combine flour and baking powder; gradually add to creamed mixture. Cover and chill overnight.

In a bowl, combine filling ingredients (mixture will be thick). Divide dough into fourths (dough will be sticky). On a well-sugared surface, roll out each portion into a 12-in. x 10-in. rectangle. Cut into 2-in. squares. Place about 1 teaspoon filling in the center of each square. Fold over two opposite corners; seal tightly.

Place 2 in. apart on ungreased baking sheets. Bake at 350° for 15-18 minutes or until lightly browned. Remove to wire racks to cool.

Candied fruits give a stained-glass look to these cookies. They're like shortbread, but dressed up.

jeweled cookies

yield 12-14 dozen

1	pound butter, softened
2-1/2	cups sugar
3	eggs
5	cups all-purpose flour
1	teaspoon baking soda
1-1/2	cups raisins
1	cup coarsely chopped walnuts
1/2	cup *each* chopped red and green candied cherries
1/2	cup chopped candied pineapple

In a mixing bowl, cream butter and sugar. Add eggs, one at a time, beating well after each. Combine flour and baking soda; add to creamed mixture. Stir in raisins, nuts, cherries and pineapple; mix well. Shape into 2-in. rolls; wrap in waxed paper or foil. Freeze at least 2 hours.

Cut into 1/4-in. slices; place 1 in. apart on greased baking sheets. Bake at 350° for 8-10 minutes or until lightly browned. Remove to wire racks to cool completely.

ginger poppy seed cookies

yield about 17 dozen

3	cups butter, softened
1-1/2	cups sugar
1-1/2	cups packed brown sugar
3	eggs
2	teaspoons vanilla extract
7-1/2	cups all-purpose flour
1/2	cup poppy seeds
4	teaspoons ground cinnamon
2	teaspoons ground ginger
1-1/2	teaspoons baking soda
3/4	teaspoon salt

In a very large bowl, cream the butter and sugars until light and fluffy. Add eggs and vanilla. Combine the remaining ingredients; add to creamed mixture. Shape into four 13-in. rolls. Wrap each in plastic wrap. Refrigerate for 2 hours or overnight.

Unwrap dough and cut into 1/4-in. slices. Place 2 in. apart on ungreased baking sheets. Bake at 375° for 9-11 minutes or until edges are golden brown. Remove to wire racks to cool.

Mary Priesgen ✳
Theresa, Wisconsin
Poppy seed and ginger pair up nicely in these popular treats. The refrigerated dough slices easily and bakes quickly.

BAKING tip

finely chopping nuts — A food processor takes just seconds to finely chop nuts and just a few more to turn them into nut butter. To avoid that problem, try these tricks. Combine 1 or 2 tablespoons of flour (from the amount called for in the recipe) with the nuts. Then process with short bursts of chopping. If the nuts on top are still too large, stir them up and continue processing.

✳ Sandy Nace, Greensburg, Kansas
I have fond memories of baking and frosting these cutout cookies with my mom. Now I carry on the tradition with my kids, which makes for a messy but fun day!

frosted butter cutouts

yield about 8-1/2 dozen

1	cup butter, softened
2	cups sugar
2	eggs
1	cup buttermilk
1	teaspoon vanilla extract
1/2	teaspoon almond extract
5	cups all-purpose flour
2	teaspoons baking powder
1	teaspoon baking soda
1/4	teaspoon salt

FROSTING:

1/4	cup butter, softened
2	cups confectioners' sugar
1/2	teaspoon almond extract
2	to 3 tablespoons heavy whipping cream

Green and red food coloring, optional
Red-hot candies, colored sugar, Cake
   Mate snowflake decors and colored
   sprinkles

In a large bowl, cream butter and sugar until light and fluffy. Add eggs, one at a time, beating well after each addition. Beat in the buttermilk and extracts. Combine the flour, baking powder, baking soda and salt; gradually add to creamed mixture and mix well. Cover and chill overnight or until easy to handle.

On a lightly floured surface, roll out dough to 1/4-in. thickness. Cut with floured 2-1/2-in. cookie cutters. Place 1 in. apart on greased baking sheets.

Bake at 350° for 6-7 minutes or until lightly browned. Remove to wire racks to cool.

For frosting, in a small bowl, combine the butter, confectioners' sugar, extract and enough cream to achieve spreading consistency. Add food coloring if desired. Decorate as desired with frosting and candies.

✳ Beverly Launius
Sandwich, Illinois
My mom and I make these delicate cookies every Christmas. Hazelnuts give a little different flavor from the usual pecans.

hazelnut crescents

yield about 10 dozen

1	cup butter, softened
1/4	cup sugar
1	teaspoon vanilla extract
2	cups all-purpose flour
1	cup whole hazelnuts, ground

Confectioners' sugar

In a large bowl, cream butter and sugar until light and fluffy. Beat in vanilla. Gradually add flour and mix well. Stir in nuts. Cover and refrigerate for 2 hours or until easy to handle.

Shape dough by teaspoonfuls into 2-in. rolls. Form into crescents. Place 2 in. apart on ungreased baking sheets.

Bake at 350° for 12 minutes or until lightly browned. Cool for 2 minutes before removing from pans to wire racks. Dust cookies with confectioners' sugar.

Tami Burroughs, Salem, Oregon ✳

These golden, cake-like cookies are my favorite, especially around the holidays. They disappear quickly from my dessert trays. The subtle pumpkin and cinnamon flavors pair nicely with chocolate chips.

pumpkin chip cookies

yield 10 dozen

1-1/2	cups butter, softened
2	cups packed brown sugar
1	cup sugar
1	can (15 ounces) solid-pack pumpkin
1	egg
1	teaspoon vanilla extract
4	cups all-purpose flour
2	cups quick-cooking oats
2	teaspoons baking soda
2	teaspoons ground cinnamon
1	teaspoon salt
2	cups (12 ounces) semisweet chocolate chips

In a large bowl, cream butter and sugars. Beat in the pumpkin, egg and vanilla. Combine flour, oats, baking soda, cinnamon and salt; gradually add to creamed mixture. Stir in chocolate chips.

Drop by tablespoonfuls 2 in. apart onto ungreased baking sheets. Bake at 350° for 10-12 minutes or until lightly browned. Remove to wire racks to cool.

ginger diamonds

yield 7 dozen

1	cup shortening
1-1/2	cups sugar
1/2	cup molasses
2	eggs
3-1/2	cups all-purpose flour
1	teaspoon baking soda
1	teaspoon ground cinnamon
1	teaspoon ground cloves
1/2	teaspoon salt
1/2	teaspoon ground ginger

Additional sugar

In a large bowl, cream shortening and sugar until light and fluffy. Beat in molasses. Add eggs, one at a time, beating well after each addition. Combine the flour, baking soda, cinnamon, cloves, salt and ginger; gradually add to the creamed mixture and mix well. Cover and refrigerate for 30 minutes or until easy to handle.

Divide dough in half. On a lightly floured surface, roll out each portion to 1/4-in. thickness. With a sharp knife, make cuts 1-1/2 in. apart in one direction, then make diagonal cuts 1-1/2 in. apart in the opposite direction. Generously sprinkle with additional sugar.

Place 1 in. apart on ungreased baking sheets. Bake at 350° for 10-11 minutes or until edges are golden brown. Remove to wire racks to cool completely.

Fran Williamson ✳
Washington, Indiana

These soft delicious cookies were one of my son's favorite. I know your family will enjoy them, too.

✳ Diane Myers, Meridian, Idaho
Dozens of these citrusy delights travel along with me to the school and church functions. The abundant orange flavor is refreshing, and they make a nice change from the typical molasses-based cookies.

orange cookies
yield about 12 dozen

1	cup shortening
1-1/2	cups sugar
1	cup buttermilk
3	eggs
2/3	cup orange juice
4-1/2	teaspoons grated orange peel
3	to 3-1/2 cups all-purpose flour
1	teaspoon baking soda
1	teaspoon baking powder

ICING:

4-1/4	cups confectioners' sugar
1/4	teaspoon orange extract
1/3	to 1/2 cup orange juice

In a large bowl, cream shortening and sugar until light and fluffy. Beat in the buttermilk, eggs, orange juice and peel. Combine the dry ingredients; gradually add to the creamed mixture and mix well.

Drop by teaspoonfuls 2 in. apart onto ungreased baking sheets. Bake at 375° for 10 minutes or until lightly browned. Remove to wire racks to cool.

For icing, combine the confectioners' sugar, orange extract and enough orange juice to achieve desired consistency. Spread over cooled cookies.

✳ Ann Petereson
Camano Island, Washington
Flaked coconut, oats, walnuts and a touch of cinnamon jazz up this take on traditional chocolate chip cookies. Warm from the oven, what could be more tempting?

ann's chocolate chip cookies
yield about 9 dozen

1	cup shortening
1	cup sugar
1	cup packed brown sugar
2	eggs
2	teaspoons vanilla extract
2	cups old-fashioned oats
2	cups all-purpose flour
1	teaspoon baking soda
1	teaspoon baking powder
3/4	teaspoon salt
1/2	teaspoon ground cinnamon
2	cups (12 ounces) semisweet chocolate chips
1	cup flaked coconut
1	cup chopped walnuts, optional

In a large bowl, cream shortening and sugars until light and fluffy. Beat in eggs and vanilla. Combine the oats, flour, baking soda, baking powder, salt and cinnamon; gradually add to creamed mixture and mix well. Stir in the chips, coconut and walnuts if desired.

Drop by rounded teaspoonfuls 2 in. apart onto greased baking sheets. Bake at 375° for 8-10 minutes or until edges are lightly browned and cookies are set. Cool for 2 minutes before removing from pans to wire racks.

Jane Ficiur, Bow Island, Alberta ✳

This version of shortbread is fragile, but not too sweet and melts in your mouth. Mostly I make it for the holidays…but I'll also prepare it year-round for wedding showers and ladies' teas.

whipped shortbread

yield 16-18 dozen

3	**cups butter, softened**
1-1/2	**cups confectioners' sugar, sifted**
4-1/2	**cups all-purpose flour**
1-1/2	**cups cornstarch**

Nonpareils *and/or* halved candied cherries

Using a heavy-duty mixer, beat butter on medium speed until light and fluffy. Gradually add dry ingredients, beating constantly until well blended. Dust your hands lightly with additional cornstarch.

Roll dough into 1-in. balls. Press balls lightly with a floured fork. Dip in the nonpareils or top with the cherry halves. Place 1 in. apart on ungreased baking sheets.

Bake at 300° for 20-22 minutes or until cookies are set but not browned. Remove to wire racks to cool.

Jolene Davis, Minden, Nevada ✳

Brimming with candied fruit, coconut and pecans, these sweet morsels resemble fruitcakes. My grandmother baked and served the cookies in decorated miniature paper or foil muffin liners, and I have carried on her tradition.

coconut fruitcake cookies

yield 8 dozen

3	**cups chopped pecans**
2-1/2	**cups flaked coconut**
1-1/4	**cups chopped candied cherries**
1-1/4	**cups chopped candied pineapple**
1	**cup chopped dates**
2	**cups sweetened condensed milk**

In a large bowl, combine the first five ingredients. Stir in the milk. Fill paper-lined miniature muffin cups two-thirds full.

Bake at 300° for 20-25 minutes or until brown. Cool for 10 minutes before removing from pans to wire racks to cool completely. Let stand for 24 hours in an airtight container at room temperature before serving.

※ Bonnie Baumgartner, Sylva, North Carolina
At first glance, these look a bit like traditional chocolate chip cookies. But one bite quickly reveals white chocolate chunks plus spicy dashes of ginger and cinnamon.

white chocolate holiday cookies

yield 10 dozen

1/2	cup butter, softened
1/2	cup shortening
3/4	cup packed brown sugar
1/2	cup sugar
1	egg
1/2	teaspoon almond extract
2	cups all-purpose flour
1	teaspoon baking soda
1/4	teaspoon salt
1/4	teaspoon ground cinnamon
1/4	teaspoon ground ginger
6	squares (1 ounce *each*) white baking chocolate, coarsely chopped
1-1/2	cups chopped pecans

In a large bowl, cream the butter, shortening and sugars until light and fluffy. Beat in egg and extract. Combine the dry ingredients; gradually add to creamed mixture and mix well. Stir in white chocolate and pecans.

Drop by rounded teaspoonfuls 2 in. apart onto greased baking sheets. Bake at 350° for 8-10 minutes or until lightly browned. Remove to wire racks to cool.

chunky oatmeal cookies

yield 24 dozen

※ Donna Borth
Lowell, Michigan
Adults and kids alike love these morsels dotted with M&M's. I made these flourless cookies to serve at a housewarming party, and they were a hit.

12	eggs
1	package (32 ounces) brown sugar
4	cups sugar
2	cups butter, softened
18	cups old-fashioned oats
3	jars (1 pound *each*) peanut butter
1/4	cup ground cinnamon
1/4	cup vanilla extract
8	teaspoons baking soda
3	cups (18 ounces) semisweet chocolate chips
1	package (16 ounces) M&M's

In a large bowl, combine eggs and sugars. Add butter; mix well. Add oats. Add the peanut butter, cinnamon, vanilla and baking soda; mix well. Stir in chocolate chips and M&M's.

Drop by rounded tablespoonfuls 2 in. apart onto ungreased baking sheets. Flatten if desired. Bake at 350° for 12-14 minutes or until set. Remove to wire racks to cool.

editor's note: This recipe does not use flour. Reduced-fat or generic brands of peanut butter are not recommended for this recipe.

Elaine Million, Denver, Indiana ✳

White candy coating adds sweetness to these bite-sized treats. Adding sprinkles and colored sugar to my mom's recipe makes them as much fun to bake as they are to eat.

holiday miniatures

yield 10 dozen

1	cup butter, softened
1/4	cup sugar
1	teaspoon vanilla extract
1	teaspoon lemon juice
2	cups plus 2 tablespoons all-purpose flour
1	pound white candy coating, chopped

Colored sugar *and/or* nonpareils

In a large bowl, cream butter and sugar until light and fluffy. Beat in vanilla and lemon juice. Gradually add flour to creamed mixture and mix well. Divide dough in half. Wrap in plastic wrap; refrigerate for 30 minutes or until easy to handle.

On a lightly floured surface, roll out each portion of dough to 1/4-in. thickness. Cut with floured 1-in. cookie cutters. Place 1 in. apart on ungreased baking sheets.

Bake at 350° for 10-12 minutes or until lightly browned. Remove to wire racks to cool.

In a microwave, melt candy coating; stir until smooth. Dip cookies in coating; allow excess to drip off. Place on waxed paper-lined baking sheets. Sprinkle with colored sugar and/or nonpareils. Refrigerate for 30 minutes or until set.

chewy cinnamon cookies

yield about 13 dozen

2-1/2	cups shortening
5	cups sugar
4	eggs
1/3	cup molasses
1	tablespoon vanilla extract
4-3/4	cups quick-cooking oats
4-1/3	cups all-purpose flour
4	teaspoons baking powder
4	teaspoons ground cinnamon
1	teaspoon baking soda
1	teaspoon salt

In a large bowl, cream shortening and sugar until light and fluffy. Add eggs, one at a time, beating well after each addition. Beat in molasses and vanilla. Combine the remaining ingredients; gradually add to creamed mixture and mix well.

Drop by tablespoonfuls 2 in. apart onto greased baking sheets. Bake at 350° for 10-12 minutes or until edges are firm. Remove to wire racks to cool.

Terri Crum ✳
Fort Scott, Kansas
A hint of cinnamon makes these chewy oatmeal cookies stand out from all others. The recipe makes a big batch, so it's perfect when you need a snack for a crowd.

Bev Martin, Shippensburg, Pennsylvania
These soft cookies are almost like little pieces of cake. With chopped pecans sprinkled over a confectioners' sugar frosting, they're a pretty addition to any dessert table.

pumpkin spice cookies
yield 7 dozen

1	package (8 ounces) cream cheese, softened
1-1/2	cups packed brown sugar
1/2	cup sugar
2	eggs
1	cup canned pumpkin
1	teaspoon vanilla extract
3-1/2	cups all-purpose flour
1	to 1-1/2 teaspoons pumpkin pie spice
1	teaspoon baking soda
1	teaspoon salt
1/2	teaspoon baking powder

FROSTING:

2	cups confectioners' sugar
1/4	cup butter, melted
1	teaspoon vanilla extract
2	to 3 tablespoons boiling water
2	cups chopped pecans

In a large bowl, beat cream cheese and sugars until smooth. Add eggs, one at a time, beating well after each addition. Beat in pumpkin and vanilla. Combine the dry ingredients; gradually add to pumpkin mixture and mix well.

Drop by rounded teaspoonfuls 2 in. apart onto ungreased baking sheets. Bake at 350° for 10-12 minutes or until golden brown. Remove to wire racks to cool.

For frosting, in a small bowl, combine confectioners' sugar, butter, vanilla and enough water to achieve frosting consistency. Frost cookies; sprinkle with pecans.

Kathy Henson
Alice, Texas

This recipe came from a church cookbook. I altered a few ingredients, and everyone who tries these crescents likes the nice nutty flavor and texture.

pecan crescents
yield 9 dozen

1	cup butter, softened
3/4	cup sugar
1-1/2	teaspoons almond extract
2-1/2	cups all-purpose flour
1	cup ground pecans
1	cup confectioners' sugar

In a large bowl, cream butter and sugar until light and fluffy. Beat in extract. Gradually add flour to creamed mixture and mix well. Stir in the pecans.

Shape teaspoonfuls of dough into crescents. Place 2 in. apart on ungreased baking sheets. Bake at 300° for 18-20 minutes or until firm. Roll warm cookies in confectioners' sugar. Cool on wire racks.

Berniece Wallace, Van Meter, Iowa

These rich, soft cookies are convenient to make ahead of time. Both the dough and the cookies freeze well, which is wonderful because this recipe makes a huge batch.

mocha fudge cookies

yield 18-1/2 dozen

4	cups (24 ounces) semisweet chocolate chips, *divided*
2	cups butter
3	cups sugar
3	cups packed brown sugar
1	cup baking cocoa
1	tablespoon instant coffee granules
8	eggs, lightly beaten
3	tablespoons vanilla extract
8	cups all-purpose flour
2	teaspoons baking powder
1	teaspoon salt
1-1/2	cups chopped walnuts

In a microwave-safe bowl, melt 2 cups of chocolate chips and butter; stir until smooth. Transfer to a very large bowl. Combine the sugars, cocoa and coffee; add to chocolate mixture. Stir in eggs and vanilla. Combine the flour, baking powder and salt; gradually add to chocolate mixture and mix well. Stir in the walnuts and remaining chocolate chips.

Drop by rounded teaspoonfuls 2 in. apart onto ungreased baking sheets. Bake at 350° for 10-11 minutes or until edges are set. Remove to wire racks to cool.

cookies for a crowd

yield about 20 dozen

4	cups shortening
4	cups packed brown sugar
4	cups sugar
8	eggs
4	cups peanut butter
4	teaspoons vanilla extract
10	cups all-purpose flour
4	teaspoons baking soda
4	teaspoons salt
1	cup chopped salted peanuts, optional

In a very large bowl, cream shortening and sugars until light and fluffy. Add the eggs, peanut butter and vanilla; mix well. Combine the flour, baking soda and salt; gradually add to the creamed mixture well. Stir in the peanuts if desired.

Drop by rounded teaspoonfuls 2 in. apart onto ungreased baking sheets. Flatten with a fork if desired. Bake at 350° for 10-12 minutes or until set. Remove to wire racks to cool.

editor's note: Reduced-fat or generic brands of peanut butter are not recommended for this recipe.

Mary Green
Mishicot, Wisconsin

I'm a cook at a 4-H camp. Our campers go wild over these crisp cookies with an excellent peanutty flavor.

✳ Lisa Varner, Greenville, South Carolina
I tried substituting rum extract for vanilla in a classic Christmas recipe, and the end result was this cookie that tastes a lot like eggnog! These delicate, buttery cookies are always welcomed wherever I take them.

holiday spritz

yield 7 dozen

1	cup butter, softened
1	cup confectioners' sugar
1	egg
1-1/2	teaspoons rum extract
2-1/2	cups all-purpose flour
1/4	teaspoon salt
Colored sugar	

In a small bowl, cream the butter and confectioners' sugar until light and fluffy. Beat in egg and extract. Combine flour and salt; gradually add to creamed mixture and mix well.

Using a cookie press fitted with the disk of your choice, press the cookies 1 in. apart onto ungreased baking sheets. Sprinkle with the colored sugar.

Bake at 375° for 6-9 minutes or until lightly browned. Cool for 2 minutes before removing to wire racks.

✳ Anna Free
Cleveland, Ohio
If you're looking for an oatmeal cookie recipe that has it all, you've found it! These treats include two types of oats, chocolate chips, nuts, raisins and coconut. Yum!

raisin-chip oatmeal cookies

yield 12 dozen

2	cups butter, softened
1-2/3	cups sugar
1-2/3	cups packed brown sugar
4	eggs
3	teaspoons vanilla extract
4	cups all-purpose flour
2-1/2	cups quick-cooking oats
2-1/2	cups old-fashioned oats
2	teaspoons baking powder
2	teaspoons baking soda
1	teaspoon salt
1	teaspoon ground cinnamon
4	cups (24 ounces) semisweet chocolate chips
3	cups coarsely chopped nuts
2	cups raisins
1	cup flaked coconut

In a large bowl, cream butter and sugars until light and fluffy. Add eggs, one at a time, beating well after each addition. Beat in vanilla. Combine dry ingredients; gradually add to the creamed mixture and mix well. Stir in the chocolate chips, nuts, raisins and coconut.

Drop by heaping tablespoonfuls 2 in. apart onto ungreased baking sheets. Bake at 350° for 12-14 minutes or until golden brown. Remove to wire racks to cool.

Sue Gronholz, Beaver Dam, Wisconsin
These buttery cookies are one of my favorites. I added the rosemary and substituted golden raisins for the regular raisins.

rosemary raisin cookies

yield about 8 dozen

1/2	cup butter, softened
1/2	cup shortening
2	eggs
1/2	teaspoon lemon extract
1	tablespoon minced fresh rosemary
1	tablespoon grated lemon peel
3-1/2	cups all-purpose flour
1-1/2	teaspoons cream of tartar
1-1/2	teaspoons baking soda
1/2	teaspoon salt
1	cup golden raisins

In a large bowl, cream the butter, shortening and sugar until light and fluffy. Beat in eggs and extract. Stir in the rosemary and lemon peel. Combine the flour, cream of tartar, baking soda and salt; gradually add to creamed mixture. Stir in raisins.

Roll into 1-in. balls. Place on ungreased baking sheets. Flatten with a fork. Bake at 400° for 8-10 minutes or until golden brown. Remove to wire racks to cool. Cookies may be frozen for up to 3 months.

soft gingersnaps

yield 11 dozen

1-1/2	cups butter, softened
2	cups sugar
2	eggs
1/2	cup molasses
4-1/2	cups all-purpose flour
3	teaspoons baking soda
2	teaspoons ground cinnamon
1	teaspoon ground ginger
1	teaspoon ground cloves
1/2	teaspoon salt
1/2	teaspoon ground nutmeg

Additional sugar

In a large bowl, cream the butter and sugar. Add the eggs, one at a time, beating well after each addition. Beat in molasses. Combine the flour, baking soda, cinnamon, ginger, cloves, salt and nutmeg; gradually add to creamed mixture. Refrigerate for 1 hour or until dough is easy to handle.

Roll into 1-in. balls; roll in the additional sugar. Place 2 in. apart on ungreased baking sheets. Bake at 350° for 8-12 minutes or until puffy and lightly browned. Cool for 1 minute before removing to wire racks.

Shawn Barto
Clermont, Florida
Loaded with molasses and plenty of spices, these cookies deliver an old-fashioned flavor everyone loves.

✳ Adina Skilbred, Prairie du Sac, Wisconsin
Is it a cookie or a candy? No matter which answer folks choose, they find these minty morsels yummy.

mint morsels

yield about 10 dozen

1/3	cup shortening
1/3	cup butter, softened
3/4	cup sugar
1	egg
1	tablespoon milk
1	teaspoon vanilla extract
1-3/4	cups all-purpose flour
1/3	cup baking cocoa
1-1/2	teaspoons baking powder
1/4	teaspoon salt
1/8	teaspoon ground cinnamon

PEPPERMINT LAYER:

4	cups confectioners' sugar
6	tablespoons corn syrup
6	tablespoons butter, melted
2	to 3 teaspoons peppermint extract

CHOCOLATE COATING:

2	packages (11-1/2 ounces *each*) milk chocolate chips
1/4	cup shortening

In a large bowl, cream shortening, butter and sugar until light and fluffy. Add egg, milk and vanilla; mix well. Combine flour, cocoa, baking powder, salt and cinnamon; add to creamed mixture and mix well. Cover and chill for 8 hours or overnight.

On a lightly floured surface, roll dough to 1/8-in. thickness. Cut with a 1-1/2-in.-round cookie cutter. Place 2 in. apart on ungreased baking sheets. Bake at 375° for 6-8 minutes or until set. Cool for 2 minutes; remove to wire racks to cool completely.

Combine peppermint layer ingredients; mix well. Knead for 1 minute or until smooth. Shape into 120 balls, 1/2 in. each. Place a ball on each cookie and flatten to cover cookie. Place on waxed paper-lined baking sheets; refrigerate for 30 minutes. In a microwave, melt the chips and shortening. Spread about 1 teaspoonful over each cookie. Chill until firm.

shortbread meltaways

yield 7 dozen

✳ Ruth Whittaker
Wayne, Pennsylvania
You'll need just five everyday ingredients to stir up a batch of these bite-size cookies. Although they don't cost much, they're rich and melt-in-your-mouth good.

1	cup butter, softened
1/2	cup confectioners' sugar
1	teaspoon vanilla extract
1	cup all-purpose flour
2/3	cup cornstarch

In a small bowl, cream the butter and confectioners' sugar until light and fluffy. Beat in the vanilla. Combine the flour and cornstarch; gradually add to the creamed mixture and mix well.

Drop by 1/2 teaspoonfuls onto ungreased baking sheets. Bake at 350° for 11-13 minutes or until bottoms are lightly browned. Cool for 5 minutes before removing from pans to wire racks.

Sue Seymour, Valatie, New York ✳

Many of our holiday traditions center around the foods my mother made while I was growing up. These cookies, which we called "Strufoli," bring back wonderful memories.

italian holiday cookies

yield about 15 dozen

1	tablespoon sugar
1	teaspoon grated lemon peel
1	teaspoon vanilla extract
1/2	teaspoon salt
4	eggs
2-1/2	cups all-purpose flour

Oil for deep-fat frying

1	cup honey

Candy sprinkles

In a large bowl, combine sugar, lemon peel, vanilla and salt. Add eggs and 2 cups flour; mix well. Turn onto a floured board and knead in remaining flour (dough will be soft).

With a floured knife or scissors, cut into 20 pieces. With hands, roll each piece into pencil shapes. Cut the "pencils" into 1/2-in. pieces. In an electric skillet or deep-fat fryer, heat oil to 375°. Fry pieces, a few at a time, for 2 minutes per side or until golden brown. Drain on paper towels. Place in a large bowl.

Heat honey to boiling; pour over cookies and mix well. With a slotted spoon, spoon onto a serving platter and slowly mound into a tree shape if desired. Decorate with candy sprinkles. Cool completely.

double-chip cookies

yield about 10 dozen

2	cups butter, softened
1-1/2	cups sugar
1-1/2	cups packed brown sugar
4	eggs
3	teaspoons vanilla extract
5	cups all-purpose flour
3	teaspoons baking soda
1	teaspoon salt
3	cups chopped walnuts
1	package (10 to 12 ounces) vanilla *or* white chips
1	package (10 ounces) peanut butter chips

In a large bowl, cream butter and sugars until light and fluffy. Add eggs, one at a time, beating well after each addition. Beat in vanilla. Combine the flour, baking soda and salt; gradually add to the creamed mixture. Stir in walnuts and chips.

Drop by rounded tablespoonfuls 2 in. apart onto ungreased baking sheets. Bake at 350° for 10-12 minutes or until golden brown. Remove to wire racks to cool.

Diana Dube ✳
Rockland, Maine

These buttery cookies are packed with vanilla and peanut butter chips plus walnuts. I'm never left with any to take home after a potluck dinner.

alphabetical recipe index

Refer to this index for a complete alphabetical listing of all recipes in this book.

general recipe index

This handy index lists every recipe by food category and major ingredient, so you can easily locate recipes that suit your needs. Plus, it lists all the tips that are given throughout the book.